BW

2

WITHDRAWN

COMMAND UNDER SAIL

COMMAND UNDER SAIL

MAKERS OF THE AMERICAN NAVAL TRADITION
1775–1850

EDITED BY JAMES C. BRADFORD

Library of Congress Cataloging in Publication Data
Main entry under title:
Command under sail.
Bibliography: p.
Includes index.
1. United States. Navy—Officers—Biography—
Addresses, essays, lectures. 2. United States—
History, Naval—To 1900—Addresses, essays, lectures.
I. Bradford, James C.
V62.C662   1984   359'.0092'2 [B]   84-29584
ISBN 0-87021-137-4

Printed in the United States of America

To my parents,
Raymond and Eleanor

CONTENTS

LIST OF ILLUSTRATIONS

PREFACE

The U.S. Navy was born just as the Age of Sail reached its climax. During this era the traditions and the style that would guide and characterize the Navy for the next century and a half were set. It was a trying time. Until well after the Revolution there were Americans who seriously doubted the desirability of having a navy, and during the early nineteenth century the appropriate type of navy remained under debate. During the next fifty years all navies would begin the transition to the modern era as propulsion changed from sail to steam, hulls from wood to iron and steel, and armaments from smoothbore cannon to rifled guns; but the basis of the U. S. Navy was already laid.

The history of the early Navy has been told in terms of battles and wars, ship construction, and administration, but there has been not a single volume of history spanning the Age of Sail that surveys all these fields. In addition, as a modern naval leader has written, "Important as ships are, naval history is made by men."[1] This is a truism worth remembering. The biographical approach to naval history makes the era more concrete and vivid. Viewing it through the eyes and careers of participants one can more fully understand the strengths and weaknesses of the young service and the variety of roles played by early naval forces.

The American sailing navy did not decisively defeat its European rivals in the American Revolution, the Quasi-War with France, or the War of 1812; but it did win important battles that influenced the outcome of those conflicts. It is not too much, for example, to credit the victories of Oliver Hazard Perry on Lake Erie and Thomas Macdonough at Plattsburgh with paving the way for the status quo ante bellum Peace of Ghent which ended America's second war with Britain. Triumphs such as John Paul Jones's capture of the *Serapis* and Isaac Hull's defeat of the *Guerriere* raised public morale in particularly difficult times.

But all was not gunsmoke and grapeshot, cannon and cutlass. The young Navy needed more than battle leaders to launch it. Strategists, administrators, and educators were equally important. The quality of the men called upon to fill these roles was not always high, and the problems they faced were not easily solvable. The provincialism of Esek Hopkins represented one of the main weaknesses of the Continental Navy. The nepotism John Paul Jones complained about during the Revolution did not disappear but continued into the nineteenth century, exemplified by such "naval families" as the Perrys and the Rodgerses. However precarious its start, the U. S. Navy soon became institutionalized (some would say ossified) and in need of reform, and leaders emerged from within the officer corps to press for change.

These biographical studies, all written especially for this volume, are interpretive rather than merely descriptive. One element of interpretation is the authors' choice of which aspects of their subjects' lives to emphasize. Robert Stockton, for example, is most commonly remembered for his command of the Pacific Squadron that helped capture California during the Mexican War, but Harold D. Langley emphasizes his role as a reformer because it was in this capacity that he had the most lasting influence on the Navy. John Rodgers is most famous for his operations in the Mediterranean, but they are not so important in American history as his actions in defense of Baltimore during the War of 1812 or so important to the Navy as his long service on the Board of Naval Commissioners. David Porter's service in the Mexican Navy and John Paul Jones's in the Imperial Russian Navy are virtually ignored because they had very little impact on the U. S. Navy. Thus, the essays are not simply short biographies.

For this reason authors have been selected whose knowledge of America's naval heritage extends beyond the individual about whom they write. Some have written on their subject before, but all offer more than distillations of the views presented elsewhere. There has been no attempt to impose a uniformity of interpretation upon the essays. In his essay, Edward Eckert identifies Edward Preble as a major influence upon the development of young Thomas Macdonough as a naval officer. Christopher McKee questions the validity of accepting the common belief that most of the American officers winning victories in the War of 1812 were "Preble's Boys." He concludes that the evidence supporting this view is circumstantial and that Preble's direct impact upon such officers as Macdonough is difficult to document. The author's views are their own, and each contributor has provided suggestions for additional reading to guide those whose interest they arouse.

The selection of subjects for this volume was not easy. The officers chosen neither were "representative" in the sense of being average or common, nor were they the "great men" that a Thomas Carlyle or Sidney Hook might choose. They include many of the most famous, such as John Paul Jones, Oliver Hazard Perry, and Stephen Decatur. But influence and importance are not necessarily linked to fame or battle command, and a number of the selections, for example, Esek Hopkins and Robert Stockton, are less obvious. Some, such as David Porter, were selected because their careers illustrated multiple themes. The exclusion of other officers, such as Thomas Truxtun and James Biddle, is not a judgment on their importance but reflects the desire to keep this work a manageable size. In selecting the subjects, an effort was made to avoid Whiggish anachronism. The events of the Navy's early history did not lead inexorably to the present. The U. S. Navy was not predestined to become the world's supreme service.

Thus the early Navy cannot be understood nor its officers judged solely in terms of the present. The conditions under which these officers served influenced their actions. The Age of Sail placed a premium on seamanship in both war and peace. The storm that caught the *Ariel* on the coast of France in 1780 could have destroyed the ship of a less able mariner than John Paul Jones; the five British ships pursuing the *Constitution* might have overtaken her, had not a man with the skill of Isaac Hull been in command. William Bainbridge's loss of the *Philadelphia* shows that not all American officers shared such abilities. Communications were notoriously slow and erratic during the era, thus conferring much greater independence on the officers of the sailing navy while at the same time placing much greater responsibility upon them than on their successors. At Foxardo, David Porter had to act without consulting his superiors in Washington. Robert F. Stockton's decisive actions in California during the war with Mexico stand in contrast to the timidity of his predecessor. Officers were called on to operate without logistical support from home, as was demonstrated by Porter's extended cruise in the Pacific Ocean during the War of 1812.

Lessons of seamanship, strategy, and tactics drawn from events of over a century ago are unlikely to be directly applicable to today's conditions, but there are connections, however metaphysical, between the eras. No modern admiral will choose to fight at anchor as Thomas Macdonough did at Plattsburgh, but the principles of fitting strategy to conditions and of thorough preparation for all battle contingencies remain valid. During most of its early history the Navy was unable to promise steady employment to its officers, and even in wartime most captains could have chosen service in privateers and amassed greater fortunes, but they did not. The patriotism of John Barry and the self-sacrifice of others remains commendable.

Few could deny the crucial importance of leadership in naval affairs. Some of the qualities required during the Age of Sail are the same ones required today, though the emphasis is perhaps a bit different. A sailing ship was a close community in which virtually every sailor saw every officer daily. The quality of personal courage under pressure, be it in storm or battle, could not be hidden from the ship's company. Perry's courage at Lake Erie, Macdonough's at Plattsburgh, and Decatur's at Tripoli are legendary. A leader's loyalty to the officers serving both above and below him was clear for everyone to observe. John Paul Jones probably did not give enough credit to his subordinates, whereas Oliver Hazard Perry would err in the opposite direction. Isaac Hull's receptivity to advice from his officers, his giving credit to his men for the victory over the *Guerriere*, and his concern for their physical needs won him their support. The enlisted men of the era were less "professional" than those of later eras. The ships of the Continental Navy in particular were manned by sailors with little experience in naval warfare. Officers of the sailing navy had to have the support of their men in a more personal way than is necessary in modern mechanized navies. At bottom was trust. The officers and men needed to have confidence that their commander knew his profession thoroughly and that he would use good judgment. When a commander lost this trust, as, for example, in the case of Esek Hopkins after the battle with the *Glasgow*, his effectiveness was severely impaired.

Taken together, these essays illustrate the bad as well as the good character traits of many officers. Most of the men were self-confident; many were hypersensitive. Porter, Jones, Preble, and Decatur all shared a thirst for glory that could have either positive or negative consequences. Other officers exhibited particular qualities. John Rodgers, for example, exemplified the conservative forces that gave the Navy stability, whereas Robert Stockton represented the reformers who forced progress upon the Navy. Stockton, it should be noted, had his greatest effect as a naval reformer not while in the Navy, but in the Senate where he blocked the reintroduction of flogging. The Navy has always had officers such as Rodgers and Stockton, as well as men such as Isaac Hull, who steered a middle course, guiding reform slowly but steadily. Certain officers virtually personify their era. John Paul Jones and Stephen Decatur embodied all the characteristics held dear by their contemporaries and by nineteenth-century naval officers. Both were men of action who seemed to act more on impulse and intuition than on education and reason. The age preferred men who struggled against overwhelming odds to men of contemplation. The early republic looked for heroes, and the Navy provided them.

Not everything can be explained logically. In human affairs there is always an element of chance, and the measure of luck has not been ignored in these essays. Oliver Hazard Perry was lucky; William Bainbridge was not.

The question of whether leadership is innate or learned is insoluble, and no attempt is made here to answer it.[2] The focus is on the infant Navy and the men who led it. Men, much more than ships or administrative agencies, link today's Navy with its past. The U. S. Navy has never had a dominating figure like Horatio Nelson, but its traditions were forged during Nelson's era. The group of men who launched the Navy, shaped its character, and set its course were a mixed lot. They lived in an age of adventure, a time when much was demanded of individual officers. Some met the challenge; others did not. All were makers of the American naval tradition. This is their story. It is also the story of the sailing navy.

NOTES

1. James Calvert, *The Naval Profession*, 6.

2. Older studies include Alfred Thayer Mahan, *Types of Naval Officers* and Charles Benedict Davenport, *Naval Officers: Their Heredity and Development*. The latter classified officers by "temperament," "juvenile promise," and hereditary traits, including "hyperkinetic qualities," "nomadism," and "Thalassophilia" (love of the sea). The subject of leadership continues to intrigue authors. Even modern authors retain the focus on leadership in battle. See, for example, John Horsfield, *The Art of Leadership in War: The Royal Navy from the Age of Nelson to the End of World War II* and Oliver Warner, *Command at Sea: Great Fighting Admirals from Hawke to Nimitz.*

ACKNOWLEDGMENTS

The deepest debt of gratitude must go to the authors, who co-operated so fully in this joint enterprise, suffering the editor's sometimes heavy-handed commentary and acquiescing to pleas for brevity. The product was made more attractive by the assistance of three individuals—Charles R. Haberlein, Head of the Photographic Section of the Naval Historical Center; Patty M. Maddocks, Director of Library and Photographic Services at the Naval Institute; and James W. Cheevers, Senior Curator of the Naval Academy Museum—who provided advice and assistance in illustrating the essays. At the Naval Institute Press, our editor, Deborah Guberti, showed remarkable patience, and our manuscript editor, Constance M. MacDonald, saved us from infelicities and inconsistencies of style. Carole R. Knapp, Mary L. Watson, and Laurie V. Caldwell of the Texas A&M University Department of History typed the manuscript, and Shirley C. Dunn assisted in proofreading. Nancy L. Underwood ably assisted in a variety of tasks including assembling the bibliography, editing the notes, proofreading, and compiling the manuscript and index. Less tangible but equally important assistance was provided by John W. and Dorothy B. Huston, my wife Judy, and our sons, Jim and John, without whose support much less would have been accomplished.

COMMAND UNDER SAIL

Courtesy of U.S. Naval Historical Center.

THE STRUGGLE
FOR INDEPENDENCE

ESEK HOPKINS: COMMANDER-IN-CHIEF OF THE CONTINENTAL NAVY

BY WILLIAM M. FOWLER, JR.

In the summer of 1797, John Adams, the newly inaugurated President of the United States, was on his way home to Quincy, Massachusetts. En route he decided to spend an evening in Providence, Rhode Island. The arrival of the President caused quite a stir. A company of dragoons escorted him to the Golden Bull Tavern where a gala reception complete with pealing bells and sounding cannon fire was offered. Never indifferent to public accolades, Adams was pleased at his warm reception.

After an evening of innumerable toasts and endless feasting, Adams and his family retired to their quarters. An unexpected knock at the door brought a servant to announce that a gentleman begged to see the President. In the anteroom the President "found an old man bowed with years and infirmities." His visitor was Esek Hopkins, late commander in chief of the Continental Navy.

He came, he told the President, to pay his respects and to tell him how grateful he was that Adams had stood in his defense twenty years before when his enemies in Congress had sought to destroy him. Old, wan, and barely able to walk, this man was hardly the vigorous and sharp-tongued seaman Adams remembered from those heady days of the Revolution. The veil of age obscured the traces of a naval career that had begun most promisingly many decades earlier.

Esek Hopkins was born on 26 April 1718 into a large and well-known Rhode Island family. Two of his older brothers had gone to sea before him, when, at age twenty, upon the death of his father, young Esek left the family farm and signed on board a merchantman out of Providence. Within a very few years he had his own command

Esek Hopkins.

in the West Indies trade and was a frequent visitor to Surinam and the neighboring sugar islands. Married at twenty-three to Desire Burroughs, daughter of a prosperous Newport merchant and ship master, Hopkins moved to his wife's town and continued his voyaging. Two years later, in 1743, sensing greater opportunities in Providence, he returned home.[1]

By 1750 Hopkins had settled easily into the predictable life-style of a Yankee shipmaster: frequent voyages to the West Indies; a good and respectable marriage at home; numerous children (five in the first seven years of marriage); and growing investments and responsibilities shoreside. In 1754 he joined many of his Rhode Island shipmates and went "a privateering" against the French during the

French and Indian War (1754–63). He quickly proved to be as good a warrior as a trader, increasing both his fame and fortune.

Like most other colonials, Hopkins celebrated the peace and looked forward to reestablishing the old trade. Events in America and England precluded that, and in the dozen tumultuous years from the end of the war to the battles at Lexington and Concord, Esek Hopkins found himself enmeshed in local affairs. He served on several town committees and in the General Assembly. Most important, however, his elder brother Stephen was elected governor, and, in the rough and tumble of Rhode Island politics, Esek became his close ally, sharing both his friends and his enemies.

At the summons for the First Continental Congress in the fall of 1774, Rhode Island, not surprisingly, elected Stephen Hopkins one of its delegates. From the moment the body came to order it was clear that sectionalism would play a key role in decision making. For his part Stephen Hopkins was loyal to Rhode Island and New England. He allied himself closely with his New England colleagues and struck up a particularly close association with John and Sam Adams. Never one to forget his friends, Hopkins emerged as a key member of Congress, accustomed to using his influence on behalf of his constituents.

With the outbreak of hostilities, Rhode Islanders quickly discovered their vulnerability by sea. In Newport Captain James Wallace had been busy terrifying the populace from his frigate, HMS *Rose*. In reaction to Wallace, the Assembly commissioned two small vessels to patrol the waters of Narragansett Bay, and in October appointed Esek Hopkins a brigadier general and placed him in command of Rhode Island's defenses. In Philadelphia too there was action. On 26 May 1775 Congress resolved that the colonies be put in a state of military readiness so that they might be able to defend their rights and liberties; on the 29th it called upon the people of Canada to join the rebellious colonies in their common cause. By the end of June Congress had voted to raise and equip an army, appointed George Washington as commander in chief, and voted to issue two million dollars in bills of credit to finance the new government's operation. In July Congress entered into negotiations with the Indians and elected Benjamin Franklin postmaster general.[2] Although the Declaration of Independence was still more than a year away, the Continental Congress was taking on the power of a sovereign body. In one noticeable area, however, its members held back. They did not authorize a navy.

Congress was skeptical of creating a navy. It was one thing to appoint a commander in chief over a rabble in arms surrounding "ministerial Butchers" in Boston. After all, that could be justified on strictly defensive grounds. But a navy was another matter, for the mobility and striking capability of armed vessels give them an inherent offensive character. This factor, plus sectional politics and concern over the high cost of a navy, prevented them from acting on a naval program.

Congress's inaction distressed Rhode Island, and on 26 August, the General Assembly resolved:

> this Assembly is persuaded, that the building and equipping an American fleet, as soon as possible, would greatly and essentially conduce to the preservation of the lives, liberty and property, of good people of these Colonies and therefore instruct their delegates, to use their whole influence at the ensuing congress, for building, at the Continental expense, a fleet of sufficient force, for the protection of these colonies, and for employing them in such manner and places as will most effectively annoy our enemies, and contribute to the common defense of these colonies.[3]

On 3 October 1775, the Rhode Island delegation presented the resolution to Congress. Four days later, when the resolve was put on the floor for debate, it was obvious Rhode Island had set off a powder keg. Samuel Chase of Maryland called it "the maddest Idea in the World to think of building an American fleet." Others, mainly southerners, chimed in, calling attention to the huge expense involved while alluding to the fact that the region most likely to benefit from the creation of a navy was New England, whence both ships and men might come.[4]

As tempers in Congress heated up, events were taking place at sea that made some kind of action unavoidable. Washington's forces were in desperate need of supplies. The quickest and most direct source for the Americans were the British themselves, who, believing the rebels could not harm them at sea, were sending out unarmed and unescorted store ships. These were ideal targets, and on 13 October Congress agreed to fit out two vessels "to cruise eastward, for intercepting such transports as may be laden with warlike stores."[5] A committee was appointed to prepare a plan. With a bit of clever politicking, the pro-navy faction took control and brought back a report that startled Congress. Instead of two vessels, the committee called for ten. It was too bold a plan for the temper of Congress; instead of ten, it authorized four. Nevertheless, this was a great victory for the New England navalists, who had secured twice the number of vessels originally debated, and, more important, now had a naval commitment from Congress.

To manage this fleet of four, Congress elected a seven-man committee. The Naval Committee consisted of Stephen Hopkins, Joseph Hewes of North Carolina, Richard Henry Lee of Virginia, John Adams, Silas Deane of Connecticut, John Langdon of New Hampshire, and Christopher Gadsden of South Carolina.

Eager to get under way, the committee arranged for quarters in a local tavern and agreed to meet every evening at six to conduct its business. The meetings were productive, lively, and convivial. John Adams remembered his service on the committee as "the pleasantest part of my labors . . . in Congress." With unusual nostalgia he recalled the men he had met with those fall and winter evenings of 1775, especially Stephen Hopkins, "Old Grape and Guts" as some called him. According to Adams, the old gentleman greatly enlivened the meetings with his wit and wisdom, and after adjournment many remained behind with him until very late—smoking, drinking, and swapping stories in a room swimming with the heavy warm odor of port and rum.[6] These sessions were more than social, however. In the weeks to come, Hopkins's influence in the committee would become abundantly clear as Rhode Island reaped the benefits of those late-night meetings.

On 2 November, Congress granted the committee $100,000 to fit out four vessels and "to agree with such officers and seamen, as are proper to man and command said vessels."[7] As the committee scouted for commanders, the assignment turned out to be a family affair, the jovial storyteller Hopkins displaying all his political dexterity. Esek, still busy in Rhode Island, was made commander in chief of the fleet. His son, John Burroughs Hopkins, was commissioned a captain, as was another Rhode Islander and kinsman, Abraham Whipple. Whipple and Esek Hopkins had sailed together on many privateering voyages. A third captain was a Connecticut mariner, Dudley Saltonstall, brother-in-law to Silas Deane. The fourth and only non–New Englander and unrelated officer was Nicholas Biddle, a well-known Philadelphia captain. All in all, the appointments were a marvelous manifestation of Hopkintonian influence.

Having appointed officers, the Congress next needed to provide rules and regulations by which their infant navy was to be governed. For reasons that are not altogether clear, the Naval Committee assigned that task to John Adams. Although a lawyer and a man reasonably acquainted with maritime law, he had no seagoing experience. Nevertheless, with his usual passion for detail, Adams undertook the duty, and on 28 November Congress approved Adams's "Rules for the Regulation of the Navy of the United Colonies." In general they followed the pattern of the Royal Navy but tended to be less severe.[8]

In Rhode Island, Esek Hopkins received the news of his appointment with glee. However, it can hardly be said that he rushed to his post. He spent several weeks tending to private and public business, and did not arrive in Philadelphia until very early in January.

In the absence of the commander in chief, the Congress had not been idle. Neither time nor funds permitted the construction of new warships; so the Naval Committee sent agents on the prowl seeking likely merchantmen to be converted to warships. They found four: the *Black Prince*, renamed the *Alfred* and given to the command of Saltonstall; the *Sally*, renamed the *Columbus*, Captain Whipple; the *Andrea Doria*, Nicholas Biddle; and the *Cabot*, John Burroughs Hopkins. These four, considered to be the most powerful members of the fleet, were joined by four additional lightly armed vessels: the *Wasp* and the *Fly*, eight-gun schooners; the *Hornet*, a ten-gun sloop; and the 12-gun sloop *Providence*, formerly the *Katy* of the Rhode Island navy.

On 4 January 1776, with Hopkins on board the *Alfred*, 24 guns, the fleet cast off and moved out into the Delaware. This first movement lasted only long enough, about four hours, to get over to Liberty Island, where they tied up again to avoid ice flows coming down the river. The next day Hopkins received two sets of orders from the Naval Committee.[9] The first were general in nature, setting out procedures and protocols. He was addressed as "Commander in Chief of the Fleet of the United Colonies," leading some to suggest that Congress intended to place him on a par with Washington. However, closer scrutiny reveals otherwise, for in a key paragraph he was told:

> You are by every means in your power to keep up an exact correspondence with the Congress or Committee of Congress aforesaid, and with the Commander in chief of the Continental forces in America.

Clearly, in Congress's mind, Hopkins was subordinate to Washington, though the relative rank of the two officers was never seriously contested and thus not clearly defined.

The second set of orders Esek opened on 5 January were his sailing instructions outlining his first mission. For reasons of strategy and politics, this Yankee fleet was being sent south to rid those coasts of British raiders.

> You are instructed with the utmost diligence to proceed with the said fleet to sea and if the winds and weather will possibly admit of it to proceed directly for Chesapeake Bay in Virginia and when nearly arrived there you will send forward a small swift sailing vessel to gain

The *Alfred* (formerly the *Black Prince*), 1775. Twenty-four-gun ship and flagship of Hopkins's Nassau fleet. Painting by Harry W. Carpenter, n.d. Courtesy of the National Archives.

intelligence. . . . If . . . you find that they are not greatly superior to your own you are immediately to enter the said bay, search out and attack, take or destroy all the naval force of our enemies that you may find there. If you should be so fortunate as to execute this business successfully in Virginia you are then to proceed immediately to the southward and make yourself master of such forces as the enemy may have both in North and South Carolina. . . . Notwithstanding these particular orders, which it is hoped you will be able to execute, if bad winds, or stormy weather, or any other unforseen accident or disaster disable you so to do, You are then to follow such Courses as your best Judgment shall suggest to you as most useful to the American Cause and to distress the Enemy by all means in your power.

It took more than six weeks to get the fleet to sea. Ice in the river as well as difficulty in filling out the crew delayed Hopkins until 18 February, when, with a fair wind blowing, men were sent aloft to "loose the Fore topsail and sheet it home."

An experienced mariner, Hopkins knew the risks of a winter sail. He was not disappointed. Gale force winds out of the north bore down on the fleet. The *Hornet* and the *Fly* proved to be poor heavy weather boats and were separated from the remainder of the fleet. The other six plowed on.

Ignoring his orders, Hopkins bypassed both Chesapeake Bay and the southern coast; instead he laid a course off shore that took him to the Bahamas. Because nowhere in his orders were the Bahamas mentioned (unless one construes them to be included in the "best Judgment" clause), it is difficult to divine the commodore's motives. Later, when he was questioned about his changes of plans, he laid his decision to the fact that so many of his crew were sick. A far more likely explanation is simply that sailing the southern coast was, in his judgment, too risky. In Chesapeake Bay, Lord Dunmore, former royal governor of Virginia, was busy terrorizing the folks along the shore. Although the governor's force was technically inferior to Hopkins, the American commodore knew full well that in combat his ersatz navy would most likely collapse at the first sight of the Royal Navy. As for the southern coast, Hopkins had already taken a beating just getting off soundings; coming along the shore would have meant hazarding Cape Hatteras. Esek Hopkins had no desire to challenge either the Royal Navy or nature.

It was a bad decision. Hopkins was behaving more like a privateersman whose main concern was to minimize danger and maximize profits. By completely bypassing the southern coasts he displayed a callous disregard for southern interests and reinforced southern suspicions about a Yankee navy. Hopkin's insensitivity to sectional and political concerns ill-suited him for command of a navy created by a Congress where these elements counted so heavily.

On 1 March, the fleet came to anchor on the lee side of Abaco Island, where for the next two days the Americans took on water and made preparations for an assault against Nassau on New Providence Island only a few more miles to the south. Hopkins hoped to catch the garrison by surprise and carry away its reportedly large supply of gunpowder.

On Sunday 3 March, the Americans landed on the northeast tip of New Providence about four miles to the west of Fort Montague.[10] After firing a few token shots, the garrison left the fort and retired to the town of Nassau. The Americans spent the night in the fort and the next day marched on the town and Fort Nassau; neither offered any resistance.

With everything secured, Hopkins brought his ships into the harbor and went looking for gunpowder. Herein lay disappointment. While the Americans were spending their evening at Fort Montague, the governor of the Bahamas had been busy moving his gunpowder out of the magazine and into the hold of a commandeered sloop which had taken off for another island. By the time Hopkins's men broke into the fort, all they found were twenty-four barrels. However, some solace could be taken from the fact that their opponents had not had enough time to remove their cannon and various other military supplies. It took two weeks to load the booty.

On the same day that the British were evacuating Boston, 17 March 1776, Esek Hopkins evacuated Nassau. At first, according to his testimony, the commodore gave thought to taking his fleet to Georgia to help rid that coast of enemy ships. Whether he really intended to undertake such a cruise is questionable; at any rate, he gave up the idea when he learned that the enemy was there in force. Instead of Georgia, the American captains were ordered to keep company with the *Alfred* and, if separated, then to sail alone and rendezvous in Block Island channel. Clearly Hopkins was headed home to Rhode Island.

Homeward bound, the men and the commodore stayed alert for any signs of enemy shipping. They saw none until 4 April, when the fleet drew near to the east end of Long Island. Cruising in the same area was the schooner *Hawk*, tender to HMS *Rose*. She was spotted and easily overtaken by the American force. The next day a second British vessel, the bomb brig *Boston*, was sighted and pursued. She proved to be a tartar and put up a fierce resistance until finally the Americans overwhelmed her.

The *Hawk* and the *Boston* were only small fry. On 6 April a truly worthy foe came into view: HMS *Glasgow*, a 20-gun ship under the command of Captain Tyringham Howe.[11] Howe, apparently unaware that the Americans were in the area, came down toward the rebel fleet. It was not until they were within hailing distance that he realized his mistake. He then made a run for it with Hopkins in hot pursuit. Although the *Glasgow* was greatly outnumbered and outgunned, she managed to inflict heavy damage on the Americans, to elude them, and to escape into the safety of Newport. Captain Howe had shown himself to be not only a fine fighter, but a clever ship handler as well. For their part, the engagement with the *Glasgow* showed the Americans to be neither. In the first place, Hopkins had not bothered to disperse his ships in a proper squadron formation. If he had done that, he might well have trapped the *Glasgow*. Furthermore, during the battle, which lasted for several hours, Hopkins made no attempt to control or coordinate the movement of his fleet. It was a typical privateering operation—that is, every man for himself.

After breaking off the engagement with the *Glasgow*, Hopkins ordered the fleet onto a southwest course intended to bring them into New London. Despite thick fog, on Sunday afternoon, 7 April, the Americans came abreast of New London Light and dropped anchor. The commodore went to finishing his dispatches for the Congress.

His report was well-received, as it deserved to be. After all, with marginal warships and inexperienced men, he had managed to sail into enemy waters, land his forces, and return with a considerable store of material. The brush with the *Glasgow* was not a particularly proud moment; but, considered in the context of the entire cruise, it was, if not excusable, at least understandable to members of Congress.

What was neither excusable nor understandable was the commodore's subsequent behavior ashore. Unlike Washington, who once he took command of the army seemed to rise above sectional politics and petty disputes, Esek Hopkins never was able to make that leap. Whatever he might have thought about Congress, the commander in chief of the army always consulted with it and kept its members informed of his decisions. Hopkins, on the other hand, seemed more inclined to find ways to annoy them. At New London his ships were crammed with military stores that were continental property. Instead of asking Congress for its pleasure, Hopkins went ahead and wrote to the governors of Rhode Island and Connecticut offering those gentlemen these stores for the defense of their colonies. It was a foolish and graceless move.

Compounding his problems with Congress were mounting vexations within the fleet. Only a day after their arrival at New London, the first wisp of trouble appeared when the crew of the brig *Cabot* presented a round robin petition to Hopkins asking to be paid. That stir among the enlisted men was soon followed by a storm among the officers.

Ever since they had landed, rumors had circulated about the alleged cowardice or incompetence of certain captains during the engagement with the *Glasgow*. Among them was Hopkins's old and dear friend Abraham Whipple.In the face of these allegations, Whipple asked his commander to summon a court-martial to clear his name. Hopkins agreed, and in its finding the court determined that indeed Whipple had made an error during the battle, but the fault was "in Judgment and not from Cowardice."[12]

Whipple's trial was only the beginning. Two days after rendering their decision on him, the same court, with the acquitted captain now joining them as a member, heard charges against John Hazard. Hazard was not so fortunate; after hearing the evidence, the court found "The Prisoner, John Hazard Esqr., had rendered himself unworthy of holding his Commission in the Navy of the United States of North America. . . ."[13]

Deserved or not, the spate of courts-martial, petitions, and nagging rumors of unrest put Hopkins in a poor light. Nor was his situation improved when on the same day that Hazard was being cashiered, Congress had decided to conduct its own investigation into Hopkins's conduct. By congressional order Hopkins's orders of 5 January were read on the floor and then sent to a special committee to determine if the commodore had in fact complied with them. Southern resentments over his failure to protect the coasts was surfacing and slowly merging with an already festering anti–New England sentiment.

Had Hopkins been able to point to a naval success, he might well have survived the gathering storm. Such was not the case. His fleet was so weakened by disease that he had to "borrow" nearly 200 soldiers simply to bring his fleet around from New London to Providence. When Washington, who was facing a disaster of his own at New York City, asked for the return of his men, the commodore naturally complied, but had to report that their loss made his fleet "useless." He did manage, by stripping all his other ships of men and supplies, to get the *Andrea Doria* and the *Cabot* to sea.

Not the least of Hopkins's problems was the fact that he had moved his fleet to Providence. Aside from the obvious reason that it was home, it is not clear why he decided to make the move; in fact he probably would have been better off had he remained at New London. In December 1775, the Congress had authorized the construction of thirteen frigates; two of these, later to be named the *Providence* 28 and the *Warren* 32, were ordered built in Providence. The construction of these vessels, among the largest yet built in America, consumed huge amounts of money, men, and supplies. Within a short time the Providence waterfront witnessed a three-way struggle for men and material among Hopkins's fleet, the frigates abuilding, and voracious privateersmen. With such competition the opportunities for profiteering were enormous, and the local merchants were not slow to take advantage. In the face of such greed, Hopkins was helpless; and while others outbid and outmaneuvered him, he could only lament "that Private Interest bears more sway than I wish it did."[14]

Having invested heavily in the Navy, Congress was in no mood to listen to Hopkins's excuses explaining why he and his fleet were still snug in the harbor. After all, other continental captains—John Paul Jones, Nicholas Biddle, and Abraham Whipple—had managed to get to sea during this time. On 14 June the President of the Congress, John Hancock, acting on the instructions of the full body, summoned Hopkins, Saltonstall, and Whipple to appear in Philadelphia to answer for their "frequent Neglect or Disobedience of Orders" and the "numberless Complaints against them.[15]

Saltonstall appeared and was let off, the charges being not "well founded." Whipple received a mild rebuke and was told "to cultivate harmony with his officers." It was for Hopkins that the Congress saved its full fury. Having been forced to cool his heels for several days, on 12 August he was called to defend himself. It was an unpleasant experience. Recalling the scene, John Adams remarked that the affair was yet another example of the rising "Anti New England Spirit, which haunted Congress." Still, even in defending the commodore, Adams had to admit that while he "saw nothing in the Conduct of Hopkins, which indicated Corruption or Want of Integrity . . . Experience and Skill might have been deficient, in several Particulars. . . ."[16] Lawyer Adams and other New Englanders skillfully defended Hopkins. They were successful in preventing the commodore from being cashiered, but not in preventing a humiliating censure. On 16 August, Congress voted "That the said conduct of Commodore Hopkins deserves the censure of this house, and the house does accordingly censure him."[17]

With that, Congress sent the commodore back to Providence to resume command. It might better have dismissed him from the service, for his authority and reputation were now so severely eroded that his effectiveness as a commander was reduced to virtually nothing. For his part, Hopkins vented his wrath on Congress. With great indiscretion he referred to the gentlemen in Philadelphia in highly unflattering terms, cursing them and calling them "ignorant fellows—lawyers, clerks, persons who don't know how to govern men." He even went so far as to swear that he would not obey the orders of Congress. Naturally such actions were quick to come to the attention of Congress, where not even his friends could defend the old man's intemperance.[18] On 26 March 1777, Hopkins was suspended from command. He was kept in that limbo until 2 January 1778, when he was summarily dismissed from the service.

Bitter at his firing, but hardly surprised, Hopkins retired to his farm in North Providence. He continued to serve his state as a member of the Assembly from 1777 to 1786 and served as a trustee of Rhode Island College, later renamed Brown University, from 1783 until his death. Never again, though, did he go to sea, and by the time of his death on 26 February 1802, few aside from his neighbors and friends remembered him as the commander in chief of the Continental Navy.

Esek Hopkins was an ordinary man who had the misfortune to live in extraordinary times. He was at heart a provincial person, loyal to his relatives, friends, and state. His localism blinded him to the greater needs of the revolutionary cause and made him insensitive to the legitimate concerns of other regions as well as the prerogatives of Congress. Hopkins's decision to attack New Providence rather than the enemy forces harassing the southern colonies and his presenting the captured munitions to Connecticut and Rhode Island rather than to the continental government combined to heighten southern hostility toward the Navy. His infelicitous manner of dealing with Congress compared very unfavorably to Washington's deference, a comparison many were wont to make.

As a commander Hopkins failed in many respects, but nowhere were his shortcomings more apparent than in his inability to bridle his temper and tongue in the face of congressional control. It was his intemperate behavior toward his civilian superiors more than his failures at sea that eventually caused his professional demise.

Despite his failures, Hopkins ought not to be judged too harshly. His provincialism was perhaps no greater than that of many of his contemporaries. Most of those who fought in the Revolution thought of themselves as Virginians, Georgians, Rhode Islanders—the concept of being an American was still in its infancy. Furthermore, it is difficult to imagine how any officer in Hopkins's position could have effectively controlled the pack of rascally privateersmen put under his command. The debacle with the *Glasgow* was a product of both his and his officers' inexperience, whereas the scandalous business in Providence was not of his doing. In attempting to create a naval force, Congress was trying to build a preposterous structure on a pitiful foundation. Navies are expensive and complex; the Americans had neither the material resources nor the manpower to put an effective force to sea. It is true that the American Revolution was decided at sea, but not by the American cockleshells; rather the decisive battles were fought by the wooden giants of Great Britain, France, and Spain.

If the Continental Navy had never existed, it is hard to see how the outcome of the Revolution could have been any different. But a citation of failures should not be read as a condemnation of effort. As a contributor to the American naval tradition, Esek Hopkins ought to be remembered as a man who was asked to do the impossible and failed.

FURTHER READING

There is only one full-length biography of Esek Hopkins: Edward Field, *Esek Hopkins, Commander-in-Chief of the Continental Navy During the American Revolution, 1775–1778*. It is, unfortunately, a very uncritical work written more as a defense of Hopkins than as an examination of his life. This ought to be supplemented by William James Morgan, *Captains to the Northward: The New England Captains in the Continental Navy*, a series of very good biographical sketches.

Field drew very heavily upon the Hopkins manuscripts at the Rhode Island Historical Society, which were later edited by Alverda S. Beck and published as *The Letter Book of Esek Hopkins, Commander-in-Chief of the United States Navy, 1775–1777* and *Correspondence of Esek Hopkins, Commander-in-Chief of the United States Navy*. These papers also provide the source material for several articles written about Hopkins that are listed in Myron J. Smith, Jr., *Navies in the American Revolution: A Bibliography*. None of these is particularly useful. The best brief treatment on Hopkins and the Nassau expedition (one that was published too late to be included by Smith) is John J. McCusker, *Alfred: The First Continental Flagship*.

Published documentary material for the Continental Navy is in good supply. First among these sources is the superb William Bell Clark and William James Morgan, eds., *Naval Documents of the American Revolution*. Scholars interested in Hopkins should also consult Charles Oscar Paullin, ed., *Out-Letters of the Continental Marine Committee and Board of Admiralty, August, 1776–September, 1780* and W. C. Ford, ed., *Journals of the Continental Congress, 1774–1789*, supplemented by the National Archives microfilm edition of the *Papers of the Continental Congress*. The Rhode Island Continental Congress political settings are discussed in the author's *William Ellery: A Rhode Island Politico & Lord of Admiralty*.

NOTES

1. Edward Field, *Esek Hopkins, Commander-in-Chief of the Continental Navy During the American Revolution, 1775–1778*, 1–35.

2. W. C. Ford, ed., *Journals of the Continental Congress*, II, 15, 68–70, 89, 91, 93, 209. Hereafter cited as *JCC*.

3. John R. Bartlett, ed., *Records of the Colony of Rhode Island and Providence Plantations in New England*, VII, 347.

4. L. H. Butterfield, ed., *Diary and Autobiography of John Adams*, II, 198.

5. *JCC*, III, 293–94.

6. Butterfield, *Diary*, III, 350.

7. *JCC*, III, 315–18.

8. Ibid., III, 378–87.

9. William Bell Clark and William James Morgan, eds., *Naval Documents of the American Revolution*, III, 636–38. Hereafter cited as *NDAR*.

10. John J. McCusker, Jr., "The American Invasion of Nassau in the Bahamas," *The American Neptune*, XXV, 189–217.

11. For reports detailing the *Glasgow* engagement see *NDAR*, IV, passim.

12. Court Martial of Abraham Whipple, *NDAR*, IV, 1419–21.

13. Court Martial of John Hazard, *NDAR*, IV, 1458–59.

14. Hopkins to Marine Committee, 2 November 1776, *NDAR*, VII, 17.

15. John Hancock to Hopkins, 14 June 1776, *NDAR*, V, 528–30.

16. Butterfield, *Diary*, III, 405–6.

17. *JCC*, V, 660–62.

18. Field, *Hopkins*, 189.

JOHN PAUL JONES: HONOR AND PROFESSIONALISM

BY JAMES C. BRADFORD

As the strains of "The Star-Spangled Banner" died, Secretary of the Navy Charles J. Bonaparte rose, walked to the lectern, and began to speak. "We have met to honor the memory of that man who gave our Navy its earliest traditions of heroism and victory." With these words, the Secretary began his introduction of the President of the United States, Theodore Roosevelt, the first of several dignitaries to deliver addresses at the 1906 commemorative exercises held in honor of John Paul Jones at the U.S. Naval Academy. Before the podium stood a star-draped casket containing the body of Jones, recently returned to the United States after lying for over a century in an unmarked grave in France. Upon the casket lay a wreath of laurel, a spray of palm, and the sword presented to Jones by Louis XVI of France in honor of his victory over the *Serapis*. The ceremony's date had been selected by President Roosevelt—24 April, the 128th anniversary of Jones's capture of the *Drake*—and the observance in Annapolis capped a series of activities that included a White House reception and an official visit by a French naval squadron. Congress ordered the publication of a commemorative volume whose introduction stated, "There is no event in our history attended with such pomp and circumstances of glory, magnificence, and patriotic fervor."[1] This may have verged on hyperbole, but there can be no doubt that the splendor surrounding America's reception of the remains of John Paul Jones, and their reinterment in a crypt

The author wishes to thank Dale T. Knobel for his advice and comments on this essay.

John Paul Jones. Portrait bust executed in marble by Jean-Antoine Houdon. Jones was one of four leaders of the American Revolution sculpted
by the renowned French artist. Jones was so pleased with the bust that
he ordered plaster copies for a dozen friends and acquaintances. Courtesy of Naval Academy Museum.

below the chapel of the U.S. Naval Academy, contrasted sharply
with the treatment accorded him at the time of his death in Paris.

In July of 1792, as Jones lay mortally ill in rented rooms near the
Luxembourg Palace, America's Minister to France, Gouverneur Morris, seemed to have trouble finding time between social activities for
a visit to his deathbed. In his diary Morris recorded: "A Message
from Paul Jones that he is dying. I go thither and make his Will. . . .
Send for a Notary and leave him strugling with his Enemy between

four and five. Dine en famille with Lord Gower and Lady Sutherland. Go to the Minister of the Marines's. . . . I go to the Louvre. . . . Take [my mistress] and Vic d'Azyr [a physician] to Jones's Lodgings but he is dead, not yet cold."[2] Morris ordered Jones's landlord to arrange for as private and inexpensive a burial as possible, but others interceded, and the French Legislative Assembly, wishing to "assist at the funeral rites of a man who has served so well the cause of liberty," took charge of the arrangements. Two days later a cortege of soldiers, representatives of the Assembly, and Masonic brethren from the Lodge of the Nine Sisters accompanied Jones's body to the Protestant cemetery outside the city walls for interment. Gouverneur Morris was giving a dinner party that evening and did not attend. Such was the sad ending to the life of the man whom Benjamin Franklin had once considered the chief weapon of American forces in Europe, and whom Thomas Jefferson had described as the "principal hope" of Americans in their struggle for independence. What kind of a man was Jones to be so heralded during his lifetime, ignored at the time of his death, and honored a century later?

The answer is complex, just as Jones was complex. From humble origins he rose through sheer force of character and combat success to prominence in the Continental Navy. More than any other American of his era, he wrote about naval policy and offered suggestions to foster professionalism in the service; but congressional leaders refused to heed his advice. When the war ended, the Continental Navy was disbanded and its officers returned to civilian endeavors. For Jones the transition was difficult. For a few years he served the United States as a diplomat, but he was a military man whose ambition focused on naval command. When he accepted service in the Russian navy of Catherine the Great to increase his naval knowledge, there were those who mocked his earlier contention that he fought in the American Revolution for the cause of liberty. When he died in Paris, he seemed a man passed by time.

If Jones feared he would be forgotten by history, he need not have. His image might change, but his name was etched on the Anglo-American memory. For a century Americans would recall him as a battle leader, a brave, almost foolhardy captain who inspired his men with "I have not yet begun to fight." To Britons his name conjured up images of treason and piracy. But this would change. At the start of the twentieth century when the United States was building a modern navy and Britain and America were drawing closer together, this image began to shift. Britons began to view Jones more positively, and Americans rediscovered his ideas. With these changes came a desire to know more about all aspects of Jones's life, a life of enough adventure to satisfy any biographer.

John Paul Jones rose from humble stock, a fact he seems never to have forgotten. Born in 1747 the fifth child of a gardener, John Paul, as he was then known, received only a rudimentary education. His father worked for William Craik, owner of "Arbigland," an estate on the Scottish shore of the Solway Firth. Young Paul's contacts with Craik and other area landowners helped instill in him a desire to better his position in society. There being little chance for advancement at home, John Paul was apprenticed at age thirteen to a shipowner from Whitehaven, a town on the Cumbrian coast of the Solway.

His first voyage took him to Fredericksburg, Virginia, where his older brother William was a tailor. A number of voyages between England, the West Indies, and the Chesapeake followed until his master went bankrupt and released Paul from his apprenticeship. At least his next two voyages were on board slavers, but he could not long abide what he called that "abominable trade," and in 1768 took passage home from Kingston, Jamaica. En route both the ship's master and mate died of a fever, and Paul assumed command. The owners rewarded him by giving him permanent command of the vessel, the sixty-ton brig *John*. Only twenty-one years old, he had risen quickly. His biggest handicaps were his temper and his inability to get along with people whom he considered incompetent or lazy. In 1770, on a voyage from Scotland to Tobago, he had Mungo Maxwell, the son of a prominent Kirkcudbright resident, flogged for neglect of duty. Maxwell lodged a complaint against John Paul with authorities in Tobago, but it was dismissed. Maxwell then boarded a packet ship for home, but died en route from a fever. Learning of his death, Maxwell's father had Paul arrested on a charge of having inflicted fatal wounds on his son. John Paul was jailed briefly before being allowed bail to gather evidence that cleared his name.

In the meantime, he joined the Masons in Kirkcudbright, probably with the knowledge that membership was a step up socially and that it could help clear any blemish on his character left from the Maxwell affair. Years later his Masonic membership would open doors to him in Boston, Portsmouth, Philadelphia, and Paris.[3]

By age twenty-five, John Paul formed a partnership with a merchant-planter in Tobago and commanded ships in the triangular trade between Britain and her colonies in North America and the Caribbean. In 1773 his crew mutinied, and he killed the ringleader in self-defense. Friends in Tobago advised him to "retire incognito to the continent of America and remain there until an Admiralty Commission should arrive in the Island" to hear his case. The young captain took their advice, fled to Virginia, and adopted the surname "Jones" as a precaution.[4]

Still in Fredericksburg at the outbreak of the Revolution, Jones traveled to Philadelphia where he became friendly with Joseph Hewes, a congressman from North Carolina whose partner was a brother of Jones's sponsor when he joined the Masons. Through Hewes, he obtained a commission as the senior lieutenant in the Continental Navy on 7 December 1776. When offered command of the sloop *Providence* (21 guns) he refused, choosing instead to serve on board the frigate *Alfred* (30 guns) in the hope that he could expand his knowledge of ship handling and fleet maneuvering. It was characteristic of Jones throughout his career to seek such opportunities to add to his professional education. In this capacity he took part in the New Providence raid and the squadron's engagement of HMS *Glasgow*. The latter convinced him that he had nothing to learn from Esek Hopkins, the commander in chief, and when he was again offered command of the *Providence* in the shuffling of positions that followed the *Glasgow* affair, he eagerly accepted.

Assigned to convoy and transport duty in May and June of 1776, in August Jones set sail on his first independent cruise. Operating off the Grand Banks, he captured sixteen British prizes and destroyed the local fishing fleets at Canso and Isle Madame in Nova Scotia. In recognition of his achievement, he was promoted to the rank of captain on 10 October 1776 and transferred to command of the *Alfred*. In a second cruise to the Grand Banks, Jones took seven more prizes, including the armed transport *Mellish* and her much-needed cargo of winter uniforms.

Upon his return to port, Jones learned that he had been placed eighteenth on the seniority list established by Congress and that he had been reassigned to the *Providence*. Incensed, Jones wrote letters of complaint to congressmen, charging in one of them that several men placed senior to him were "altogether illiterate and utterly ignorant of marine affairs."[5] Congress had not purposely slighted Jones when it compiled the list; clearly he was the most successful officer to date. Family relationships and place of residence, not ability, were the main criteria. The four most senior officers on the 1775 list were related to members of the congressional committee that directed naval affairs. The 10 October 1776 list was drawn up shortly after Congress had ordered the building of thirteen frigates, and, in order to enlist local support in the construction of the vessels and to facilitate the recruitment of sailors, local men were assigned to command the vessels. Jones was an outsider. He had no relative in Congress to press his appointment, no shipyard interest to support him, and no local community to put forward his name. This may have saved him from the provincialism of an Esek Hopkins, but it certainly did not help him gain advancement. It is perhaps of more note that his name appears on the list at all than that it appears so low. But it is also natural that Jones should resent what he took to be a slight. That he should continue to complain throughout the war of what he considered to be an insult is a testament to his personal sense of honor, though he also believed that there was a principle involved. Jones regarded the existing system as unfair and wanted to replace it with one based on merit and seniority. "Perhaps it would have been good policy to have commissioned five or seven old mariners

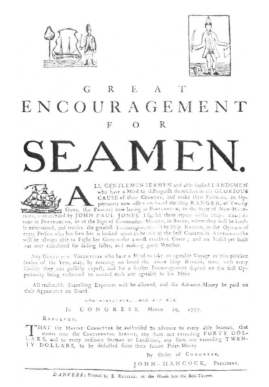

Recruiting poster, 1777. Issued in mid-1777 when Jones was fitting out the *Ranger* in Portsmouth, New Hampshire, this is the only extant American naval poster from the Revolution. Courtesy of Essex Institute, Salem, MA.

who had seen War, to have examined the qualifications of the candidates . . . ," he wrote. At the least, no officer should have been superseded by another unless such a change in seniority was based on the proven abilities of the men involved.[6]

Jones traveled to Philadelphia and pressed his case without success. He also proposed a strategy for carrying the war beyond American waters. Specifically, he suggested a voyage along the unprotected coasts of Africa to prey on British trading outposts and the India fleet. Robert Morris, speaking for Congress, endorsed such an overseas strategy but suggested that the Caribbean was a better place to attack the British than Africa.[7] When plans for the Caribbean expedition were canceled—through the jealousy and backwardness of Esek Hopkins, Jones suspected—he was given command of the *Ranger*, a sloop-of-war under construction in Portsmouth, New Hampshire.[8]

For months Jones worked to ready the *Ranger* for sea. Cordage, sails, and cannon were collected from all over New England.[9] Though he anticipated only a single voyage in the ship—once in Europe his orders called for him to take command of a frigate under construction in Holland—Jones took great pains in his work. A perfectionist, he was rarely satisfied with the condition of a ship when he took command. His seasoned eye told him that the *Ranger* was too lightly built to carry the 20 guns her sides were pierced for, and he reduced the number to 18.

On 1 November 1777, the outfitting and alterations complete and a crew enlisted, Jones set sail for Europe. The passage was not used for rest after the months of work on the ship, but for exercising his officers and crew. Jones was a hard but fair commander who had the best interests of the entire ship's company at the heart. "The care . . . of our seamen is a consideration of the first magnitude," he wrote to Robert Morris soon after his arrival in France.[10] Before proceeding to Paris, Jones advanced spending money to the crew from his own account, ordered the purchase of fresh meat and vegetables for them, purchased new sails for the *Ranger*, altered her rig, and reballasted her.

In mid-December he was summoned to the capital by the American commissioners to France. Jones quickly became friends with the first two of them, Benjamin Franklin and Silas Deane, but probably because of this, did not enjoy good relations with Arthur Lee. The divisions among the commissioners reflected political alignments in Congress. Because of the friendships he had developed with Morris, Franklin, and other members of the Middle States faction, Jones became almost anathema to many of the Adams–Lee faction, of which Arthur Lee and John Adams, who succeeded Deane, were principals.

Jones was disappointed to learn that the ship promised to him would not be available because the British had learned of her intended use and convinced the Dutch not to deliver her to the Americans. He then sought and obtained orders from the commissioners allowing him to retain command of the *Ranger* and to "proceed with [her] in the manner you shall judge best, for distressing the enemies of the United States by sea, or otherwise. . . ."[11] The final phrase reflects Jones's strategic ideas. The Continental Navy could best contribute to victory by preying on British commerce and raiding its coast. The Royal Navy should be left to the French, who had a fleet capable of engaging it in a pitched battle. Thinking in broad strategic terms, Jones proposed a plan to bring the war to a speedy close:

> Were any continental marine power in Europe disposed to avail of the present situation of affairs in America . . . a single blow would now do the needful. Ten or twelve sail of the line with frigates . . . would give a good account of the fleet under Lord Howe. . . . Small squadrons might then be formed to secure the coast and cut off the enemies supplies while our army settled the account current.[12]

Jones's ideas were ahead of their time. The French had greater interests in the West Indies, but his belief that a French fleet in American waters could bring victory was correct.

In February and March, Jones cruised the Bay of Biscay to prey upon British commerce and familiarize himself with the area. On 14 February 1778, during a visit to Quiberon Bay, he arranged the first official salute of the American flag by a foreign power. Early in April he set sail for the Irish Sea with plans to raid a coastal town to repay Britain for her raids on towns in Connecticut and to seize one or more prisoners who could be exchanged for American seamen held in British prisons. Jones was always concerned about Americans so incarcerated. One of his objections to the use of privateers was the fact that they captured so few English seamen who could be used to gain prisoners' release.[13]

Within a month Jones fulfilled both his goals, though not in the way he had planned. On the night of 22 April, he led an attack on Whitehaven where he spiked the guns of the fort and set fire to colliers in the harbor. The damage was minimal in financial terms, but the alarm it spread was great. Not since the Dutch burned Sheerness in 1667 had foreign forces so treated a British seaport. On the following day he led a party ashore on St. Mary's Isle in Kirkcudbright Bay, across the Solway Firth. Jones planned to seize the Earl of Selkirk as a hostage to force the release of Americans held prisoner by Britain. To a boy raised in a nearby gardener's cottage, the earl seemed worthy of such a price. In fact he was a minor Scots peer at best and by his own admission "scarce known" to the king. When Jones learned from a servant that the earl was away, he ordered his men back to their ship, but the men "were disposed to pillage, burn, and plunder all they could," and refused to obey. Faced with mutiny, Jones proposed that a small group go to the house and "politely demand the family plate." His plan was accepted, the silver taken, and violence averted. In a letter to Lady Selkirk written upon his return to France, Jones informed her of his original plan to kidnap the earl, promised to purchase and return the plate, and explained his motives:

> It was my intention to have taken [the earl] on board the Ranger, and to have detained him till thro' his means, a general and fair Exchange of Prisoners, as well in Europe as in America had been effected. . . . I have drawn my Sword in the present generous Struggle for the right of Men; yet I am not in Arms as an American, nor am I in pursuit of Riches . . . I profess myself a Citizen of the World. . . .

Some of Jones's contemporaries and many historians since have discounted his claim to have fought for the "rights of men" and to be a "Citizen of the World," sentiments he would repeat on a number of occasions. To do so is wrong. Such statements were common during the Enlightenment. Thomas Jefferson, Samuel Adams, and Edward Gibbon expressed similar ideas, and James Otis adopted "Ubi Libertas, Ibi Patria," meaning "Where liberty is, there is my country," as his motto. Jones was as serious as any of them when he stated the idea, though he may have been a bit naive in stating it such in a letter. He certainly made himself appear foolish when later in the letter he said to Lady Selkirk: "let not therefore the Amiable Countess of Selkirk regard me as an Enemy. I am ambitious of her esteem and Friendship, and would do anything consistent with my duty to merit it." It was important to him that the Selkirks consider him a gentleman. In his biography of Jones, Admiral Morison speculates that Jones might even have thought of returning to live in the area after the war.[14]

The Earl of Selkirk did not prove to be the key to gaining the release of American prisoners, but the action of the next day did effect the freedom of some of them. On 24 April 1778, Jones crossed the Irish Sea to Carrickfergus where he enticed HMS *Drake* into battle. It was an even match; the *Drake* mounted 20 six-pounders, the *Ranger*, 18 nine-pounders, but the *Drake* had more men. Jones concluded that it was in his interest to disable the *Drake* with cannon fire and prevent her from closing, so that her larger crew could not board the *Ranger*. Such tactics would also preserve the value of the sloop as a prize. In an hour-long action described by Jones as "warm close and obstinate," the captain of the *Drake* was killed, her second-in-command mortally wounded, and her rigging virtually cut to pieces. When the *Drake* surrendered, a more cautious captain might have burned his prize and sailed away before the Royal Navy could send ships after them, but not Jones. Understanding the impact that a British prize would have on the French if brought into port, he calmly remained in sight of the coast for most of the next night and day, refitting the badly damaged *Drake*. Finally, on 8 May, he led the *Drake* into Brest "with English Colours inverted under the American Stars." On board were 200 prisoners who were later exchanged for Americans held in Forton and Old Mill prisons in England.[15]

The entire cruise was a huge success; "what was done," Jones said later, "is sufficient to show that not all their boasted navy can protect their own coast, and that the scene of distress which they have occasioned in America may soon be brought home to their own shores." The Royal Navy and the British government might assail him as a pirate, but American knew better. John Banister, a Virginia delegate to Congress, called his attack on Whitehaven "intrepid & bold," saying that it gave the British "a small specimen of that Conflagration & distress, we have so often experienced from our Enemies, in a much higher degree." Fellow delegate James Lovell recognized the strategic value of the attack, writing that Jones's "conduct alone will make England keep her ships at home."[16]

If Jones expected immediate recognition and promotion as a reward for his actions, he was disappointed. The Continental Congress had few ships to assign, and Jones was too far away to press his claim, in any case. The American commissioners in France, especially Benjamin Franklin, appreciated his achievements but commanded even fewer resources, a fact not fully appreciated by Jones. In June the French Minister of Marine called Jones to Paris to discuss various operations, but nothing was agreed upon, and Jones returned to Brest, where he sought to make profitable use of his time.[17] He had by this time become proficient enough in French that he felt comfortable using the language. He undoubtedly brought to mastering it the same determination that characterized his self-study of every subject that he considered of value to a naval officer. When word arrived of the outbreak of war between Great Britain and France,

Jones sought permission to join the French fleet as an observer to study fleet maneuvering and battle tactics firsthand. To his displeasure, permission did not arrive before the fleet sailed, and Jones missed the chance to observe the Battle of Ushant.

The search for a suitable command for Jones continued. The task was not easy. Several vessels were suggested but rejected. "I wish to have no connection with any Ship that does not Sail *fast* for I intend *to go in harms way*," wrote Jones.[18] Finally a ship was found. She was an old East Indiaman, the *Duc de Duras*, which Jones almost wholly rebuilt and transformed into the *Bonhomme Richard*, renamed in honor of his friend and patron Benjamin Franklin.

Jones proposed "several plans related to different important operations [that he] wanted to undertake" in the vessel, but "was not reluctant" when asked in early April to join the Marquis de Lafayette in launching a raid on Liverpool.[19] Work continued on the *Richard* and the ships assigned to join her, but in May, France and Spain agreed to a joint invasion of England and the Jones—Lafayette expedition was canceled.[20] In June, Jones made a cruise of the Bay of Biscay, and, after some changes in the crew and recovery from the first illness to strike him in years, he was ready to execute his own plans.

On 14 August he put to sea from L'Orient with a squadron composed of the frigates *Bonhomme Richard* (40 guns), *Alliance* (36 guns), and *Pallas* (32 guns), and the corvette *Vengeance* (12 guns), the cutter *Cerf* (18 guns), and two privateers that left the squadron soon after it sailed. Jones planned first to intercept ships expected from India, then to lay Leith, the port city of Edinburgh, under contribution, and finally to intercept the Baltic convoy laden with naval stores. He proceeded clockwise around the British Isles, taking seventeen prizes before he reached the southeast coast of Scotland. Two of the prizes were sent into the neutral port of Bergen in Norway. On 13 September, Jones, with the *Richard, Alliance*, and *Pallas*, was off the Firth of Forth. Writing later, he assessed his position and stated goals in the enterprise:

> Though much weakened and embarrassed with prisoners, [I] was anxious to teach the enemy humanity, by some exemplary stroke of retaliation, and to relieve the remainder of the Americans from captivity in England, as well as to make a diversion in the north, to favour a formidable descent which [I] then expected would have been made on the south side of Great Britain, under cover of the combined [French and Spanish] fleet.[21]

His plan was to sail up the Firth to Leith where he would put a small party ashore and demand payment of 200,000 pounds, under the threat that otherwise the town would be burned. On the point of execution, he reported, a "sudden storm rose and obliged me to run before the wind out of the Gulf of Edinburgh."[22] Jones next attempted to convince his captains to attack the city of Newcastle-on-Tyne to destroy coal supplies destined for London. Seeing no profit in such a plan, his subordinates refused, but after further pleading from Jones agreed instead to cruise along the Yorkshire coast to prey on British shipping.

On 23 September, between two and three in the afternoon, a fleet of forty-one sail was sighted off Flamborough Head. Jones realized immediately that this had to be the sought-after Baltic convoy and set course to engage. As the wind was very light, he was not able to close with the enemy until dark. There ensued one of the hottest naval engagements in the Age of Sail.

The opponents appeared to be evenly matched. The *Serapis*, rated at 44 guns, actually carried 50 and was supported by the 20-gun *Countess of Scarborough*. The *Bonhomme Richard* was rated at 44 guns, like the *Serapis*, but, in fact, carried only 40. With the *Alliance* (36 guns), the *Pallas* (32 guns), and the *Vengeance* (12) to support him, Jones should have had an advantage. However, the *Vengeance* took no part in the battle, and the *Alliance*, captained by the erratic Pierre Landais, did nothing to support the American effort; on the contrary, her only part in the battle was to fire three broadsides into the *Bonhomme Richard*. In addition, the *Serapis* was a newer (less than six months off the stocks), faster, and more maneuverable ship, and her crew of Englishmen were almost certainly superior to Jones's polyglot mix of 174 French, 79 Americans, 59 English, 29 Portuguese, 21 Irish, and representatives of six other nationalities.

By seven o'clock the *Richard* and the *Serapis* were within pistol range of one another and opened fire almost simultaneously. On the first or second broadside, two of Jones's 18-pounders exploded, killing their crews and blowing a hole in the deck above. Fearing the other 18-pounders would also explode, Jones abandoned his main battery. Now sensing that his only hope for victory lay in boarding the more powerful *Serapis*, Jones ran the *Richard* against the starboard quarter of the *Serapis* and ordered his men to board. The British drove the Americans back, and Jones sheered off to seek a better position. When Captain Pearson of the *Serapis* tried to cross the *Richard*'s bow to rake her, Jones ran the bow into the *Serapis*'s stern. Cannonading continued with, in Jones's words, "unremitting fury," the *Richard* receiving most of the damage. The American flag was shot away, and Captain Pearson shouted, "Has your ship struck?" Jones responded with his immortal, "I have not yet begun to fight."

Their ships entangled, the two captains continued to maneuver as best they could until Jones was able to get the two vessels lashed together bow to stern. With his own hands he tied a loose forestay from the *Serapis* to his mizzenmast. "Well done, my brave lads," he cried, "we have got her now." For two hours the ships lay in deadly embrace with the *Serapis* pouring devastating cannon fire into the *Richard*, while the seamen and French marines of the *Richard* swept the enemy's deck with small arms and swivels. Jones remained on the quarterdeck directing fire and working with the guncrew of a 9-pounder. Near exhaustion, he rested for a moment on a hencoop. A sailor begged him, "For God's sake, Captain, strike." "No," responded Jones, "I will sink, I will never strike," and he jumped to his feet.

At ten o'clock the battle swung in favor of the Americans when a grenade thrown from one of the *Richard*'s yardarms fell through an open hatch on board the *Serapis* and exploded among a pile of loose cartridges, killing at least twenty British sailors, horribly burning others, and causing panic on the gundeck.

Jones then focused the fire of his three remaining 9-pounders on the enemy's mainmast. Growing desperate, Captain Pearson ordered his men to board the *Richard*. They were thrown back, and he sought to continue the battle, but within half an hour his mainmast began to tremble. Seeing no hope of victory, he surrendered. The casualties were high. Between 75 and 80 died in each ship during the three-and-a-half-hour battle, and some 100 others were wounded. Thus, almost half of the *Bonhomme Richard*'s crew of 322 were casualties, and Captain Pearson lost almost the same number of the *Serapis*'s 325-man crew. Lieutenant Richard Dale boarded the *Serapis*, and Jones, in a typical eighteenth-century gesture, invited Richard Pearson to his cabin for a glass of wine.[23]

Meanwhile the crews of both ships worked frantically to extinguish fires and patch holes. In a memoir, Midshipman Fanning described the "shocking sight" of "the dead lying in heaps . . . the groans of the wounded and the dying . . . the entrails of the dead scattered promiscuously around, [and] the blood over ones shoes. . . ." For two days, Jones tried to save the *Bonhomme Richard*, but she was "mangled beyond my power of description," and "with inexpressible grief" he watched her sink into the North Sea.[24]

For a week the battered ships drifted and sailed across the North Sea. Jones wanted to try to reach the French port of Dunkirk, but the captains of the *Alliance, Pallas,* and *Vengeance* insisted on going directly across the sea to the Texel in Holland, arriving there on 3 October. A combination of foul weather and good fortune allowed the squadron, including the *Countess of Scarborough*, which had been captured by the *Pallas* while Jones battled the *Serapis*, to escape the dozen British ships sent in their pursuit. Most of the Royal Navy's ships searched the English and Scottish coasts in response to wild rumors and false sightings. When the Admiralty learned that Jones was in the Texel, ships were sent to blockade the port. Now something of a celebrity, Jones was both hated and admired in Britain. "Paul Jones resembled a Jack o' Lantern, to mislead our marines and terrify our coasts," said London's *Morning Post*. He is "still the most general topic of conversation," the paper said a month later. Poems and ballads celebrated his victory and attacked him as a traitor.[25] In America, news of his victory was eagerly embraced; 1779 had not been a good year for American arms. The Dutch people greeted Jones as a hero. He was applauded when he attended the theater, and crowds gathered when he walked the streets. British ambassador Sir Joseph Yorke was appalled at his reception and demanded that Jones be forced to leave Holland and that the Dutch government turn the *Serapis* and the *Countess of Scarborough* over to the the Royal Navy. Jones, supported by France's ambassador, asked that he be allowed to land his sick and wounded, send his 504 British prisoners ashore, and repair his ships so that he could put to sea. For the next two months Jones was the center of partisan political maneuvering in Amsterdam where the House of Orange was basically friendly to Britain, and the Patriot Party favored France and sympathized with the United States. Some Dutch officials even suspected that Jones had been sent to Holland to try to provoke a war between Britain and the Netherlands.[26]

Jones had no desire to remain in Dutch waters and made his repairs as quickly as possible. He did try, unsuccessfully, to trade his English captives for Americans held in British prisons, but otherwise he focused his attention on his men and ships. Finally, he was forced to turn control of his prisoners and ships over to the French and set sail in the *Alliance* on 27 December. Leaving the Texel, Jones called his officers together and informed them that he planned to cruise for twenty days before going to L'Orient. "Gentlemen," he told them, "you cannot conceive what an additional honour it will be to us all, if in cruising a few days we should have to good luck to fall in with an English frigate of our force and carry her in with us. . . . This would crown our former victories, and our names, in consequence thereof would be handed down to the latest posterity." His crew was hesitant, indeed near mutiny, but Jones imposed his will upon them, and the *Alliance* sailed through the English Channel and on to Corunna, Spain, where she took on supplies and made repairs before crossing the Bay of Biscay to arrive at L'Orient on 19 February. Jones immediately set the crew to making alterations in the ship that he felt had been shown essential by the cruise. Many of his crew did not believe the work was necessary and had an additional grievance: they had not been paid either wages or prize money since they left America almost a year before. This latter was not Jones's fault, but the crew blamed him, and in mid-April he set out for Paris to see if he could obtain funds either from the American commissioner or from Le Ray de Chaumont, the French agent who had handled the financial arrangements for fitting out the *Bonhomme Richard* squadron.[27]

Jones proved unable to obtain money but was flattered by the welcome he received. His capture of the *Serapis* contrasted sharply with the failure of the combined French and Spanish fleet. His personal conduct during the battle appealed to the French sense of valor, and all Paris lionized him. Louis XVI awarded him the Ordre du Mérite Militarie and presented him a gold-hilted sword. France's leading Masons, the brethren of the Lodge of the Nine Sisters, invited Jones to join and engaged the renowned Jean-Antoine Houdon to sculpt his bust. Crowds applauded him everywhere he went. A handsome war hero, fluent in French, and genteel in manner, Jones was in great demand for dinners and receptions. His wit became famous. At a dinner given his honor by the Duc de Biron, Jones was informed that the king of England had recently knighted Richard Pearson for his conduct during the battle with Jones; and Jones replied, "Let me fight him again and I'll make him a lord!" Women seemed to be irresistibly drawn to Jones, who often responded with poetry. His six weeks in the capital flew by.

In June, Jones returned to L'Orient with plans to sail to America with a cargo of military supplies. In his absence Pierre Landais had been busy undermining Jones's command of the *Alliance* by telling the crew that Jones was acting in league with Chaumont to deny them their prize money. Arthur Lee was in L'Orient ready to sail to America and promised to use his influence with Congress to help them get their wages if they backed Landais. Benjamin Franklin warned Jones that trouble was brewing, but Jones seems to have underestimated the gravity of the situation and allowed himself to be outmaneuvered. Landais took control of the ship and sailed in June. Most of the sailors who had served on board the *Bonhomme Richard* under Jones were left behind and formed the nucleus of a crew for the *Ariel*, a sloop-of-war built for the British navy but captured by the French and lent to the United States to carry supplies to America. When given command of the *Ariel*, Jones was, as usual, dissatisfied with the ship and ordered her rerigged, thus further delaying his departure.

While the *Ariel* lay at anchor, the *Independence*, an American privateer, entered the harbor under the command of Thomas Truxton. Like many other privateers, Truxton had little respect for the Continental Navy and thus refused to accord to Jones and the *Ariel* the traditional signal of respect. Rankled, Jones sent an officer to remind Truxton of the congressional resolution prohibiting privateers and merchant vessels from flying pennants when in the presence of ships of the Continental Navy. When Truxton refused to remove the pennant, Jones wrote to him "It is not me you have offended. You have offended the United States of America," and sent his first lieutenant Richard Dale and two boat loads of seamen to forcibly haul it down. When Truxton again flew the pennant, Jones sent a letter to the Board of Admiralty describing the incident and asking, "Is not this bidding defiance to Congress and the Continental Flag?" There is no evidence that Congress took any action on Jones's complaint, but Truxton's biographer believes that the incident had an effect on Truxton, who "put some of Jones's ideas away in the corner of his mind" and recalled them later when he became the commander of an American man-of-war.[28]

Work was finally finished on the *Ariel* in September, and Jones put to sea only to be caught in a vicious gale that destroyed ships along the entire Breton coast. The survival of the *Ariel* was due to Jones's consummate seamanship. The French commander of the port of L'Orient wrote: "The Commodore showed in this gale the same strength that he had exhibited in battle. . . . The crew and passengers all credit him with saving the ship."[29] The *Ariel* lost two masts, and repairs delayed Jones's departure so that he did not reach America until February of 1781.

Upon his arrival in Philadelphia, a group of congressmen sought to launch an investigation of Jones's conduct in France to show that it had delayed the sending of supplies to America. They hoped through Jones to embarrass Benjamin Franklin but abandoned their plan when it appeared it might backfire. Instead, they decided to have Jones examined in private by the Board of Admiralty. The secretary of the board gave Jones forty-seven questions to which he skillfully responded, giving a detailed account of his triumphs and laying blame for any delays on Landais and Chaumont. Governmental restraint soon turned to acclaim as France's ambassador formally invested Jones with the eight-pointed star of the Ordre du Mérite Militarie, the highest award the French could give to a foreigner. Congress showed its regard for Jones by voting "that the thanks of the United

States in Congress assembled, be given to Captain John Paul Jones, for the zeal, prudence and intrepidity with which he has supported the honor of the American flag; [and] for his bold and successful enterprizes to redeem from captivity the citizens of these states." Jones was particularly pleased by the last section. Congress rewarded him more concretely by voting unanimously to give him command of the *America*, the Continental Navy's only ship-of-the-line, then building at Portsmouth, New Hampshire.[30]

In mid-August, Jones left Philadelphia for Portsmouth, where he arrived on the last day of the month. For a year Jones struggled to find the supplies and skilled workmen necessary to ready the *America* for launching, but just as she was ready for sea, command of the ship was taken from him. Peace negotiations were under way with the British, and the war seemed almost over. The Continental Congress, even shorter on funds than usual, doubted the need for the ship. When a French ship-of-the-line was lost on a sandbar outside Boston Harbor, Congress voted to give the *America* to the French navy as a replacement.[31] Jones supervised her launching on 5 November 1782, and two days later set out for Philadelphia. Unable to procure another command, Jones sought and was given permission to join a French fleet for a cruise to the Caribbean. As in 1778, his goal was to increase his professional knowledge by firsthand study of fleet maneuvering and French naval tactics. Jones sailed with the fleet on Christmas Eve 1782 for what turned out to be a mixed experience. The wardroom company must have been pleasant, but for part of the voyage Jones was gravely ill. He was able to observe fleet evolutions, but there was no combat. When the fleet reached Puerto Cabello, Venezuela, it learned that a peace treaty had been signed with Britain. From there Jones sailed to Cape Haitien, where, sick again, he left the ship.

By May, Jones was back in Philadelphia, his health so bad that Robert Morris feared for his life; and in July, he entered a sanatorium in nearby Bethlehem where he remained for over a month, thinking, perhaps brooding, about the future. Back in March he had tried to purchase an estate in New Jersey, and in August he wrote to a friend that "I hope that I have occasion 'to learn War no more,' " indicating that he hoped to visit Portsmouth, New Hampshire in the fall.[32] Such thoughts of domesticity may have been induced by his illness. By fall he had recovered and was planning far more ambitious enterprises. To Robert Morris he wrote suggesting he be sent to Europe "in a handsom Frigate to display our Flag in the Ports of the different Powers," to negotiate commercial treaties, and to study the administration of foreign navies. In mid-October he wrote to the President of Congress concerning prize money owed to the officers and men of the *Bonhomme Richard* squadron in France and Denmark. Jones was confident that he could succeed where others had failed. "I beg leave to acquaint you that I am ready to proceed to Europe in order to make the necessary application at those two Courts, provided I can go honored with the Sanction of Congress."[33] On 1 November 1783 Congress gave its sanction, and nine days later Jones boarded a packet ship for France.

Negotiations in France dragged on for two years. Jones's success in finally extracting money from the distressed French treasury is a mark of both his continued prestige in Paris and the tenacity with which he pursued almost all his objects. During this period, "the Chevalier," as Jones was known in France, renewed old friendships and cast about for future employment. He considered several commercial ventures and invested in a few with mixed results. At the same time he yearned for more active service. In 1784 Thomas Jefferson joined Franklin and Adams in Paris as an American commissioner to France. The three were empowered to deal not only with France but also with the Barbary states, whose corsairs had been taking American ships captive under the pretext of war. The North Africans wanted tribute, and the American commissioners were divided on how to deal with them. Jefferson opposed such payments in principle:

> We ought to begin a naval power, if we mean to carry on our own commerce. Can we begin it on a more honourable occasion, or with a weaker foe? I am of opinion Paul Jones with half a dozen frigates would totally destroy [the Barbary states'] commerce . . . by constant cruising and cutting them to pieces by piecemeal.[34]

Jones would no doubt have welcomed such an enterprise.

Only a month before leaving America he had addressed a long letter to Robert Morris, who as "Agent of the Marine" headed the Navy. "In the time of peace it is necessary to prepare, and be always prepared for war by sea," wrote Jones. In succeeding paragraphs he discussed strategy, the officer corps, and naval education and training. "It is the work of many years' study and experience to acquire the high degree of science necessary for a great sea officer," he wrote. He claimed that service in the merchant marine does not adequately prepare a man for naval command, nor does "cruising after merchant ships, (the service on which our frigates have generally been employed), afford . . . the knowledge necessary for conducting fleets and their operations." Officer candidates must be carefully selected and promoted on a merit basis. Jones recognized the financial constraints imposed on the young nation:

My plan for forming a proper corps of sea officers, is by teaching them the naval tactics in a fleet of evolution. To lessen the expense as much as possible, I would compose that fleet of frigates instead of ships of the line: on board of each I would have a little academy, where the officers should be taught the principles of mathematics and mechanics, when off duty. When in port the young officers should be obliged to attend at the academies established at each dockyard, where they should be taught the principles of every art and science that is necessary to form the character of a great sea officer.

In addition to training officers, the fleet of evolution would provide an opportunity to develop and practice signals and tactics. In his draft of the letter to Morris, Jones analyzed current French and English signaling and maneuvering systems and concluded that the French system was far superior.

Reform of the officer system was also necessary, he believed. The Continental Navy's ranks of midshipmen, lieutenants, and captains were inadequate. In 1775 Congress had established three grades of lieutenants, but Jones saw the need for "the same number of sub-altern grades" below lieutenant. "The charge of the deck of a ship of the line should . . . never be entrusted to an officer under twenty-five years of age." The increase in the number of grades would allow the Navy "to raise young men by smaller steps" and thereby avoid the "uneasiness" of mind that results "when they are continued too long in any one grade." Regular promotions would also give officers a sense of accomplishment. In the same letter he commented on Congress's failure to mention his name when transferring the *America* to France. "Such little attentions to the military pride of officers are always of use to a state, and *cost nothing*." Perhaps Jones was learning. During the war he had not always been liberal in his praise of his subordinates in official reports.[35]

By the time Jefferson made his suggestion concerning the Barbary states, Jones appears to have given up hope of any immediate service in an American navy. As early as 1782, he had written to Hector McNeill that his voice was "like a cry in the Desert" when he made suggestions to improve the Navy.[36] During the fall of 1785 he wrote his "Memoir" for Louis XVI, probably with the hope that should the threatening war with Britain become real, he might be offered a commission in the French navy. If so, he was disappointed. There was no war in 1785 or 1786, and Jones decided to return to America before proceeding to Copenhagen to press the claims of the *Bonhomme Richard* squadron before the Danish court.

Jones sailed from France to New York City in July 1787. There he presented his accounts for the French prize money negotiations to Congress and again sought to be named rear admiral. As in the past, officers senior to him blocked the promotion. Such an action would have been honorary at best because the United States lacked a navy at the time. Congress did honor Jones by unanimously voting him a gold medal and instructing that Thomas Jefferson have it executed in Paris. Jones was the only Continental Navy officer so recognized, and was much pleased. Congress also asked the king of France, probably at Jones's request, to allow him "to embark with one of his fleets of evolution; convinced that he can no where else so well acquire knowledge which may hereafter render him more extensively useful." In addition, Congress renewed his authority to press the Danish government for payment for the prizes handed over to the British.

In 1788 Jones left America for the last time. He arrived in Copenhagen in March and was received with ceremony. He met with the Danish foreign minister and dined with the royal family, but could do nothing to obtain the money. By mid-April he was presented a far more appealing opportunity and gave up on the prize money. He certainly was not willing to devote two years to the project as he had in France.

The offer was a commission in the Imperial Russian Navy. Attracted by an opportunity to command a fleet, as well as the promise of adventure, glory, and profit, Jones accepted immediately and set out for Saint Petersburg. However, several British officers served in Catherine the Great's navy in the Baltic, and they threatened to resign rather than serve with a "pirate"; so Jones was ordered to the Black Sea.

Jones was commissioned a rear admiral, but the limits of his authority were not clearly delineated. Prince Potemkin, one of Catherine the Great's favorites, was the overall commander in the region. Jones thought that he was to command all naval forces, but there were three other rear admirals already serving in the Black Sea. One commanded the arsenal at Kherson, another the flotilla of galleys, and the third a separate fleet at Sevastopol. Jones was given command of the sailing ships and had to deal closely with only one of the other admirals, Prince Nassau-Siegen, an international adventurer who was very jealous of Jones and had the ear of Prince Potemkin, their common superior.

Jones boarded his flagship, the *Vladimir*, on 29 May 1788. With a Turkish attack imminent, Jones took strategic control of the Russian forces, deploying them across the Liman, or estuary of the Dnieper River. Eight days later the Russian forces repulsed an assault by the Turks. A second attack broke down when the Turkish flagship ran aground. During the following night Jones personally reconnoitered the enemy fleet in a rowboat and skillfully shifted the position of his ships to meet the next day's onslaught. The Second Battle of the Liman lasted two days and resulted in the capture or destruction of ten large and five small Turkish vessels against the loss of only a single ship by the Russians. Nassau-Siegen, with the support of his friend Potemkin, took credit for the victory although the strategy of fighting a defensive battle had been Jones's and was adopted over Nassau-Siegen's protests. In fact, the victory would have been greater had Nassau-Siegen followed Jones's orders during the battle. After four months of political bickering over credit for the victory, Jones emerged the loser and was recalled to Saint Petersburg under the pretense of reassignment to the Baltic fleet. For several more months he languished in the capital, devoting much of his time to drafting plans for a Russian–American alliance, the reorganization of the Black Seas fleet, and Russian-led operations against the Barbary corsairs. He also compiled a "Narrative of the Campaign of the Liman," which he meant to submit to Catherine in the hope that it would regain her favor. In April of 1789 a trumped-up scandal linking Jones to a young girl ended any chance for his restoration to command, and he decided to leave Russia. It took him until the end of August to put his affairs in order and to obtain the necessary exit papers. From Saint Petersburg he went to Warsaw, Alsace, and Vienna, before reaching Amsterdam in December. In May 1790 he visited London and finally settled in Paris. Jones was clearly drifting. His health was deteriorating. Without money or employment he settled into rented rooms near the Luxembourg Palace. There he spent his final days, all but ignored. To Gouverneur Morris, American minister to France, he became a bore. "Paul Jones calls on me," Morris recorded in his diary. "He has nothing to say but is so kind as to bestow on me all the Hours which hang heavy in his Hands. . . ." A few days later Morris wrote "Paul Jones calls and gives me his Time but I cannot lend him mine."[37]

It was a sad ending to a career filled with highlights. Jones must have sensed the attitude of Morris and have been hurt by the inattention of men like Lafayette who had once sought him. When death claimed him in July 1792, just days after his forty-fifth birthday, he may have welcomed it as a relief after two months of suffering from jaundice and other diseases brought on by long exposure to the elements. Had he known that President George Washington and his Secretary of State Thomas Jefferson remembered him and valued his services, it would have been a great comfort. Only days before his death, the two leaders signed a commission appointing "John Paul

Jones a citizen of the United States . . . a Commissioner . . . to confer treat and negotiate with the [Dey of] Algiers . . . concerning the ransom of all citizens of the United States of America in captivity with the Said Dey."[38] Jones died before the commission was delivered. It was a strange and lonely death.

Jones's life paralleled that of the Continental Navy. Both rose from humble origins, appeared briefly on the world scene, and then passed with few mourners. Jones gave to it some of its brightest moments, including the capture of the two largest Royal Navy ships to strike their flags to Americans during the Revolution. He always made the most of the limited resources available to him. In the battle against the *Serapis*, he left a legacy of dauntless courage and unconquerable persistence in the most desperate of circumstances. Every fighting service needs a tradition of refusal to surrender in the face of seemingly overwhelming odds. "It was [John Paul Jones] who . . . created the spirit of my country's infant Navy." wrote a mid–nineteenth-century naval officer.[39]

This was the dominant image of Jones during a century when naval officers, in particular, shared his great sense of personal honor. The era of Jacksonian Democracy found much to admire in the rise of a Scots gardener's son to glory in the Continental Navy and to flag rank in the Imperial Russian Navy.

Early American naval officers were not an introspective group. Few conducted extensive correspondence, and fewer still left memoirs of their service. No account exists of the mundane contacts between Jones and those who served with him, of the long hours shared on the quarterdeck, the inspection tours of the ship, and the relaxing dinners in his cabin. Still, it is clear that he directly influenced such future officers as Richard Dale, Thomas Truxton, and Joshua Barney.

At the start of the twentieth century when the U.S. Navy took its place among leaders of the world, the image of Jones held by the general public and by naval officers began to change. The Navy's rising professionalism led it to value Jones not simply as a courageous leader in time of battle but as a complete naval officer. Jones understood the basics of his vocation. His grasp of naval architecture was demonstrated by his supervision of the construction of the *Ranger* and the *America*, the virtual reconstruction of the *Bonhomme Richard*, and alterations to the masts and rigging of almost every ship he commanded. His victories were not won by courage and superior tactics alone, but were the result of careful preparation. Jones took a motley crew on board the *Bonhomme Richard* and welded them into a team. His letters and actions show the respect he had for his subordinates, though he often failed to give enough credit to the officers who served under him.

His writings also suggest a nascent professionalism. His opposition to nepotism and desire to establish boards to evaluate officers for promotion were visionary for his time. His proposals for a fleet of evolution and naval academies predated the establishment of such institutions in the United States by over half a century. Consequently, quotations from his writings, sometimes imaginary, appeared on the fitness report forms of the Navy's Bureau of Personnel and on examination books at the U.S. Naval Academy in the early twentieth century.

Jones's strategic ideals were equally sound. As clearly as anyone, he understood the limitation of the Continental Navy and advocated operations congruent with its capabilities. The need for French assistance in ejecting the British army from America was apparent to Jones. It is not surprising that Admiral DeGrasse's biographer credits Jones with suggesting the strategy that ultimately brought victory at Yorktown.[40]

John Paul Jones's great fault was his egotism. He could express his gratitude to men such as Hewes, Franklin, and Morris who appreciated his abilities and helped him, but he always resented anyone who did not measure up to his standards and was in a position to control his affairs. As an individual, Jones was jealous and vain. A man of strong opinions, he generated strong feelings in others. To some he was an arriviste whose pride smacked of overweening hubris. This partly explains his nation's treatment of him at the time of his death.

That he was a man of talent cannot be denied, nor can his patriotism. His disappointments in terms of recognition and command rivaled those of Benedict Arnold, but their reactions differed sharply. Jones's reputation rests on his exploits of 1778 and 1779, when he took the war to the British people and strengthened American morale at times when it was sinking. Sadly, he was destined never to test his talents on a broad scale. With the end of the war, America thought it no longer needed a navy and thus had no use for Jones as a naval officer.

But Jones never fully adapted to peace. His success as a diplomat was no compensation for his disappointment when his plans for an American navy were rejected. Throughout the Revolution, he had remained optimistic, convinced that the Continental Navy, no matter how low its fortunes, could win respect from Europe for the new United States. That he sought personal fame at the same time is not surprising. His pursuit of glory as a reward for self-sacrifice and service to the nation was fully in keeping with the spirit of the time.[41] In the end, John Paul Jones's legacy rests not so much on what he accomplished as on how he did it. As the inscription on his tomb reads: "He gave to our navy its earliest traditions of heroism and victory."

FURTHER READING

John Paul Jones is almost certainly America's most famous naval officer. He has been the subject of over a score of biographies and even more works of fiction. Only four of the biographies are worthy of attention. These are John Henry Sherburne's 1825 *Life and Character of the Chevalier John Paul Jones*; Anna DeKoven's two-volume *The Life and Letters of John Paul Jones*, published in 1913; Lincoln Lorenz's *John Paul Jones, Fighter for Freedom and Glory*, published in 1941; and Samuel Eliot Morison's 1959 Pulitzer Prize–winning *John Paul Jones: A Sailor's Biography*. Other biographies contain so many errors that they should be avoided. Most important in this group is Augustus C. Buell's two-volume *Paul Jones, Founder of the American Navy: A History*, which was published in 1900 and served as the basis for later biographies such as Norman Hapgood's *Paul Jones* and M. MacDermot Crawford's *The Sailor Whom England Feared*. Valentine Thomson, *Knight of the Seas*, accepts most of Buell's tales and adds several of her own. Gerald W. Johnson, *The First Captain: The Story of John Paul Jones*, describes episodes, such as Jones's service in the Royal Navy and his career as an actor, for which there is no documentation.

The largest collections of Jones manuscripts are held by the Library of Congress, the National Archives, and the U.S. Naval Academy, but there has never been a complete or accurate edition of his papers. During the nineteenth century, Jones's niece, Janette Taylor, arranged for the publication of the *Memoirs of Rear-Admiral Paul Jones*, probably by Sir John Malcolm, and Robert Sands's *Life and Correspondence of John Paul Jones, Including His Narrative of the Campaign of the Liman*. The *Naval Documents of the American Revolution*, eight volumes to date, include Jones's most important papers for the first two years of the war, and Frank A. Golder's *John Paul Jones in Russia* includes transcriptions of most of his important papers relating to his service in the Black Sea. John S. Barnes edited *The Logs of the Serapis–Alliance–Ariel Under the Command of John Paul Jones, 1779–1780*, and Louis F. Middlebrook edited *The Log of the Bon Homme Richard*. Gerald W. Gawalt translated the *Memoir of the American*

Revolution that Jones prepared for the king of France, and it was published by the Library of Congress for the U.S. Bicentennial.

Jones's operations are described in Gardner W. Allen's *A Naval History of the American Revolution*, his command of the *Providence* is included in Hope S. Rider's *Valour Fore & Aft: Being the Adventures of the Continental Sloop Providence, 1775–1779, Formerly Flagship Katy of Rhode Island's Navy*, and the battle between the *Bonhomme Richard* and the *Serapis* is analyzed by John Evangelist Walsh in *Night on Fire: The First Complete Account of John Paul Jones' Greatest Battle*. Don C. Seitz's *Paul Jones, His Exploits in English Seas During 1776–1780, Contemporary Accounts Collected from English Newspapers with a Complete Bibliography* will guide the reader to eighteenth- and nineteenth-century works.

The administration of the Continental Navy and early naval policy and strategy have not received the attention they merit. Charles O. Paullin's *The Navy of the American Revolution: Its Administration, Its Policy, and Its Achievements* has been superseded by Frank C. Meyers's doctoral dissertation, "Congress and the Navy: The Establishment and Administration of the American Revolutionary Navy by the Continental Congress." Both works focus on administration rather than strategy and policy. William Bell Clark discusses the goals and achievements of operations in European waters in his *Ben Franklin's Privateers*, but no work surveys the entire war.

Three officers who served with Jones left varying accounts of their commander. *Diary of Ezra Green, M.D., Surgeon on board the Continental Ship-of-War Ranger Under John Paul Jones, from November 1, 1777 to Sept. 27, 1778 ...* , edited by George H. Preble, pictures Jones in positive terms, as does Lt. Richard Dale's "Particulars of the Engagement Between the Bonhomme Richard and the Serapis," which is printed in Sherburne's biography. Nathanial Fanning, author of *Fanning's Narrative: Memoirs of Nathaniel Fanning*, edited by John S. Barnes, served as a midshipman on board the *Bonhomme Richard* and is more critical of Jones. His "memoir" and the sketch of Jones's life that follows contain a number of amusing but apocryphal stories.

NOTES

1. Charles W. Stewart, comp., *John Paul Jones Commemoration*, 13.

2. Gouverneur Morris, *A Diary of the French Revolution*, II, 468, 471.

3. Documents relating to the Mungo Maxwell episode, including the warrant for Jones's arrest, his petition for bail, dated 10, 13, and

15 November 1776, are in the Kirkcudbright Sheriff Clerk's Records, Scottish Record Office, Edinburgh. Jones's petition for admission to the Masonic Lodge is in the Naval Academy Museum.

4. Jones to Benjamin Franklin, 6 March 1779, Franklin Papers, American Philosophical Society, Philadelphia.

5. Jones to Joseph Hewes, 17 August and 1 September 1777; Jones to Robert Morris, 24 August and 30 October 1777 (from which the quotation is taken) and 10 October 1783; Jones to Jonathan Williams, 20 November 1780; Jones to John Ross, 23 November 1778, Jones Papers, Library of Congress (henceforth Jones Papers, DLC).

6. Jones to R. Morris, 10 October 1783, Jones Papers, DLC; Jones to Franklin, 6 March 1779, American Philosophical Society.

7. Jones to R. Morris, 12 January 1777 and the Marine Committee to Jones, 1 February 1777, Jones Papers, DLC; R. Morris to Jones, 5 February 1777, Jones Papers, Papers of the Continental Congress, National Archives (henceforth PCC 168).

8. Jones to R. Morris, 10 October 1783, Jones Papers, DLC.

9. Jones to John Brown, 31 October 1777, Pierpont Morgan Library.

10. Jones to William Whipple, 11 December 1777, Dreer Collection, Historical Society of Pennsylvania, and Jones to R. Morris, 11 December 1777, Jones Papers, DLC.

11. American Commissioners to Jones, 16 January 1778, Benjamin Franklin Letterbook, DLC.

12. Jones to American Commissioners, 10 February 1778, PCC, item 193.

13. Jones to R. Morris, 11 December 1777, Jones Papers, DLC.

14. *John Paul Jones' Memoir of the American Revolution*, translated and edited by Gerald W. Gawalt; Jones to Lady Selkirk, 8 May 1778. Original in possession of Sir David Hope-Dunbar, Kirkcudbright, Scotland. Virtually all of Jones's biographers quote the letter.

15. Jones to Commissioners, 9 May 1978, Jones Papers, PCC 168. William Bell Clark, *Ben Franklin's Privateers*, discusses previous attempts by Americans in Europe to obtain British prisoners for use in an exchange for American prisoners.

16. John Banister to Theodorick Bland, Jr., 31 July 1778 and James Lovell to William Whipple, 14 July 1778. Paul H. Smith, ed., *Letters of the Delegates to Congress*, IX, 278, 376. G. J. Marcus, *A Naval History of England: The Formative Centuries*, 418.

17. Gawalt, ed., *Jones' Memoir*, 25.

18. Jones to Le Ray de Chaumont, 16 November 1778, Jones's Letterbook, U.S. Naval Academy Museum.

19. Lafayette to the Comte de Vergennes, 1 April 1779. Stanley J. Idzerda, ed., *Lafayette in the Age of the American Revolution*, II, 251–53.

20. Lafayette to Sartine [16–20 April]; Lafayette to Vergennes, 26 April 1779; Lafayette to Jones, 27 April and 22 May 1779; Franklin to Jones, 27 April 1779; Jones to Chaumont, 30 April 1779. Idzerda, *Lafayette*, II, 255–68.

21. Quoted from the lost English copy of Jones's memoir in Robert Sands, *Life and Correspondence of John Paul Jones*, 171.

22. Gawalt, ed., *Jones' Memoir*, 31.

23. All of Jones's biographers recount the battle. The most recent and most complete account is John Evangelist Walsh, *Night on Fire: The First Complete Account of John Paul Jones' Greatest Battle*. Samuel E. Morison reconstructs Jones's words and actions that evening in *John Paul Jones: A Sailor's Biography*, 221–42.

24. Fanning, *Narrative*, edited by John S. Barnes, 53. Jones to Franklin, 3 October 1779, Jones Papers, DLC.

25. Morison, *Jones*, 247–49 contains excerpts from several.

26. Jan Willem Schulte Nordholt, *The Dutch Republic and American Independence*, Chapter V, "Here Comes Paul Jones!"

27. Fanning, *Narrative*, 78–79, 81.

28. Eugene S. Ferguson, *Truxton of the Constellation*, 40–42.

29. Quoted in Morison, *Jones*, 306.

30. *Journals of Congress*, 27 February, 14 April, 26 June 1781.

31. Ibid., 3 September 1782.

32. Jones to Major John Sherburne, 1 August 1783, U.S. Naval Academy Museum.

33. Jones to R. Morris, 10 October 1783, Jones Papers, DLC; Jones to Boudinot, 18 October 1783, PCC 168.

34. Thomas Jefferson to James Monroe, 11 November 1784. Paul L. Ford, *The Writings of Thomas Jefferson*, IV, 10–11.

35. Jones to R. Morris, 13 October 1783. The draft containing Jones's comments on the current state of the French and British navies is in the Jones Papers in the Library of Congress.

36. Jones to Hector McNeill, 25 May 1782; DeKoven, *Jones*, I, 195.

37. Gouverneur Morris, *Diary*, II, 59, 64.

38. The commission is in Jones's crypt at the U.S. Naval Academy.

39. Lt. Alexander B. Pinkham quoted by Edouard A. Stackpole, *A Nantucketer Who Followed An Ideal in a Far Country*, 2–3.

40. Charles Lee Lewis, *Admiral DeGrasse and American Independence*, 70–71.

41. This is the central theme of Douglas Adair's "Fame and the Founding Fathers." Every war produces individuals whose talents seem of little value, or whose temperaments prevent them from achieving success in peace commensurate with that in war. George Rogers Clark and Light Horse Harry Lee—as well as Jones—come to mind as examples for the American Revolution.

JOHN BARRY: A MOST FERVENT PATRIOT

BY WILLIAM JAMES MORGAN

A Pennsylvania letter of marque brigantine mounting 10 guns and a crew of forty-five, the *Delaware*, was homeward bound from a fruitful West Indian cruise in October 1779. Shortly after the brigantine came inside the Delaware Capes, word was received that the *Confederacy*, a 32-gun Continental Navy frigate desperately in need of seamen (a chronic condition suffered by all American naval vessels throughout the Revolutionary War), lay in the river above, impressing seamen from incoming merchant ships. This disturbing news, quite understandably, was a cause of concern to the *Delaware* crewmen, but it did not intimidate her master. He held his course, meanwhile clearing the small ship for action should resistance prove necessary. As she came up with the *Confederacy*, a warning shot brought the *Delaware* to. Unbeknownst to Lieutenant Stephen Gregory, temporarily commanding the frigate, he had caught a tartar when he stopped the *Delaware*. Here he confronted a shipmaster willing to give battle, regardless of the overwhelming disparity in strength between the warship and the brigantine, to protect his men from impressment, whether the antagonist be American or British. When his identity became known on board the *Confederacy*, Lieutenant Gregory decided that discretion was the better part of valor. The *Delaware* was allowed to continue unhindered to Philadelphia with her crew intact.

Who was this captain whose very name caused a powerful American man-of-war to back off despite an urgent need to fill her complement and put to sea with a minimum of delay?

It was John Barry, a prominent senior Continental Navy captain who had achieved spectacular success against the British earlier in

John Barry. Courtesy of Naval Academy Museum.

the war. By 1779 American naval fortunes had sunk so low that there was no public vessel available for him to command. In such circumstances it was common practice for naval officers to request a leave of absence and to undertake a private adventure in a letter of marque, a privateer, or simply a plodding merchant ship. Even had service by a naval officer on board a private vessel seemed a contradiction, it would have been in keeping with Barry's life.

Philadelphia became home to Barry in 1760 when the fifteen-year-old seaman and native of County Wexford, Ireland, first arrived at the city. In the ensuing years he prospered as ship owner, master, and investor in the West Indies trade. Barry was highly respected by the mercantile community for his integrity and ship handling skill, and Robert Morris and other leading Philadelphia merchants sought him out to command their ships. He was an anomaly, standing well over six feet tall at a time when the norm was perhaps five feet six. And, he was a practicing Catholic in a predominantly Protestant society. As relations between England and her American colonies deteriorated, Barry fervently espoused the cause of his adopted land. It can be safely assumed that his patriotic ardor was heated several extra degrees by an Irishman's inborn antipathy for anything British.

At the close of the year 1774, John Barry was commanding a new 300-ton ship, the *Black Prince*, which belonged to the prominent house of Willing, Morris and Company and several other investors. He loaded a cargo of grain and wood for Bristol, England, and after a stormy crossing arrived at Bristol at the end of January 1775. After an unexceptional return passage, Barry found Philadelphia electric with news of events to the northeast at Lexington and Concord. Merchants were frantically getting their cargo-laden ships off for a final voyage before all commercial exchange with Britain came to a halt. Barry made a rapid turnaround, and once again plowed the Atlantic, this time to London. On the homeward run, the remarkably fast *Black Prince* logged an incredible 237 miles in one day.[1]

Barry returned to a turbulent city. These were days of decision in Philadelphia. Rhode Island had instructed her delegates to the Continental Congress to press for the founding of a national navy. Opposition was vocal and vehement. Nevertheless, the New England navalists prevailed, and on 13 October 1775 (a date now officially recognized as the birthday of the U.S. Navy), Congress resolved to outfit two vessels "with all possible despatch," and on 30 October two additional vessels were authorized.[2]

The four ships prescribed by Congress were wanted for immediate service. Time did not allow building the ships from the keel up as men-of-war. Converted merchantmen would have to do. Robert Morris, an astute businessman as well as a congressman, was acutely aware of the impact the imminent war would have on normal ocean commerce. Accordingly, he offered to sell the fast-sailing *Black Prince* to the government. The offer was accepted, and renamed the *Alfred*, for the founder of the British navy, she became the first ship in the Continental Navy.

Purchase of other merchant ships followed quickly to form the fleet which would sail under Commodore Esek Hopkins. Congress employed Joshua Humphreys, celebrated local ship designer and builder, to undertake hull strengthening and alterations to change merchant ships into warships. To supervise the refitting and rerigging necessary to improve sailing qualities, Congress turned to Barry.

Since Barry was the last commander of the *Black Prince/Alfred* and a mariner of known quality, it may seem logical that Congress would name him captain of that ship. Not so; the first American naval effort was virtually an exclusive New England affair. All three members of the initial Naval Committee were New Englanders. Esek Hopkins, commander of the fleet, was from Rhode Island. Captains of the major ships with one exception, Nicholas Biddle, were New Englanders.* Dudley Saltonstall of Connecticut, and the brother-in-law of Naval Committee member Silas Deane, was appointed captain of the *Alfred*. What Barry's reaction, if any, was to being passed over for command of his old ship is not known.

Early in March 1776, while the Continental Navy fleet under Commodore Hopkins was loading booty from captured Nassau in the Bahamas, an armed brig, the *Wild Duck*, arrived at Philadelphia. She had been obtained at Saint Eustatius by Maryland and was loaded with 2,000 pounds of gunpowder, small arms, and other warlike stores. She was a tight vessel, a fast sailer, and pierced for 16 guns. Congress directed the Marine Committee, which had replaced the Naval Committee, to purchase the *Wild Duck*. Application was made to the Maryland congressional delegates, and the sale was approved by the Maryland Council of Safety. The *Wild Duck* was immediately renamed the *Lexington* as more befitting a naval vessel.

Robert Morris, recent employer, friend, and admirer of John Barry, was now a member of the Marine Committee. This powerful sponsor was determined that Barry would not again be overlooked for a command in the Continental Navy. Morris's recommendation carried the necessary weight. Barry received a captain's commission and command of the *Lexington*. Thus, this thirty-year-old seasoned seafarer began a naval career that spanned the American Revolution and the first war the new republic waged in defense of her freedom on the high seas.

Although Barry, like most other Continental naval officers, had no previous naval experience, he was no stranger to the use and sound of the cannon. During the eighteenth century, merchant ships went armed for protection against incursions by warring nations and

---

*Biddle was a member of a prominent and politically active Philadelphia family. He had served a tour in the British navy where he was a messmate of young Horatio Nelson.

pirates, and thus Barry entered the Navy with a working knowledge of naval ordnance.

Joshua Humphreys completed any minor refitting the *Lexington* required in a matter of days. Captain Barry with characteristic knowledge and ardor had the brig ready and manned two weeks after he received his commission. He sailed on 28 March "with a determined resolution of distressing the enemy as much as in my power."[3] He outdistanced HMS *Roebuck* off Delaware Bay and made the open sea.

"In sight of the Capes of Virginia, April 7, 1776," Captain Barry sent the following dispatch to the Marine Committee:

> Gentlemen, I have the pleasure to acquaint you, that at one P.M. this day I fell in with the sloop *Edward*, belonging to the *Liverpool* frigate. She engaged us near two glasses. They killed two of our men, and wounded two more. We shattered her in a terrible manner, as you will see. We killed and wounded several of her crew. I shall give you a particular account of the powder and arms taken out of her, as well as my proceedings in general. I have the pleasure to acquaint you that all our people behaved with much courage.[4]

Unknown to him, Barry had captured the first Royal Navy vessel to be taken by a Continental Navy ship.

Barry's laconic victory message reached Philadelphia on board the prize sloop *Edward*. The Marine Committee responded with applause for the "zeal and bravery" of the *Lexington*'s officers and men. They warned her captain that "the Men of War in Virginia, Delaware and New York will undoubtedly hear of you. They will probably lay some plans to surprise or decoy you, but we dare say a continued vigilance will enable you to avoid the Snares and power of those who are too strong for you, as well as to send us some more of those who are not an over match for the *Lexington*."[5] He avoided the "Snares" and was again safely inside Delaware Bay as May opened.

For Captain Andrew Snape Hamond, RN, patrolling the Delaware's mouth in the heavy frigate *Roebuck*, Barry's success and the Britisher's inability to bring the elusive *Lexington* to bay were matters of deepening rancor. He poured out his frustrations to Lord Dunmore, Virginia's royal governor:

> I would give more than I can express to have the *Otter*, or even the *Otter*'s Tender here for a few days, as without a small Vessel that can go in shallow water it is totally impossible (or at least very unlikely) that I shall be able to do anything with this brig *Lexington*. All the North side of Delaware Bay is encompassed with shoals and shallow water, having a channel of about 13 or 14 foot water within them:

and this passage Mr. Barry is at present master of. I have chaced him several times but can never draw him into the Sea. . . . However, I trust if my good stars will be but propitious enough to me to send me any Vessel that can carry 50 Men, his reign will be of short duration, especially as his success of late had made him bold.[6]

During the spring and summer of 1776, Barry was employed in the defense of the Delaware, salvaged a valuable gunpowder cargo from a grounded ship about to fall into enemy hands, served on courts-martial, and made another cruise in the *Lexington*. One of the prizes taken on this second cruise, and Barry's last in the brig, was the privateer sloop *Lady Susan*. She was three days out of Bermuda, and her master was William Goodrich of the infamous Goodrich Tory family of Virginia. Later from a Philadelphia jail he wrote to his brother John: "I was treated Extreamly Jenteal by Capt Berry, and when carryed onboard of the Brig Capt Berry received me with A Grate deal of Joy giveing me a harty welcom onboard of the *Lexenton* Saying that he never was glader to see any man in all his life altho we neaver Saw each other before."[7] The befuddled Goodrich was the unsuspecting butt of John Barry's Irish humor.

Congress approved a naval captain seniority list on 10 October 1776. John Barry was placed seventh. He was now ranked by three officers—including James Nicholson, number one on the list—who had seen no service in the Continental Navy. If Barry complained, no record of such survived. By contrast, John Paul Jones, number eighteen, was infuriated and fired off protest letters in all directions. Samuel Eliot Morison, in his definitive biography of Jones, states that the seniority list "continued to anger him as long as he lived."[8]

Barry was detached from the *Lexington* to oversee construction and take command of the *Effingham*, 28 guns, one of four Philadelphia-built frigates. The *Effingham* touched the water on 31 October 1776, the last of the Philadelphia frigates to launch. William Hooper, North Carolina signer of the Declaration of Independence, declared her "the finest vessel of the whole."[9] Fine lines she may have had, but the *Effingham* was afflicted with the chronic illness of every Continental Navy ship—acute shortage of men and cannon. Both were required to turn a trim new hull into an active man-of-war, but they were siphoned off by privateers and to fill the local defense needs of the Pennsylvania State Navy.

November 1776 witnessed a major British thrust southward from New York through New Jersey, pushing Washington's inferior army before it. At Philadelphia panic mobilization of manpower and resources to defend the capital doomed any small possibility Barry might have had of mustering a crew and arming the *Effingham*.

It was not in this fervent patriot's nature to stand by idly with an inactive and impotent frigate in time of crisis if he could be of service elsewhere. His offer "to take some heavy Cannon with a Company of Vollenteers" to join the army and "defend the banks of the Delaware" was readily accepted.[10] Barry was in the field at Princeton and met with General Washington at his Morristown headquarters. The naval officer, temporarily turned soldier, was back in Philadelphia by mid-January 1777. Of his role in Washington's critical winter campaign, Barry simply said that his service "is best known to his Excellency and the Officers who then served under him."[11]

The *Effingham* remained in the same desolate state as when Barry had last seen her. Robert Morris wrote to the Secret Committee of Congress that "there is no guns for the *Effingham*," and if she could just enlist enough men to work her, "think she had best load and send her to France to be compleated."[12] Months of inactivity, frustrations, and uncertainties led inevitably to frayed nerves and irritability. Barry accused the Philadelphia-based Navy Board of the Middle District of not taking vigorous efforts to supply his ship. In turn, Francis Hopkinson, board chairman, called Barry a "grumbler."[13] Twelve lieutenants refused to serve on board any Continental Navy ship until their pay grievances were settled. It was Captain Barry's lot, as senior officer present, to come to grips with this mutinous confrontation. Vexatious as these matters were, they faded into the background when news arrived that a British force exceeding 250 warships and transports led by General Howe and his brother, Vice Admiral Richard Lord Howe, after being sighted briefly off the Delaware Capes, had entered Chesapeake Bay on 22 August. The British troops were disembarked at Head of Elk, Maryland, to move by land against Philadelphia. Meanwhile, Admiral Howe's fleet doubled back to the Delaware to force the river defenses of the American capital.

While the enemy closed in on the city overland and by water in a huge pincers movement, Barry rounded up enough crewmen to move the *Effingham* up the Delaware River to the vicinity of Bordentown, New Jersey. In a memorial to Congress several years after the Revolution summarizing his wartime services, Barry recounted an amazing incident that transpired at this time. An unidentified individual came on board the *Effingham* and offered Barry a bribe of 15,000 guineas and command of the frigate in the Royal Navy if he would bring her back to Philadelphia. The irate captain "spurned the eydee of being a treater to his Country and returned for an answer that he scorned any offer they could make him."[14] The Royal Navy was the most powerful in the world, and surely had no urgent need for an ungunned partially rigged frigate. Captain Barry himself was the principal object of this audacious attempt to have him defect. The large amount of the bribe clearly reflects the high value placed on luring John Barry into the British camp.

Barry again ran afoul of Francis Hopkinson when he loudly and vehemently protested a Navy Board order to sink the *Effingham* to prevent her falling into enemy hands. The captain had been through too many trials and tribulations with this frigate to see her destroyed without a struggle and without ever putting to sea. He argued that she was secure and could be indefinitely defended at her present location. Nevertheless, he ultimately bowed to authority, and the *Effingham* was scuttled. Hopkinson brought formal charges against Barry. The Marine Committee found that he had treated the board member "with indecency and disrespect," and recommended that the captain be given a mild slap on the wrist.[15]

Winter 1778 found John Barry commanding a flotilla of armed barges and small boats on the Delaware. With Washington's approval and backing, he carried out hit-and-run attacks against incoming British supply shipping in the frigid river, ferried Continental troops and militia, and put landing parties ashore to torch hundreds of tons of hay intended for the occupying enemy army in Philadelphia. On one day, Barry's marauding band captured two forage-laden transports and a schooner carrying, among other engineering items, much-needed entrenching tools. The transports were destroyed and the schooner given up after a running fight with British warships, but not until the cargo had been put on shore.

Washington wrote Barry from Valley Forge congratulating the captain "on the success which crowned your gallantry and address, in the late Attack upon the Enemy's ships. Altho circumstances have prevented you from reaping the full benefit of your conquest, there is ample consolation in the degree of Glory which you have acquired. You will be pleased to accept of my sincere thanks for the good things which you have been so polite as to send me. . . ."[16] Barry had sent the general a cheese and a jar of pickled oysters from the captured schooner. The same day Washington wrote to the President of Congress: "I have the pleasure to transmit you an Extract of a Letter from Capt. Barry, which will inform you of his successes. The two ships he burnt, after stripping them; and he was obliged, it seems two days after the capture, to ground and abandon the Schooner, after a long and severe engagement with some of the Enemy's Frigates and smaller armed Vessels. It is said he saved her Guns and most of her tackle."[17]

Barry's memorable tour in the *Lexington*, his disappointments with

the *Effingham*, and his spirited actions on the Delaware River emi-
nently entitled him to a major naval command with a fair chance of
operating at sea. The *Raleigh* was at Boston without a commanding
officer; Captain Thomas Thompson had been relieved and was await-
ing court-martial. Barry was appointed to command this 32-gun frigate and "repair immediately" to Boston as ordered by the Marine
Committee 30 May 1778.[18]

John Barry's reputation had preceded him, but area-conscious naval authorities in Boston would have preferred a New England captain for the *Raleigh*. When Barry came on board his new command,
he found the all-too-familiar problems—need of stores, need of crew,
and need of guns. On her last cruise, the frigate's cannon had been
jettisoned to lighten ship and aid her escape from enemy pursuers.

Filling multitudinous needs for the frigate occasioned long months
of delay. It was not until 24 August that the Marine Committee sent
Barry orders to cruise "between Cape Henlopen and Occracock
[Ocracoke] on the Coast of North Carolina, with a view to take
certain armed Vessels fitted out by the Goodriches, or any other of
the enemies Vessels that may be infesting that Coast."[19] The Tory
"Goodriches" were not strangers to Barry. As mentioned earlier in
this chapter, one of the captures he made was captained by a member
of the Goodrich clan.

Another month passed before the *Raleigh* was able to put to sea
giving convoy to a brigantine and a sloop. Within hours of leaving
Boston harbor, two sail were sighted southeast by east, distant five
or six leagues and closing the *Raleigh*. They were the Royal Navy's
50-gun ship *Experiment* and the frigate *Unicorn*, 22 guns. The *Raleigh*
was cleared for action, and the men held at quarters throughout the
night. A chase of more than fifty hours followed before a shot was
fired. The *Unicorn*, the faster of the two British ships, came up and
exchanged broadsides with the *Raleigh*, opening a British cannonade
which lasted seven hours. The *Raleigh* was severely damaged in her
sails, masts, and rigging, and the 50 guns of the *Experiment* had come
within range. After consulting with his officers, Barry decided that
an attempt would be made to run the *Raleigh* on shore. To interdict
this effort, the *Experiment* poured a withering fire into the wounded
Raleigh, which an American officer reported was returned with "re-
doubled vigor." And, "Encouraged by our brave commander, we
were determined not to strike."[20]

The *Raleigh* grounded on a rocky uninhabited island off the Maine
coast, still firing her guns defiantly. Preparations were made to burn
the frigate, but through either a midshipman's treachery or misun-

derstanding of his orders this plan was not carried out. The British were able to get the frigate off the rocks, and she was taken into the Royal Navy under the same name. Captain Barry and the remaining crewmen able to travel made their way back to Boston.

Barry detailed the battle and loss of the *Raleigh* to the Boston Navy Board. The board members notified the Marine Committee of Congress, and expressed their conviction that Captain Barry had weathered an unequal conflict with "great gallantry," and, "though he has lost his ship, he has gained laurels for himself and honour to his country; perhaps no ship was ever better defended. . . . Capt. Barry's conduct is highly approved of here . . . his officers and men are greatly pleased with him."[21] The formality of a court of inquiry found Barry guiltless.

The Boston Navy Board urged the Marine Committee to assign Barry to the frigate under construction at Norwich, Connecticut. Command of that ship, to be named the *Confederacy*, had already been given to Seth Harding, a Connecticut man. However, the board's strong recommendation on Barry's behalf demonstrates their respect for and appreciation of the captain's qualities, which these New Englanders came to recognize in a relatively short time.

Congressional planning for an invasion of East Florida coincided with Barry's return to Philadelphia. He was directed to take charge of all armed vessels on the expedition, which was to be under the overall command of Major General Benjamin Lincoln. Barry was less than enthusiastic about the assignment, considering it a personal diversion from more important activities; but his view was of little moment because the invasion scheme was dropped. At this juncture, with his prospects of being called to public service in the immediate future at best remote, Barry signed on as master of the letter of marque *Delaware*. We met him in this capacity at the beginning of the chapter when he stood fast and prevented his men from being impressed into the Continental Navy frigate *Confederacy*.

Barry remained in private employ, on leave from the Navy, until November 1779 when he was named to command the *America* "on the Stocks at Portsmouth in New Hampshire."[22] She was the only 74-gun ship-of-the-line built by the Americans during the Revolution, and command of her did great honor to John Barry. But like the *Effingham* and the *Raleigh* before her, the *America* was another disappointment for the captain. Building was painfully slow, and money to complete her nonexistent. The *America* was not launched until 1782, and immediately thereafter was presented to France as a gift. Barry had long since given up all hope of ever treading the

America's quarterdeck. It can only be speculated what results might have been achieved, had Barry been able to take this powerful war machine to sea.

Two years before the *America* launched, the Continental Navy, which had never been a major factor in the conflict, had eroded to a few ships. Among those still in service was the Massachusetts-built *Alliance*, a 36-gun frigate. She arrived at Boston from France with her erratic, if not totally demented, captain, Pierre Landais, having been relieved during the passage by his first lieutenant.[23]

When Barry was given command of the *Alliance* on 5 September 1780, it was the second time in his naval career that he had replaced a deposed captain. A French observer described the *Alliance* as a ship "equal to any in Europe . . . there is not in the [French] King's Service, nor in the English navy a frigate more perfect and complete in materials or workmanship."[24]

Upon reaching Boston, Barry's first order of business was to preside over Captain Landais's long court-martial. The *Alliance* was crewless, a deficit that as always proved no mean obstacle. In desperation Barry requested authority to impress, which was denied. Although the *Alliance* was to carry Washington's aide-de-camp, Colonel John Laurens, to Europe with an urgent appeal to France for money and a naval force to operate on the American coast, Barry's manning problems extended into the new year 1781.

The *Alliance* finally did get under way on 11 February with a crew so deficient that the captain lamented that he did not have ten men including officers "that could steer her."[25] Colonel Laurens was joined by Thomas Paine as a passenger on board the frigate.

Barry arrived at L'Orient on 9 March where he debarked his distinguished passengers. A British privateer had been taken en route. The *Alliance* left the French port three weeks later giving convoy to the *Marquis de Lafayette*, a large ship heavily burdened with munitions and uniforms for the Continental Army. Just one day out of L'Orient, Barry had to deal rapidly and decisively with a plot to mutiny, kill most of the officers, take over the ship, and sail her to an Irish port. An informer named the three main perpetrators, who were immediately placed in irons. Midshipman John Kessler described what happened the following morning: "The three designated men were brought out of their irons on the quarterdeck, and being stripped and hoisted by the thumbs to the mizzen stay, underwent a very severe whipping before either would make any confession. The names of 25 of their accomplices were obtained from them before the whipping was discontinued."[26] Strong medicine, but mutiny threatened the safety of the ship and the lives of all on board. It had to be crushed severely as a deterrent to other would-be malcontents below deck.

Continuing on what proved to be an extremely stormy westward voyage, Barry seized several prizes. The supply-laden *Marquis de Lafayette* deliberately parted from the *Alliance* and was subsequently captured. One prize, the *Mars*, a 22-gun brig, mistakenly judged the *Alliance* to be a merchantman. She ran close aboard the frigate and without the customary hail fired a broadside that the *Alliance*'s log notes was returned "double fold."[27] The *Mar*'s gunners realized their fatal error. They deserted their stations and ran for cover. When the brig struck and the crew was taken on board the *Alliance*, they were all put in irons without rank distinction—"Captain Barry considering them as not meriting other treatment in consequences of their firing on us with no intention of bravely fighting."[28] An unwritten code of chivalry and honor still prevailed in eighteenth-century sea warfare.

On 28 May 1781, shortly after being struck by lightning which split the main topmast in two and severely burned a number of men on deck, the *Alliance* encountered a Royal Navy ship and a brig. They were the *Atalanta*, 16, and the *Trepassey*, 14, on a cruise out of Newfoundland. Together they were no match for the American frigate, but in a dead calm by using their sweeps the Britishers placed themselves athwart the *Alliance*'s stern and quarters. From this position they poured in a withering raking fire for hours. The *Alliance* "laying like a log" could not bring her great guns to bear.[29] Captain Barry was hit in the left shoulder by a large grape shot. He remained on the quarterdeck until loss of blood forced him below to have the wound dressed. Midshipman Kessler relates that some time after Barry had left the deck, Lieutenant Hoysteed Hacker, second in command, came to the surgeon's cockpit to see the captain. Because of great damage to the ship, the many killed or wounded, and no wind, Hacker asked Barry "whether the colors should be struck." Heatedly Barry replied, "No, sir; and if the ship cannot be fought without me I will be brought on deck."[30] Hacker retreated to his post topside and found there was now a breeze, light but sufficient to allow the *Alliance* to make headway. Her broadsides were brought to bear and fired. The Union Jack quickly fluttered down on both enemy warships.

The shattered *Alliance* limped into Boston on 6 June after a passage of sixty-three days from L'Orient. The three mutiny ringleaders were sentenced by court-martial to be hanged. Sentence was later reduced, and because Barry would have no part of them, they were turned over to the army to serve for the duration of the war. By the last week in July, Barry had so recovered from his wound that he expected to return to duty before the beginning of August.

The captain declared himself fit for duty, but his ship was not. At his urging, the *Alliance* had been copper-bottomed, but she still needed extensive repairs. The universal shortfall, finding enough officers and men willing to sign on, continued as before. The entire Continental Navy now consisted of two ships, the *Alliance* and the *Deane*, and all naval affairs were under Robert Morris's direction.

Morris's original orders were for the *Alliance* and the *Deane* to make a joint cruise, with Barry, senior captain, selecting the area and duration of the cruise. The surrender of Cornwallis at Yorktown altered the picture, and these orders were countermanded. Washington was sending Lafayette to France to seek more money and a continuing strong French naval presence in American waters. "No land force can act decisively," wrote the commander in chief to Lafayette, "unless it is accompanied by a Maritime superiority. . . . It follows then as certain as that night succeeds the day, that without a decisive Naval force we can do nothing definitive, and with it, every thing honourable and glorious."[31]

John Barry was to give the Marquis de Lafayette and a small company of French officers passage in the *Alliance*. Special sea stores, including some luxury items, had to be laid in for the guests. Morris, walking on both sides of the street, directed that this be done with discretion. He cautioned Barry to "remember that we are not rich enough to be extravagant nor so poor as to act meanly." Lafayette informed Washington that he had received "all possible civilities" on board Barry's command.[32] French sailors fleshed out the crew, and the *Alliance* took the wind from Boston harbor 23 December 1781.

Morris's sailing instructions to Barry stressed that his sole mission was to bring Lafayette to France safely and as quickly as possible. Accordingly, he was to avoid contact with all vessels. This meant that potentially rich captures could cross the *Alliance*'s path and sail on unmolested. Prize money was, of course, a prime inducement to ship on, and this restriction did not sit well with the forecastle hands or the wardroom. Again we turn to Midshipman Kessler for an eyewitness account. He tells of an oft-expressed wish of the crew "that the Marquis was in France."[33] To which, we may be sure, Captain Barry added a silent "Amen." The Atlantic crossing was otherwise uneventful, and the *Alliance* came to at L'Orient 18 January 1782.

The *Alliance* made a short unproductive cruise out of L'Orient before Barry turned the frigate's bow homeward. Not one prize was taken on the passage. Barry tried to get inside the Delaware Capes where he was chased by HMS *Chatham*, 64 guns. The *Alliance* outran the ship-of-the-line, logging a remarkable fifteen knots an hour.[34] Off New York two British frigates took over the chase. Barry ducked into Long Island Sound and ran up the Thames River to sanctuary at New London, Connecticut. It was now mid-May.

New London was not to John Barry's liking. He confided to John Brown, long-time close friend and congressional secretary to naval committees, that "I never was in such a damb country in my life." And, of Thomas Mumford, Continental Agent in Connecticut, he said, "I wood not trust him farther than I could see him."[35]

Morris ordered the *Alliance* around to Rhode Island to operate with and place herself under orders of a French frigate commanded by an officer of a rank equivalent to midshipman in the American navy. This offended Barry's pride in rank, which he shared with every naval officer. He was indignant and told Brown that Mr. Morris "will be much offended," but "altho I serve the country for nothing I am determined that no Midshipman in any service shall command me let him be a Chev. [Chevalier] or what he will."[36] Apparently Barry's adamant objections to the offensive orders were effective. The *Alliance* never joined a French frigate in Rhode Island.

Barry did not have a hundred men left on board, and manning was, as always, a problem. A rendezvous was opened in New London, and, after the recruiting drums had been beating for a fortnight, one man signed. By the first week in August, crew enough had been somehow fashioned to enable the *Alliance* to leave New London behind and embark on a cruise stretching from Bermuda to the Newfoundland banks. Captain Barry was now unencumbered by noble passengers.

The Jamaica fleet bound for England was struck and widely scattered by a vicious storm.* Barry made a field day out of the enemy's misfortune as he easily picked off unprotected stragglers. In all, eight prizes heavily laden with rum and sugar were taken. Four of the prizes were dispatched to America, and four were escorted by the *Alliance* to L'Orient, arriving 17 October 1782.

Barry found L'Orient buzzing with rumors of peace. He twice wrote to Lafayette in Paris asking about "any Expectations of Peace soon."[37] Should war's end be close, Barry was anxious to be off on one more profitable cruise before the guns fell silent. Circumstances intervened to make his quick departure impossible. Barry became

---

*This storm sank the huge *Ville de Paris*, 110 guns, flagship of Admiral de Grasse at Yorktown in 1781, which had been captured by the British the following year at the Battle of the Saints.

ill, and, while he was recovering, six officers, including the first lieutenant, refused to return on board the *Alliance* until they received wages long due them. After telling the disgruntled officers that they would have to wait the ship's return to the United States to make a demand on Robert Morris for their wages, he addressed letters to each ordering his return to duty. When the orders were ignored, Barry placed the six under arrest, recommended that their prize money be withheld until they had been tried by court-martial, and left them in France to find their own way back to America. Shortly before he sailed, 8 December, preliminary peace terms had been signed.

The crossing to the West Indies was uneventful, yielding no prizes. The *Alliance* came into St. Pierre, Martinique, on 8 January 1783. Here Barry found orders to go to Havana and there take under his protection the *Duc de Lauzun*, which had on board seventy-two thousand dollars for Congress. The American ships were detained by Spanish authorities at Havana until the beginning of March when permission to depart was given. It was soon discovered that the *Duc de Lauzun* was an indifferent sailer. Barry had the public money transferred to the *Alliance* for safekeeping.

On 10 March while the *Duc de Lauzun* pressed on all sail to escape, the *Alliance* was locked in a severe engagement with HMS *Sybil*, 32 guns. Much damaged after forty-five minutes of close fire, and sighting a 60-gun French ship coming up, the *Sybil* sheered off. The *Alliance* suffered ten casualties, and her sails, spars, and rigging were slightly hurt. Captain Vashon of the *Sybil* was reported, some years later, as saying "he had never seen a ship so ably fought as the *Alliance*," and that he had never before "received such a drubbing."[38]

The *Alliance–Sybil* was the final battle of the American Revolution, and it had been fought by the same John Barry who in 1776 made the first capture of a British warship by a Continental Navy vessel.

Barry brought the *Alliance* into Rhode Island waters, then to the Chesapeake, and ultimately back to Philadelphia, after a voyage to Amsterdam with a cargo of tobacco on government account aborted when the ship proved leaky. He continued to command the *Alliance*, the only naval officer remaining on active duty, until 1785 when the frigate was sold. She was the last ship in the Continental Navy.

In the years that followed, John Barry, like many other naval veterans, returned to the merchant service whence he came. He made a long commercial voyage to Canton, China. When in Philadelphia, he divided his time between his home in town and his country estate, Strawberry Hill, some miles north of the city. Hospitality and as-

Alliance vs. *Sybille*. In the last naval action of the Revolution, Barry in the 36-gun *Alliance* engaged the British 32-gun *Sybille* on 7 March 1782. Courtesy of The Mariner's Museum, Newport News, VA.

sistance were available to relatives, close or distant, who found their way to America. Appeals for money from needy family members in Ireland never went unanswered. By the terms of his will, lifetime support was provided for his two household slaves. Barry was a strong proponent of the federal Constitution, and played an active part in gaining Pennsylvania's ratification. He also devoted much time and effort to preparing memorials and submitting petitions seeking to have his wage and prize money accounts settled.

By 1794, the revered Washington was President of the United States. France was in the throes of bloody revolution and at war with England. The expanding American merchant marine, with no navy to protect it, was subject to interference by both combatants and depredations in the Mediterranean by the corsairs of Barbary. The situation became increasingly desperate. Finally, on 27 March 1794, Congress passed naval legislation calling for the construction of six frigates. This marked the beginning of the U.S. Navy under the Constitution.

Barry was convinced that Congress was about to act "for the protection of our trade against the Algerines." He wrote the President a week before the naval resolution passed "to offer myself for the Comd of the Squadron conceiving myself competent thereto. . . ."[39] Washington knew Barry well, not only by reputation but by personal association during the struggle for independence. The chief executive may also have savored the memory of the pickled oysters and cheese Barry had thoughtfully sent him at Valley Forge.

A letter signed by Secretary of War Henry Knox, under date of 5 June 1794, notified John Barry that the President had appointed him a captain in the Navy, and that he stood first in the relative rank order among the captains. He was ordered to superintend construction of the 44-gun frigate to be built in Philadelphia.

A fragile peace was bought in the Mediterranean, and work on the frigates was suspended as provided in the original authorizing legislation. However, yielding to pressure from Washington, Congress allowed building to start again on the three most advanced ships, including the one at Philadelphia. The *United States*, as Barry's handsome and powerful frigate was named, launched on 10 May 1797 and "the pleasantness of the day seemed to give a zest to the flattering prospect of an American Navy."[40]

Relations with revolutionary France continued to deteriorate. French privateers lurking in the Caribbean and off the Atlantic coast seized American trading vessels with impunity. This condition was unbearable, and during the summer of 1798, in retaliation, Congress au-

THE PRESIDENT of the UNITED STATES of AMERICA,

To John Barry.

I GEORGE WASHINGTON, President of the United States,

First commission in the U.S. Navy. Notation on the left indicates that John Barry was commissioned the senior captain in the new U.S. Navy in 1797. Courtesy of Naval Academy Museum.

thorized the capture of French armed vessels anywhere on the high seas.

Barry was now addressed as commodore because the Navy's senior officer was given command of a squadron of ships. The commodore's squadron made several deployments to the West Indies, and the *United States* carried peace envoys to France. Although the ships under Barry's command ran down several French privateers, retook a number of captured American vessels, and provided convoy to homeward-bound merchantmen, the commodore achieved no spectacular successes or victories such as he had during the Revolution. The laurels of this quasi-war with France went to Captain Thomas Truxtun and the USS *Constellation*.

Commodore Barry was disappointed with the barren results of his cruises, and Secretary of the Navy Stoddert was critical of his conduct of operations. "Barry is old and infirm," the Secretary confided to Alexander Hamilton. Stoddert questioned his ability to employ a group of ships, telling President Adams that "Barry no doubt is brave, and well qualified to fight a single ship."[41] Yet, in spite of his harsh and unwarranted faultfinding, it is not surprising that Secretary Stoddert sent his son to the *United States* to serve under Barry as a midshipman.[42]

Peace with France coincided with the coming to office of the Jefferson administration. All naval vessels were at once ordered home from the West Indies. Barry sailed the *United States* up the Potomac River to the Washington Navy Yard where the frigate was laid up. The commodore came on shore 6 June 1801. His long and illustrious sea service in the cause of his beloved country was ended.

Jefferson's peacetime naval establishment allowed for the retention of nine captains. Barry was included among the nine named by the President.

Congress struck a gold medal for Captain Thomas Truxtun as it had for John Paul Jones and other naval notables. Commodore Barry was never so honored. The Secretary of the Navy sent Barry one of the Truxtun medals enclosed with a letter that read: "Considering you as the Senior Officer of the Navy and entitled to the most respectful consideration I cannot resist the inclination I feel of presenting one to you."[43] Barry, his health failing rapidly, must have received this "thoughtful" gift with a measure of cynicism. The commodore, fifty-eight years of age, died at Strawberry Hill 13 September 1803. Both of his marriages were childless.

What is John Barry's legacy to the U.S. Navy? He was a master seaman and ship handler, and a proven leader. As a disciplinarian, he was eighteenth-century firm but fair. He placed the welfare of his men foremost. Commodore Barry's bravery, integrity, and honor are beyond question. He was not above riling out against the naval bureaucracy as occasion demanded, and avidly and proudly protected the prerogatives of his rank.

John Barry was not the father or founder of the U.S. Navy, contrary to the claims made in a wealth of partisan writings. Nor was John Paul Jones or any other individual. The U.S. Navy can be said to have had many fathers, including George Washington, John Adams, and even the Rhode Island Assembly.

More significant than any claim to fatherhood is the fact that numerous junior officers whose names were destined to shine brightly in American naval history and traditions, including Stephen Decatur, Jr., Richard Dale, Richard Somers, Charles Stewart, and Jacob Jones, served at sea under the watchful eye and tutelage of Commodore Barry.

In this writer's view, John Barry's place in the galaxy of the U.S. Navy's immortals rests not only on his triumphs as the cannon roared, but also—and no less—upon his total devotion to his adopted land, the United States of America. He advised a young Irish correspondent that America was "the best country for a man to live in under the sun."[44] Speaking at the dedication of a Barry monument in Washington, D.C., in 1914, President Wilson simply and eloquently phrased the commodore's love for America. "John Barry," he said, "was an Irishman, but his heart crossed the Atlantic with him."[45]

FURTHER READING

Although John Barry has been the subject of considerable writing effort, there is precious little worth recommending to the reader. There have been several full-length biographies, for example, Joseph Gurn, *Commodore John Barry: Father of the American Navy*. Such books as Bryan Hannon's *Three American Commodores* devote a portion to Barry's career.

Much of what has been written lacks objectivity, and is deficient by the standards of modern biography. Wide usage of subtitles acclaiming Barry the "father" of the Navy, such as Leo Gregory Fink's *Barry or Jones—"Father of the U.S. Navy,"* clearly demonstrates that the writers started with the fixed purpose of establishing John Barry as the "father."

Martin I. J. Griffin's book *Commodore John Barry: The Record of His Services for Our Country*, while not without errors, is of interest. Griffin must be counted among the never-questioning Barry champions, but his work is of value because it contains extensive correspondence and other primary materials including the eyewitness accounts of Midshipman John Kessler, who saw extensive sea service under the commodore.

The best biography of Barry remains William Bell Clark's *Gallant John Barry, 1745–1803: The Story of a Naval Hero of Two Wars*. Clark forgoes the usual scholarly apparatus of footnotes, quotation identification, and so on, and generates imagined conversation, but it is a thoroughly researched book, authoritative, and excellent reading. The bibliography is extensive and comprehensive.

NOTES

1. William Bell Clark, *Gallant John Barry, 1745–1803: The Story of a Naval Hero of Two Wars*, illustration opposite p. 54.

2. William James Morgan, *Captains to the Northward: The New England Captains in the Continental Navy*, 14–15.

3. Clark, *Barry*, 73, 75.

4. "Barry to the Marine Committee, 7 April 1776," William Bell Clark and William James Morgan, eds., *Naval Documents of the American Revolution*, IV, 702. Hereafter cited as NDAR.

5. "Marine Committee to Barry, 11 April 1776," NDAR, IV, 772.

6. "Captain Andrew Snape Hamond, R.N., to Lord Dunmore, 26 April 1776," NDAR, IV, 1268–70.

7. "William Goodrich to John Goodrich, Jr., 5 September 1776," NDAR, VI, 716.

8. Samuel Eliot Morison, *John Paul Jones, A Sailor's Biography*, 89.

9. "William Hooper to Joseph Hewes, 1 November 1776," NDAR, VII, 11.

10. Clark, *Barry*, 107.

11. Ibid., ms. illustration opposite p. 221.

12. "Robert Morris to the Secret Committee of the Continental Congress, 19 February, 1777," NDAR, VII, 1236–37.

13. Clark, *Barry*, 120.

14. Ibid., ms. illustration opposite p. 221.

15. Ibid., 139.

16. John C. Fitzpatrick, ed., *The Writings of George Washington from the Original Manuscript Sources 1745–1799*, XI, 67.

17. Ibid., XI, 73–74.

18. Charles Oscar Paullin, ed., *Out-Letters of the Continental Marine Committee and Board of Admiralty, August, 1776–September, 1780*, I, 250.

19. Ibid., I, 287.
20. Martin, I. J. Griffin, *Commodore John Barry*, 96.
21. Ibid., 97.
22. Paullin, ed., *Out-Letters*, II, 126.
23. Clark, *Barry*, 189.
24. Griffin, *Barry*, 119.
25. Clark, *Barry*, 200.
26. John Kessler's narrative quoted in Griffin, *Barry*, 133.
27. Griffin, *Barry*, 135 and Clark, *Barry*, 213–14.
28. John Kessler's narrative quoted in Griffin, *Barry*, 134.
29. Griffin, *Barry*, 136.
30. John Kessler's narrative quoted in Griffin, *Barry*, 137.
31. Fitzpatrick, ed., *Writings of Washington*, XXIII, 341.
32. Griffin, *Barry*, 156, 159.
33. John Kessler's narrative quoted in Griffin, *Barry*, 160.
34. John Kessler's narrative quoted in Griffin, *Barry*, 163.
35. John Barry to John Brown, 4 June 1782, quoted in Griffin, *Barry*, 165.
36. Ibid., 165.
37. Griffin, *Barry*, 186.
38. *Portfolio*, 1 July 1813, quoted in Griffin, *Barry*, 227.
39. Griffin, *Barry*, 291.
40. *Philadelphia Gazette*, 11 May 1797, quoted in Griffin, *Barry*, 317.
41. Clark, *Barry*, 448–50.
42. Ibid., 471–72.
43. Griffin, *Barry*, 410.
44. Ibid., 286.
45. John Barry file, Historical Research Branch, Naval Historical Center, Washington, D.C.

Courtesy of *The U.S. Navy: An Illustrated History.*

BAPTISM BY FIRE

EDWARD PREBLE AND THE "BOYS": THE OFFICER CORPS OF 1812 REVISITED

BY CHRISTOPHER MCKEE

Fletcher Pratt was a prolific writer. He had to be; that was the way he kept bread on the table. Between 1934 and his death in 1956 Pratt published more than fifty books on topics as diverse as criminal detection, science fiction, culinary arts, space exploration, Julius Caesar, and cryptography. But the center of his writing was always popular works on military and naval subjects.

Sometime during the 1930s Pratt apparently contemplated writing a full-scale biography of Commodore Edward Preble, looked into the first volume of Preble manuscripts at the Library of Congress, made a few notes, and then abandoned the project. But what Pratt did not abandon was his fascination with Preble, his personality, his career, and his influence on the U.S. Navy. Instead, he began writing a series of interpretative and biographical essays on Preble and on the Navy's principal commanding officers of the War of 1812. These essays, based on readily available printed sources, were published in book form in 1950 as *Preble's Boys: Commodore Preble and the Birth of American Sea Power*. Never one to linger over checking his facts too carefully, and often guilty of interpretations and speculations that make more cautious and scholarly historians wince with pain, Pratt stated the central thesis of *Preble's Boys* with a clarity that could not be mistaken: save for Perry's victory on Lake Erie in 1813, all of the United States naval victories in the War of 1812 were won by officers

The author wishes to thank Grinnell College students Dana Leach and Karin Stein for their careful assistance in compiling portions of the data used in this essay and his indefatigable secretary, Jetta Lentz, for her seemingly endless patience and astonishing accuracy in preparing several drafts of the manuscript.

Edward Preble. Forty-three-year-old Edward Preble had just returned
from his command of the U.S. Mediterranean squadron and was at the
height of his fame when he sat for Rembrandt Peale at Philadelphia in
March 1805. In his left hand Preble holds a chart of his attacks on Tripoli, which Peale has copied with great accuracy. Unfortunately, such carefully observed detail is lost when the painting is reduced for reproduc-
tion. Courtesy of Naval Academy Museum.

who had been Preble's subordinates during his command of the U.S.
Mediterranean squadron in 1803–4, and to those officers he had
been the supreme role model. To prove his point Pratt argued that,
although Preble's former subordinates accounted for only one-third
of the command-rank officers in 1812, they—with the single trou-
bling exception of Oliver Hazard Perry—won all the naval battles

that were won by the United States in that war. And when Pratt went looking for common threads in the lives of these victorious officers, he found only one: their service under Edward Preble.[1] Since 1950 Pratt's vision of Preble as the towering figure who shaped the officer corps of the War of 1812 and with it the United States naval tradition has been an all-pervasive one—even among historians who have been appalled by Pratt's sloppy scholarship.

Was Pratt correct in his intuition that Preble was perceived as the great model for the officers of 1812? The weight of the evidence suggests that he was. In the opening days of the War of 1812, Secretary of the Navy Paul Hamilton decided to send Captain John Cassin, longtime second-in-command at the Washington Navy Yard, to take charge of the yard at Gosport, Virginia. A public dinner to say goodby to an old friend and associate and to salute him as he assumed a still more responsible post was clearly in order, and at 4:30 P.M. on Tuesday, 4 August 1812, the highest civilian officials of the Navy Department, senior commissioned officers who chanced to be in Washington, and the section heads at the Washington Navy Yard assembled at Tomlinson's Hotel to honor Cassin. "After the table was cleared of viands and vegetables," says the newspaper report of the festivities, "the following toasts were given spontaneously and extempore, interspersed with enlivening songs." Because there were as yet no known War of 1812 victories at sea to be saluted, the toasts at Captain Cassin's testimonial dinner provide a special opportunity to discover those events in its pre-1812 history to which the naval establishment looked as sources of pride and inspiration.

Two points catch one's attention immediately. First, no event during the naval warfare of the American Revolution was in any way mentioned. That war formed no part of the 1812 Navy's mythic past—apparently because it was seen as providing no useful historical lessons of a positive nature. For the U.S. Navy of 1812, its mythic as well as its institutional history began only with 1798 and the Quasi-War with France. Second, and less understandably, one notices that none of the recorded toasts saluted Commodore Thomas Truxtun and his Quasi-War battles with *L'Insurgente* and *La Vengeance*. Indeed, the only Quasi-War allusion was to then-Captain and now-Washington Navy Yard Superintendent Thomas Tingey's supposed response to the British officer who boarded the *Ganges* and asked to examine the men's seamen's protective certificates of U.S. birth and citizenship: "There's their protection [pointing to the flag over his head]. They want none other." The Tingey incident apart, the only three recorded toasts that mentioned events or people in the Navy's pre-1812 history all pointed to Edward Preble and his 1803–4 Tripolitan

War campaign. "The memory of Commodore Preble" was the third toast drunk; it was offered by Captain Cassin, the guest of honor, and came immediately after toasts honoring the President of the United States and George Clinton, the late Vice-President. "Preble's flame, lighted in the midst of enemies by the Intrepid Ketch [at the burning of the *Philadelphia* in Tripoli harbor], and only extinguished by the ocean," was another. Charles W. Goldsborough, Chief Clerk of the Navy Department, saluted "The memory of Eleven to Thirty-Six," an allusion to the moment during Preble's 3 August 1804 attack on the Tripolitan gunboats when Sailing Master John Trippe boarded a Tripolitan boat to discover that only ten of his crew had been able to follow him and that he was outnumbered thirty-six to eleven— in spite of which formidable odds he and his comrades had succeeded in capturing the enemy vessel.[2]

Beyond a doubt Fletcher Pratt was right. As the War of 1812 began, Edward Preble was the great model for the officer corps, a man whose memory almost completely dominated the Navy's vision of its own short history. But what of Pratt's contention that, among the fifteen War of 1812 commanders whom he called *Preble's Boys*, "if there is any common background factor in this group besides service under Preble, it fails to meet the eye"? Actually Pratt's use of this title for the group, Preble's *boys*, alludes to another supposed common denominator: all were thought to be unusually young officers when they came under Preble's influence. According to a possibly apocryphal story told by James Fenimore Cooper, early in Preble's Mediterranean command the commodore summoned a meeting in the *Constitution*'s cabin that was attended by the commanding officers of four of his small cruisers—Lieutenants Charles Stewart, Stephen Decatur, John Smith, and Richard Somers—as well as by Tobias Lear, the U.S. consul general at Algiers.

> The four gentlemen of the service who thus met Preble, almost for the first time, were all young in years, and they held a rank no higher than that of lieutenants. Preble had been very little known to the service during its brief existence of five years. . . . In addition to these circumstances, the commodore's reputation for severity of discipline and a hot temper was so well established as to produce little confidence and sympathy between these young men and himself. The former fought shy at the council, therefore, letting the commodore have things very much in his own way. They fancied it was their office to obey and his to plan. After his lieutenants commandant had withdrawn, Preble and Lear remained alone together in the *Constitution*'s cabin. The former seemed thoughtful and melancholy, leaning his head on his arm, the latter resting on a table. Lear, observing this, inquired if he were unwell. "I have been indiscreet, Colonel Lear," answered

Preble, raising himself up to answer, "in accepting this command. Had I known how I was to be supported, I certainly should have declined it. Government has sent me here a parcel of children, as commanders of all my light craft." A year later Lear reminded Preble of this speech and asked him if he remembered it. "Perfectly well," said Preble, smiling, "but the children turned out to be good children."[3]

For more than thirty years Pratt's thesis has prevailed among historians. Should it continue to do so? Is it supported by discoverable fact? What was it about Preble and his professional life that made him the mythic model for the War of 1812 officer? Was his 1803–4 campaign against Tripoli really a latter-day Children's Crusade? Can one discover to what extent the successful War of 1812 officers were actually molded and influenced by Preble? Were there other, but historically unnoticed role models for the corps of 1812?

In 1803 Edward Preble seemed an unlikely candidate for anybody's model. Preble's career since his 1798 appointment as a naval lieutenant had, outwardly at least, been neither distinguished nor unusually promising.[4] The brig *Pickering*, his first command during the Quasi-War with France, had made a purely routine cruise to the West Indies in 1799, convoying American merchantmen and failing to find, let alone capture, any French privateers. Later that same year, Preble, by then a captain, was appointed to the command of the frigate *Essex* as the junior commander in a two-ship squadron ordered out to Java to convoy home richly laden merchantmen. Early in the outward-bound voyage to Java, the frigate *Congress*—with the squadron commander, James Sever, embarked—became separated, dismasted, and forced to put back for repairs. As a consequence of this accident, Preble was given an opportunity to display first-rate energy and initiative when he went on to complete the mission alone and successfully.[5] But this year-long cruise, good omen though it might be of capability of a high order, had taken Preble to remote waters. Under his command the *Essex* became the first ship of the U.S. Navy to sail beyond the Cape of Good Hope. He was far out of the public eye, and almost as far out of that of the Navy Department, while his peers were winning more visible laurels fighting the French in the West Indies. Moreover, Preble's health had begun to deteriorate on the *Essex* cruise when a disorder of his digestive system appeared for the first time, at least in noticeable form, during the Java voyage. Although selected as one of the small number of captains to be retained in the reduction of the Navy at the end of the Quasi-War with France in 1801, Preble was too sick a man to assume command of any ship that was sent to the Mediterranean in either of the first two squadrons dispatched there in consequence of Tripoli's declaration of war on the United States in May 1801.

This apparently undistinguished record apart, Preble's very personality seemed a formidable obstacle to anyone's seeing him as a man to be emulated. His marine lieutenant in the *Essex* complained loudly and repeatedly to the Commandant of the Corps of having "spent a very disagreeable time on board the *Essex*, the most so I have ever encountered through life, and, was it not delicacy forbids me to wound your feelings at the treatment I received from Captain Preble, my pen should find no rest till that information was given."[6] A little later, Sailing Master James Trant, himself reputed to be a "man of obdurate feelings and of a cruel disposition,"[7] resigned from the Navy rather than serve under Preble, whom he characterized as "cross, peevish and ill-tempered, surly and proud." The problem was a hair-trigger temper, which Preble either would not or could not keep under control, and under the lash of which his officers often writhed. At the other end of the ship's hierarchy Preble's sailors often writhed under a decidedly more physical lash, for he was one of the Navy's harshest disciplinarians, administering whippings more frequent and more severe than those awarded by almost any of his peers.[8]

But to perceptive men such as Secretaries of the Navy Benjamin Stoddert (1798–1801) and Robert Smith (1801–1809) there was something about Preble that spoke of the potential for distinction and, perhaps, even for greatness. One does not know how much these civilian leaders were aware of the details of Preble's Revolutionary War service in the Massachusetts state navy, but evidence existed therein to confirm intuitions. Particularly impressive had been Preble's performance as first lieutenant of the Massachusetts state sloop *Winthrop* when she singlehandedly waged war on the Loyalist privateers operating out of Bagaduce (now Castine), Maine, in the summer and fall of 1782. And no event of that service had been more memorable than Preble's dark-of-night boarding and capturing, with the aid of only fourteen men, of the privateer brig *Merriam* while she lay anchored under the protection of shore-based guns in the harbor of Bagaduce.

As salient a personality trait as his temper was Preble's driving ambition to distinguish himself. Although he had been born (15 August 1761) at the summit of Maine's eighteenth-century elite— his father, Jedidiah Preble of Falmouth (now Portland), Maine, was an admired provincial soldier, a successful businessman, a community leader, and a powerful state legislator—Edward Preble was consumed by the desire to make an even greater name for himself through public service. The psychological roots of this drive for fame through military achievement almost certainly lie beyond hope of rediscovery, but there can be little doubt that such ambition gave the spur to Preble's decision to abandon a moderately successful sixteen-year career (1783–98) as master and supercargo in the merchant marine and to accept a lieutenant's commission when the newly established Federal Navy began active cruising upon the outbreak of the Quasi-War with France.

It was this drive toward fame that provided the fuel Preble burned when he energetically accepted the opportunity to command the U.S. Navy's Mediterranean squadron in the spring of 1803. Fortunately, for one intent on fame, he had easy acts to follow. The first Mediterranean squadron, commanded by Richard Dale, had been handicapped by limited instructions drawn up before the Tripolitan declaration of war was known in the United States. The second suffered from a worse handicap: its commodore, Richard V. Morris, had been placed in a situation that demanded abilities beyond those he possessed. Easily distracted by threats and rumblings at Tunis and Morocco, Morris was unable to focus his attention on the war with Tripoli. Nor was he able to act decisively in any other way, to carry his discretion to the maximum limit required for success. Doing so would have demanded mental and physical energy of a high order, and these Morris lacked. Disgusted with this performance when they had expected his relatively large squadron to end the Tripolitan War, the Jefferson administration recalled Morris before his designated tour of duty was up. From the new Mediterranean commander, Edward Preble, it anticipated better things.*

---

*The precise reasons why Preble, who stood seventh on the list of ten captains in the spring of 1803, was selected by Secretary of the Navy Robert Smith for the Mediterranean command cannot be determined from any known records. Preble's appointment may have owed as much to the fact that he was one of the few captains who was actually available for the assignment as it did to any perception by the administration that he was *the* officer with the genius of command to succeed where Morris had failed. Because the new squadron was to include two frigates, at least one captain junior to the squadron commander would be required. Of the three captains below Preble on the list, both James Barron and Hugh G. Campbell had commanded ships in the Morris squadron. Under customary practice they would be expected to bring those ships home and to have periods of leave before their next tours of active duty. Hence, of the captains junior to Preble, only William Bainbridge, who had not commanded at sea since August 1802, was available for a new assignment. He was given the frigate *Philadelphia*. Six captains stood senior to Preble on the list. But John Barry was dying at his home in Philadelphia; Samuel Nicholson was old, incompetent to hold a responsible command afloat, and occupied a sinecure post ashore; Richard V. Morris was, as noted, being recalled under an

Such hopes were quickly fulfilled. When Preble, in the frigate *Constitution*, arrived at Gibraltar in September 1803 he found that Morocco had declared clandestine war on the United States, and that its ships were at sea to capture American merchantmen. Fortunately, the other frigate of Preble's squadron, the *Philadelphia* under Captain William Bainbridge, had preceded him to Gibraltar and had already captured the Moroccan cruiser *Mirboha*. Equally fortunate was the arrival at Gibraltar of several elements of the old Morris squadron, now under the command of John Rodgers and en route to the United States. After some initial friction—superficially over relative rank, but actually a personality clash—Preble and the senior Rodgers soon decided to rise above counterproductive squabbling and to cooperate in joint operations against Morocco, with Preble assuming de facto leadership of the combined squadrons. The *Mirboha*'s capture and Preble's ability to mass a greatly superior force all along the Moroccan coast quickly led the Sultan of that country to repudiate every warlike

---

ominously dark cloud; and Alexander Murray stood poorly in Smith's estimation, though perhaps undeservedly so, and would never have been entrusted by the Secretary with the command of a major squadron. That left Samuel Barron, John Rodgers, and Edward Preble as the available pool from which to select the squadron commodore. Barron, who had commanded the *Philadelphia* in the Dale squadron, was eligible for another tour of sea duty had Smith elected to tap him. John Rodgers was highly regarded by Secretary Smith. However, he had been in the Mediterranean since November 1802 as part of the Morris squadron. Rodgers's ship, the *John Adams*, had to return home more or less immediately because of expiring enlistments, but some arrangement might have been made to transfer Rodgers to a fresh ship—and Rodgers certainly would have been eager to accept the squadron command if given the opportunity. But keeping John Rodgers on station would have involved so many complications, which space does not permit detailing here, that Smith must quickly have rejected this option, if he considered it at all. Robert Smith had only two real choices for the squadron command: Samuel Barron and Edward Preble. No paper record exists as to why Smith chose Preble, but then neither does such a record exist for any other command choice Smith made during his seven and a half years in office. A reason may, however, be surmised. The War and Navy Departments shared the same building, known as the "War Office," hard by the White House. Daily informal contact and cordial personal relations existed between Robert Smith and Secretary of War Henry Dearborn. From the small fragment of their personal correspondence that is available, one knows that Preble was a reasonably intimate friend of Dearborn; the latter was in a position to serve as advocate for Preble's desires, merits, and abilities when the Secretary of the Navy was making his choice. On the other hand, Smith knew both Barron and Preble to some degree, and he may have selected Preble as the more able of the two possibilities without ever discussing the matter with Henry Dearborn. Charles W. Goldsborough, the Chief Clerk of the Navy Department, with whom Smith certainly would have discussed the choice, almost surely backed Preble. What role President Jefferson played in the choice of squadron commanders is unknown.

intention and to agree to negotiations, which were held at Tangier in early October. Throughout the Moroccan crisis Preble was supported by sound advice from Tobias Lear, the newly appointed consul general at Algiers, who was traveling to his post in the *Constitution*. In the actual negotiating sessions Preble was joined by the veteran U.S. consul at Tangier, James Simpson. The combination of overwhelming naval force and skillful, face-saving diplomacy terminated in the return of the vessels captured by each side during the brief war and in the reaffirmation of the treaty of 1786 between Morocco and the United States—the latter a desired, but hitherto elusive, goal of America's Barbary policy.[9]

Preble's decisive and effective handling of the Moroccan hostilities appeared to promise a quick and satisfactory end to the Tripolitan War as well, but his hopes were soon shattered. On his passage up the Mediterranean he learned that the frigate *Philadelphia*, which had gone ahead of the *Constitution*, had run aground off Tripoli and had been captured by the Tripolitans on 31 October 1803. Preble's mercurial temperament was plunged into depression by this catastrophic event, for his frigate force was cut in half, and he was left with only five small cruisers: the schooners *Enterprise* (12 guns), *Nautilus* (12), and *Vixen* (12) and the brigs *Argus* (16) and *Syren* (16). Preble's visceral response to discouragement and depression was always vigorous action. Late in December he found an excuse sufficient to enable him to seize and condemn an Ottoman ketch that had allegedly aided the Tripolitans in their capture of the *Philadelphia*. Doubtless remembering his own boarding of the *Merriam* under the guns of Bagaduce, Preble sent the ketch, now renamed the *Intrepid*, on a secret mission, under Lieutenant Stephen Decatur, to board, capture, and destroy the *Philadelphia* at her moorings in Tripoli harbor, a mission that was flawlessly and brilliantly executed on the night of 16/17 February 1804.

Though this spirit-elevating event solved the immediate problem of the frigate *Philadelphia*, Preble still had to discover a means of defeating Tripoli militarily and of securing the release of the more than 300 officers and men captured in that frigate. He acted with his usual monomaniacal energy. "Busied with his summer's operations against Tripoli," wrote one frankly admiring midshipman of Preble, "he feels no pleasure in anything which does not forward his favorite plans." Preble's problem lay in the fact that, of his squadron, only the *Constitution* was heavily enough armed to attack Tripoli's forts and batteries, while his brigs and schooners could not enter the shoal waters of Tripoli harbor to do battle with the gunboat flotilla that defended it. At length, and aided by some minor bribery, Preble succeeded in borrowing six gunboats and two bomb ketches from the Neapolitan government, and, with this additional force, he set out to assault Tripoli in the summer of 1804.

The first attack, that of 3 August, was the most successful. Three bloody hand-to-hand combats resulted in the capture of three Tripolitan gunboats which were promptly added to Preble's force. A second attack, on 7 August, did more damage to the American attackers than it did to the enemy: one of the recently captured gunboats blew up when a piece of flaming wadding from a friendly ship fell into its magazine. Later that same day Preble was once more plunged into depression when he learned that the Jefferson administration, acting in response to the capture of the *Philadelphia*, had resolved to send a much larger squadron to the Mediterranean. The lack of sufficient captains junior to Preble to command the increased number of ships meant that he must be superseded by a senior officer in the squadron command. As usual, Preble's response to depression and hurt was intensified activity: he sought to defeat Tripoli militarily or to negotiate a peace before his successor arrived on the scene.

In neither task did he succeed. Preble's effective action against Morocco in the fall of 1803 had owed nearly as much to the diplomatic skill of James Simpson as it did to Preble's guns. Now, in the spring and summer of 1804, Preble decided to conduct negotiations himself. But the personality traits that helped make Preble a great leader of men in action, vigor and decisiveness, were not necessarily assets at the bargaining table. Preble was too impatient and too irritable to be a good diplomat. He quickly developed a profound, and apparently unjustified, distrust of the French consul, Bonaventure Beaussier, who was attempting to serve as mediator between Tripoli and the United States. He was maladroit in knowing when to fight and when to parley. He was insensitive to the Tripolitan *mentalité* and would not listen when Beaussier tried to elucidate it for his benefit. No peace was negotiated in the summer of 1804.

Nor was Preble the combatant any more successful. After 7 August his squadron made several more attacks on the city of Tripoli and its shipping, but none inflicted serious damage. Finally, in an attempt to exceed even his previous triumph in destroying the *Philadelphia*, he filled the ketch *Intrepid* with explosives. Another picked crew would sail her into the harbor and detonate her in the midst of the Tripolitan gunboats' nightly anchorage. The *Intrepid* sailed on her daring mission during the night of 3 September, only to explode short of her target, leaving not one soul of her ship's company of thirteen alive to explain what had happened.

Six days later, on 9 September 1804, Preble was relieved by his successor, Commodore Samuel Barron. Preble returned to the United States early in 1805, there to receive a hero's welcome that included public dinners in his honor at Philadelphia, New York, Boston, and Portland and a gold medal commemorating his attacks on Tripoli. Preble's age—he turned forty-four during the summer of 1805—made it unlikely that he would ever again command a fighting squadron at sea, but his ambition to make a famous name for himself through service to his country appears to have been satisfied, and he settled rather comfortably into the role of a naval elder statesman.

In spite of his quick and harsh temper, Edward Preble was a man who set high value on harmonious relations with a wide circle of friends and acquaintances. As a consequence, he consciously avoided the postwar wrangling and recrimination over the treaty that terminated the Tripolitan conflict in June 1805—quarrels that embittered these years for several of his peers. Preble looked, rather, to the Navy's future. Late in 1805 he led the first recorded lobbying effort by a group of U.S. naval officers, a campaign in which he and associates William Bainbridge, James Barron, and Thomas Tingey sought to persuade the administration and Congress to commence the construction of ships-of-the-line, to increase the pay of captains, and to establish a board of navy commissioners. Although this effort failed in all of its immediate aims, it pointed to a future role for its leader. Preble's was a respected voice in naval matters. Secretary Smith, Chief Clerk Goldsborough, and, to a lesser extent, President Jefferson sought and heeded his counsel. This advice would be nearer at hand and Preble's influence the greater if he resided in the national capital rather than amid remote Maine's woods and rocks. The establishment of at least a winter residence by the commodore in the District of Columbia, with Preble thereby assuming the mantle of a formal or informal professional advisor to the Navy Department, was sporadically considered by both Preble and members of the administration circle during 1806 and the early months of 1807. Such was not to be. Sometime during the winter of 1806–7 Preble's old digestive disorder reappeared with renewed virulence and eventually brought him down—a slow, wasting death ending his life at his home in Portland on 25 August 1807.

Those War of 1812 officers whose careers may have been directly shaped, or at least influenced, by service under Edward Preble can readily be identified. On 1 January 1813, as closely as can now be calculated, the Navy's officer corps consisted of 927 men. Of these 927, some 89 (9.6 percent) were on the roll of the Navy's officers on 1 August 1803 and were, consequently, available to have served under Preble's command during his Tripolitan campaign.[10] But to say that less than 10 percent of the War of 1812 officer corps *might* have served under Edward Preble risks understating the realities of the situation. By 1 January 1813 these 89 veteran officers were distributed among the Navy's ranks in this fashion:

	Total number in rank on 1 January 1813[11]	Preble-era veterans
Captains	16	15
Masters commandant	10	9
Lieutenants	71	41
Midshipmen	486	4
Sailing masters	197	7
Surgeons	32	8
Pursers	38	5

Virtually all of the Navy's captains and masters commandant whose names stood on the roll of officers on the first day of 1813 had entered the corps before August 1803.[12] More than half (57.7 percent) of its lieutenants were senior enough to have been available for duty with Preble during his 1803–4 Mediterranean command. Practically no one who had held a midshipman's warrant in 1803 was still a midshipman nine and a half years later.[13] In other words, with the exception of the sailing masters[14]—less than 4 percent of whom had been in service in time to have gone out with Preble in 1803— the leadership ranks of the War of 1812 Navy, and more particularly those leadership ranks that had direct command responsibility in combat, were totally or heavily dominated by officers who could have come under the immediate influence of Preble's leadership.

To examine the ranks these 89 veteran officers held on 1 August 1803 is to document further the likelihood that Preble might have served as a shaping influence and model for their professional lives. Then the 89 had been:

Captains	5
Lieutenants	18
Midshipmen	46
Sailing masters	6
Surgeons	4
Surgeon's mates	4
Pursers	3
Captain's clerks	2
Gunner's mate	1[15]

Lewis Warrington. In every way typical of the midshipmen who served under Edward Preble's command during his Mediterranean campaign, Lewis Warrington of Virginia was twenty years old in the summer of 1803. Warrington had received his appointment early in the year 1800. Since that time he had been on active duty in the frigates *Chesapeake, President,* and *New York* so continuously that the only opportunities he would have had to pose for Rembrandt Peale in his midshipman's uniform were brief leaves in the spring of 1801 and the summer of 1802. Courtesy of The Minneapolis Institute of Arts.

The five men who had been captains on 1 August 1803 and who were still captains as 1813 began—Alexander Murray, John Rodgers, James Barron, William Bainbridge, and Hugh G. Campbell—were all mature men, ranging in age from twenty-nine to forty-eight years.

Each possessed a fully formed professional personality derived from many years of command, and each marched to his own inner drummer. They were more likely to—and, indeed, did—see Preble as a potential rival rather than as a model to be emulated. It is most improbable that Preble was a shaping influence on any of their careers, except *possibly* that of William Bainbridge. But the lieutenants and midshipmen of August 1803, who comprised more than two-thirds (71.9 percent) of the Preble-era officers still on the rolls as 1813 began, were all men at stages in their lives at which service under a leader of Preble's caliber was likely to leave a lasting imprint on their professional personalities.

The great preponderance of the Preble-era veterans whose names stood on the Navy's rolls at the beginning of January 1813 had been young enough in their professional careers nine and a half years earlier to have been malleable to Preble's example and influence. Does it follow that the officer corps with which Preble had to fight his Tripolitan campaign really was comprised of *children?* Although ages can be discovered for only 70 of the 89 Preble-era officers still on the rolls on 1 January 1813, that number is sufficient to establish an age profile of acceptable accuracy. In August 1803, just a few weeks before Preble supposedly lamented that "government has sent me here a parcel of children," the age distribution of the 50 lieutenants and midshipmen (among the 89 veterans) about whom this information is known[16] looked like this:

Age, August 1803	Lieutenants	Midshipmen
17		6 ⎫
18		7 ⎪
19	1	6 ⎬ 78.8%
20		7 ⎭
21	2 ⎫	2
22	1 ⎪	2
23	3 ⎬ 58.8%	2
24	1 ⎪	1
25	3 ⎭	
26		
27	1	
28		
29	1	
30	1	
31 . . .	1	
35 . . .	1	
44	1	

More than half of the lieutenants were twenty-one to twenty-five years old at the beginning of Preble's campaign, while nearly eight out of ten of the midshipmen were between seventeen and twenty. But, clearly, both groups were made up of young adults, some of them less than half the age of their forty-two-year-old commodore.

However wistfully Preble may have imagined having one or two captains of mature years to aid him, the age of the officer pool from which his subordinates were drawn can scarcely have come as a surprise to him. Seafaring was, in the early-nineteenth-century United States, an occupation almost exclusively dominated by young adults. As Ira Dye has discovered in his investigations of American merchant seamen of the 1796–1818 period, the median age of merchant mariners fluctuated between twenty-two and twenty-four years. In a typical merchant ship's crew a mere 19 percent of the men would be over thirty years of age, while 64 percent would fall into the eighteen- to thirty-year-old category. (The remaining 17 percent of the ship's company were, of course, under eighteen.)[17] What was true of the merchant marine was true of the Navy as well, for both drew on the same pool of potential mariners. Indeed, Preble himself had been only twenty in 1782 when he was appointed first lieutenant of the Massachusetts sloop *Winthrop*, a post at least as responsible as that held by most of his 1803–4 lieutenants. What may be surprising is the age profile of the Navy's midshipmen in August 1803. The immature adolescents of thirteen and fourteen who are often supposed to have crowded the midshipmen's mess are nowhere to be found. All of them, so far as can now be determined, were seventeen or older.

Even more impressive than the maturity of the midshipmen was the amount of active duty the typical lieutenant or midshipman displayed on his record in August 1803. Two-thirds of the lieutenants had entered the corps as long ago as 1798. Indeed, 72 (80.9 percent) of the 89 Preble-era veterans actually received their first appointments between 1798 and 1800. Since that commencement almost all of these officers had been continuously employed on active duty in naval vessels or had filled up their furloughs with self-improving voyages in the merchant service. Whether or not, in a moment of depression and irritation, Preble referred to his officers as "children," he was as aware as any later social historian can be that he was setting off on his Mediterranean campaign with an officer cadre drawn from a pool that was young enough to be vigorous, but mature enough to bear heavy responsibilities; an officer corps thoroughly trained and socialized by previous naval service; and one largely purged by that long service of members more likely to be liabilities than assets.*

To this point the focus has been on officers who *might* have served with Edward Preble—the 89 officers on the roster of 1 January 1813

*Is the case here being made for the age and experience of the officer cadre available to Preble questionable because it is based only on the 89 Preble-era officers still on the rolls in January 1813? Might these 89 *not* be representative of the entire corps of August 1803? Could they, indeed, have been the more successful in their later careers because they were more mature when they came under Edward Preble's influence? A total of 257 officers have been identified who were members of the corps in August 1803 and who, consequently, were potentially available for service under Preble. The 89 veterans of January 1813 thus constituted about one-third of the corps as it had stood at the outset of Preble's campaign. Among the 37 lieutenants of August 1803, ages have been discovered for 25. For this larger group of 25 the youngest is still the lone nineteen-year-old and the eldest remains the man of forty-four. Fifteen lieutenants (60.0 percent) stand clustered in the twenty-one- to twenty-five-year-old age grouping, while the comparable figure for the smaller corps of Preble-era veterans is 58.8 percent. Midshipmen among the August 1803 officer cadre totaled 146; ages were established for some 66 of them. Because of the prevalent misconceptions regarding the supposedly juvenile character of the early Navy's corps of midshipmen, a detailed age profile of the 66 may be of value:

Age, August 1803	Number	
15	1	
16	1	
17	9	
18	14	
19	9	63.6%
20	10	
21	3	
22	6	
23	4	
24	3	
25	3	
26+	3	

Among this much larger group of 1803 midshipmen, only two have been identified who are younger than seventeen. Sixty-one of the 66 (92.4 percent) fall in the seventeen- to twenty-five-year-old bracket. These were most definitely young men—not boys.

The same pattern holds true on the score of experience. When the service records of the 37 lieutenants on the Navy's register in August 1803 are examined, one discovers that all but one of the 37 had entered the Navy in 1798 or 1799. Of the 146 midshipmen available for service in the summer of 1803, three-quarters (74.0 percent) had been appointed in the year 1800 or earlier, whereas only 24.0 percent were comparatively recent appointments of 1802 and 1803. (Combining the lieutenants and midshipmen of August 1803, one learns that 145—79.2 percent—had entered the Navy between 1798 and 1800.) In terms of both age and experience as of August 1803, the 89 Preble-era veterans still on the roster of officers in January 1813 were quite typical of the entire corps at the outset of Preble's campaign.

who had entered the corps before 1 August 1803. Now it is time to return to Fletcher Pratt, *Preble's Boys*, and those among the 89 Preble-era veterans who actually *did* serve under the commodore's stern eye. What of Pratt's contention that, with the exception of Oliver Hazard Perry, only those officers who had served with Edward Preble won naval victories in the War of 1812? Had service with Preble marked these officers with a special spirit that set them apart from the rest of the corps?

The answer to the first of these questions must be: Yes, Preble's former subordinates did win the War of 1812 victories, but they won them because they *were* the Navy's fighting commanders. Of the entire 89 Preble-era veterans still on the rolls on 1 January 1813, three-quarters (77.5 percent) had—using Fletcher Pratt's own criteria[18]—actually served with Preble. And, if one isolates from among the 89 those who held the primary command ranks in January 1813, this picture appears:

	Number in rank on 1 Jan. 1813	Number in service before Aug. 1803	Percent in service before Aug. 1803	Number serving under Preble	Percent serving under Preble
Captains	16	15	93.8	11	68.8
Masters commandant	10	9	90.0	6	60.0
Lieutenants	71	41	57.7	35	49.3
	97	65	67.0	52	53.6

These figures require exegesis. True, only 11 of the 16 captains of January 1813 had served under or with Preble. But, of the five who had not, one (James Barron) was suspended from the Navy by sentence of a court-martial, and four (Alexander Murray, Thomas Tingey, John Shaw, and John Cassin) were confined to shore duties. Of the latter four, only John Shaw, who was thirty-nine years old as 1813 began, was young enough to have been considered for a command at sea. It was absolutely impossible for any captain who was not a Preble veteran to win a victory at sea in the War of 1812, for there was not one afloat! Among the masters commandant there was a greater probability that a non-Preble veteran would win a distinguished victory. One of them, Oliver Perry, did so. Another, Arthur Sinclair, who spent almost the entire war in commands afloat, did not. Jacob Lewis was confined to harbor defense at New York; and Charles Ludlow resigned in 1813 without having performed any significant active duty at sea during the War of 1812. As for the lieutenants, Preble veterans may have constituted only half the total number of men holding that rank, but they also constituted 85.4 percent of those lieutenants who had entered the Navy before August 1803. The latter, being the oldest lieutenants among the 71 in service, were the ones most likely to be placed in positions of command and responsibility. The hegemony of the Preble veterans was unchallenged among the fighting officers of the War of 1812. But this hegemony came about not, as Pratt seems to suggest, because service under Preble had cast some sort of mystic spell that destined those who bore it to victory and those who lacked it to oblivion. The hegemony of the Preble veterans came about because the demographic dynamics of the corps itself brought the professionally successful among those officers who had had a chance to serve under him to positions of command responsibility by the time war was declared by Congress in June 1812.

The most significant questions remain thus far unanswered: To what extent was Edward Preble really a conscious role model for the officer of the War of 1812? And, how exactly did he influence him? Answers to these questions are elusive—and probably always will be. The historian may only be able to speculate. The typical officers of 1812–15 were men of action more than men of reflection. So far as this historian is aware, none of the Tripolitan War veterans ever made a detailed statement of how Preble's example shaped his later life. Neither did they create records that captured the dynamic, day-to-day interaction between Preble and his subordinates—work together on the quarterdeck in battle or in danger of the sea, conversation over dinner in the cabin, oral reprimands for duties less than carefully performed—interactions that were the bedrock of his influence on their professional careers. When the officer of the War of 1812 adopted the autobiographical mode, usually in expostulating with the Secretary of the Navy over alleged delays and injustices in promotion, it was normally to detail his own merits and services—with scarce a passing mention of any shaping influences by his former commanding officers. Even Captain Charles Morris, the most reflective and self-aware of the group, is more intent in his autobiography on telling how he weathered Preble's wrath, secured his good opinion, and thereby advanced the career of Charles Morris than in saying how Preble's example illuminated his future conduct.[19]

Nor should the thoughtful student of history ever forget that each of the 89 Preble-era veterans had served under other senior officers whose positions, abilities, and personalities made them as much role models as was Edward Preble. One may list these shapers of young men: Thomas Truxtun, Alexander Murray, John Rodgers, Hugh George Campbell, William Bainbridge. If the names of Murray and Campbell are less than household words, even with naval historians, that does not lessen their roles as key molders of the professional lives of their young subordinates. When Campbell, by then confined through disability to a shore command in Georgia, wrote to congratulate his old subordinate, Oliver Hazard Perry, on his September 1813 victory on Lake Erie, the latter responded:

> My dear and much respected Sir: Among all my friends who have offered me their congratulations on my good fortune, none has given me more pleasure than your kind and flattering letter. If I have any respectability in the service as an officer, you, my dear Sir, are entitled to a great share of the credit. It was to your friendly and frequent admonitions that I obtained a standing with my brother officers. I shall never cease to recollect with gratitude how much I am indebted to you, not only for kindness shown me when sick and at all other times, but for examples of activity which I never witnessed on board any other ship than yours. I have uniformly declared that, if you had an active command, you would show us all how to dash, and I regret most sincerely that your country is deprived by your ill health of that activity which would reflect so much honor on the service.[20]

And when Master Commandant Daniel Todd Patterson looked back to the events of 1803–5, when he was a prisoner in Tripoli as a result of the capture of the *Philadelphia*, it was not Preble's attacks on the city that he recalled, but a different leadership:

> It would not become an officer of the Navy to complain of the sufferings and privations attendant on a confinement of more than nineteen months, but, whatever they might be, the friendly care of Captain Bainbridge and of Lieutenants [David] Porter and [Jacob] Jones enabled [me] to profit essentially by the seeming misfortune, as these gentlemen daily devoted a portion of their time to the instruction of the younger officers in naval affairs and a scientific knowledge of their profession; and the confinement was productive of the farther good of making [me] and [my] comrades fully acquainted with the value of their great commander and of the said two lieutenants, who have all since signalized themselves in the eyes of the world and shed lustre on their profession and their country.[21]

One can go beyond recognizing that other models influenced and shaped younger subordinates just as powerfully as did Preble to see Fletcher Pratt's *Preble's Boys*, readable though it may be, as an example of a simplistic approach that has dominated and distorted the study of the U.S. Navy's history. One speaks here of the focus on individual combat commanders, often accompanied by the implied or explicit claim that the officer in question was *the* premier shaper of the American naval tradition. Even at the biographical level this is lamentable because it results in ignoring almost anyone who was not a command combat leader. To cite one example: Charles W. Goldsborough, longtime key civilian official of the Navy Department, did as much to shape the U.S. Navy as many of the commanders who appear in *Preble's Boys*—indeed, probably did more than many of them; yet he is an unknown and ignored figure. Individual biography will continue to be written—and to be read. The confrontation between the individual and the larger historical forces of his time is too innately appealing ever to cease to be a major vehicle of historical exploration. Scholars ought, however, to investigate those larger historical forces as well.

The process by which the U.S. Navy's officer corps had, by the eve of the War of 1812, developed into a highly competent professional body, while the contemporary U.S. Army had failed to do the same, was the result of complex historical and social factors.[22] A comprehensive discussion of these factors lies beyond the scope of this essay. But for Fletcher Pratt to say that the U.S. Navy was a successful fighting force in the years 1812–15 only because particular combat leaders had been trained by Edward Preble is just too simpleminded. The lieutenants and midshipmen whom Preble had helped to form were, by 1812 to 1815, positioned to win victories at sea as much because of the demographics of the corps itself as because of their experience under Preble. Had the War of 1812 occurred ten years later, the U.S. Navy might have demonstrated as excellent a professional performance, but its victories would have been won by a different set of men, fewer of whom would have been Preble-era veterans. Not only must demographics have its due recognition, but historical context as well. When the War of 1812 began, all of the 89 Preble-era veterans had been serving as officers anywhere from nine to fourteen years, and always under wartime or near-wartime conditions. Can one seriously maintain that two years of exposure to Edward Preble's leadership did more to shape their professional personalities than seven to twelve years of other experience?

If one rejects reductionist explanations for the Navy's professional success in the War of 1812, that is not to denigrate the high importance of teachers and role models. Among the complex factors that shaped that successful corps, the example of a leader such as Edward Preble must always be seen as a major component. Perhaps Preble's volatile and forbidding personality accounts for the absence of later testimonials recounting the ways he had shaped distinguished careers.

Save for a relatively small number of immediate associates—Stephen Decatur and Isaac Chauncey would be examples—not many officers ever got close enough to Edward Preble to know him as a human being. He was not someone whose stern but kindly advice one recalled with affection in later years. All that said, and although the point is impossible to document quantitatively, there can be no doubt from what references to him do exist that his old subordinates admired and respected Preble as a commander—if often from a substantial psychological distance. That admiration and respect were usually qualified by Preble's failure to command himself and his temper. But there are many other positive ways in which Preble can be seen as a model for the younger men.

His patriotism, apparently born of his participation in the Revolution, was deep, sincere, and a principal motive force in his life. He frequently made statements during his Mediterranean command that said, in substance: "I value the national character of my country too highly to consent to a peace which the most powerful nation in Europe would blush to make." More significant as a model was his own conduct of policy, which lived up to that standard. Nor could any subordinate have failed to be struck by Preble's willingness to spend himself for a larger good: the welfare of his country and its people. If he sought fame as a reward for that sacrifice, it must never be forgotten that, in the ethos of the times, pursuit of fame through self-sacrifice and service to the republic was a worthy and, indeed, a highly regarded life motive.[23] Preble, in common with contemporaries Thomas Truxtun, Hugh G. Campbell, Alexander Murray, and John Rodgers, held his subordinates to the highest standards of professional conduct and ethics. Young men who showed no promise of ever disciplining themselves sufficiently to be a credit to the Navy were ruthlessly harried out of the corps by Preble. The momentarily wayward, who might yet be made into good and useful officers, were admonished and encouraged, and a proper line of conduct marked out for them. Able subordinates could count themselves lucky to have served under a commodore willing to delegate important and responsible assignments to promising junior officers, thus providing opportunities to test and to demonstrate ability. But Preble's supreme example was that of a commander who never gave up in the face of reverses and discouragements; for whom—no matter how unpromising the chances—vigorous action was always better than succumbing to despondency. He demonstrated that, when led by a determined, decisive man, the small U.S. Navy could win the respect and admiration both of its own countrymen and of the officers of more powerful navies. Edward Preble fulfilled the requirement Secretary of the Navy Benjamin Stoddert defined in 1799 for the new nation's naval leaders: "Our Navy at this time, when its character is to form, ought to be commanded by men who, not satisfied with escaping censure, will be unhappy if they do not receive and merit praise; by men who have talents and activity, as well as spirit, to assist a judicious arrangement for the employment of the force under their command or to cure the defects of a bad one."

Preble's victories were primarily moral ones. They were his greatest legacy to the U.S. Navy. And they made him the preeminent mythic hero and model to the officer corps of the War of 1812.

FURTHER READING

Edward Preble's most recent and most comprehensive history is Christopher McKee, *Edward Preble: A Naval Biography, 1761–1807.* The notes of either edition, the preface to the 1980 reprint, and the notes to the present essay, taken together, provide a guide to all known sources for Preble's life. Lorenzo Sabine's *Life of Edward Preble* and James Fenimore Cooper's essay in his *Lives of Distinguished American Naval Officers* are earlier biographies still worth reading. Those interested in studying the original texts of Preble's letters, journals, incoming correspondence, and other documents of the Tripolitan War, 1801–5, will find the U.S. Office of Naval Records and Library, *Naval Documents Related to the United States Wars with the Barbary Powers*, a copious source of such material. A detailed reconstruction of the principal ship of Preble's squadron as she was during his command is provided by William P. and Ethel L. Bass, *Constitution, Second Phase 1802–07—Mediterranean, Tripoli, Malta & More.* Of new research on the Navy during the Tripolitan War years, the most interesting and original is J. Worth Estes's investigation of the medical records of Surgeon Peter St. Medard; the first published results are to be found in his "Naval Medicine in the Age of Sail: The Voyage of the *New York*, 1802–1803." A recent English-language history of Tripoli that focuses on the years 1711–1835 is Seton Dearden's *A Nest of Corsairs: The Fighting Karamanlis of Tripoli.* It provides the framework essential to understanding Tripoli's war with the United States. The overarching context of U.S. involvement in the Mediterranean, with ample attention to its naval aspects, is provided by James A. Field, *America and the Mediterranean World, 1776–1882.* One cannot fully appreciate the internal functioning of the Preble-era U.S. Navy without an understanding of how the national government of the day operated. Such insight is found in two outstanding and complementary works: Leonard D. White, *The Jef-*

fersonians: A Study in Administrative History, 1801–1829, and Noble E. Cunningham, *The Process of Government under Jefferson.*

NOTES

1. Fletcher Pratt, *Preble's Boys: Commodore Preble and the Birth of American Sea Power,* especially 398–404. For Pratt see *Current Biography,* 1942, 679–80; 1956, 502; *New York Times,* 11 June 1956, 31.

2. *National Intelligencer,* 8 August 1812. Tingey had been present at the dinner before the toast was offered that cited his Quasi-War riposte to the officer from the British ship *Surprise.*

3. James Fenimore Cooper, *Lives of Distinguished American Naval Officers,* I, 197–98. As far as this historian has ever been able to determine, there was no time when the six men who were supposed to have attended this meeting were all in the same geographical location at the same time during Preble's Mediterranean command. However, there almost certainly is some factual basis for the story because Lorenzo Sabine in his *Life of Edward Preble,* 167, quotes a letter from Charles Stewart to Preble—the original of which cannot now be found—in which the former refers to Preble's "*boys*" of the infant squadron."

4. With the additions cited in the notes that follow, this brief sketch of Preble's life is based on Christopher McKee, *Edward Preble: A Naval Biography, 1761–1807,* and the sources detailed therein.

5. To the sources for the voyage of the *Essex* cited in the notes to Chapter 4 of McKee, *Preble,* there should be added Philip Chadwick Foster Smith, *The Frigate Essex Papers: Building the Salem Frigate, 1798–1799,* and especially the important William Mumford letter quoted at p. 189. In *Preble,* 76–78, this historian told of a French privateer "identified as [Robert] Surcouf's *Confiance,*" shadowing the merchantmen under the *Essex's* convoy in the Sunda Strait on 22–24 June 1800. According to Auguste Toussaint, *Les Frères Surcouf,* 138–39, Robert Surcouf in the privateer *Confiance* did indeed capture the American letter-of-marque *Alknomack* on 15 June and was off Anjer on 19 June. At Anjer, however, Surcouf learned that Preble was in Java waters and, fearing to encounter the *Essex,* had left Sunda Strait by 20 June. This historian is not entirely persuaded that the ship that stalked Preble's merchantmen on 22–24 June was not the *Confiance*—if not the *Confiance,* what ship was she?—but the evidence is contradictory.

6. James Porter to William Ward Burrows, 11 December 1800, Letters Received by the Commandant of the Marine Corps, 1799–1818, Record Group 127, National Archives.

7. James Fenimore Cooper, *History of the Navy of the United States of America*, II, 280n.

8. Substantial additional study of the Navy's disciplinary practices has convinced this historian that he underrated the comparative severity of Preble's punishments in McKee, *Preble*, 221–24.

9. To the printed sources for the Tripolitan War of 1801–5 and the activities of the U.S. Mediterranean squadron cited in McKee, *Preble*, 364–75, there should be added the letters of William Lewis, excerpted in Mary Lewis Cooke and Charles Lee Lewis, "An American Naval Officer in the Mediterranean, 1802–7," U.S. Naval Institute *Proceedings*, LXVII (1941), 1533–39.

10. All statistics on the Preble-era veterans who were still members of the officer corps on 1 January 1813, as presented in the balance of this essay, are drawn from the author's biographical profiles for each of the individuals who entered the U.S. Navy's officer corps between June 1794 and February 1815. A full bibliography of sources from which these profiles were compiled will appear in the author's in-progress social history of the officer corps to the end of the War of 1812.

No officer who sailed from the United States in one of the ships of Preble's squadron was appointed to the officer corps later than July 1803, but the 89 men here counted include Sailing Master Samuel B. Brooke, who was appointed to that rank on 17 October 1803. Brooke joined Preble's squadron by April 1804, apparently via the storeship *Woodrop Sims*, and he participated in the summer campaign against Tripoli.

11. The difference between the total of this column and the 927 officers in rank on 1 January 1813 is accounted for by ranks that included no Preble-era veterans.

12. The exceptions were Captain Thomas Tingey, who although superintendent of the Washington Navy Yard, did not hold rank as an officer between October 1801 and November 1804, and Master Commandant Jacob Lewis, who had been appointed directly to that rank, 27 November 1812, to command the flotilla for the defense of New York Harbor.

13. The four pre-August 1803 midshipmen (actually one had then been a captain's clerk who acted as a midshipman) who were still midshipmen on 1 January 1813 were all officers whose careers were under one or another kind of cloud. Two of them eventually and grudgingly obtained their lieutenant's commissions. None advanced beyond that rank.

14. Sailing master, a rank that has no equivalent in the contemporary U.S. Navy, was a non-promotion-track appointment much

used in the pre-1815 Navy as a means of bringing into the officer corps older, experienced civilian master mariners—men who could not be appointed to the promotion track ladder of midshipman to lieutenant to master commandant to captain without harmfully disrupting the established system of seniority and advancement. Sailing masters were occasionally able to transfer to the promotion track at the lieutenant level. Although each cruising ship had a sailing master attached to her to perform certain specific duties under the direction of the captain, the great mass of the Navy's sailing masters commanded gunboats and other small patrol vessels.

15. The seemingly anomalous gunner's mate here included was Edmund P. Kennedy. He had been an acting midshipman in the frigate *John Adams* during the Quasi-War with France and was discharged from the corps in the 1801 peacetime reduction. Kennedy accepted the gunner's mate's berth in the hope of being eventually reappointed as a midshipman, a reward he received as a result of heroic conduct during Preble's 7 August 1804 attack on Tripoli.

16. More precisely, ages are known for 17 of the 18 men who were lieutenants in 1803, but for only 33 out of the 46 midshipmen. The age distribution of Preble's midshipmen might be modified in a substantial way if ages could be discovered for more of them. Note, also, that the data on ages here presented can only claim to be accurate plus or minus a year. In many cases they must be based on statements similar to that Master Commandant Michael B. Carroll made on 26 June 1815: "am now 39 years of age." (M. B. Carroll to Board of Navy Commissioners, 26 June 1815, ZB File, Early Records Section, Naval Historical Center, Washington Navy Yard.) If this is taken literally, Carroll might have been born any time between 27 June 1775 and 25 June 1777, though for purposes of these calculations his birthdate is assumed to be 26 June 1776.

17. Ira Dye, "Early American Merchant Seafarers," American Philosophical Society *Proceedings*, CXX (1976), 331–60.

18. Pratt credits *any* service under Preble, no matter how tenuous the connection. Of his 15 "Preble's Boys" no fewer than 5—Jacob Jones, William Bainbridge, David Porter, James Biddle, and Daniel T. Patterson—sat out almost the whole of Preble's campaign as prisoners of war in Tripoli as a result of the capture of the frigate *Philadelphia*.

19. Charles Morris, *Autobiography*, especially 19–34.

20. O. H. Perry to Hugh G. Campbell, 21 December 1813, in Cooper, *History of the Navy*, extra-illustrated by John S. Barnes, II, pt. 4, New-York Historical Society, New York City.

21. Daniel T. Patterson, Memorial to William Jones, 30 Novem-

ber 1813, R.G. 45: Letters Received by the Secretary of the Navy from Masters Commandant, National Archives.

22. The pre-1812 army leadership's failure to coalesce professionally is investigated by William B. Skelton as part of his in-progress book, "The United States Army Officer Corps, 1784–1861: A Social History."

23. This is, of course, the central point of Douglass Adair's well-known essay, "Fame and the Founding Fathers," in Trevor Colbourn, ed., *Fame and the Founding Fathers: Essays by Douglass Adair*, 3–26.

WILLIAM S. BAINBRIDGE: BAD LUCK OR FATAL FLAW?

BY CRAIG SYMONDS

In the pantheon of American naval heroes, the figure of Commodore William S. Bainbridge is one that most naval historians pass over quickly, perhaps in some embarrassment. Although he won a bloody slugfest with a British frigate and returned home a hero in the War of 1812, "Hard Luck Bill" (as at least one prominent authority labels him) is more often remembered for his blunders. He was the only American captain to surrender a ship in the Quasi-War in 1798, and he did so without firing a single shot. In another war he ran the frigate *Philadelphia* aground in broad daylight on a hostile shore and lost both the ship and his entire crew to the enemy, thus reversing at a single blow the balance of power in the Mediterranean. It is not without justification that Bainbridge lamented to his friend Edward Preble that "misfortune has attended me through my naval life."[1]

But Bainbridge's series of misfortunes cannot be passed off simply as the result of hard luck. Rather they were the product of his own inherent weaknesses, the principal one of which was a tendency toward a reliance on clear codes and rules of conduct. Such a dependence made him dogmatic when he needed to be flexible, made him hesitate when the rules did not provide ready answers, made him cautious when caution was fatal, and made him careless when he thought the rules protected him. In short, he was a man of very precise but very limited vision. He was a man who was more at home revising the Navy's penal code or drafting long letters about squadron maneuvers than he was in dealing with people. He was well liked by his fellow officers, but feared rather than loved by his men. Their attitude did not trouble him. He never thought very much of sailors

William Bainbridge. Courtesy of Naval Academy Museum.

anyway, for he was convinced that the only thing that prevented their becoming a perfect rabble was a stern discipline and a strict adherence to the rules.

Bainbridge's attitude toward the common sailor was not untypical of naval officers of his day, but it was heightened by two circumstances peculiar to him. First, as a captain in the merchant trade during his early manhood, he often had to use his own imposing presence (he was a beefy six-footer) to face down a restless crew. He thus came to think of sailors as men to be cowed and subdued rather than as comrades to be encouraged. Second, he never held any position in an American warship other than captain. He was never a midshipman, never a first lieutenant; he received a direct commission to the command of a sloop-of-war during the crisis with France in 1798. As ship's master his authority was absolute, and he did not quail or waver in applying force to uphold it. Rules were rules, and Bainbridge was punctilious in enforcing them.

On the positive side, he was a good seaman—an accurate navigator, a good ship handler, a man with a keen eye for the design of a seaworthy vessel; but in the U.S. Navy of the nineteenth century, good seamanship was not enough. A man with his literal mind was simply not prepared to deal with the subjective nature of the many problems that naval officers on distant stations had to face. In the nineteenth century the political–military circumstances that led to the dispatch of a vessel often changed dramatically by the time the ship reached her destination. Decisions then had to be made by a ship's captain without recourse to higher authority, decisions on which the question of war and peace often hung in the balance. Technical competence and determination were not enough; a ship's commander also had to be able to survive in a politically complex world peopled by wily princes of minor city states and devious and clever representatives of great European powers. For a man such as William Bainbridge, who possessed a delicate sense of both personal and national honor as well as an almost desperate eagerness for public and official approval, these were troubled waters indeed.

Bainbridge embarked on his naval career in August 1798. News of the so-called XYZ Affair had put Congress in a fighting mood and led to a series of acts designed to put the nation in a condition to fight back against the French privateers that were pillaging American commerce in the Caribbean. Bainbridge's reputation as a skilled merchant seaman who, on at least one occasion, had fought off a British effort to board and search his vessel led to his consideration as a prospective U.S. naval officer. He was commissioned lieutenant and assigned to command the small (107-ton) schooner *Retaliation*, which carried 14 six-pounders. His ship was the first vessel of France captured in this "Quasi-War," and Bainbridge had the distinction of taking her to war against her former masters as part of a three-vessel American squadron under the command of Alexander Murray, who flew his flag on board the small frigate *Montezuma*.

During the first few weeks on station, the American squadron succeeded in recapturing several American merchantmen that had fallen to French privateers. Then on 19 November, while the *Retaliation* was temporarily separated from her consorts, the masthead lookout sighted two large frigates hull down on the horizon. Because Bainbridge had been told that the French had no vessel larger than a sloop in the Caribbean, he presumed that these two must be British.

He hoisted the British recognition signal, but it elicited no response. He tried the American recognition signal, but the approaching frigates replied with a flag that he could not read. If he became suspicious by this behavior, it was not enough to provoke an effort to escape. He probably assumed that the ships were officered by skeptical British skippers who suspected the tiny *Retaliation* of being a Frenchman. After all, six months before, she *had* been a French vessel. As the two unidentified ships ranged up within gunshot, the lead frigate fired a full broadside into the *Retaliation* and simultaneously hoisted French colors. Resistance at this point would have been futile, and Bainbridge ordered the flag lowered, thus becoming the first U.S. naval officer to strike his flag to an enemy.[2]

Despite this ignominious end to his first command, the disaster did not hurt Bainbridge's career. The loss of the *Retaliation* was adjudged not to be his fault, and upon his return to the States in February 1799, he found himself not only forgiven but promoted to master commandant and entrusted with another command. But Bainbridge's loss of the *Retaliation* was not simply a product of misfortune. More than anything else, it was a clear error in judgment. He had convinced himself that the two unidentified frigates offered no danger, and had acted accordingly.

Bainbridge took his new command to sea in the spring of 1799. His second cruise was more productive than his first—how could it be otherwise?—but it was not dramatically successful. Nevertheless, upon his return from this second cruise in May 1800, the twenty-five-year-old Bainbridge found himself promoted to captain and given command of a frigate, the *George Washington*.

Bainbridge's new assignment was a delicate one: he was to deliver a cargo to Algiers as payment on a treaty that obligated the United States to make an annual contribution to that North African city state in exchange for its friendship. Because of the large cargo, the fighting efficiency of the *George Washington* would be somewhat impaired, a matter of some importance because of the continuing war with France. If Bainbridge encountered a French man-of-war, his undermanned ship would have a difficult time fighting the enemy. For that reason, Bainbridge's orders specified that after delivering his cargo, he should immediately return to the United States.[3]

The *George Washington* arrived in Algiers on 17 September. One of the first to scramble onto the deck of the American frigate to greet Bainbridge was the American consul, Richard O'Brien. While the pilot guided the *George Washington* to its anchorage, O'Brien filled Bainbridge in on the political situation in Algiers. The next morning, a pleasant Mediterranean day with light breezes that cut the late summer heat, Bainbridge prepared for the offloading of his cargo of lumber, coffee, sugar, and other staples. O'Brien again came on board, this time bringing with him the English consular representative, John Falcons. While they talked, the ship's crew took on board grapes, figs, oranges, and other exotic Mediterranean fruits.[4] Later, O'Brien and Bainbridge paid a courtesy call on the ruler of Algiers, Bobba Mustapha, whose title "Dey," literally translated "uncle," meant that he ruled the city as the representative of the Ottoman Empire. At their meeting Bobba Mustapha mentioned that he desired the *George Washington* to carry an embassy to his own political master, Selem III, the Grand Seignor of the Ottoman Empire. It seems that for all his imperiousness within Algiers, the Dey was not in favor at Constantinople. His most serious crime was failing to declare war on the French at a time when the Turks were battling Napoleon in Egypt. To assuage the imperial anger, Mustapha planned to send him a virtual treasure on board the *George Washington.*

O'Brien remonstrated. The American captain, he said, had no orders from his government authorizing him to perform such a mission. Indeed, he had very explicit orders to return to the United States after delivering the original cargo. The Dey was not pleased with this response. Nor was the Algerine Prime Minister, to whom the Americans spoke next. To Secretary of State John Marshall, O'Brien wrote, "I have tryed all in my power to evade this, but, I am afraid I shall be obliged to give way . . . ."[5]

The announcement put Bainbridge in a very awkward dilemma. His orders were clear—he was to proceed immediately to the United States. To violate these orders would no doubt bring official disfavor. But to refuse the Dey would bring war, and he did not want to be held responsible for that. At noon on 9 October, Bainbridge and O'Brien returned to the Algerine Ministry of Marine to plead their case once again. For Bainbridge it must have been very frustrating; most of the communication had to be done through official translators or by O'Brien with Bainbridge standing by anxiously. But the Minister of Marine was resolute. There was no alternative; the Dey must be obeyed. They retreated to O'Brien's office in the American consulate to discuss their next move. A half-hour later they received word that the Algerine flag must be hoisted at the main on the *George Washington.* Only now did Bainbridge realize that he had been incautious in anchoring his ship within Algiers Harbor under the guns of the Dey's forts. Bainbridge urged O'Brien to request another audience of the Dey.

That afternoon, standing again before Bobba Mustapha, they ran through the litany of reasons why Bainbridge could not make the voyage to Constantinople. The Dey listened to what was becoming a very familiar speech, but then he assured O'Brien and Bainbridge that not only was there no alternative, but that he would never forget this favor done for him by the Americans, and he guaranteed that they would be glad for having done it. Presumably Bainbridge expressed his concern that in acceding to the Dey's demands he would, himself, be court-martialed upon his return, for the Dey made a special point to assure him that the U.S. government "would be highly pleased at the conduct of the Consul & Captain in obliging the Dey and Algrs."[6]

Giving up hope of avoiding the mission altogether, Bainbridge now focused his efforts on preventing the Dey and his minions from hoisting the Algerine flag at the main truck of the *George Washington.* He argued that if the American flag did not fly at the main, the ship could not be considered to be in commission. He was willing to fly the Algerine flag at the main topgallant masthead, but the stars and stripes, he insisted, should continue to fly at the main. The Dey replied that he was not an expert on naval protocol, but that his Minister of Marine would make the right decision. Bainbridge and O'Brien therefore took themselves to the Minister of Marine. That official was not happy to see them. He thought all their arguments and protestations petty and obstructionist. He claimed that the Americans were just being difficult and evasive, and that other nations had flown the Algerine flag at the main. On this point O'Brien had to nod in agreement. Though no American ship had done so, it was in fact the custom for European ships to fly the Algerine flag at the main when on a mission for the Dey. Determined as he was not to yield on this point, Bainbridge found that it was necessary to do so. Immediately following this conversation, the whole party went on board the *George Washington* where the American flag was lowered and the Algerine flag hoisted in its place. The official log of the *George Washington* reported that "some tears fell at this instance of national Humility."[7]

The entire experience was gall and wormwood for Bainbridge. Throughout his naval career, his particular strength was a determination to fulfill the precise letter of his official instructions, and being unable to conform to Secretary of the Navy Benjamin Stoddert's very clear instructions was mortifying to him. He did not make a conscious decision that acquiescence would be better for the national interest than refusal; he simply could not think of a way to get out of it. The more he thought about it, the more outraged he became. The next day he took pen in hand to write a bitter letter to Stoddert explaining his predicament and justifying his decision to acquiesce.

In this letter he claimed that the Dey's attitude was: "You pay me tribute, by that you become my slaves." It is possible that the Dey did in fact make this statement, but is more likely that he did not. The Dey's tactics at the meeting the day before had been to soothe rather than bluster. But Bainbridge was angry and frustrated, and no doubt he wanted his letter to make Stoddert appreciate the difficulty of his situation. His claim that the Dey looked upon all Americans as his "slaves" might have been a calculated effort to stir up Stoddert's anger. Bainbridge also offered a potential solution to the dilemma. "Had we 10 or 12 frigates and sloops in these seas," he argued, "I am well convinced in my own mind that we should not experience those mortifying degradations that must be cutting to every American who possesses an independent spirit."[8]

The "treasure" that Bainbridge was now required to carry to Constantinople included a virtual Noah's ark of animals—tigers, antelopes, lions, ostriches—as well as more than a hundred black slaves, both men and women. In addition he had to transport the ambassador's suite and servants, numbering nearly a hundred more. Altogether his "guests" outnumbered his crew. It must have occurred to him that he might have tried to chuck the ambassador overboard once he was beyond the guns of Algiers, but even assuming that his 130-man crew could have done so, the Dey had made it very clear that he would hold the United States responsible for any losses incurred en route. Bainbridge thus set a course for Constantinople and resolved to make the best of it.[9]

He did make one gesture of defiance once he was beyond Algiers harbor. He removed the Algerine pennant from the main and replaced it with the American flag. Thus when the *George Washington* approached the entrance to the Dardanelles on 10 November, she was flying the stars and stripes. The pilot Bainbridge had taken on at Milo Harbor informed him that all vessels entering the Dardanelles must first be inspected by the commander of the forts at the entrance. Bainbridge was in no mood to commence negotiations with yet another self-important Turk, so he avoided this obligation by incorporating a ruse. He ordered his crew into the tops and the men began to gather in sail while the gun crew began a 21-gun salute to the castle on the shore. The salute was returned, and while the smoke from the guns billowed about the estuary, he ordered his topmen to sheet home the sails, and he navigated the ship past the forts before its commander realized what was happening.

That afternoon Bainbridge spied the spires of Constantinople from the deck of his own frigate, the ship's log reporting that the city was "beautifully situated on the sides of 7 hills gently ascending from the sea making a most beautiful appearance."[10] The next morning Bainbridge navigated the *George Washington* into the harbor, which was crowded with exotic vessels, and anchored opposite the palace of the Grand Seignor himself.

Once again Bainbridge's diplomatic acumen was about to be tested. For this encounter he had luck on his side. The Grand Seignor, Selem III, was angry with the Dey at Algiers and used the occasion of Bainbridge's visit to demonstrate his displeasure. He underscored his mood by treating Bainbridge with ostentatious kindness while ignoring Mustapha's personal envoy. At first Selem's representatives could not understand the flag flying from the gaff of the *George Washington*—they had never heard of the United States. Bainbridge told them that his country was in the new world discovered by Columbus, and that seemed to be sufficient explanation. He was offered a lamb (representing peace) and flowers (representing welcome) and given a warm reception.

The *George Washington* was in Constantinople harbor for a week discharging the cargo. Bainbridge noted on 12 November that he "Set on shore 2 lions 3 tigers 5 antelopes 2 Ostriches and 20 Parrots." But after that, both ship and crew had to wait until the Algerine ambassador was ready to return. Bainbridge spent the next two weeks exploring the area. He took the ship's boat up through the Bosporus to raise the American flag for the first time on the Black Sea; he made exploring expeditions with Edward Daniel Clarke, a famous British world traveler of the day; and he sampled the local delicacies. At one dinner party given on board the *George Washington*, he placed four decanters of water on the table, each containing fresh water from a different continent: America, Africa, Europe, and Asia.[11]

By mid-December Bainbridge was growing restive. How long would he have to wait in this port—however interesting and hospitable—before he could sail out again and fulfill his original orders to return to the United States? He had already written to Secretary Stoddert that if the delays dragged on much longer, he would insist upon departing regardless of the consequences. But it never came to that. The Algerine ambassador, thoroughly chastized and burdened with orders that the Dey must immediately declare war on France, and make further amends by sending more treasure, was finished by Christmas, and the *George Washington* got under way on 30 December.[12]

Upon his return to Algiers in January, Bainbridge anchored well outside the harbor beyond the range of the guns of the Algerine forts. He was determined that he would not again place himself or his ship in a position to be blackmailed. He even had the opportunity to turn the tables a little on the Dey. Much chastened by the reception of his entourage in Constantinople, the Dey immediately released the Europeans he held in captivity and dispatched a party to chop down the flagpole of the French consul—the traditional Algerine signal of a declaration of war. But he wanted one more favor of Bainbridge: to return again to Constantinople with more gifts. This time Bainbridge was ready for him. He produced a "firman" given him by Selem as a gesture of his high esteem. The Dey was impressed. It was very unusual for a Westerner to bear the firman of the Grand Seignor. Bobba Mustapha's tone changed immediately. Bainbridge decided to press his luck and demand the release of all the French prisoners with whom the Dey had hoped to replace the captives he had set free. Though the United States and France were still fighting an undeclared naval war, Bainbridge felt he had to attempt to prevent the imprisonment of any Christian Europeans. The Dey was reluctant. Without captives to hold for ransom, a significant amount of his income would be jeopardized. Besides, did not the Grand Seignor himself want war with France? But Bainbridge argued that Selem did not want the Dey to war on women and children, and Bobba Mustapha gave in. The French would be released, he said, but only if Bainbridge himself would carry them off. Bainbridge readily agreed and took on board a retinue of French officials and their families, whom he transported to the Spanish port of Alicante. There he learned that France and the United States had negotiated a peace, the Convention of Môrtefontaine, signed the previous fall.[13]

Throughout his mission to Constantinople, Bainbridge had worried himself over two points. First, it concerned him that his own unavoidable decision to carry the Dey's embassy to Constantinople would not be sanctioned by his superiors, and second, it galled him that the United States was being subjected to demeaning acts by a minor prince, acts he believed ought to be resisted by force.

The news of Bainbridge's humiliation reached the United States in December via the American merchant ship *Brutus* and was only one more argument in favor of a policy decision that had already been made: As soon as peace with France was established, an American squadron would be sent to the Mediterranean to deter the imperiousness of Algiers, Tunis, Morocco, and especially Tripoli, the most belligerent of the North African states. Bainbridge's role in helping bring this policy change about was a minor one, but illustrative of how naval officers on the scene were expected not only to render their technical expertise, but to propose and even carry out policy.

For a year after his return, Bainbridge commanded the 32-gun

Essex, whose job it was to escort American merchantmen through the Mediterranean. Then after a year's shore duty, he again received orders to sea, this time in command of the 36-gun *Philadelphia*. Along with the *Constitution*, flying the commodore's pennant of Edward Preble, Bainbridge's new command would provide the power of the American squadron while four smaller ships would perform crucial inshore work around Tripoli. This time the American squadron was going to war.

Bainbridge's loss of the *Philadelphia* off Tripoli Harbor was the absolute low point of his career, perhaps of his entire life. Though he spilled a great deal of ink justifying his every action on that fateful day, he did so with such earnestness and frequency that, like Hamlet's mother, perhaps he did protest too much. He described the events many times, and the chronology is a matter of clear historical record. Preble had entrusted Bainbridge with the command of a two-vessel squadron charged with the blockade of Tripoli Harbor. On 23 October a storm forced Bainbridge to take the *Philadelphia* out to sea. Not until the 31st could he stand back in for Tripoli. At nine o'clock in the morning, he was approaching his station when a lookout reported a Tripolitan ship close to shore trying to make its way into the harbor. Pursuit of this vessel would ordinarily have been a job for the *Philadelphia*'s consort, the schooner *Vixen*, but several days before, on hearing that a Tripolitan cruiser was at sea, Bainbridge had sent the *Vixen* off to patrol the Straits of Sicily. This decision was questionable because blockading Tripoli was Bainbridge's primary mission. As a result the *Philadelphia* was alone off Tripoli on the 31st, and Bainbridge conned her toward the Tripolitan vessel which immediately headed into shoal water and tauntingly raised Tripolitan colors. Bainbridge's only hope was to cripple the Tripolitan with a ranging shot. He opened fire at eleven o'clock, but after half an hour decided that he was coming too close to shore and gave up the chase. He brought the *Philadelphia* about and began to beat out to windward to gain searoom when the ship struck hard on an uncharted reef. Thinking that it was a narrow sand bar, Bainbridge first ordered a heavy press of sail in hopes of driving his ship up and over, but it served only to wedge the vessel tighter. Soundings at bow and stern showed deeper water astern, and so swinging the yards around, he laid all sails aback and lightened ship forward by cutting away the bow anchors. The ship did not move.

Bainbridge called a council of his officers to solicit their advice. The officers' deliberations were hastened by the sight of Tripolitan gunboats putting out from the harbor; having devined the predicament of the *Philadelphia*, the Tripolians were coming out like jackals

Loss of the *Philadelphia*. Courtesy of Naval Historical Center.

to harry the trapped American bear. Bainbridge and his officers determined to lighten the ship further by tossing the great guns overboard. It was a desperate step, but it was a desperate crisis. Two of the guns were moved to bear directly aft where the Tripolitan gunboats were gathering, but the others were manhandled over the side one by one until the ship was disarmed. But still the frigate did not rise from the shoal, and Bainbridge called another council of officers. What else could be done to lighten ship and restore mobility before the gunboats shot them to pieces? They decided to cut away the foremast, and a party of sailors went to work on the mast which soon went over the side, taking the main topgallant mast with it in a tangle of rigging. But even this did not free the ship, and shortly before four o'clock, Bainbridge huddled with his officers for the third and last time as captain of his ship. He asked each of his officers what else could be done. He got no answer.

> A Council of Officers was called [he wrote later] when they were unanimously of opinion that it was impossible to get her off the rocks; and that continuing in our present situation would be only a sacrificing [of] lives without affecting our enemy or rendering the least service to Our Country; in such a dilemma too painful to relate, the Flag of the United States was struck.[14]

Had Bainbridge in fact done all that could be done to save the vessel? The hull itself was still very much intact, and though the gunboats fired regularly, they did little damage, perhaps in a conscious effort to capture the ship basically undamaged. There were over 300 American sailors and marines on board, and though they had jettisoned the great guns, they still had a large supply of small arms. Surely they could have repelled a boarding attempt. What convinced Bainbridge to capitulate was the fact that he believed the Tripolitans had time on their side. They could hover beyond the range of small arms and simply shoot the *Philadelphia* to pieces. Still Bainbridge's decision has remained controversial, and Bainbridge himself was aware of how his act would look back home. For most of the rest of his life, he would defend himself against the charge that he had been too ready to haul down the national flag.[15]

His campaign began almost immediately. The very day after the capture of the *Philadelphia*, Bainbridge solicited a certificate from his ship's officers on his conduct, and he sent copies of it to Preble and Stoddert along with letters of his own explaining and excusing his action. To Commodore Preble, whose plan for the conduct of the war in the Mediterranean would be thoroughly disrupted by the loss of half his frigate force, Bainbridge wrote half a dozen letters in the first three weeks of captivity. Preble did not learn of the loss of the *Philadelphia* until nearly a month later when the *Constitution* touched at Malta. Though he wrote Bainbridge a soothing reply, it was not forwarded until February, causing Bainbridge some anxiety. Nevertheless Bainbridge continued to write, often repeating whole paragraphs from earlier letters in the assumption that his letters were not getting through. In one of his first letters to Preble, Bainbridge wrote, "Some Fanatics may say that blowing the ship up would have been the proper result. I thought such conduct would not stand acquitted before God or Man, and I never presumed to think I had the liberty of putting to death the lives of 306 souls because they were placed under my command." Indeed Preble himself might have been classified as one such "Fanatic." Upon learning of the circumstances of the event, Preble wrote Stoddert, "Would to God, that the Officers and crew of the *Philadelphia*, had one and all, determined to prefer death to slavery; it is possible such a determination might [have] save[d] them from either."[16]

Preble was not alone in this reaction. The former American consul at Tripoli, James Leander Cathcart, likewise thought, "How glorious it would have been to have perished with the Ship . . . our national honor and pride demanded the sacrifice." Others could not imagine that the ship had been given up without a struggle. As word of the incident made its way through the Mediterranean, the events became enlarged in the telling. Bainbridge must have been embarrassed to receive a letter from Tobias Lear, the new U.S. consul in Algiers, in which Lear wrote that he had heard that "many lives were lost in the engagement from day light until 4 P.M." when the frigate was carried by boarding. . . ." This scenario had the *Philadelphia* holding out for twelve rather than four hours and the men of the ship surrendering only after a bloody struggle across the decks. How much more surprised must Lear have been to learn later that the ship surrendered without a single casualty, and so precipitously that Bainbridge had to send Porter out in a ship's boat to inform the incredulous Tripolitans that the *Philadelphia* had in fact surrendered.[17]

Though eventually Preble sustained Bainbridge's decision, and they remained good friends throughout long naval careers, in December 1803 he could not help but wonder publicly why the *Philadelphia* was not "rendered useless before the Colours were struck."[18] For as fate would have it, a high tide two days later refloated the American frigate, and the enterprising Tripolitans raised the guns from the shallows where they had been dumped. Soon a fully armed frigate floated freely in Tripoli Harbor.

This event served to increase Bainbridge's mental discomfort, as he knew that his capitulation not only deprived the United States of half its major combatants in the Mediterranean, but increased the strength of its enemy several times over. His response, however, was to redouble his epistolary attempts to justify his action by stating that it was unavoidable. Twice he suggested to Preble the possibility of a few ship's boats sneaking into Tripoli Harbor to destroy the *Philadelphia*. He later cited these letters to support his claim that he was responsible for suggesting Stephen Decatur's daring enterprise. But, in fact, Preble had already determined to attempt the destruction of the *Philadelphia*. Indeed, he would have been derelict in his duty if he had not.[19]

Bainbridge's mental anguish over the loss of his ship was severe. To his wife he admitted a nagging fear that he would be held censurable for the loss by his countrymen:

> My anxiety and affliction does not arise from my confinement and deprivations in prison—these, indeed, I could bear if ten times more severe; but is caused by my absence, which may be a protracted one, from my dearly loved Susan; and an apprehension which constantly haunts me, that I may be censured by my countrymen. These impressions which are seldom absent from my mind, act as a corroding canker at my heart. So maddened am I sometimes by the workings of my imagination, that I cannot refrain from exclaiming that it would have been a merciful dispensation of Providence if my head had been shot off by the enemy, while our vessel lay rolling on the rocks.

He came back to the topic of public censure again and again: "If I am censured, if it does not kill me, it would at least deprive me of the power of looking any of my race in the face. . . . I cannot tell why I am so oppressed with apprehension. . . ."[20] It is not unlikely that some of his obsessive fear resulted from an inner guilt—a guilt that he took great pains to deny for as long as he lived. Eventually it did become a canker that ate away at him, making his last years bitter and acrimonious.

Bainbridge, his officers, and men remained prisoners of the Bashaw of Tripoli, Yusuf Caramanli, for three months short of two years. He was not merely turning a nice phrase when he wrote his wife that the deprivations of confinement were not a great burden to him. Indeed, Bainbridge and the other officers of the *Philadelphia* found their lengthy imprisonment in Tripoli little worse than boring. They were sent first to the previously abandoned consular home of the American representative James Cathcart, and later to private rooms in the stone castle overlooking the harbor. Though there were many long days of strict confinement, the officers were occasionally given their parole so that they could walk about the city. The fact that Bainbridge was allowed to write his wife, his commanding officer, the Secretary of the Navy, and just about anyone else suggests that the American officers were allowed remarkable freedoms. Much later, after his return to the United States, Bainbridge asked a friend to present his respects to the Bashaw and expressed a hope that he was in good health.[21]

To attack the boredom, the officers plotted various escape plans including digging a tunnel under the wall or climbing out of a barred window on lengths of cloth tied together. Once a group of officers actually managed to get outside the window and onto the rampart before retracing their steps upon the approach of a guard. For his part, Bainbridge declined to join in any escape attempts. He claimed later that he did so because the men left behind would feel abandoned by their commanding officer, but the fact that virtually all the escape plans involved swimming out to a small boat must also have had something to do with his decision. Though he had been at sea since the age of fifteen, William Bainbridge did not know how to swim.[22]

When they were not planning an escape, the Americans spent much of their time reading. Bainbridge ordered the younger officers to set up study groups for the furtherance of their professional education. He directed his executive officer, David Porter, to see to it that after breakfast each day midshipmen should "repair to their rooms to study Navigation and read such books as we are in possession of that they will improve their minds."[23] For this suggestion Bainbridge was much praised after his release, and his role in sponsoring a "school for sailors" much exaggerated. This order, and Bainbridge's later practice of holding school sessions on board his ships, led the Navy to name the Naval Education Center in Maryland after him.

If the officers suffered mostly from boredom, the crew of the *Philadelphia* suffered from everything except boredom. Unlike the officers, they were confined to a crowded prison with little light, poor food, and no sanitation. The crew were sent on daily work details building roads and improving already strong fortifications. They felt themselves much abused and underfed, and appealed to Bainbridge to intercede with the Bashaw on their behalf. As a result of his intercession they were allotted meat twice a week for a brief period, but soon this ration was discontinued and they went back to their diet of brown bread and oil.[24] In fact, Bainbridge made no sustained effort to improve their lot. His only reference to their treatment was in a letter he wrote in late November to protest the Bashaw's decision to throw the *Philadelphia*'s officers into that same prison for a day in response to rumors that Preble had been mistreating Tripolitan prisoners. Bainbridge insisted that the rumor was unfounded, and he and his officers were soon released. But Bainbridge nevertheless complained to Preble that "myself and Officers were confined one day to the loathsome prison of our Crew, without anything to eat. . . ." His outrage, however, was not directed at the "loathsome" conditions of the crew's prison, but at the fact that the officers were made temporarily to share those conditions. As for the sailors, Bainbridge had little sympathy for their plight: "I believe there never was so depraved a set of mortals as Sailors are," he wrote; "under discipline they are peaceable and serviceable;—divest them of that and they constitute a perfect rabble."[25]

By the time Bainbridge and his ship's company were released as part of the peace settlement, the war had reached a satisfactory end, and there was little enthusiasm or apparent reason to prosecute anyone. The court of inquiry on Bainbridge's loss of the *Philadelphia* was all but pro forma. Bainbridge's officers, all of whom shared in the decision to strike the flag, were the principal witnesses, and Bainbridge's good friend Edward Preble, glowing in the aftermath of the successful war, presided. The court listened to the witnesses and then concluded that "no degree of censure should attach itself to him [Bainbridge] from that event."[26] Indeed, his return to the United States in the fall of 1805 took on the aspect of a triumphal procession. He landed at Hampton Roads, Virginia, and remained there two days, "feasting and indulging in all the Luxuries of Epicurus, and the flowing libations of Bacchus."

> We then proceeded to Head Quarters, but the hospitality of the Citizens of Richmond detained us there 3 days, and those of Fredericksburg one. On the 25th of Septr. arrived in Washington, found the Chief and heads of our Department absent, but the hearts of our fellow citizens at Washington as warm as those of Virginia—they gave us an equal reception.

He continued to receive "kind congratulations all along the road to my home" in Perth Amboy, New Jersey, where he was reunited with his family.[27]

The interval between Bainbridge's triumphal return from Barbary in 1805 and his participation in the War of 1812 found him involved in various business enterprises in an effort to improve his financial situation. He now had a wife and three children to support (a fourth was born in 1814) and was finding that difficult on the salary of a naval captain, especially in peacetime when he could not look forward to the possibility of prize money.

Bainbridge did not cease to be interested in naval affairs. He continued to believe that the United States could assure itself of adequate protection from potential enemies only by committing itself to the construction of a significant naval force. Though he counted himself a Republican (presumably because of their Anglophobia, which he shared), he had little sympathy for President Jefferson's gunboat policy. Gunboats, he admitted, were useful in coastal defense—after all, a swarm of them had not only kept the U.S. Navy out of Tripoli for a half decade, but a handful of them had captured his last command. But gunboats, he argued, were of very limited utility. They could not go onto the open ocean to defend trade; they could not hope to stand up to enemy warships in hull-to-hull combat. In addition to gunboats, therefore, Bainbridge, along with most naval officers of his generation, believed strongly in the necessity of building some ships-of-the-line. At least in part, his policy views were a product of his own operational aspirations. It was his greatest ambition to command an American 74-gun battleship in combat with a British two-decker.

A few months after his return from the Mediterranean, Bainbridge joined his friend Preble and Captain Samuel Barron on a trip to the nation's capital as self-appointed lobbyists to support naval expansion. Alas for their cause, Congress was still dominated by an anti-naval ideology, and the only successful naval legislation that year was an appropriation of a quarter of a million dollars for the construction of more gunboats.

Active blue water commands were scarce in the U.S.Navy of 1806–7. Of Bainbridge's two companions in that journey to Washington, only Samuel Barron succeeded in gaining an appointment. No doubt Bainbridge envied him his orders to command the frigate *Chesapeake*. Several months later, Bainbridge learned that Barron's ship, manned by a green crew and with her gunports triced down for a transatlantic voyage, was stopped, fired upon, and forced to submit to a search by the British frigate *Leopard*. Considering Bainbridge's hatred of the British, he must have fumed with anger and frustration.

Not for two more years did Bainbridge get a chance to command an American frigate at sea. Meanwhile he devoted himself to more entrepreneurial pursuits. Bracketing a brief and uneventful tour as commander of the frigate *President* in 1809–10, Bainbridge took extended furloughs in order to pursue a fortune in the merchant trade. He was in St. Petersburg, Russia, in the fall of 1811 when he heard about the accelerating animosity between the United States and Britain. Though he had planned to winter over in Russia, he now changed his mind and sought to get back to the United States before a declaration of war made his return impossible. Because St. Petersburg's harbor was already frozen, he traveled overland across

Sweden, finally arriving in Boston in February 1812 after a genuinely harrowing land and sea journey. The trip left him physically weakened and marked the first appearance of a persistent and wracking cough that was to plague him the rest of his life, and would eventually kill him.

His trips to the Baltic had brought him a substantial estate, sufficient to ease his concerns for his family's well-being, and Bainbridge was eager to put to sea in uniform in command of a frigate. He was still every bit an Anglophobe, eager to cross swords with the Royal Navy. He forbore from campaigning openly for a declaration of war, however, insisting that the duty of a naval officer was not to discuss policy but to carry it out.[28]

Reinstated to active duty, Bainbridge was first assigned to command the Charlestown Navy Yard, but after the declaration of war in June, he lobbied for an active command and was promised the frigate *Constellation*, a 38-gun veteran of the Quasi-War. But when the 44-gun *Constitution* came into Boston Harbor fresh from her victory over the *Guerriere*, Bainbridge learned that her commanding officer, Issac Hull, would plead ill health and ask for a shore station. Bainbridge lost no time in applying for command of the larger vessel. His request was accepted, and, in addition, he was appointed to command one of three naval squadrons, each of which was to be made up of a heavy frigate, a light frigate, and a smaller vessel. All the squadron commanders vied to have the best ships assigned to their command. Decatur thought that the *Essex* would be assigned to him because she was based near his flagship, the *United States*, but Bainbridge invoked his seniority to get the Secretary of the Navy to reverse an earlier decision and to assign the *Essex* to him.

On 6 October, the *Constitution* and the *Hornet* sailed in company out of Boston while the third vessel of Bainbridge's squadron, the *Essex* sailed separately from the Delaware Bay. Bainbridge sent Porter, captain of the *Essex*, a detailed itinerary suggesting various spots where they might rendezvous, but in fact the two vessels never did meet, and Porter, taking advantage of a clause in Bainbridge's orders to "act according to your best judgment," took the initiative and carried the war into the South Pacific where, after a successful cruise, he was eventually cornered and defeated by a superior British force.[29]

For his part, Bainbridge encountered only one vessel of any interest en route to his South Atlantic cruising ground—an American merchantman out of Glasgow, the *South Carolina*, which possessed a British license to trade. Eager to secure a capture, Bainbridge construed this to signify disloyalty on the part of the ship's owner, and he put a prize crew on board and sent the ship off for adjudication. Much later the prize court would refuse to condemn the ship, and Bainbridge would be held liable for the costs incurred by the owners.

In early December the *Constitution* made landfall off the coast of Brazil at Fernando de Noronha, one of the rendezvous points Bainbridge had suggested to Porter. Failing to encounter the *Essex*, Bainbridge left a message behind and continued on to Brazil where he put in at St. Salvador or Bahia. Henry Hill, the American consul there, proved to be an excellent source of information, though the Brazilian governor had little sympathy for either Bainbridge or his mission. Indeed, the governor became quite upset when James Lawrence in the *Hornet* pursued a British vessel too close to Brazilian waters. So terse was the governor's letter of complaint that Bainbridge responded belligerently (through Hill), threatening to "act accordingly" if the governor wanted to count himself as an enemy.[30]

Both the *Constitution* and the *Hornet* cruised in and about St. Salvador for several days, hoping to entice out a British vessel reputed to be loaded with specie. In the hope of encouraging the ship to head for open water and a "fair fight" with the *Hornet*, Bainbridge left St. Salvador on 26 December and headed southeast for his fated encounter with the *Java*.

A few leagues off the Brazilian coast on the morning of 29 December, lookouts in the *Constitution* spied the topsails of two vessels in the northeast. Almost immediately the sails separated, one making for land, the other holding course to intercept the *Constitution*. Shortly before eleven, Bainbridge ordered the royals and mainsail reset, explaining later that he did so to draw the enemy farther away from the neutral coastline. Possibly, too, he wanted to assess more carefully the strength of his probable enemy.

A few minutes before two under a clear sky and light winds, Bainbridge again put the *Constitution* under topsails and closed with what proved to be the enemy frigate. He was almost certain of her nationality, but he nevertheless fired a gun across her bow in formal challenge and inquiry. The vessel responded by hoisting English colors and firing a full broadside.

The enemy was HMS *Java*, a relatively new 38-gun frigate under the command of Captain Henry Lambert, RN. The *Java* was a refitted French prize laden with stores for the British garrison in India and carrying on board the new governor general, Lieutenant General Sir Thomas Hislop. Though the ship was sound, her crew was untested and composed largely of resentful conscripts. Considering both his crew's inexperience and his passenger's safety, Lambert might have been excused if he had given the *Constitution* a wide berth. But bolstered by an English tradition of superiority at sea, and perhaps unwilling to appear cowardly before an army officer, Lambert held course to bring the American to battle.

Here at last was a naval problem unencumbered by North African potentates, French diplomats, or politicians of any stripe, and one for which Bainbridge had a clear and uncomplicated solution. His immediate desire was to close with the *Java* as rapidly as possible and slug it out with her, relying on his superiority of fire power to overwhelm the enemy. But whenever the *Constitution* began to close the range, Lambert pulled away. The cannonade was furious on both ships. After about a half hour the *Java* crossed the stern of the *Constitution* and delivered a raking broadside that smashed the wheel housing and shot away the wheel. A piece of langrage, or shrapnel, embedded itself in Bainbridge's leg. But he was not about to quit the ·deck now. Supporting himself by clinging to the rigging, he ordered men below to rig steering cables so that the ship could be maneuvered by orders shouted down from the quarterdeck. Ten minutes later the *Java* mistimed her tack, and Bainbridge was finally able to close, raking from the stern as he did so. From close range the *Constitution*'s fire was devastating, and in a period of only fifty minutes all three masts on board the *Java* were felled. At that moment Bainbridge knew that victory was assured. The British frigate was little more than a hulk, incapable of maneuver and helpless before Bainbridge's guns.

At four, Bainbridge hauled off to repair his own rigging and give the Briton a chance to consider his hopeless situation. Lambert, however, was not yet ready to give up. Severely wounded himself and with more than a hundred other casualties lying about his blood-smeared decks, he, nevertheless, set his crew to work clearing the wreckage and in futile attempts to jury-rig something from the stump of the mainmast. But it was indeed hopeless. After a twenty-minute respite, Bainbridge carefully maneuvered the *Constitution* across the bow of the *Java* in a silent but eloquent demonstration of dominance. With Lambert mortally wounded, the decision to strike was made by the senior lieutenant, Henry Chads.[31]

In two and a half hours the *Java* had been pounded into a leaking hulk. Besides Lambert, another hundred had been wounded, and sixty more lay dead. On board the *Constitution* the losses were remarkably lighter: only nine killed and twenty-five wounded including Bainbridge. It was an unquestionable and unsullied victory, the absolute high point of Bainbridge's career. Finding himself in a situation where nautical skill and raw courage were the essential attributes, Bainbridge proved that he had them to spare. It was full and satisfying

Capture of HMS *Java*. The low and high points of Bainbridge's career were the grounding and loss of the *Philadelphia* to Tripoli in 1803 and his destruction of the *Java* off the coast of Brazil in 1812. Courtesy of Naval Historical Center.

vindication for a man eager to eradicate memories of his earlier defeats.

The *Java* was so wrecked that Bainbridge rejected all thought of trying to patch her up and bring her back to an American port as a prize. Escorting a crippled frigate over a thousand miles through an enemy blockade would be dangerous as well as time-consuming. Instead, Bainbridge ordered the two remaining ship's boats on board the *Constitution* to shuttle the *Java*'s crew to the American frigate and then ordered his prize destroyed. He did not attempt to salvage the small cargo of stores or other valuables on board, but he did bring off the officers' baggage.

It was characteristic of Bainbridge to be so conscientious in his thoughtful treatment of captive officers. Like most other officers of his day, he took his personal code of conduct as a gentleman very seriously—invoking it when he was himself a prisoner, and supporting it to the hilt when he was the captor. His first act of generosity was to return Lambert's sword to the dying man, telling him that he had defended his vessel with great honor. By itself such an act was merely a thoughtful courtesy, but as part of an overall pattern Bainbridge's treatment of captive enemy officers suggests that he was striving to demonstrate his own high quality as a gentleman by exaggerated solicitousness. Significantly, this treatment did not extend to enlisted men. Indeed, the crew of the *Java* was very roughly handled, even considering the necessarily crowded conditions on board the *Constitution*. Bainbridge made a clear and unbridgeable distinction between officers and enlisted men. In effect he believed that the two were different species altogether. This attitude was displayed in a letter he wrote a friend a few days after the battle, in which he expressed a hope that prize money would be granted by Congress for the destroyed *Java*. How else, he asked rhetorically, could anyone expect enlisted men to continue to fight. "It is prize money which stimulates the sailor; patriotism and fame guide the officer."[32]

Though the *Constitution*'s cruise was to have lasted until the spring, Bainbridge now planned to return immediately to Boston, not necessarily because his ship required some minor repairs as a result of the battle with the *Java*, but because he knew that news of the victory would be well received at home. In the letter to a friend mentioned earlier, he admitted that "The applause of my countrymen has for me greater charms than all the gold that glitters."[33] Lambert's successor in command of the *Java*, Lieutenant Henry Chads, defending himself before a British court of inquiry, argued later that Bainbridge had been forced to return to port rather than embark on what surely would have been a devastating cruise in the Pacific because of the punishment inflicted on the *Constitution* by the *Java*. But Bainbridge's desire to hear the applause of his countrymen had more to do with his decision to return to the United States than the physical condition of his ship.

Bainbridge conned the frigate into Boston Harbor in February with the Union Jack flying beneath the stars and stripes. Forewarned by Bainbridge's dispatches, the citizens of Boston welcomed him with huzzahs and participated in a triumphal procession to his hotel, through a town draped in bunting and past a huge banner linking Bainbridge's name with the names of Hull, Jones, and Decatur. There was the obligatory public dinner and a "Naval Ball" in celebration of the victory, and then an outpouring of official appreciation. Massachusetts and New York passed legislative thanks, President Madison sent his own congratulations, and Congress voted to strike a gold medal to Bainbridge which he later helped to design. Perhaps the most useful thanks was the fifty thousand dollars of prize money voted by Congress to reward the officers and men of the *Constitution*. Bainbridge's share was seven thousand dollars—a fortune equal to what he had earned as a merchant trader in five years of peace.

For Bainbridge the rest of the war was anticlimatic. He was named commandant of the Charlestown Navy Yard and commanding officer of the nation's first ship-of-the-line, the massive *Independence*. Alas for his hopes of further victories, the giant *Independence* was still unready for sea when the war ended.

Bainbridge lived eighteen years after the end of the war with Britain, but never again reached the peak of popularity he enjoyed in 1812 and 1813. His last best hope to gain further success and recognition came in 1816 when he commanded a squadron to the Mediterranean with orders to protect American commerce from the renewed aggressive actions of the Algerines and, if possible, to defeat them in battle and force upon them a permanent solution to the problem. But Bainbridge's appointment to this important command came more than a month after the Navy Department had issued nearly identical orders to Stephen Decatur. Decatur was desperately eager to assuage his loss of the frigate *President* in the last year of the war against Britain, and he rushed his preparations for sea with almost unseemly haste. Bainbridge, meanwhile, was plagued by manpower and material shortages, and Decatur proved more resourceful in overcoming both, with the result that when Bainbridge finally arrived in Gibraltar, he learned that Decatur's smaller squadron had not only arrived there first, but had defeated the Algerine navy at sea and virtually brought the war to an end. Bainbridge reported rather forlornly to the Secretary of the Navy:

> Altho sir this squadron of which the President honored me with the Command in Chief have not owing to previous arrangements of the first squadron [Decatur's] had an opportunity of doing more than shewing its forces off the Barbary ports and exercising in evolutions of Naval service, I beg leave through you to assure the President that had occasion required or opportunity offered that the gallant officers and men under my command would have proved that devotion to their country which our small navy has to often exhibited.[34]

The officer corps of the U.S. Navy in the early nineteenth century was a small and exclusive club. Those few who had retained membership after the reductions that had followed the Quasi-War and the onset of the Jefferson administration had, by 1816, become very senior officers. But they were also men who knew that they stood very little chance of ever being promoted again. Despite occasional congressional resolutions to create a rank of admiral in the U.S. Navy, the national prejudice against military and naval hierarchies was too strong. Most officers compensated by jealously guarding the privileges of rank which to them represented official recognition and approval. The result was the creation of informal rivalries and alliances within this small but competitive fraternity. Of course there were officers who were above it all—Edward Preble seems to have been one of them—but more commonly professional relations among naval officers in the second decade of the nineteenth century resembled the politics of the Roman senate: polite words masked deep animosities.

In this context the relationship between Bainbridge and Stephen Decatur is one of the more titillating aspects of both careers. Decatur had hurried his departure for the Mediterranean precisely so that he would not have to serve under Bainbridge, and having won his race to glory, he delayed returning to Gibraltar, where Bainbridge's squadron lay at anchor, for the same reason. When Decatur finally did bring his flagship into the harbor, he timed his arrival to coincide with the departure of Bainbridge, who was leading the combined American squadron on its trip back across the Atlantic. As the *Guerriere* entered Gibraltar, her crew put out the jolly boat, and every eye in the fleet watched as Decatur leaped into the sternsheets with the apparent intention of having himself rowed over to the *Independence* to pay a call on Bainbridge. But the *Independence* was already under way, and Bainbridge was reluctant to stop the entire squadron in order to receive Decatur. He held his course. Decatur's friends claimed then and later that this was a deliberate snub by Bainbridge growing out of his jealousy of the junior, but more successful, Decatur. For three years afterward the two men remained personal and professional enemies.[35]

Not until December of 1819 did they reconcile. As Bainbridge later recalled the incident, he saw Decatur on the street, and in one of those spontaneous bursts of sentimentality that had become characteristic of him in his later years, he rushed up to Decatur and offered his hand. All was forgiven in an instant. But the timing of their reconciliation was curious, for in December of 1819 Decatur was embroiled in the midst of a messy war of words with Samuel Barron that was about to fester into open conflict. For reasons known only to himself, Decatur asked Bainbridge to serve as his second in the forthcoming duel. Bainbridge agreed, and met with Barron's second, Jesse Elliot, on board the *Columbus* in March 1820.

The duel took place later that month at a notorious dueling ground outside Washington on the Bladensburg road. Witnesses then, and historians since, have suggested that Bainbridge was partly at fault for neglecting an opportunity to stop the duel when Decatur told Barron, "I was never your enemy." Instead Bainbridge called for silence and ordered the duel to proceed. The two duelists fired nearly simultaneously, and both fell wounded. Barron would recover, but Decatur's wound was mortal. Why had Bainbridge been unwilling to permit an apparent reconciliation? Decatur's young widow, distraught at the news of her husband's death, accused Bainbridge of participating in a plot with Jesse Elliott. Personal and professional jealousy, she claimed, had led Bainbridge to feign friendship and bring her husband to this sad end. But Bainbridge's conduct was not the product of a sinister plot; rather it proceeded from his lifelong veneration for propriety and his firm belief that the rules must be obeyed. Duelists were not supposed to speak to one another; that, after all, was why they had seconds to speak for them. He called for silence on the battlefield to quiet the unseemly conversation. The rules had to be obeyed.[36]

In a few weeks Bainbridge was at sea in the *Columbus* on his way to the Mediterranean. It would be his last sea command, and when he returned, he would be remembered not so much as the man who had stood on the deck of Old Ironsides with a piece of langrage in his leg and fought the *Java*, but as the man who, as most of Washington now suspected, had conspired in Decatur's death. Even in his dying Decatur had bested him—exiting the martyred hero and leaving Bainbridge on stage alone before a hostile audience.

Bainbridge died in 1833, a victim of poor health and worse medical care. (The pain-killing and cough-suppressing drugs prescribed for him turned him into a near addict, prone to violent shifts of mood in his later years.) Because of his canonization in 1812, naval historians have felt compelled to explain away Bainbridge's early failures as the product of "hard luck." Though his seamanship was excellent—and none dared dispute his commitment and determination—his dogmatism, inflexibility, and reliance on precise codes of behavior blinded him to opportunities and tied him to conventional responses in times of crisis. What he never learned, even in his twilight career as president of the Board of Navy Commissioners in the 1820s, is that codes, rules, and written orders can provide guidance only to a certain point. Beyond that point successful captains must rely on breadth of vision and insight, and these were not Bainbridge's strongest suits.

FURTHER READING

Because few Bainbridge letters have survived other than the official letters in the published naval documents collections and the microfilmed Captain's Letters from the National Archives, most biographical information about Bainbridge comes from one of two early biographies written by admirers. The first is by General Henry A. S. Dearborn (*The Life of William Bainbridge, Esq., of the United States Navy*), written in 1816 just after the end of the war with Britain for the purpose of praising the conqueror of the *Java*. The manuscript was not published, however, until it was discovered many years later by James Barnes, who was working on his own biography of Bainbridge. Barnes added a final chapter to Dearborn's work covering the years 1820–33 and published the book in 1931. In it Bainbridge's career is depicted as a modern parable illustrating the triumph of personal courage, determination, and virtue over an evil fate. General Dearborn was a personal friend of Bainbridge, and his "research" consisted of asking Bainbridge himself to provide the details. Many of the stories associated with Bainbridge's early career as a merchant captain, as well as details of his subsequent career as a naval officer, come from Dearborn.

The second early biography is by Thomas Harris, another personal friend, who wrote *The Life and Services of Commodore William Bainbridge, United States Navy*. Harris makes a greater effort to be critically objective, but for background information about Bainbridge's early years he too relied heavily on Bainbridge's memory, and apparently he had access to Dearborn's manuscript, for many of the passages in Harris's book are remarkably similar to passages in Dearborn. For all practical purposes, the Dearborn and Harris biographies are only as good or as reliable as Bainbridge's own selective memory.

A third "biography" is by James Barnes, who "discovered" and published Dearborn's manuscript. Barnes's book is entitled *Commodore Bainbridge, From the Gunroom to the Quarter-Deck*. It is a "boy's book" written to show how courage and perseverance lead eventually to success even if fate throws obstacles in the way. To dramatize his work, Barnes made up dialogue and put thoughts into the minds of his characters much as a novelist might.

Another dramatic narrative of Bainbridge is in Glenn Tucker's *Dawn Like Thunder: The Barbary Wars and the Birth of the U.S. Navy*, which opens with Bainbridge's confrontation with Bobba Mustapha over the impressment of the *George Washington*. It is good drama and very readable, but unreliable as history. A much better study is the sketch of Bainbridge in Leonard F. Guttridge and Jay D. Smith, *The Commodores: The United States Navy in the Age of Sail*. They conclude that insofar as Bainbridge was concerned, ". . . it was as much miscalculation and uncertainty as bad luck that precipitated disaster."

Only in the last few years has a scholar undertaken a serious full-length study of Bainbridge. David Long (author of the essay on David Porter in this volume) wrote *Ready to Hazard: A Biography of Commodore William Bainbridge, 1774–1833*, which was published in 1981. Far more detailed and accurate than any of the earlier studies, it is more balanced in its treatment of the commodore. Long finds Bainbridge to have been clearly at fault, for example, in his loss of the *Philadelphia*.

A definitive account of Bainbridge's life and career, however, will continue to elude historians. There are episodes of his life and aspects of his character that will never be known. The reason is that Bainbridge's daughters burned nearly all of his private letters after his death in 1833. Many scholars, including David Long, have speculated that they did so in order to prevent the details of his involvement in the Barron–Decatur duel from becoming public. Of course, we can never know for sure. But that uncertainty is part of what makes Bainbridge a continuing paradox.

NOTES

1. The "prominent authority" is E. B. Potter in *Sea Power*, 91. The quotation is from a letter of Bainbridge to Preble, 12 November 1803, in Dudley Knox, ed., *Naval Documents Related to the United States Wars with the Barbary Powers*, III, 74. (Hereafter cited as *NDBP*.)

2. Murray to Stoddert, 23 November 1798. Dudley Knox, ed.,

Naval Documents Related to the Quasi-War Between the United States and France, II, 40–41. (Hereafter cited as *NDQW*.)

3. Stoddert to Bainbridge, 25 June 1800, *NDBP*, I, 361–62. Stoddert to Bainbridge 12 July 1800, *NDQW*, VI, 141.

4. See the log of the *George Washington* in *NDBP*, I, 370. Accounts of the voyage of the *George Washington* and of Bainbridge's confrontation with the Dey of Algiers are based on Thomas Harris, *The Life and Services of Commodore William Bainbridge, United States Navy*, 43–61. Remarkably similar accounts appear in Gardner Allen, *Our Navy and the Barbary Corsairs*, 75–87; Henry A. S. Dearborn, *The Life of William Bainbridge, Esq., of the United States Navy*, 18–24; and Glenn Tucker, *Dawn Like Thunder: The Barbary Wars and the Birth of the U.S. Navy*, 11–41. See also David F. Long, *Ready to Hazard: A Biography of Commodore William Bainbridge, 1774–1833*, 41–46.

5. O'Brien to Marshall, 20 September 1800, *NDBP*, I, 371.

6. O'Brien to Bainbridge, 9 October 1800, *NDBP*, I, 377.

7. Logbook of the *George Washington* in *NDBP*, I, 378.

8. Bainbridge to Stoddert, 10 October 1800, *NDBP*, I, 378–79.

9. O'Brien to Bainbridge, 10 October 1800; O'Brien to Eaton, 19 October 1800, *NDBP*, I, 380, 384–85.

10. Logbook of the *George Washington, NDBP*, I, 400.

11. See Harris, *Life and Services*, 43–61.

12. Bainbridge to Stoddert, 17 November 1800, *NDBP*, I, 401.

13. Logbook of the *George Washington, NDBP*, I, 417.

14. Principal sources for the loss of the *Philadelphia* are two letters written by Bainbridge soon after the event. The quotation is from Bainbridge to Smith, 1 November 1803. Both letters are in *NDBP*, III, 171–74. See also the testimony of David Porter at the Court of Enquiry held in June 1805, in *NDBP*, III, 189–94.

15. Bainbridge's earlier biographers strongly sustain his decision to strike. More recently David Long has concluded that "Bainbridge erred on the side of caution and . . . his decision to yield his command was premature and precipitate." Long, *Ready to Hazard*, 77.

16. Bainbridge to Preble, 12 November 1803; Preble to Smith, 10 December 1803, *NDBP*, III, 339.

17. Cathcart to Secretary of State, 15 December 1803; Lear to Bainbridge, 16 December 1803; Lear to Davis, 17 December 1803, *NDBP*, III, 272–73, 274–75, 277.

18. Preble to Secretary Smith, 10 December 1803, *NDBP*, III, 258.

19. Bainbridge to Preble, 5 December 1803; Preble to Bain-

bridge, 19 December 1803; Bainbridge to Preble, 18 January 1804, *NDBP*, III, 253–54, 280, 347.

20. Bainbridge to Susan Bainbridge, 1 November 1803, *NDBP*, III, 178–79.

21. Bainbridge to John Ridgely, 27 January 1806, Bainbridge Papers, Naval Historical Collection, Library of Congress. (Hereafter cited as LC.)

22. Dearborn, *Life of Bainbridge*, 71–72.

23. Bainbridge to Porter, 5 November 1803, Charles T. Harbeck Papers, box 2, Henry E. Huntington Library, San Marino, California.

24. Crew of the *Philadephia* to Preble, 7 November 1804, Bainbridge Papers, LC.

25. Bainbridge to Preble, 25 November 1803, *NDBP*, III, 175–76.

26. Printed in *NDBP*, III, 194.

27. Bainbridge to John Ridgely, 27 January 1806, Bainbridge Papers, LC.

28. Bainbridge to John Ridgely, 22 February 1811, Bainbridge Papers, LC.

29. Bainbridge to Porter, 13 October 1812, R.G. 45: Letters Received by the Secretary of the Navy (Captains' Letters), 1805–1885, National Archives. (Hereafter cited as Captains' Letters.)

30. Harris, *Life and Services*, 139; Long, *Ready to Hazard*, 144.

31. See Bainbridge's report to Secretary Hamilton dated 3 January 1813 in Captains' Letters, reel 26. See also the account in Harris, *Life and Services*, 163–66 and Dearborn, *Life of Bainbridge*, 129–31.

32. Bainbridge to "a friend," 24 January 1813, quoted in Harris, *Life and Services*, 163–66 and Dearborn, *Life of Bainbridge*, 129–30.

33. Harris, *Life and Services*, 163–66, Dearborn, *Life of Bainbridge*, 129–30.

34. Bainbridge to Crowninshield, 6 September 1815, Captains' Letters, reel 45. (Misfiled as part of the packet of letters dated 26 July.)

35. See Alexander Slidell Mackenzie, *The Life of Stephen Decatur*. Mackenzie, as a junior officer on board the *Chippewa*, was a witness to the event.

36. Mackenzie, *Life of Decatur*, 320–25; Helen Nicolay, *Decatur of the Old Navy*, 204–19; Charles L. Lewis, *The Romantic Decatur*, 190–327; and Long, *Ready to Hazard*, 227–46. See also the Memorandum of Samuel Hambleton printed in Mackenzie, *Life of Decatur*, 439–41.

OLIVER HAZARD PERRY: SAVIOR OF THE NORTHWEST

BY JOHN K. MAHON

Perry's short life is almost exclusively a naval one. He came into the world with navy in his blood; his father, Christopher Raymond, was in naval combat during the American Revolution, and in British prisons for long stretches. When the Navy Department was created in 1798, he was commissioned captain. Oliver Hazard, born 20 August 1785, was the oldest of four sons and three daughters. All of the sons became officers in the Navy, and two of the daughters married naval officers.[1] Oliver's brother, Matthew Calbraith, junior to him by nine years, became famous for commanding the U.S. expeditionary squadron during the Mexican War, and for opening Japan to American trade.

In 1799, fourteen-year-old Oliver went on board the US Frigate *General Greene*, 28 guns, as a midshipman under his father's command. Thereafter, he never left the service until his premature death at age thirty-five. From the start, he learned his profession well; both afloat and ashore he studied navigation, seamanship, and mathematics, and read Hackluyt. He worked with the guns too, becoming as fine an ordnance officer as there was in the service. Apart from professional manuals, he read Shakespeare and Montaigne. He became an accomplished flutist, horseback rider, and fencer. The distinguished officers under whom he served contributed to his development: his own father, Edward Preble, James Barron, Charles Morris, and, above all, John Rodgers. These and other senior officers were impressed with him, and took pains to advance his career. But he owed more to diligence and to the consequent mastery of skills for his rise in the profession than to other contributants.[2] When he

Oliver Hazard Perry. Courtesy of Naval Academy Museum.

became a captain, he closely supervised the education of the young midshipmen under his command.

Perry rose rapidly in the young Navy. He was commissioned lieutenant at seventeen while serving in the Mediterranean squadron, took command of the schooner *Nautilus*, 12 guns, when he was twenty, and was chosen to direct the building of seventeen of Jefferson's gunboats when he was twenty-two. Each of the gunboats was to be armed with a long 24-pound gun, and manned by thirty persons.[3] Two years later he took command of the schooner *Revenge*, 12 guns. The *Revenge* came near to interrupting his upward mobility when on 2 February 1811 she ran aground in a heavy fog and broke up on the rocks off Newport, Rhode Island. Perry was suspended from command pending a hearing on this loss. The panelists of the inquiry charged the grounding to the pilot, who was supposed to know the coastal waters, and exonerated Perry; but the loss of a ship, nonetheless, marred his record.[4]

Throughout the *Revenge* affair, Perry seems to have tried to spare the feelings and protect the reputation of Lieutenant Jacob Hite, notwithstanding that he had suspended Hite from duty for reasons that are not known. In spite of Perry's protection, the panelists decided that Hite's performance during the wreck was discreditable, and they broke him to midshipman and suspended him from active duty.[5] This episode reveals a tendency in Perry to shelter subordinates from their just deserts. One who was thus sheltered plagued the later years of Perry's life, and did his best to destroy his superior's image in history.

The same day that President Madison proclaimed a state of war against Great Britain, 18 June 1812, the Secretary of the Navy directed Perry to take command of the gunboats that he had helped build at Newport. Perry instituted a rigorous training, putting the gunboats and their crews through fleetlike maneuvers, and engaged in sham battles.[6] But in time of war this was not enough; like his peers, Perry needed the glory and honor that were only to be attained in combat. Accordingly, he steadily sought assignment to a seagoing fighting ship, and as steadily failed to receive it. Finally, therefore, he requested transfer to the Great Lakes theater where John Rodgers assured him, salt water or not, that there would be brisk fighting.[7]

On 8 February 1813, the Secretary of the Navy ordered Master Commandant Perry to proceed with 150 of his best gunboat sailors to report to Captain Isaac Chauncey, commander of the Great Lakes. Eager to see action, Perry lost no time in carrying out this directive.[8]

On 28 February, only twenty days later, he met his new commanding officer, not on the Lakes, but in Albany, New York. Chauncey—who was to be a central character in the events that placed Perry prominently in American history—personified one strain in the officer corps, Perry the opposite. Chauncey was an administrator, Perry an operational commander. Chauncey, the manager, ordered Perry, the combat officer, to travel westward with some of his Rhode Island men to Presque Isle on the south shore of Lake Erie, and there to build a naval squadron with which to wrest control of the lake from the British, who, at that time, dominated it. In carrying out this gigantic task, Perry was able to draw on his experience building the Jefferson gunboats. Having built, he must become supreme on the lake, 200 miles long and 60 miles wide, and over both tips of the Ontario Peninsula.[9]

Perry traveled in the bitter cold, partly by sled on the frozen lake, to reach Presque Isle on 27 March. The spot was one of natural beauty with a fine harbor, but virtually undefended. The garrison was insignificant, with but one cannon. As for building materials, the wood stood in the forest: cedar, black oak, white oak, chestnut, and pine for the decks. Non-wood materials had to come from Pittsburgh, 130 miles away, or Philadelphia, farther yet, via a series of small rivers and creeks. With the aid of army ordnance at Pittsburgh, Perry collected a few artillery pieces and some essential building material. Authorities canvassed homes in the town for iron that could be put to naval use. At this time, as at all others, Perry doggedly held to his duty, and the building went forward.

Manpower was even scarcer than materials. A few blacksmiths could be drawn from the local militia, but more were needed and had to be trained as they worked. "Give me men, Sir," Perry wrote to Chauncey, "and I will acquire both for you and myself glory and honor . . . or perish in the attempt."[10] Chauncey, who was hard-pressed to hold his own against Sir James Lucas Yeo on Lake Ontario, sent small detachments, but often retained the best sailors for his own command. Perry suspected as much, and desperate as he was for reinforcements, he complained about one of the detachments sent to him. Had the commodore ever seen these men? Chauncey, it happened, had had to curb his own operations to make that particular shipment, and replied sharply. Perry was offended by the tone of the response, and wrote to the Secretary requesting transfer. "I cannot serve," he said, "under an officer who has been so totally regardless of my feelings."[11] Here Perry displayed the hypersensitivity common to the officer corps. Feelings were deep with them, and they were touchy on matters of honor, glory, and pride. Chauncey became conciliatory, the secretary denied the transfer request, and Perry characteristically stood to his duty. Although he continued to believe that his crews were composed of Chauncey's rejects, he did his best with them.[12]

Such supplies as reached Presque Isle came at prices so high that the secretary often required Perry to justify them. For example, it cost $1,000 to ship one cannon from Albany to the lake region, the price of 500 acres of good land around Pittsburgh. A barrel of flour came at $100. Small wonder that the secretary demanded to know why Perry requisitioned expensive lead for ballast when big heavy stones lay about for free. Perry made the rational and plausible response that the runs (i.e., the shape of his ship's underbodies) were such that sufficient stones could not be placed in them, that pig iron, the usual ballast material, was not available, and that the lead he purchased for ballast could, at any time, be sold for the price he paid for it and the money returned to the treasury.[13]

With the advent of spring Perry surveyed his resources for the upcoming campaign season. His Lake Erie command included, in addition to the vessels he was building, five small craft at Black Rock on the Niagara River. The problem lay in uniting his squadron. The Black Rock ships were immobilized by the guns at Ft. Erie on the Canadian side of the Niagara, and it would be difficult to get them out of the river and the eighty miles to Presque Isle because the British dominated the lake. In addition, the harbor at Presque Isle was blocked by a bar at its mouth. Even at times of high water there was no more than seven feet of water over it; at other times, as little as four. The two brigs building there would draw nine feet. Jesse Elliott, soon to loom large in Perry's life, had told his supervisors that the place was unsuitable for the American base on Lake Erie because of the bar. Perry, who did not create the situation, accepted it as part of what he must overcome to do his duty and earn honor and glory.[14]

The opportunity to free the vessels at Black Rock came late in May 1813. Chauncey, for the Navy, and General Henry Dearborn, for the Army, agreed to assault Ft. George, which sat at the northern end of the Niagara River. Chauncey summoned Perry to take part, and turned the naval action ashore over to him. Perry had scant respect for the Army, but found himself able to work well with Colonel Winfield Scott, to whom Dearborn had delegated the Army's role. Perry planned the river crossing and personally led the landing party that established the beachhead. The joint American force captured Ft. George on 27 May, whereupon the British evacuated Ft. Erie at the other end of the Niagara without a fight. Now the Black Rock ships could emerge onto Lake Erie, but only after a herculean effort in which sailors yoked up with oxen and 200 soldiers sent by General Dearborn dragged them against the swift current of the river as it rushed toward Niagara Falls. By 12 June, the vessels were on the lake hugging the south shore for the eighty miles to Presque Isle in order to elude the British.[15]

Why had the enemy not wiped out Perry's precarious base when it was virtually defenseless? One part of the answer is that they, like the Americans, were at the tip of their line of communications; supplies had to come up the St. Lawrence, go through Lake Ontario, and only then reach Erie. Perforce, the end-of-the-line forces were chronically short of everything they needed. Added to this difficulty was another, the complicated layers of command interposed between a commander on Erie and supplies, men, and strategy.

Sir John Borlase Warren, British naval commander in North America, sent Captain Robert Heriot Barclay, a veteran who had lost an arm at Trafalgar, to the Great Lakes in February 1813, but some of his superiors retained Barclay on Lake Ontario for too long. Finally, he was told to go to Erie and take charge, but it was 3 June before, with the utmost effort, he could reach Amherstburg. There he joined the ships of the British squadron, and took to the lake at once to try to intercept the Black Rock vessels. Because they were on the lake on 12 June, he had scant time for preparations. In any case, Perry got them inside the Presque Isle bar on 19 and 20 June. Barclay reported that the Americans had slipped by him in heavy fog. He knew now that added forces were necessary to attack Presque Isle, and he pleaded for them to every commander, army and naval, who might help. His requests ricocheted around among Brigadier John Vincent, Governor General George Prevost, Brigadier Henry Procter, Major General Francis DeRottenburg, and Sir James Yeo, but none of them could find soldiers or sailors to wipe out Perry's menacing establishment.[16] Perry, who would have resisted, however futilely, any attack, never stopped putting together an American squadron to contest for the control of Lake Erie.

There is an ingredient in martial achievement, that—combined with diligence and determination in the commander—must be present: luck. Perry was lucky that the British did not strike him when he was all but defenseless. Nor did luck desert him later.

By 10 July, Perry's squadron was ready to cross the bar, except for a shortage of sailors. His twin brigs were 141 feet long by 30 feet wide, with two masts. Each mounted 20 guns, two of them long, the rest carronades, shorter in range but able to throw heavier projectiles. Perry knew that Barclay was hurrying to finish one ship equal to one of his brigs, and that whoever got onto the lake first with a superior squadron might dominate it afterward. Sometime in July, he learned that his closest friend in the Navy, James Lawrence, had been killed on board the *Chesapeake* in a battle with the frigate *Shannon* on 12 July. He named the brig he had chosen as his flagship the *Lawrence*, and he saw to the sewing of a battle flag with Lawrence's last words worked onto it: "Don't Give Up the Ship!" The twin brig received the name *Niagara*. Noah Brown, who had supervised building the two, said that they were good for one battle, no more. Constructed as they were of green wood, a musket ball could penetrate their two inches of planking.[17]

It was a mile from deep water in the harbor to deep water in the lake. The two brigs would have to be mounted on "camels" to pass over the bar and the shoal water beyond it. The camels would be filled with water in the harbor and pumped dry at the bar, at which time they would lift the vessels high enough to pass over. Because of their weight, the guns would have to be dismounted; thus, while in transit, the vessels would be utterly helpless. In spite of this vulnerability, and in spite of being short about 250 men, Perry decided that he must go over. He positioned the dismounted guns and the light craft to give as much defense to the operation as was possible, and on 1 August started the movement. As it was a Sunday, the country people from far and near came to watch, and the local militia pitched in to help with the heavy hauling. By 2 August the five Black Rock vessels were over and posted defensively. On 4 August the *Lawrence* was afloat on the lake, but the *Niagara* was stuck in the shoals. At that critical moment, Barclay's squadron, minus his big ship which was not yet finished, appeared. Perry now demonstrated the audacity that marks him as a combat commander by sending the *Ariel* and the *Scorpion* out to sail straight at the foe, firing their long 24-pounders. Thinking he saw a formidable squadron over the bar, Barclay failed to realize the American's vulnerability, and sailed back toward Amherstburg, not to emerge again until his flagship *Detroit* was able to join. Perry, for his part, remounted the armament on his big ships, and prepared them to cruise. His audacity, supported by luck, had brought him success. Barclay had always asserted that he could prevent Perry's crossing the Presque Isle bar.[18]

During the second week of August 1813, Master Commandant Jesse D. Elliott reported to Perry, bringing with him about 100 men and the letter from Chauncey that caused Perry to ask for transfer. Perry's sailing master, William V. Taylor, noted that Elliott detailed the best of the replacements to the *Niagara*, which he was to command. Taylor protested to Perry, but the latter, showing his tendency to avoid ruffling the feelings of subordinates, let the matter pass.[19]

Perry now pointed his squadron up the lake the 150 miles toward the British base. Illness appeared to be draining away his luck. Half of his crews were down with typhoid or malaria, and he, himself, was too sick to be on deck during the latter part of August; but good fortune returned, and he could resume active control on 1 September.[20]

As Perry's place on the roster of American military immortals depends on one battle, the details of that fight, bearing on his leadership, are here essential. Major General William Henry Harrison, commander of the land forces across the lake from Amherstburg, had been waiting many months for American domination of Erie so that he could cross and invade Upper Canada. It was grievous to Perry to have to tell Harrison from time to time that he must wait longer. Now he informed the general that a lack of manpower held him up. Harrison offered soldiers, and Perry accepted those who could be of help. The Secretary of the Navy rebuked Perry mildly for informing an army officer of his deficiencies. Such shortcomings, he said, ought to be kept within the naval service.[21] Perry and Harrison together reconnoitered the upper lake and selected South Bass Island as the staging point for action against the British. Thirty-five miles from the enemy's base, the island has a good harbor—later designated Put-in-Bay—and it was a logical place to move the army from the American mainland if and when it could invade.[22]

While Perry positioned his squadron to ensure that there would be a climactic battle, his superior was maneuvering on Lake Ontario in such a way as virtually to ensure that there would be no battle. For ten weeks or so, he and Sir James Lucas Yeo engaged in Virginia-reel-like action, falling back, and advancing, over and over again. Neither commander was willing to bring on the climactic battle on that lake. Chauncey, for example, would never risk his fast ships to overtake the enemy, trusting to the laggards to catch up in time to turn the tide. Instead he caused the swift ones to take the dullards in tow.[23]

Developments in the British side on Lake Erie were pushing toward the showdown that Perry sought. Supplies had piled up at Long Point that were desperately needed at the head of the lake, 150 miles away. They could not be transported by land, only via the lake. Barclay launched the *Detroit* on 20 July, but without stores or crew, arming her with 19 long guns of four different calibers and two howitzers removed from the forts. Filling out his crews with men from the foot regiments, he prepared for combat.

Perry knew in general terms of Barclay's preparations and took pains to avoid being taken by surprise. Should Barclay attack his squadron at anchor, the ships should weigh anchor and form a line with the *Lawrence* in the lead. Should there not be time for such a maneuver, the ships should cut their cables and make sail behind the leewardmost vessel. Passwords were devised to avoid confusion during darkness. Twice Perry reconnoitered Barclay's fleet at Fort Malden and surveyed the coast, looking for suitable places to land Harrison's army.

By the beginning of September, Barclay had to act. Perry's anchorage in the Bass Islands virtually blockaded the British at Malden and cut their supply lines from the East. With 20,000 troops and Indian allies to feed, Barclay's stores ran low, and he was forced to put his men on reduced rations. On 6 September he informed his commanders that he was prepared to leave his base and fight. He knew that his squadron was inferior, but not to what degree, and his only alternative was to abandon his ships and withdraw overland. The obvious choice was to fight.

The balance of forces slightly favored the Americans:[24]

	Ships	Brigs	Schooners	Sloops	Men	Guns	Weight of Broadside
U.S.	2	1	5	1	530	54	896 pounds
British	2	2	1	1	440	63	459 pounds

Barclay's advantage lay in his superiority in long guns, but Perry knew this and planned to bring his squadron into close action rapidly, where his superior weight of broadside would count. Thus, he directed each ship captain to close with the opposite of his class and engage at close range. The *Lawrence*, Perry commanding, would duel the other flagship, the *Detroit*, and the *Niagara*, Jesse Elliott commanding, would fight the *Queen Charlotte*.[25]

American lookouts sighted the British squadron nine miles west of Put-in-Bay and nine miles from the U.S. mainland. The direction of the wind made it difficult for Perry to leave harbor, but so determined was he to engage that he ordered the line to move anyway, working from the lee side. He made the rounds of the guncrews, and his visit strengthened their determination. Forty-seven of his guns were manned by Rhode Islanders, for whom he had special encouragements. Next he ran up the banner "Don't Give Up the Ship," and urged the sailors to follow the motto; they responded with a great shout. Then the Perry luck reasserted itself, as the wind swung around ninety degrees giving him the weather gauge. His squadron straightway fanned down upon the enemy at an angle of about twenty-five degrees in order to get within carronade range the fastest way. The oblique approach subjected the *Lawrence*, in the lead, to heavy fire before she could bring her own broadsides to bear. Moreover, Barclay, who had decided that his best tactic was to knock out the American flagship, concentrated 35 of his 63 guns on the *Lawrence*. Beginning at a range of a mile and a half, the British long guns began to take effect. Because Elliott for some reason did not bring up the *Niagara* to close, the *Queen Charlotte* could also concentrate on the *Lawrence*. In spite of the punishment, Perry got his vessel to within 300 yards of the *Detroit*, and pounded away at her. Now for two and one-half hours the American flagship absorbed as severe a shelling as any ship ever has. By 1:30 P.M. the *Lawrence* was dead in the water, but still fighting. Half an hour later only 19

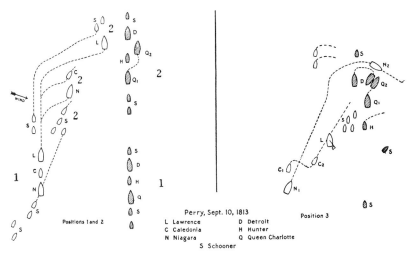

Perry, Sept. 10, 1813	
L Lawrence	D Detroit
C Caledonia	H Hunter
N Niagara	Q Queen Charlotte
S Schooner	

Positions 1 and 2

Position 3

DIAGRAM OF THE BATTLE OF LAKE ERIE SEPTEMBER 10, 1813

Battle of Lake Erie. The diagram from Alfred Thayer Mahan's *Sea Power in Its Relations to the War of 1812* illustrated Jesse Elliott's failure to support Perry. The engraving shown is representative of the many phileopiestic depictions of the battle produced in nineteenth-century America. Courtesy of Naval Academy Museum.

135

of her crew of 142 men were fit for duty. In the midst of the mael-
strom, however, the Perry luck was holding: Perry, dressed as a
common sailor in order to deceive marksmen, stood at his post,
where he was slightly wounded once, while men fell all around him,
spattering him with their blood and brains.[26]

With the *Lawrence* dead in the water, Jesse Elliott finally brought
the *Niagara* forward, keeping the *Caledonia*, which had closely supported Perry throughout the battle, and the shattered *Lawrence* between his ship and the enemy broadsides. When the *Niagara* was
about half a mile from the flagship, Perry decided to shift to her,
perfectly unharmed as she was. He boarded the gig, providentially
intact, and with five sailors and his brother Alexander, made for the
Niagara. Once the British saw the movement, they opened fire on
the little boat, but in fifteen minutes Perry was across the bullet-
churned water and on board his new flagship. Although there were
precedents for this transit in the English–Dutch wars, it was rare
enough to be astonishing. Numerous pictures of it have been painted
by artists who were not there, more than one of which depicts Perry
standing upright in full dress uniform with his sword pointed straight
out like a lance. Perry, who knew better than to posture in this
critical moment, was, of course, still in common sailor's garb, and
sitting because the rowers begged him to sit.[27]

It can never be known for sure what passed between the two
master commandants when Perry came on board. There are several
versions of the conversation, all of them suspect because of bias.[28]
It is certain, however, what took place next. Elliott got into a small
boat and was rowed to the lesser warships to bring them into closer
action. His passage, like Perry's, was hazardous. Perry curbed the
speed of the *Niagara*, which seemed to him about to run out of the
battle, and turned into what was left of the British line so as to cross
the "T" on both broadsides. The *Niagara* raked the vessels to her
left and right from stem to stern. At 3:00 P.M., fifteen minutes after
Perry's transit, the *Detroit* struck her colors, and the other British
ships soon did the same. Here, for the first time in history, a full
British squadron was surrendered.[29] That great historian Henry Adams said of the result, "More than any other battle of the time (this)
was won by the courage and obstinacy of one man."[30] Perry reported
his victory in simple, powerful words. To the Secretary he wrote,
"It has pleased the almighty to give the arms of the United States a
signal victory over our enemies on this Lake . . . "; and to General
Harrison, "We have met the enemy and they are ours, two ships,
two brigs, one schooner and one sloop."[31]

This tiny action, involving fifteen vessels, 117 guns, and about

1,000 men, ranks as one of the decisive battles in American history when one considers the results. By gaining control of Lake Erie, and with it the waterways between Upper Canada and Michigan, it transferred the initiative to the Americans. The British found their position in Michigan and Ohio untenable; they were forced to withdraw, and the Northwest was preserved for the United States. William Henry Harrison was now able to invade Upper Canada. Beginning on 20 September, Perry transported Harrison's troops to Canada. Thereafter, his squadron kept the invading army supplied, while Perry himself joined the general and on 5 October 1813 was in the forefront of the Battle of the Thames, which broke the fighting power of the British west of the Niagara River.[32]

Only ten days after his great achievement, Perry requested to be relieved from the Erie command. Why he did so is not known. He had found it trying to work under Chauncey, and perhaps to function as Jesse Elliott's superior. Moreover, little honor seemed available while Chauncey continued his combat-free maneuvering on Ontario. In any case, the Navy Department granted his request. On 25 October he transferred the Erie command to Elliott and began a hero's progress across the northeastern United States to his home in Newport. Chauncey protested the department's decision to release Perry because it would make it difficult to hold competent officers in the lake zone. To him Perry was deserting his post, and to a degree, he was.[33]

In reporting the battle, Perry had made a grave mistake. Dissatisfied as he had been with Elliott's performance, he yet wrote in his official account that "At half past two, the wind springing up, Captain Elliott was enabled to bring his vessel . . . gallantly into close action." Without adding that he had personally assumed command of the *Niagara*, Perry went on to say that "In this action, [Elliott] evinced his characteristic bravery and judgment. . . ."[34] Later, he acknowledged that it was foolish of him to have written this because it was not true. He explained his lapse thus: "At such a moment, there was not a person in the world whose feeling I would have hurt." Almost immediately after the battle Elliott began to demand more recognition than was in the after-action report. In response, just nine days from the fight, Perry informed Elliott his conduct had his commander's "warmest approbation."[35]

This distortion of what Perry really believed, in order to spare the feelings and the record of a subordinate, dogged him the rest of his life. Elliott persisted in his demand that the report be changed. Finally, in 1818, he challenged his former commander to a duel.[36] By this time Perry no longer cared about the man's feelings. He replied that he could fight only a gentleman, which Elliott had proved he was not, and that he would file formal charges against him. If the resultant court-martial exonerated him, then, and only then, would there be a duel. The charges went to the Secretary of the Navy on 10 August 1818, nearly five years after the battle. They stipulated that Elliott had disobeyed his orders; had hung a mile behind the *Lawrence*; had handled his sails to keep clear of the melee; and through "cowardice, negligence, or disaffection" had not done his utmost to destroy the vessel he had been assigned to attack. The Secretary, not wishing to divide the officer corps on a matter so far in the past, passed the papers along to the President without recommendation. James Monroe, for political reasons, chose to pigeonhole them; so there never was a trial. As a consequence, years after Perry had died, Elliott was asserting that he, not Perry, had really won the battle.[37] His campaign did not dislodge Perry from his pedestal in American history, nor did it perpetuate Elliott's own name, but it poisoned relations within the Navy's officer corps for thirty years. Only the Sampson–Schley controversy at the turn of the twentieth century rivals it for acrimony and longevity. Writers such as the novelist–historian James Fenimore Cooper and the naval officer–biographer Alexander Mackenzie were drawn into the fray. More recent historians have preferred to overlook the bitter dispute between the naval hero and the officer who wished to replace him as hero. The one place where Elliott nearly got even was in the distribution of prize money. Congress appropriated $250,000 to distribute among officers and sailors for the capture of the British squadron. At the start Elliott received $7,140, the same sum as Perry. Chauncey, who was in overall command on the lake though not present at the battle, received more than either of the participants, his share being $12,750. Later Congress voted $5,000 more for Perry.[38]

The balance of Perry's short life is quickly told. In 1814 when the British fleet moved up the Potomac River, Perry, with John Rodgers and David Porter, was sent by the department to delay the British in any way possible. They put naval guns ashore and commanded batteries that harassed the invading ships as they returned down the river.[39]

Perry was assigned to supervise the completion of the *Java*, a frigate of 44 guns, and command her when at sea. The ship was built like a fine piece of cabinet work, but what Perry did not know was that some of the wood used was substandard. It was 1816 before the *Java* was ready to sail for the Mediterranean, and during that voyage one of the yards broke, pitching five sailors to their death on the deck and revealing rotten wood. The year 1816 was not a good one for Perry. While serving with the Mediterranean squadron he made a second serious error; he struck Captain John Heath, the commander of marines on board the *Java*. Perry reported his violation of regulations to his superiors at once, acknowledging that he had lost control of himself. There was a court of inquiry, the judges of which censured Heath and gave a light reprimand to Perry. Some of his oldest associates, senior captains, protested that Perry's sentence was too lenient. To condone striking a junior officer, they said, opened the way to arbitrary, dictatorial conduct by senior commanders. Other of Perry's peers defended him to the point of demanding that the protesters be dismissed. The sentence stood, and no one was let go.[40]

In the Marine Corps an officer could not allow a blow, whoever struck it, to go unrevenged. Therefore, Heath persisted in demanding satisfaction. Finally on 19 October 1818, two years after the event, the two met in a duel at Weehawken, where Alexander Hamilton had been killed by Aaron Burr in 1804. Like Hamilton, Perry let it be known that he would not fire at all; while he stood with his arms at his side, Heath shot and missed. Perry's second proposed to Heath that what had occurred ought to satisfy his honor; Heath agreed, and the matter ended there.[41]

Very little of historical note occurred for some time in Perry's career. Then, in 1819, the Secretary directed him to sail in the frigate *John Adams*, accompanied by the schooner *Nonsuch*, to find the leaders of Venezuela, a new nation freshly created by Simon Bolívar, and negotiate a treaty with them not to molest American merchantmen. To find the Venezuelan government, Perry had to work his way 150 miles or so up the Orinoco River, traveling in the *Nonsuch* because the frigate drew too much water. At the town of Angostura, the captain found a vice president, Francisco Zea, who seemed competent to negotiate, since Bolívar himself, the head of state, was off fighting for independence from Spain in another area. By the time Perry had secured an agreement from Zea and started down the river, it was August, with fearful heat and clouds of insects. The Navy Department, one supposes, had no way of knowing that to order a voyage into the jungle at that season was the equivalent of issuing a death warrant. Among the swarming insects were mosquitoes, carriers of deadly yellow fever. Perry's crew was decimated. The captain wrote his reaction to the conditions: "I meet this danger as I do all others, simply because it is my duty; Yet I must own that there is something more appalling in the shape of death approaching in a fever than in the form of a cannon ball." The Perry luck had finally run out. It was his fate to accept death in the more appalling form: yellow fever killed him at the mouth of the Orinoco River on 23 August 1819, just three days after his thirty-fourth birthday.[42]

The family he left behind consisted of his widow, three sons, and one daughter. Congress voted Elizabeth Mason Perry $400 per year through her life and all of the children $50 per year until they were of age. The daughter's annuity was to run for life if she did not marry. Congress here exceeded its previous provision for dependents, which ended with the life of the veteran himself.[43]

This concern for Perry's heirs reflected the commodore's treatment of others while he was alive. Perry was generally conciliatory and humane, reserved in public but warm with close associates. His best friends in the Navy were James Lawrence and Stephen Decatur, two of its finest officers. Midshipmen who were fortunate enough to serve with him received an excellent professional beginning. Perry opened his library to them, and they remembered his guidance in later life. Other subordinates, including Sailing Master William V. Taylor and Surgeon Usher Parsons, considered him a brave officer, respecting not only his ability as a fighter but also his humanity toward the sick and wounded. Among the latter, Perry's prisoner Captain Robert Barclay, terribly wounded, recorded that his captor treated him like a brother. Perry expected the best from common sailors and got it, by visiting them at their battle stations and appealing to their pride, and by standing under the same hail of bullets they endured. After the war, recruiting a crew for the *Java*, Perry had to turn away good seamen who had flocked to serve with him because he was the sort of hero who reflected credit upon them. Better than many of his peers, Perry worked effectively with competent army officers. He and Winfield Scott shared in the capture of Ft. George, and he and William Henry Harrison cooperated to bring about the final defeat of the British army in Upper Canada.[44]

Perry is remembered in the Navy, however, not as a hail-fellow-well-met, but for winning one of the decisive battles in American history. In doing so he became a national hero. While the memory of his achievement was fresh, citizens named nineteen towns and nine counties after him. Painters executed a dozen or more heroic portraits of Perry, and at least as many canvases of the Battle of Lake Erie, most of them featuring the transit from the *Lawrence* to the *Niagara*. There is a massive monument to him on South Bass Island and another, less massive but more artistic, in Newport, Rhode Island, his hometown. A third statue stands in Buffalo, New York. A replica of the *Niagara*, containing some fragments of the original, is placed on a hillside overlooking the harbor at Erie, Pennsylvania. The United States Naval Academy displays the sword Perry wore during the battle and spreads the pennant, "Don't Give Up the Ship," in Bancroft Hall. During the past half century, seven articles in which Perry is mentioned, some of them featuring him, have been printed in the *Proceedings* of the United States Naval Institute.[45]

Part of the Perry legacy is the imbroglio between him and Jesse D. Elliott. This demonstrates to all generations that it never pays to gloss over a poor performance in order to protect the feelings or the record of any person. Too late, Perry himself recognized his. When his relationship with Elliott had deteriorated as far as it could go, he wrote him: "I shall never cease to criminate myself (for giving a favorable report of your conduct) for the sake of screening you from public contempt."[46]

Perry was not a managerial officer. When caught in an inactive theater, he sought transfer to the combat zone. Once there, he bent all his energy to engage the foe in a climactic battle. In his day it was still possible to win a campaign, even a war, in a day. He drew on his reserve strength to be ready for the decisive moment; for example, when dragging the ships across the bar at Presque Isle, he went without sleep for three days and three nights. Although he stood throughout the action, he took pains, as noted earlier, to keep from being foolishly conspicuous. Perry was basically a kind man, but in battle he became so preoccupied with the outcome as to be unconscious of the misery about him. He was prepared to lose his life for three intangibles: duty, honor and glory. Certainly he was not indifferent to material rewards, yet he would not accept the percentages of the cost of ships built under his supervision, to which he was entitled by regulation. He feared this sort of financial gain might warp his judgment as a fighting officer. It is no small part of his legacy to his profession that he was first and foremost a combat officer.[47]

FURTHER READING

Biographers have widely differed in their evaluations of Oliver Hazard Perry. James Fenimore Cooper, *Lives of Distinguished American Naval Officers*, is less favorable to Perry than is any other biographer, whereas the most recent biography of Perry, Richard Dillon's *We Have Met the Enemy: Oliver Hazard Perry, Wilderness Commodore*, is one of the most positive. The latter contains neither footnotes nor bibliography, but it is apparent that Dillon has used well the Perry Papers in the William L. Clements Library, Ann Arbor, Michigan. It is not clear if he used the Perry Collection at the Northwest Ohio Great Lakes Research Center at Bowling Green State University or Perry's correspondence with the Secretary of the Navy, which is in the National Archives. He has not, however, consulted British Admiralty Records or Colonial Office records in Kew or the manuscripts in the Public Archives of Canada in Ottawa. If the reader has time for only one volume, this is the one to read. Charles J. Dutton's *Oliver Hazard Perry* is not a first-class biography, but the second choice after Dillon's. Alexander S. MacKenzie's *The Life of Commodore Oliver Hazard Perry* is essential reading for the inquirer who wishes to get below the surface. Much of the second volume is taken up with documents, among them the charges Perry made against Elliott five years after the action. Frederick L. Oliver's "Commodore Oliver Hazard Perry of Newport, Rhode Island" is a tidy summary if the reader has only a short time to read.

Much has been written about the Battle of Lake Erie, Perry's major claim to fame. Theodore Roosevelt covers the battle in *The Naval War of 1812*. He says that James Fenimore Cooper's critical analysis of the battle in *History of the Navy of the United States of America* is inaccurate. Roosevelt also believed William James's *Full and Correct Account of the Chief Naval Occurrence of the Late War Between Great Britain and the United States* to be unreliable on the lake war, but it does provide the British point of view. Benson J. Lossing's *Pictorial Field-Book of the War of 1812* may be the best short summary of all. In contains diagrams of the ship positions and pictures of the sites and participants. Alfred Thayer Mahan, *Sea Power in its Relation to the War of 1812*, is especially good in contrasting Perry's dash with Chauncey's excessive caution. On naval matters it never pays to neglect Mahan. James H. Ward's *Manual of Naval Tactics* is very instructive because it includes a technical examination of the battle and the handling of the sails and sailing accessories. James C. Mills's *Oliver Hazard Perry and the Battle of Lake Erie* was issued as a centenary tribute and tells a straightforward story, but is too eulogistic and condemns Elliott without reservation.

Richard J. Cox, "An Eye-Witness Account of the Battle of Lake Erie," U.S. Naval Institute *Proceedings*, published the account of Samuel Hambleton, who was Perry's purser during the battle. The papers of another participant, Daniel Dobbins, who was sailing master under Perry, were used by his son to produce a very useful account entitled *History of the Battle of Lake Erie (September 10 1813), and Reminiscences of the Flagships "Lawrence" and "Niagara."*

Several collections of primary sources have been published. *Anecdotes of the Lake Erie Area: War of 1812*, transcribed from the original sources by Richard C. Knopf, contains extracts from the court-martial proceedings of Robert Heriot Barclay, the British commander, and accounts of participants Usher Parsons, David C. Bunnell, and Isaac Roach.

In 1835 a volume entitled *A Biographical Notice of Commodore Jesse D. Elliott Containing a Review of the Controversy between him and the Late Commodore Perry* was anonymously published in Philadelphia. It was written or prepared by Elliott himself and contends that Elliott, not Perry, was the true victor in the Battle of Lake Erie. The following year Stephen Decatur's widow had *Documents in Relation to the Differences Which Subsisted Between the Late Commodore O. H. Perry and Captain Jesse D. Elliott* published from papers that were left with Decatur by his friend O. H. Perry. Elliott had been James Barron's second in the duel in which Barron killed Decatur in 1820. These documents do not spare Elliott.

The Battle of Lake Erie: A Collection of Documents, Charles O. Paullin, ed., contains the proceedings of the court-martial of Robert Heriot Barclay and the court of inquiry of Jesse D. Elliott.

NOTES

1. John M. Niles, *Life of Oliver Hazard Perry*, 16, 17; Richard Dillon, *We Have Met the Enemy*, 1.

2. Dillon, *We Have Met*, 4, 6, 16, 18; Niles, *Life*, 23, 25; Charles J. Dutton, *Oliver Hazard Perry*, 17.

3. Dutton, *Perry*, 24, 28, 41; Niles, *Life*, 31, 57, 223; Dillon, *We Have Met*, 13, 28, 38, 39; Frederick L. Oliver, "Commodore Oliver Hazard Perry of Newport, Rhode Island," U.S. Naval *Proceedings*, LXXX (July 1954), 778.

4. Dutton, *Perry*, 24, 28; Alexander S. MacKenzie, *The Life of Commodore Oliver Hazard Perry*, I, 99.

5. Dillon, *We Have Met.*, 39ff.

6. Dutton, *Perry*, 50; *Appleton's Cyclopaedia of American Biography*, IV, 735.

7. Dillon, *We Have Met*, 54; MacKenzie, *Life*, I, 122.

8. Secretary of the Navy to Perry, 8 February 1813, R. G. 45: Letters Sent by the Secretary of the Navy to Officers, National Archives. (Hereafter cited as Secretary of the Navy Letters.)

9. MacKenzie, *Life*, I, 130–33, 170, 171; Dutton, *Perry*, 56ff, 63, 73.

10. Quoted in Dillon, *We Have Met*, 101.

11. Chauncey to Perry, 14 July 1813, R. G. 45: Captains' Letters; Alfred Thayer Mahan, *Sea Power in its Relations to the War of 1812*, II, 63–66; Dutton, *Perry*, 113.

12. Richard J. Cox, "An Eye Witness Account of the Battle of

Lake Erie," U.S. Naval Institute *Proceedings*, CIV (February 1978), 73.

13. Dillon, *We Have Met*, 64, 66, 67, 113, 114; George D. Emerson, compiler, *The Perry Victory Centenary*, 158; MacKenzie, *Life*, I, 208, 209.

14. Dillon, *We Have Met*, 58; Fletcher Pratt, *The Navy*, 178; Glenn Tucker, *Poltroons and Patriots: A Popular Account of the War of 1812*, I, 316; Barclay to Yeo, 1 June 1813 printed in *Anecdotes of the Lake Erie Area: War of 1812*, transcribed by R. C. Knopf, 17.

15. Mahan, *Sea Power, 1812*, II, 38, 41; Dillon *We Have Met*, 85–92, 94; Chauncey to Secretary of the Navy, 29 May 1813, R.G. 45: Captains' Letters.

16. Dillon, *We Have Met*, 94, 95; Barclay's narrative in Charles O. Paullin, ed., *The Battle of Lake Erie: A Collection of Documents*, 159–61; Barclay to Yeo, 4 June 1813, same 10 July 1813, in *Anecdotes*, 23–24; Brigadier Vincent to Lieutenant General Sir George Prevost, Governor and military Commander of all Canada, 18 June 1813, Public Archives of Canada; and Brigadier Henry Proctor to Prevost, 11 July 1813, Public Archives of Canada.

17. MacKenzie *Life*, I, 136; Mahan, *Sea Power, 1812*, II, 62; Dutton, *Perry*, 86; Dillon, *We Have Met*, 98, 99, 116, 131. On carronades see Spencer C. Tucker, "The Carronade," U.S. Naval Institute *Proceedings*, IC (August 1973), 65–70.

18. Dutton, *Perry*, 98, 105; Tucker, *Poltroons*, I, 316, 317; MacKenzie *Life*, I, 178; Mahan, *Sea Power, 1812*, II, 72; James C. Mills, *Oliver Hazard Perry and the Battle of Lake Erie*, 86, 88; Dillon, *We Have Met*, 108, 109; Barclay's Narrative, Paullin, *Documents*, 161.

19. Dillon, *We Have Met*, 112; Mills, *Perry*, 91.

20. MacKenzie, *Life*, I, 203; Mills, *Perry*, 109; Dr. Usher Parsons in *Anecdotes*, 53.

21. MacKenzie, *Life*, I, 210.

22. Mills, *Perry*, 107; Dillon, *We Have Met*, 97.

23. Mahan, *Sea Power, 1812*, II, 51, 55ff, 61.

24. Ibid., II, 71; Barclay to Yeo, 6 September 1813, in *Anecdotes*, 37; the strength figures come from William James, *Full and Correct Account of the Chief Naval Occurrences of the Late War Between Great Britain and the United States*, 292.

25. Mills, *Perry*, 119, 125.

26. Mills, *Perry*, 122, 125, 130; Dillon, *We Have Met*, 133–36, 149, 150; MacKenzie, *Life*, I, 229, 230, 234; Mahan, *Sea Power, 1812*, II, 72; Dutton, *Perry*, 145, 149, 154; Oliver, "Commodore," 777; James A. Ward, *Manual of Naval Tactics*, 77.

27. C. S. Forester, *The Age of Fighting Sail: The Story of the Naval*

War of 1812, 183; MacKenzie, *Life*, I, 245; Mills, *Perry*, 130; Emerson, *Centenary*, 147.

28. Elliott's version is carried in full in *A Biographical Notice of Commodore Jesse D. Elliott*, 34; Cox, "Eye Witness," 72; Emerson, Centenary, 158; MacKenzie, *Life*, I, 283; Mahan, *Sea Power, 1812*, II, 97.

29. Mahan, *Sea Power, 1812*, II, 64, 76; MacKenzie, *Life*, I, 229; Mills, *Perry*, 145; Oliver, "Commodore," 777; Kenneth J. Hagan, ed., *In Peace and War*, 59.

30. Henry Adams, *The War of 1812*, 69.

31. Perry to the Secretary of the Navy, 10 September 1813, R.G. 45: Captains' Letters; Perry to Harrison, 10 September 1813 in Logan Esarey, ed., *Messages and Letters of William Henry Harrison*, II, 539.

32. Perry to Secretary of Navy, 24 September 1813, R.G. 45: Captains' Letters; Harrison to Secretary of War, 9 October 1813, R.G. 107: Letters Received by the Secretary of War; Henry Bathurst, Secretary of State for War and the Colonies to Prevost, 5 November 1815 in *House of Lords Sessional Papers*, 1815, IV, 332.

33. MacKenzie, *Life*, I, 303; Dutton, *Perry*, 218; Dillon, *We Have Met*, 164, 182, 183; Perry to Secretary of Navy, 25 October 1813, R.G. 45: Captains' Letters; Chauncey to Secretary of Navy, 13 October 1813, R. G. 45: Captains' Letters.

34. Quoted in Dudley W. Knox, *A History of the United States Navy*, 118.

35. MacKenzie, *Life*, I, 286.

36. Elliott to Perry, 7 July 1818, in *Biographical Notice*, 207.

37. Dillon, *We Have Met*, 209–11; Mahan, *Sea Power, 1812*, II, 78; *Biographical Notice*, 35, 207–13. The charges are printed verbatim in MacKenzie *Life*, II, 251, 252. Elliott published his last attack in *Address . . . to his Early Companions.* The controversy among nineteenth-century writers can be seen in Cooper's *History of the Navy of the United States* and *The Battle of Lake Erie* and in Mackenzie's *Life.* Compare these with Edward Channing, *History of the United States*, IV, 521–22.

38. Secretary of Navy to Perry, 18 April 1814, R. G. 45: Secretary of the Navy Letters.

39. Dillon, *We Have Met*, 187, 188; Robert G. Albion, *Makers of Naval Policy*, 186.

40. Niles, *Life*, 270; Park Benjamin, *United States Naval Academy*, 94; MacKenzie, *Life*, II, III, 128, 139; Dillon, *We Have Met*, 192–203.

41. J. Robert Moskin, *The U.S. Marine Corps Story*, 100, 101.

42. Niles, *Life*, 279, 289; MacKenzie, *Life, II, 197, 206.*

43. *Niles, Life*, 303, 304.

44. Cox, "Eye-Witness;" Dillon, *We Have Met*, xii, civ, 27, 88–92, 182, 192; William V. Taylor to his brother, 17 October 1813, in Emerson, *Centenary*, 157; MacKenzie, *Life*, I, 76, 229; II, 140, 141.

45. Ellery H. Clark, Jr., "United States Place Names Honoring the Navy," U.S. Naval Institute *Proceedings*, LXXIV (April 1948), 452–55, and "Famous Swords at the United States Naval Academy," U.S. Naval Institute *Proceedings*, LXVI (December 1940), 1769–75; Ruby R. Duval, "The Perpetuation of History and Tradition at the United States Naval Academy Today," U.S. Naval Institute *Proceedings*, LXIV (May 1938), 660–77; Emerson, *Centenary*, 8, 9, 80.

46. Perry to Elliott, 18 June 1818 in *Documents in Relation to the Differences Which Subsisted Between the Late Commodore O. H. Perry and Captain Jesse D. Elliott*, 22.

47. Dutton, *Perry*, 104, 209; Dillon, *We Have Met*, xii–xiv, 181; Knox, *History*, 119.

THOMAS MACDONOUGH: ARCHITECT OF A WILDERNESS NAVY

BY EDWARD K. ECKERT

Few days are more refreshing and beautiful than those of late summer and early autumn in upstate New York and New England. Sunday, 11 September 1814, was no exception—a clear, brisk day, the leaves having begun their annual change to their bright fall colors. Shortly after nine o'clock in the morning the *Eagle*, an American brig, fired four of her guns, shattering the calm and signaling the opening of the decisive battle of Lake Champlain. Thundering over the waters for more than two hours, the small British and American fleets tossed lethal shot back and forth. When quiet descended once again, the British fleet had been soundly beaten and a major invasion of the United States by seasoned continental veterans turned back. Commodore Thomas Macdonough was the hero of the American hour. Hearing of the battle, Secretary of the Navy William Jones proclaimed it "not surpassed by any naval victory of record; to appreciate its results, it is perhaps, one of the most important events in the history of our country."[1] Seventy-five years later Theodore Roosevelt called Macdonough "the greatest figure in our naval history" before the Civil War.[2]

What thoughts must have flashed through the thirty-year-old commodore's head as he proudly wrote to Secretary of the Navy Jones telling of his accomplishment. "The Almighty has been pleased to grant us a signal victory on Lake Champlain, in the capture of 1 frigate, 1 brig, and 2 sloops of war of the enemy."[3] Macdonough had

The author acknowledges with gratitude a faculty research grant from St. Bonaventure University which enabled him to do research at archives in the Historical Society of Delaware, the University of Vermont, and the State University of New York, Plattsburgh.

Thomas Macdonough. Courtesy of the Art Commission of the City of New York.

recognized the importance of the event. He had mimicked Horatio Nelson's signal at Trafalgar, "England Expects That Every Man Will Do His Duty," by calling on his own ships before the battle with, "Impressed Seamen Call On Every Man To Do His Duty." Following the battle, in his letter to Jones, Macdonough once again paraphrased Nelson. This time it was the British admiral's victory message after the Battle of the Nile.

Macdonough had done his homework well. He had learned the fundamentals of sailing while a midshipman under Commodore Edward Preble in the Mediterranean and had learned strategy from studying the battles of Nelson. His entire life had prepared Macdonough for this single moment. Few others have had such a dramatic chance to display their acquired prowess. That Macdonough was so successful is ample evidence of the effectiveness of his practical education as an American naval officer.

Thomas Macdonough was the sixth child and second son born to Major Thomas McDonough and his wife Mary Vance. Young Thomas was born in December 1783; conflicting records give either Christmas Eve or New Year's Eve as the day of his birth. The future commodore entered a family that was widely respected and prominent in local affairs. Thomas's mother died when he was nine, and his father left him an orphan three years later. By the time of his death in 1795, Thomas McDonough had little left of his personal estate other than his land and home to leave his children.[4]

No letters or diaries exist to provide historians with a hint about young Thomas Macdonough's early life. Much later the commodore would write to his sister Lydia, who had remained near the family home in Delaware, that, "I should like to visit the old home where I have spent some youthful happy hours; to stroll about the fields and woods as I used to do."[5] These few lines are often quoted by Macdonough biographers as an example of the commodore's sentimental affection for his birthplace. In actuality his ties could not have been very strong if he was able to break those bonds at the age of sixteen and enter one of the loneliest professions in the world—that of a naval officer on board a sailing ship.

Orphaned at twelve, Macdonough first went to work as a clerk in nearby Middletown. Meanwhile, his eldest brother, James, managed to get a midshipman's warrant through his family's political connections. James served on board the *Constellation*, was with her when the American vessel fought the French frigate the *Insurgente* in 1799, and was wounded during the fight. He returned home on a modest pension. His stories of seaborne adventure must have kindled the fire of wanderlust in young Thomas.

Their father had not left the young Macdonoughs with material possessions, but he did leave them with important friends, including Senator Henry Latimer, through whose influence young Thomas obtained a midshipman's warrant in February 1800. To a family tradition of military service was added the alluring call of adventure to a bright boy who could not imagine living out his life as a clerk. At age sixteen Thomas had had no experience with the sea or sailing when he was ordered to begin his naval career by reporting on board the *Ganges*, a converted merchantman. His family now left behind, it was up to Thomas to determine if he could make a success of his life as an officer in the U.S. Navy.

Macdonough's career began inauspiciously. The *Ganges*, a poor sailer, would have a difficult time chasing enemy privateers in the Caribbean during the Quasi-War with France. While she was anchored in Havana harbor, deadly yellow fever broke out among the crew, striking down Macdonough along with many others on board. In his autobiography Macdonough described the filthy hospital where "nearly all of the men and officers died and were taken out in carts as so many hogs would have been."[6] When he recovered from the dread disease, Macdonough took passage on board a merchantman bound for Philadelphia. Off the Capes of Delaware the ship was stopped and searched by an English warship. Found to be carrying Spanish cargo in her hold, she was sent to Halifax as a British prize. Macdonough and two other American naval officers were set down penniless at Norfolk. There the naval agent gave them enough food, clothing, and money to return to their homes. What a happy fright his family must have had when they saw Thomas walk down the lane, for they already had been informed that he had contracted the fever and was not expected to live.

Young Macdonough's service at sea had not lasted long enough to turn him into a sailor, but it had tested his innate spirit and resolution. Though he had been abandoned and left behind to die, Macdonough's constitution had proved strong enough to overcome disease. Left with only the clothes on his back, he had been resourceful enough to make his way home. It was clear that he had found a home in the Navy. From this point until his death he would never turn away from the sea.

When the American navy, and its officer corps, were drastically reduced following the ratification of a peace treaty with France in February 1801, Secretary of the Navy Robert Smith recognized that the future success of the service would depend upon the hardy young midshipmen who had never known any other profession. Smith recommended that they be excluded from the contemplated manpower reduction, saying that the midshipmen "are among the most promising young men of our country, possess all the materials to make officers equal to any in the world, and well merit the fostering care of their government."[7] Still some cuts were ordered, and Macdonough only escaped falling victim to them when Caesar Augustus Rodney, another of his deceased father's friends, intervened in his behalf. Not only did Macdonough keep his warrant; he also received a prized berth in the *Constellation*, just beginning a cruise to the Mediterranean.

It was on board the *Constellation* that Macdonough's true education as a sailor began. Captain Alexander Murray, commander of the frigate, took seriously his charge to supervise the schooling of his midshipmen. Murray not only taught them the techniques of handling a ship under sail, but he also had them instructed in navigation and gunnery, and required that all his midshipmen keep journals of the cruise as a means of improving their handwriting and observation. Thomas Macdonough's journal covers the year from 15 March 1802 until 13 March 1803, and records the daily log from the *Constellation*. It is a rudimentary notebook designed to teach professional seamanship rather than a diary of personal feelings, and thus lacks personal notes or comments.

The *Constellation*'s mission was to show the flag to the pirate princes of North Africa. For generations these freebooters had terrorized merchantmen. Only the most powerful nations were able to keep them in check with bribes and naval power. When the Revolution severed American ties with England, the pirates felt free to loot U.S. vessels. The Federalist administration had paid an annual tribute as insurance against these raids. Jefferson, however, found his personal principles violated by such an arrangement and ordered the payments stopped. Although Jefferson's efforts eventually were unsuccessful and the tribute had to be resumed, the naval action in the Mediterranean fostered professionalism and American naval leadership. American naval officers gained invaluable experience sailing vessels of all sizes in sea battles along the North African coast. The U.S. Navy, which had been born during an undeclared war with France, matured on the waters of the Mediterranean in another undeclared war.

On 22 July 1802 Macdonough noted in his journal that the *Constellation* had "discovered several small sail to the westward of the town [Tripoli]. . . . At 11 fired at them. . . . Keeping up a constant Fire at the Gunboats, some of which must have been injured, being but a few yards from the Beach many of our shott went on shore among the Troops that were Drawn up there. . . ."[8] The *Constellation* saw little other action before returning to the United States. Macdonough was given only a few days leave before he was recalled to duty, this time to serve with Captain William Bainbridge on board the *Philadelphia*, which was ready to sail for the Mediterranean.

The *Philadelphia* had no sooner cleared Gibraltar than she discovered a Tripolitan ship, the *Meshoba* (sometimes called the *Mirboka*), with an American brig in tow. The *Meshoba* was no match for the American frigate, and Captain Bainbridge soon sent a prize crew, including Macdonough, on board to take the ship back to Gibraltar.

Before Macdonough and the rest of the prize crew could return to the *Philadelphia*, the unfortunate frigate became stuck on the shoals in the harbor of Tripoli and was taken by the enemy.

Macdonough was transferred to the *Enterprise*, commanded by Lieutenant Stephen Decatur who was only five years his senior. The chemistry between these two men can only be imagined after almost two centuries. In addition to the time spent together on board ship, the two often went for walks when in port and discussed the young Navy they both loved, the recent victories of the British hero Horatio Nelson, leadership traits, and their own concerns. They were friends who could confide in one another. Their camaraderie grew, giving them a home at sea on the decks of American naval vessels. All of the American naval officers had cut family ties only to create new ties with fellow officers. They took their lives and profession seriously. Fortunately, overseeing these young men was Captain Edward Preble, commander of the Mediterranean squadron and *pater familias*, who demanded the best from his "boys." In return, Preble gave them the best naval education in the world. He stressed seamanship, careful planning, and bold action. Preble, more than any other early naval officer, was determined to make his officers professionals and leaders. It was the training these young men received under his careful eye in the Mediterranean that would prepare them to fight a major war in 1812 against the world's premiere seapower. Historians have often noted the professionalism instilled in young army officers after the creation of the United States Military Academy in 1803. This same type of esprit and professionalism was created in the American navy on the decks of its ships. As Decatur became Preble's favorite lieutenant and star pupil, Macdonough would be Decatur's favorite midshipman and best student.

Few tales of American naval history are as worth retelling as the story of the destruction of the *Philadelphia* in February 1804. If she were put into service by the Tripolitans, the ship would make their fleet stronger than the American force in the Mediterranean. Moreover, American naval officers considered her a grinning insult to the nation's power in the area, and concluded that something had to be done. Unable to retrieve her from her anchorage under the guns of the main enemy fortress, they decided that she had to be destroyed. The task was assigned to Stephen Decatur, who sailed a captured Moorish vessel with a volunteer crew, including Macdonough, into the harbor at night. Disguised as Arabs, they tied up to the *Philadelphia*'s cables, boarded the frigate, and after a sharp engagement set the ship afire, returned to the ketch, and rowed hard to get away from the burning frigate and out of the range of the guns of the fort and enemy gunboats. With only one man wounded, the American crew had succeeded in what Lord Nelson called "the most bold and daring act of the age."[9]

In August 1804 Preble decided to mount a gunboat attack against Tripolitan gunboats and galleys. The flat-bottomed American gunboats, which Preble had borrowed from the king of Naples, carried crews of thirty-five men each and a single 24-pounder mounted on the bow. They were designed for close action in protected waters. Although the gunboats were untrustworthy sailers upon open water, they were ideal for action near the shore, as well as for patrolling and attacking the enemy's smaller vessels. Two divisions of three gunboats each were sent against a far larger enemy fleet. As commander of one of the two divisions and captain of a gunboat, Decatur had chosen Macdonough to be his first officer. Decatur's boat engaged two enemy vessels that were captured after a hard-fought action in which Macdonough led one of the boarding parties. In his report to Preble, Decatur made special note of "the zeal, courage and readiness of Mr. Thomas Macdonough."[10] On 10 September 1804, the last day of his command, Preble gave the young Macdonough a "gunboat commission" which promoted him to the rank of lieutenant while retaining the pay of a midshipman.

For the next twenty-two months Macdonough served with the American fleet in the Mediterranean which was attempting to blockade the harbor at Tripoli. During these months Macdonough had enough free time to tour parts of Italy and to have his portrait painted. More important than this holiday was Macdonough's assignment to the Italian shipyard at Ancona where he supervised the construction of four vessels to be outfitted as gunboats. Observing the shipwrights there, he gained another bit of professional knowledge he would need later on. Thus the rudiments of Macdonough's professional education were completed, and he fought his first battles during the three years he served in the Mediterranean. For the next six years this knowledge would be reinforced and improved by assignments that would make him a leader as well as a sailor.

Upon his return to the United States in the summer of 1806, the young but experienced Macdonough was placed on furlough and given time to visit his family in Delaware. On 21 October he was recalled to active duty and ordered to Middletown, Connecticut, to join Captain Isacc Hull who was superintending the construction of four American gunboats. Although Macdonough stayed there only a few months, this assignment was of tremendous importance for both his professional and his personal life.

Professionally, it enabled Macdonough to observe American shipbuilding techniques firsthand. At Middletown he learned the design, construction, and outfitting of small naval vessels, kept the government accounts, and superintended the purchase of supplies. The knowledge Macdonough gained in these activities prepared him to supervise the construction of his own fleet on Lake Champlain.

Personally, it was at Middletown that Macdonough met Lucy Ann Shaler, who would become his wife on 12 December 1812. Lucy was the daughter of a wealthy merchant, and her family soon became Macdonough's surrogate family. Lucy Ann was an adventurous young woman of seventeen when they first met. At the time of their marriage six years later she traveled with her husband over winter snows to Lake Champlain, preferring to make her home in the north country with Macdonough rather than to remain behind in Middletown with her parents. She was pleased to find that Vermont had many of the comforts of Connecticut life. She wrote her mother that "Parisian manners and customs prevail in the midst of the Green Mountains."[11]

Macdonough's relationship with his mother-in-law, to judge from later correspondence between them, was more that of mother and son than mother-in-law and son-in-law. In a letter to Macdonough by his then-widowed mother-in-law, which Mrs. Shaler signed "Your affectionate Mother," she wrote, "I miss you more than I can express. Numberless things occur wherein I want your advice and assistance, and I have no male friend at hand to look up to. . . ."[12]

The Macdonoughs' married life was brief. Lucy died from tuberculosis in 1825 after thirteen years with Thomas. The couple had ten children, five of whom died at a young age. Although some writers would have us believe that their marriage and home life were ideal, the fact is that no one today can make that judgment based on the extant documents. As happened with his own parents, Macdonough and Lucy both died young, leaving behind an orphaned family. "Their only surviving child wrote [much later] . . . that the 'children were dispersed among guardians, and all traditions, memorials and correspondence were neglected or lost.' "[13] A grandson, Rodney Macdonough, tried to correct the lacunae by writing a biography of his grandfather, a family history, and numerous articles.

After less than three months at Middletown, Macdonough was ordered to leave his post supervising the construction of four gunboats. He reported to Washington to join the *Wasp* as her first lieutenant. The ship's captain, Master Commandant John Smith, sent Macdonough to Baltimore and New York City to recruit sailors for the ship. Few jobs were more frustrating to Macdonough than trying to entice sailors with the low wages offered them by the Navy.

In 1807, while the *Wasp* was carrying dispatches to Europe, a British frigate, the *Leopard*, stopped and boarded an American frigate, the *Chesapeake*, prompting President Jefferson to close all American ports to international trade. During the following year the *Wasp* cruised in coastal waters from Charleston to Boston enforcing the embargo.

On 31 March 1809 Macdonough was transferred to the *Essex* at the request of her new captain, John Smith, who had had Macdonough serve under him on two previous occasions. Macdonough remained on board the *Essex* for only a few months. His departure from the ship gave rise to an event that Fletcher Pratt, author of *Preble's Boys*, called "one of those fascinating and fugitive glimpses of a man that come through the eyes of other people." The *Essex* crew took "the extraordinary step of addressing him in a round robin."[14] The letter, with thirty-seven signatures affixed along with Jeremiah Jones who signed "for the remaining part of the within mentioned crew," read in part:

> Permit us, Sir, before your departure to return you our most Sincere thanks and acknowledgements for your officer-like Conduct and Philanthropy during the time we have had the happiness of being under your command as Second officer. We don't Wish to trouble you with a great Harrangue. We can only assure you, Sir, that we all feel as one in the Cause of Regret at your about to leave the Ship.
>
> We do sincerely Wish and hope your Successor will tread the steps which you have to Render the Crew as Comfortable as possible.
>
> We have only to add, Sir, that we wish you all the happiness that man can enjoy, and may He who holds the Destiny of Mankind guide you Safe through life and Pilot you at last to the harbour of Rest is the Hearty prayer of the Subscribers.[15]

By 1810, Macdonough clearly had more than a technical knowledge of seamanship; he also possessed the qualitative ability to be a leader. His men had shown that they not only respected him but liked him as well. Macdonough had the elusive gift of being able to make others do what he willed without forcing them to do so.

From the *Essex* Macdonough was transferred to command the gunboats on Long Island Sound. Although not so prized as service on board a frigate, the new assignment allowed Macdonough to station himself at Middletown, Connecticut. Shortly thereafter he and Lucy Shaler agreed to marry. However, the prospects of a naval lieutenant appeared bleak. Many officers were resigning from the "Gunboat Navy." In his autobiography Macdonough later summed up these feelings succinctly: "At this time the navy was unpopular. . . ."[16] Macdonough's naval experience could provide him with a good living in the merchant service. Still the Navy was his home and he did not wish to break all his ties with it. Consequently, Macdonough requested and received a furlough from active duty. He captained the merchant brig the *Gulliver* of Boston on a cruise to Britain and the East Indies. After thirteen months at sea, Macdonough returned to Boston with a rich cargo. So successful was this voyage that he promised to make another one. By August 1811, however, the Madison administration realized that war with England had become a definite probability. Secretary of the Navy Paul Hamilton refused to renew Macdonough's furlough. However, the captain already had contracted to take a second cargo to the East Indies, and needed the money to pay for what he called a "domestic engagement."

Macdonough offered his resignation to the Navy Department if it would not grant him a second leave. Hamilton was inclined to accept his resignation from the service, but, for some reason, the Secretary reconsidered his decision and permitted Macdonough to renew his furlough. By the time Macdonough had found a crew and supplies for the voyage, it was April 1812 and American commerce had been suspended.

Macdonough left the merchantman in port and returned to Middletown where, in preparation for his forthcoming marriage, he was confirmed in the Episcopal church. While his grandson and some other pious writers have made much of Macdonough's strong religious convictions, there is little primary evidence to justify such emphasis. Macdonough's family was Episcopalian, but, more important, so too were the Shalers. Other than his confirmation and the fact that he led his crew in a short Episcopal prayer on the Sunday morning of the battle of Lake Champlain, there is no evidence of a particularly pious man. Instead, one senses in Macdonough a self-confident leader who accepted providence or fate. Macdonough probably was no more or less pious than the average naval officer of that era. Religion simply did not play a very large role in their lives.

As soon as Macdonough had learned that his nation had declared war on Great Britain, he requested orders from the department for active duty. On 17 July 1812 Macdonough was ordered to the *Constellation*, which was at the Washington Navy Yard. Realizing that it would be a long time before she could get to sea, Macdonough requested a transfer to a more active post, and was placed in command of a division of gunboats in Portland, Maine. No sooner did Macdonough arrive there than he received new orders to take command of the tiny naval force on Lake Champlain. The lieutenant hired a horse and chaise for seventy-five dollars and set out for Burlington, Vermont, where fate and fame awaited his arrival.

Lake Champlain—on the New York–Vermont border—had been an invasion route since early colonial times. The lake, along with Lake George and the Hudson River to the south, slices off the New England states from the rest of the country. Lake Champlain flows north through the Richelieu River into the St. Lawrence, emptying there close to Montreal. The Lake Champlain–Richelieu River corridor made a double-ended sword pointing toward important strategic goals for both adversaries.

Lake Champlain is 136 miles long with widths of from one-quarter mile to thirteen miles. The widest point is in the center near Plattsburgh, New York. At one spot its waters reach a depth of 400 feet. On the average the lake is frozen over for sixty-eight days a year.[17]

Although Lake Champlain was isolated from coastal settlements, the area around it had grown considerably in the forty-five years since the British had last traversed it and lost an army at Saratoga. The roads, particularly along its western shore, had been improved since that time, and wilderness settlements had grown into respectable villages, especially at Plattsburgh and Burlington. The waters and the roads witnessed a lively commerce between Canada and northern New York and New England. Since 1807 American laws had tried to restrict this trade, but commerce remained active and profitable right through the war. General George Izard, in command of the American troops at Plattsburgh, complained to the War Department in June 1814 that, "the road . . . is covered with droves of cattle, and the river with rafts destined for the enemy. On the eastern side of Lake Champlain the high roads are insufficient for the cattle pouring into Canada. Like herds of buffaloes they press through the forests, making paths for themselves. Were it not for these supplies, the British forces in Canada would soon be suffering from famine."[18] During that same summer Macdonough's ships intercepted naval supplies, including masts being smuggled to the enemy shipbuilding facility on Isle aux Noix at the head of the Richelieu River.

Prior to 1814 the area largely had been overlooked in the war. The British, tied down with a war with Napoleon in Europe, permitted the Americans to take the initiative. The Americans, hindered by inept generals, lack of coordination, failure to understand strategic objectives, and antiwar opposition, condemned their own forces to make a series of ineffective invasions along the Niagara River and in the Detroit area. By 1813 it had become clear to the Madison administration that control of the northern frontier meant control of the lakes—at least Erie, Ontario, and Champlain. Secretary of the Navy William Jones wrote to Commodore Isaac Chauncey, the over-all commander of the American naval forces on all of the lakes: "It is impossible to attach too much importance to our naval operations on the Lakes—the success of the ensuing campaign will depend absolutely on our superiority on all the Lakes—& every effort and resource must be directed to that object. . . . whatever force the Enemy may create, we must surpass. . . . Indeed you are to consider the absolute superiority on all the Lakes as the only limit to your authority."[19] Neither Chauncey nor his opponent on Lake Ontario, Commodore James Lucas Yeo, ever reached a comfortable level of superiority over the other; both continued building vessels through-out the war, provoking Jones to refer to Chauncey's command as "a warfare of Dockyards and arsenals."[20] On Lake Erie, Oliver Hazard Perry met and defeated the enemy on 10 September 1813, opening the way for American armies to enter Upper Canada from the west.

When Macdonough arrived at Burlington in early October 1812, he found to his surprise that his entire fleet consisted of two gunboats, one of which leaked so badly that it was beached, plus whatever vessels he could convince the army commander at Plattsburgh to give him from the fleet of six sloops the army used as transports. To get his tiny fleet ready for action, Macdonough literally rolled up his sleeves and went to work building ships alongside his men.

In 1813 the strategic balance on Lake Champlain shifted to favor the British. In June two American sloops were captured when they foolishly attacked an enemy position on Isle aux Noix at the northern end of the lake. The British renamed them the *Pinch* and the *Chub*, repaired them, and for the first time ventured into American waters to capture some merchant vessels, raiding Plattsburgh and even threatening to raid Burlington.

In December 1813, Macdonough shifted his operations to the more easily defendable Vergennes, Vermont, and began building ships. The government in Washington provided him with firm back-ing, and though Secretary of the Navy Jones complained that "God knows where the money is to come from," the Madison administra-tion liberally supported Macdonough's construction efforts.[21]

Though remote, the lake was connected to Boston and Albany by reasonably good roads. Small manufactories were located near the lake. Vergennes, situated at the falls of the Otter Creek, seven miles upstream from the lake, had "eight forges, a blast furnace, an air furnace, a rolling mill, a wire factory and grist, saw and fulling mills. Before hostilities opened in 1814, one thousand 32-pound cannon balls had been cast there for the American fleet."[22] Trees abounded in the area, and iron deposits were close by at Monkton. Craftsmen, led by the skilled boat builders Noah and Adam Brown, could turn out warships in a miraculously short time. In general, supplies and ships were not a major concern for Macdonough as long as there was money.

Difficult to obtain at any price were experienced seamen to sail the ships. Blue-water sailors had little desire to travel into the interior and sail in a lake vessel. Lake seamen had sailed on board merchantmen but had no desire to man the guns of a warship. Experienced sailors from either could make far more money on board merchantmen as privateers or smugglers. On 22 January 1813 Macdonough complained to Jones that "there are no men to get here and soldiers are miserable creatures on shipboard, and I very much fear that unless I get the above (ordinary) seamen and not soldiers, there will be a dark spot in our Navy."[23] Macdonough was never able to solve the problem of manning his vessels. By 1814 his crews were a mixed lot of sailors, both fresh and salt water, soldiers, militiamen, and inexperienced boys looking for adventure. The lack of experienced naval seamen was one of the primary reasons Macdonough selected static tactics to meet the enemy.

By 1814 the situation had changed in Europe. Napoleon had agreed to go into exile on Elba after the disastrous campaign of 1813, which included his decisive defeat at the Battle of Leipzig and British victories in Spain. Peace in Europe meant that British veterans could be sent to America. A three-pronged invasion aimed at the Chesapeake Bay, New Orleans, and the Champlain–Richelieu corridor was planned. Just what Britain's ultimate goals would have been had all three campaigns succeeded is not known, and probably had not been clearly thought out at the time.

Canada received but 15,000 of Wellington's veterans, and Sir George Prevost, Governor-General of Canada, planned to invade the United States along the western shore of Lake Champlain. His orders were to secure Canada from invasion, and it is unlikely that the conservative, defense-minded Prevost dreamed of cutting the United States in two by marching all the way to New York City or even to Albany. More likely he sought strategic positions at Crown Point and the forts along the corridor. In any event, no matter what his ultimate objective was, Prevost had concluded that his army of invasion, some 11,000 men, could be adequately supplied and maintained only by water. Hence British naval control of Lake Champlain was an absolute requirement, in Prevost's own mind, for the success of his strategic plans.

In August Prevost began moving his army southward. On 6 Sep-

tember it crossed into American territory and proceeded along the
west bank of Lake Champlain with Captain George Downie's squadron of sixteen vessels covering its left flank. The Americans were in
a precarious position. General Alexander Macomb placed his forces—
about 1,500 regulars and 3,000 raw militia—in defensive positions
constructed by West Point engineers on the peninsula formed by
the Saranac River just south of Plattsburgh. Thomas Macdonough
anchored his fourteen-ship squadron in Plattsburgh Bay to cover
Macomb's right flank.

On balance, the two naval forces were roughly equal in number
of ships and guns, weight of metal, and manpower, though Downie's
largest ship, the *Confiance*, mounted 37 guns, 11 more than Macdonough's largest ship, the *Saratoga*. Neither squadron was ready for
battle. The *Confiance* had been launched on 25 August, and work
was so incomplete on her magazine that her powder had to be pulled
along in a rowboat tied to her stern. The second largest American
ship, the 20-gun *Eagle*, was in similar condition. Shipwrights were
still working on her when she joined Macdonough on the same day
that Prevost's advance party entered Plattsburgh.

Macdonough was not pleased with his situation. He feared that
the longer guns of the British would give them the advantage in open
water, and he hoped to avoid such a confrontation. He also knew
that a victory by Prevost on land would allow the British to use their
field artillery to force him out into the lake.

Downie was no more confident of his situation. He had only
assumed command of the British squadron on 2 September and knew
that his crew's lack of practice would severely handicap them. Prevost, however, cajoled and insulted Downie to such a degree that
the latter felt honor-bound to commit his unready fleet to battle
under conditions that he knew were unfavorable. A formal siege by
Prevost on land and a blockade by Downie at sea would almost
certainly have forced Macdonough to come out and fight on terms
much more favorable to the British. But Prevost, perhaps mindful
of the fate of Burgoyne in the last war, would not accept delay and
goaded Downie to attack prematurely.

Macdonough had used his brief time in Plattsburgh Bay to the
fullest advantage, taking every measure possible for repelling an
attack. When Downie hove to east of Cumberland Head on 11 September and rowed around the point to reconnoiter Macdonough's
position, he could not have been pleased by what he saw. The American commander had chosen his position carefully. His four major
ships were anchored in a line across the bay, with the *Eagle* at the
northern end near enough to shoals to prevent a doubling of the

Battle of Plattsburgh Bay. Courtesy of Naval Academy Museum.

van. The *Saratoga*, the *Ticonderoga*, and the *Preble* followed to the southward with Macdonough's ten gunboats held in reserve to provide reinforcement where needed. This left Downie with few tactical options. He would have to sail his ships around Cumberland Head before the wind—which usually blew from the north—then turn directly across the wind, enter the battle close-hauled, and attempt either to break Macdonough's line or, even more difficult, to run to the south and double his rear. The British sailors were no more experienced than the American, and these tricky maneuvers proved impossible for them to perform.

At first all went well for the British. Downie rounded Cumberland Head in good order, his four major ships abreast and his twelve gunboats on the left to turn the southern end of the American line. Then the wind died down, forcing the British to anchor. Downie's two lead ships, the *Linnet* and the *Confiance*, took position opposite the *Eagle* and the *Saratoga* without firing, but once anchored unleashed broadsides that cut down one-fifth of Macdonough's crew. The *Linnet* so battered the *Eagle* that her captain sought shelter behind the *Saratoga*, which was trading broadsides with the *Confiance*. The *Chub* quickly became unmanageable, drifted into the American gunboats, and was forced to strike. The *Ticonderoga* and the *Preble* poured fire into the *Finch*, which lost headway in changing direction and eventually ran aground on Crab Island to the south of the battle. When half of the British gunboats attacked the *Ticonderoga* and the *Preble*, the latter was forced from the battleline. She ran aground before the guns of the *Ticonderoga* could drive off the remaining gunboats with heavy losses.

The deciding factor in the battle was the duel between the two flagships, and it was here that Macdonough's tactical preparations brought victory. Fighting at anchor provided stable gun platforms for his inexperienced crew, meant that they would not have to handle sails, and released all his men for working the guns. Macdonough's attaching springs to his cables to allow his ships to be swung on a wide arc without setting sail was not particularly innovative, but his precaution of setting kedge anchors with lines to the *Saratoga*'s quarters so that he could turn his ship completely around was clearly original and brilliant.

The fire exchanged at the northern end of the line was particularly hot. Macdonough was struck several times by falling spars and flying splinters, but he maintained his place on deck and served as a vivid inspiration to his men. On the other side Sir George Downie, along with several other officers, was felled in the first fifteen minutes of fighting. After over an hour of firing, both flagships' broadsides were so shattered that neither could continue effective fire. Macdonough then made use of his preset kedge anchors to swing the *Saratoga* around to bring a fresh broadside of thirteen guns to bear on the *Confiance*.

The surviving lieutenant in the British flagship recognized Macdonough's tactics and attempted to turn his ship. The success of such a maneuver, however, depended upon preparation, practice, and accurate timing. The *Confiance* stopped halfway around, permitting the *Saratoga*'s fresh port battery to rake her from bow to stern. The British captains knew that they were beaten and struck their colors. Macdonough's victory was complete. In the two and a half hours of battle the Americans suffered 200 casualties, the British 300. All four major British ships had been hammered beyond control, as had the *Saratoga*, but the Americans were left in control of the lake.

On shore Prevost's feeble attack was turned back by Macomb. That night Prevost turned tail and led his continental regulars on a disgraceful retreat back to Canada, leaving behind a large number of deserters and an incalculable amount of military stores. News of Macdonough's victory and word of the repulse of the British attack on Baltimore three days later reached the peace commissioners in Europe at the same time and strengthened the American position immensely. With two of three invasion prongs blunted—particularly with a total defeat at Plattsburgh—and the results of the third, the invasion of New Orleans, in doubt, British leaders realized that they could not hope for victory in 1814, if ever, and accepted a *status quo ante bellum* treaty. This treaty was the true effect of Macdonough's victory.

On Lake Champlain Thomas Macdonough had done what no other naval commander was able to do in modern time. He had beaten the monarch of the seas at her own game with an inferior fleet. The Battle of Lake Champlain was the culmination of Macdonough's naval career. His victory had required him to use all the skills gained from his years in the Navy: leadership, seamanship, inventiveness, shipbuilding, tactics, and strategy. That he was able to combine all of these elements into a single successful moment is a tribute to his own abilities: decisiveness, self-confidence, and intelligence. It is true that Macdonough was in the right place at the right time, but it is also true that he was the right man for the position. The British naval historian William Laird Clowes has called Macdonough's victory, "a most notable feat, one which, on the whole, surpassed that of any other captain of either navy in this war."[24] Alfred Thayer Mahan, the American naval strategist and historian, labeled the action the most "decisive" battle in the War of 1812, and Theodore Roosevelt wrote that at Lake Champlain Macdonough "won a higher fame than any other commander of the war, British or American."[25] Novelist and historian James Fenimore Cooper felt that he had slighted the importance of the battle in his first edition of the *History of the Navy*, and he wrote a letter apologizing for his account to Captain Horace B. Sawyer. Cooper told Sawyer, "The Battle of Plattsburgh Bay is the most honorable affair, that has ever occurred to our arms. Hitherto it has not been sufficiently noticed, but I think it will henceforth take its proper place in our annals."[26]

The battle may not have been "sufficiently noticed" in America, but it was in Britain. There it was studied as a model of tactical preparation and execution. Often called "the False Nile," it was compared to Nelson's victory at Aboukir Bay in 1798. Macdonough's position was roughly similar to that of French Admiral François Brueys, but Macdonough had taken precautions Brueys failed to take, and nearly everything that had worked to Bruey's disadvantage had aided Macdonough. In addition to contemporary and later accolades, Macdonough received so many fine gifts of land, money, and swords that he exclaimed, "In one month from a poor lieutenant I became a rich man."[27]

Unfortunately fate is not always kind to heroes. Macdonough had achieved a brilliant victory on Lake Champlain, but he also had contracted tuberculosis while there. The story of the eleven years between Lake Champlain and his untimely death can be told quickly. After parading Macdonough around like a proper hero, the Navy Department assigned him to command the *Fulton First*, the world's first steam naval vessel. However, Macdonough confessed to his wife's grandfather that he did not "like the command of the steam frigate, not being used to such a vessel."[28]

Although a peace treaty had been signed on Christmas Eve, 1814, the news did not reach America until several weeks later. The administration, fearing a renewed British attack on Lake Champlain in 1815, transferred Macdonough back to the lake. He returned reluctantly to Burlington, fearing additional damage to his health from the extreme climate. After the war Macdonough spent three practically inactive years as the commander of the Portsmouth, New Hampshire, Navy Yard. There he supervised the construction of the *Washington*, a ship-of-the-line, and occasionally was called to serve on courts-martial or to advise the newly established Navy Board of Commissioners.

Disliking the inactivity and fearful for his health, Macdonough sought and obtained command of the frigate *Guerriere* on 22 April

1818. He remained in command of this vessel patrolling the Mediterranean until July 1819, when he and other officers of the American fleet had a squabble with Commodore Charles Stewart over a technicality during a court-martial proceeding. Stewart sent Macdonough and the other officers back to the United States without their ships. The department and the President ruled in favor of Stewart, and Macdonough and the others formally apologized to him. Macdonough could have returned to command the *Guerriere*, but he considered her a sickly ship and instead accepted command of the ship-of-the-line *Ohio*, then under construction in New York.

The *Ohio*, however, would not be launched for years, and Macdonough spent most of the next four years (1820–24) at his home in Middletown, Connecticut. During these years he wrote the brief autobiography that is one of the very few primary sources he left for posterity. At times he complained to the department and asked for active duty. Finally, on 31 May 1824, Macdonough was given command of the most famous of all American naval vessels, "Old Ironsides," the frigate *Constitution*.

Unfortunately, tuberculosis had made Macdonough a very sick man, and even the healthy, warm climate of the Mediterranean could not stop its ravages. News of his wife's death from the same disease on 9 August 1825 took away his ardor for living. Knowing his own days were numbered, Macdonough turned command of the *Constitution* over to Captain Daniel T. Patterson on 14 October 1825 and sailed for home on board the merchant brig *Edwin*. Less than a month later, 600 miles from port, Thomas Macdonough died at sea. He had told his son Augustus Rodney, who had accompanied him on this cruise, that he wished to be buried beside his wife rather than to be committed to the sea. After elaborate funeral services in New York City and Connecticut, Macdonough's remains were placed alongside Lucy Ann's. A monument was erected over their graves with an inscription that reads, "They were lovely and pleasant in their lives, and in their death they were undivided."

Throughout his life Macdonough had sought active service, fame, and glory. In a few short years on Lake Champlain, he achieved all three. In contrast to his superior, Isaac Chauncey on Lake Ontario, Macdonough gave the American navy the tradition of adapting to the resources available, and using them creatively to defeat the enemy. On Lake Champlain Macdonough demonstrated his administrative and ship-building skills, his courage under fire, his sense of tactical timing, and his seamanship. With these came victory against a superior enemy force. And with that victory came immortality.

FURTHER READING

Primary source material on Thomas Macdonough is scanty. Official correspondence is in the National Archives, Washington, D.C., and is available on microfilm. The Historical Society of Delaware, Wilmington, has a few letters from Macdonough as well as the journal he kept on board the *Constellation*. The Wilbur Collection in the Guy W. Bailey Library, University of Vermont, Burlington, has an interesting personal accounts ledger kept by Macdonough after the war. Although there is an entry dated 1813, the ledger really begins in 1817. It is logical that because Thomas Macdonough was away at sea for such long periods, he must have written many letters home; but if such a collection of documents exists, it is unknown to scholars working in the area.

Although Macdonough wrote an autobiography in 1823, it is only twelve pages in length and concerns itself solely with his naval career. Rodney Macdonough, the naval hero's grandson, made it a personal challenge to research and write about his grandfather's life. His book, *The Life of Commodore Thomas Macdonough*, is the result of his efforts. It is as objective an account as one could expect from a close relative. It traces Macdonough's professional and personal life with occasional gratuitous remarks emphasizing the commodore's religious nature or generous spirit. Rodney Macdonough included Macdonough's autobiography along with a summary of the family's ancestry and some official documents. In addition, Rodney Macdonough wrote a biographical article that appeared in two different journals: "The Hero of Lake Champlain's Great Naval Battle," *Vermonter*, 2 (1897), 149–54; and "A Paper on Commodore Thomas Macdonough, United States Navy," *Papers of the Historical Society of Delaware*, 18 (1907), 3–22. Two other authors have provided reliable brief biographies: Charles H. Darling, "Thomas Macdonough," *Vermont Historical Society Proceedings* (1905), 57–89; and L. C. Vandergrift, "Memoir of Commodore Macdonough," *Papers of the Historical Society of Delaware*, 2 (1895), 3–14. A few, unrevealing personal papers have been published by Charles G. Muller in "Commodore & Mrs. Thomas Macdonough," *Delaware History*, 9 (1960–61), 341–54. The best interpretative biography of Macdonough appears in Fletcher Pratt, *Preble's Boys: Commodore Preble and the Birth of American Sea Power*. Pratt not only seeks to recount Macdonough's professional career, but he also explains its importance and how it relates to that of the other naval figures of the era.

Although Macdonough's life lacks wide coverage, there is no dearth of materials on the War of 1812. The best complete military history of the war is John K. Mahon, *The War of 1812*. Mahon had done research in all the major American, Canadian, and British archives for his authoritative study. Harry L. Coles, *The War of 1812*, is equally reliable, but less complete and lacks footnotes. Although British historians almost ignore the war, Canadian writers have pursued it. The best Canadian study is J. Mackay Hitsman, *The Incredible War of 1812, A Military History*. Another Canadian, Pierre Berton, focused on the social impact of the war on Canada in his *The Invasion of Canada, 1812–1813* and *Flames Across the Border: The Canadian–American Tragedy, 1813–1814*.

The naval war is best covered in Alfred Thayer Mahan's two-volume study, *Sea Power in its Relation to the War of 1812*. Although some of Captain Mahan's strategic ideas have become dated, there is nothing wrong with his historical research. The best one-volume account is by Theodore Roosevelt, *The Naval War of 1812*. The young Roosevelt is a bit overly nationalistic and enthusiastic, but it is a solid study. The most exciting reliable study of the naval war is by the great British novelist C. S. Forester in *The Age of Fighting Sail*. Forester's account is drum and trumpet history at its best, exciting to read and memorable.

Studies of the Lake Champlain battle abound, especially in local history journals and societies. Most of the writing is antiquarian and myopic. However, Allan S. Everest in his *The War of 1812 in the Champlain Valley* has successfully managed to combine local history with the overall strategic concerns of the war. It is the best account of the region's importance.

For the Battle of Lake Champlain alone, the best technical account is by Alfred Thayer Mahan, "Commodore Macdonough at Plattsburgh," *North American Review*, 200 (1914), 203–21. Also reliable is William R. Folsom, "The Battle of Plattsburgh," *Vermont Quarterly*, 20 (1952), 234–59. A stirring, popular account that concentrates on missed British opportunities is C. S. Forester, "Victory on Lake Champlain," *American Heritage*, 15 (1963), 4–11, 88–90. special caution has to be given *The Proudest Day: Macdonough on Lake Champlain* by Charles G. Muller. It is a species of historical fiction that incorporates dialogue, thoughts, and feelings into what is otherwise a reliable historical narrative. Muller's detailed notes, available at the Historical Society of Delaware, Wilmington, are adequate testimony to his ability as a researcher; however, the novel should be used cautiously by any serious student.

NOTES

1. Quoted in Edward K. Eckert, *The Navy Department in the War of 1812*, 35.

2. Theodore Roosevelt, *The Naval War of 1812*, 399.

3. Quoted in A. Bowen, ed., *The Naval Monument, Containing Official and Other Accounts of All the Battles Fought Between the Navies of the United States and Great Britain During the Late War*, 145.

4. Genealogical information on Thomas Macdonough can be found in Rodney Macdonough, *The Macdonough–Hackstaff Ancestry*.

5. Thomas Macdonough to Lydia Macdonough Roberts, 1 July 1822, The Historical Society of Delaware, Wilmington.

6. Thomas Macdonough's entire autobiography appears in Chapter 2 of Rodney Macdonough, *Life of Commodore Thomas Macdonough, U.S. Navy*. This quote is from page 21.

7. Macdonough, *Thomas Macdonough*, 46.

8. Original is located at the Historical Society of Delaware, Wilmington.

9. Quoted in Edgar Stanton Maclay, *A History of the United States Navy from 1775 to 1893*, I, 268.

10. Quoted in Fletcher Pratt, *Preble's Boys: Commodore Preble and the Birth of American Sea Power*, 350.

11. Quoted in Charles G. Muller, "Commodore & Mrs. Thomas Macdonough," *Delaware History*, IX (1960–61), 345.

12. Muller, "Commodore & Mrs. Thomas Macdonough," 353.

13. Emma C. Gilman, "Hero of the Battleship 'Saratoga'—Macdonough of Connecticut," *Connecticut Magazine*, XI (1907), 554.

14. Pratt, *Preble's Boys*, 352.

15. Macdonough, *Thomas Macdonough*, 91–92.

16. Ibid., 25.

17. Information on Lake Champlain is from Sydney E. Hammersly, *The Lake Champlain Naval Battles of 1776–1814: Hudson–Champlain, 1959, 350th Anniversary Edition*, 1.

18. Quoted in Alfred Thayer Mahan, *Sea Power in its Relation to the War of 1812*, II, 364.

19. Quoted in Eckert, *Navy Department*, 30–31.

20. Quoted in Eckert, *Navy Department*, 35.

21. Irving Brant, *James Madison, Commander in Chief, 1812–1836*, 273.

22. Henry W. Hill, "Otter Creek in History," *Vermont Historical Society Proceedings*, VIII (1913–14), 138.

23. Allan S. Everest, *The War of 1812 in the Champlain Valley*, 108.

24. William Laird Clowes, *The Royal Navy, a History from the Earliest Times to the Present*, VI, 141.

25. Roosevelt, *Naval War of 1812*, 398.

26. James Fenimore Cooper to Captain Horace B. Sawyer, 16 January 1846, Horace B. Sawyer Papers, Wilbur Collection, Guy W. Bailey Memorial Library, University of Vermont, Burlington.

27. Quoted in W. S. Murphy, "Four American Officers of the War of 1812," *Irish Sword*, VI (Summer 1963), 4.

28. William Denning to Mrs. Nathaniel (Lucretia Ann) Shaler, 6 January 1815, quoted in Macdonough, *Thomas Macdonough*, 217.

David Porter.   Stephen Decatur.

John Rodgers.
Courtesy of U.S. Naval Historical Center.

DISTANT STATIONS

DAVID PORTER: PACIFIC OCEAN GADFLY

BY DAVID F. LONG

He had a flair for action; a willingness to take risks; an awareness of tactical, if not strategic ends; a talent for diplomacy on occasion; a sense of his country's coming greatness—and, yes, an impulsiveness; a hotheadedness; a vindictiveness; and a touchy appreciation of his own personal honor. In short, David Porter was somewhat typical of his contemporary "makers of the American naval tradition"—that little coterie of naval officers who had been the protégés of Commodore Edward Preble, their dour but electrifying commander during the Tripolitan War, and were known thereafter as "Preble's Boys."

Porter, from a seafaring family in Massachusetts, entered the Navy as a midshipman in 1798, and had his first tutelage under Captain Thomas Truxtun, whose "school" in the frigate USS *Constellation* was rough enough to make him consider surrendering his commission. Instead, Truxtun bellowed at him: "Why you young dog! If I can help it you shall never leave the navy! Swear at you? Damn it, sir, every time I do that you go up a round on the ladder of promotion. . . . Go forward and let us have no more whining."[1] During the Quasi-War against France in 1799, Porter proved that his instructions had taken root when he and Lieutenant John Rodgers with only eleven sailors allegedly managed to bring in to the West Indian island of St. Kitts the French frigate *L'Insurgente* and no fewer than 173 captives after Truxtun's *Constellation* had hammered the frigate into submission. This undoubtedly helped his rapid promotion to lieutenant later that year.[2]

In his first voyage as a lieutenant, Porter was second-in-command to William Maley in the schooner *Experiment* on a cruise to protect

David Porter.

American shipping in the Caribbean. On 1 January 1800, the *Experiment* and her convoy of four merchantmen were becalmed off the coast of Haiti and came under attack by about 400 pirates in ten barges. When Maley announced he would surrender, Porter shunted him aside, took command, and saved the *Experiment* and two of the merchantmen. That Porter escaped punishment for such a bold act is evidence of Maley's greater sin of cowardice in the eyes of higher naval officials.[3]

Two tours in the Mediterranean during the Tripolitan War ensued. The first was highlighted by one of the U.S. Navy's most unusual battles. During the summer of 1801 Porter was in the schooner USS *Enterprise* under Lieutenant Andrew Sterrett. The Americans fought for three straight hours at point-blank range against their enemy equivalent, the *Tripoli*. Porter went over to her after her surrender and found that of the eighty men on board, thirty had been killed or wounded; not one American had even been scratched. Little wonder that Washington's *Daily National Intelligencer* murmured, "We are lost in surprise."[4] Home on a short leave, Porter made himself notorious by killing a man. While searching for deserters in the Baltimore slums he went into a saloon, was reviled by its keeper, knocked to the floor, and stomped, but managed to extricate his sword and run his attacker through. His plea of self-defense was accepted by the Secretary of the Navy.[5]

He was soon back in the Mediterranean, this time in the ill-starred frigate USS *Philadelphia* under Captain William Bainbridge, assigned to blockade Tripoli. Late in October 1803 the *Philadelphia* chased into the harbor a Tripolitan raider, only to pile atop a hidden sand reef, unmarked on any American charts. All efforts to refloat her having failed, late the same afternoon the officers collectively advised Bainbridge that surrender was their only option. While their shipmates were trying unsuccessfully to scuttle the ship, Porter and Midshipman James Biddle were given the unenviable task of rowing out in a boat to notify the Tripolitans that resistance had ceased.[6] American spirits were further lowered when, a mere forty hours later, changes in the wind and tide refloated the *Philadelphia*, and the Tripolitans were able to keep her until she was incinerated by Stephen Decatur during February 1804.

For nineteen months until June 1805 the Bashaw of Tripoli held the Americans captive. Porter passed some of his time in starting a "naval school" for the midshipmen, acting in dramas to while away the tedium, trying without success to escape, and consoling the shattered Bainbridge—who was having to live with the realization that in the short history of the Constitutional Navy only three U.S. men-of-war had pulled down their flags, and he had commanded all three. It took a combination of separate events to end the war. The able and excitable General William Eaton's improbable little army marched hundreds of miles from Egypt to capture Derna, Tripoli's easternmost city. Tobias Lear, U.S. Consul-General to Algiers; Mediterranean Commodore Samuel Barron; and Bainbridge were the appeasers responsible for a less than satisfactory treaty with Tripoli, the latter probably quite correct in fearing for his own life and those of his people if Tripoli were stormed.[7]

Soon promoted to master commandant (commander), Porter remained abroad for another two years, and during this interim made a significant contribution to American naval policy. After being insulted by a British sailor at Valetta, Porter impulsively brought him on board the *Enterprise* and had him flogged. Under the threat of being fired upon from the city's forts should he attempt to depart, Porter was warned not to leave Malta until his case had been decided by its governor. He defied the order, and as he laconically put it, "proceeded to sea without molestation."[8] One modern naval historian compliments him:

> . . . international law was being rewritten, and the men who plied words on sheets of foolscap in the chanceries were mainly occupied with rationalizing acts already performed; yet acts which, being established as precedents, would control the movements of generations unborn. If *Enterprise* submitted to being detained for this reason, there would be some other reason for holding the next American ship that came in; and presently the right of British port officers to grant or withhold exit passes would be established.[9]

Finally back at home, Porter was assigned to command the New Orleans Station, where he remained from 1808 to 1810. It was an unpleasant tour, marred by the death of his aged father, constant bickering with the Navy Department over expenses, and the onerous burden of trying to enforce the unpopular embargo with Jeffersonian gunboats. From a family afflicted with disaster he took little David Glasgow Farragut, aged eight, into his home and brought him up, although never legally adopting him (he even had him along on his Pacific cruise from 1812 to 1814). As Farragut became the first American admiral, and David Dixon Porter, his natural son, became the second, David Porter may be said to have contributed manfully to the "makers of the American naval tradition."

During his New Orleans tenure Porter demonstrated acumen in his dealings with General James Wilkinson, commanding the U.S. Army there. Wilkinson was perhaps as slippery a character as has ever marred the rolls of the American armed forces, his actions always cloaked in a cloud of protective sepia. It is hard to discern exactly what he was up to during 1809–10; perhaps it was some kind of a filibustering expedition into Mexican Texas in collusion with the Spanish governor of West Florida. Certainly Wilkinson was familiar with Spanish officialdom; he was in the pay of their king for twenty years while commanding U.S. troops in the remote Southwest. But he needed Porter's gunboats to pull off whatever arcane scheme he had in mind, and was turned down decisively enough to ruin the plot. Indeed, Porter notified Washington about the matter, asking if the general were operating under some kind of secret orders to stir up trouble, and when the reply was negative, he later accurately

summed up Wilkinson as "Gen'l Puff—a man of duplicity[,] mean-
ness and cowardice."[10]

During this period of his life Porter had a chance to earn a fortune
for himself and his family. He captured three privateers which had
been working so effectively and pitilessly off Cuba that the merchants
of Havana offered rewards totaling $60,000 to anyone who could
bring their careers to an end. Off and on he spent the rest of his life
trying to collect this impressive sum, and David Dixon Porter pursued the same after his father's death in 1843, arguing that with
accrued interest the amount had reached "about $160,000."[11] Sadly,
however, neither the elder nor the younger ever saw a penny of it.

Porter's War of 1812 experiences were, to put it mildly, unpar-
alleled. He was promoted to "post captain," the highest official rank
in the Navy, and early in the conflict sailed on his first cruise in the
little 32-gun frigate *Essex*. He took six prizes and fought the war's
first ship-to-ship battle, although he modestly and correctly referred
to it as "so trifling an action."[12] On 13 August 1812, accosted by
the 20-gun British sloop *Alert*, Porter had posed as a panicky merchantman attempting to escape, thereby drawing the Englishman
within range. He settled the matter with a single broadside; eight
minutes later the *Alert* surrendered.[13]

It was, however, his second and last wartime cruise that made
history when he roamed the Pacific in the *Essex* from February 1813
until his return home during July 1814. The *Essex* had been assigned
to Bainbridge's squadron consisting of the fabled *Constitution* and
the sloop *Hornet*. Delayed by a necessary overhaul of his ship, Porter
could not sail until late in October 1812, well after the other two.
The squadron was supposed to rendezvous off the Brazilian island
of Fernando de Noronha, but when he arrived there he found only
a note from Bainbridge, written in secret ink, telling him to look for
the *Constitution* and the *Hornet* near Rio de Janeiro. But he soon
learned that an American frigate had smashed a British counterpart—
only later did he find out that she had been HMS *Java*—and shrewdly
surmised that the *Constitution* must have been hit hard enough to
require her to go home for repairs.[14] Hence there was no longer any
reason for him to tarry off Brazil, and he could act upon either of
the two options the Secretary of the Navy had offered to the squadron: he could lurk off St. Helena to harry British traffic to and from
the Cape of Good Hope, or he could round Cape Horn, to burst
into the Pacific on a commerce-destroying mission there. He chose
the latter, a decision that James Fenimore Cooper called "as much
characterized by wisdom and prudence as it was by enterprise and

spirit,"[15] and thus had the distinction of commanding the first American warship in the Pacific.

Until his thirst for glory wrecked his reasoning process, causing the loss of his ship and casualties to over half of his people, the beginning of Porter's three-act drama in the Pacific was a resounding success. Coming into Valparaiso, Chile, after a "boisterous" passage around and after Cape Horn, he remained there for nine days, resupplying his vessel and becoming friends with José Miguél Carrera, the temporary dictator of that country, then in rebellion against its Spanish overlords. This association would significantly affect U.S. foreign relations a few years later.

Porter next aimed the *Essex* at the Galápagos Islands, well off the coast of Ecuador. They were the centers of the British whaling industry, manned for the most part by Americans from Nantucket Island in Massachusetts. Porter fell upon the English whalers as the clap of doom, roving through the Galápagos from April into October 1813, taking no fewer than ten well-provisioned and well-armed ships, and, according to him, saving a like number of American whalers from their more potent adversaries. One of the prizes, the *Atlantic*, was refitted as a warship and named the *Essex Junior*. Porter, with breathtaking conceit, estimated that the combined value of his prizes and the American whalers he had spared amounted to over five million dollars—surely a ludicrous exaggeration because none of his prizes ever made it to the United States for sale.[16]

Nevertheless, Porter's services had considerable impact in several spheres. Incredibly, he and his 32-gun frigate had seized and retained for many months naval control of the Pacific Ocean, for the British did not have a single man-of-war in those 65,000,000 liquid square miles. Theodore Roosevelt judged Porter to have been both skillful and audacious: "It was an unprecedented thing for a small frigate to cruise for a year and a half in enemy waters, and to supply herself . . . purely from captive vessels, with everything. . . . Porter's cruise was the very model of what an expedition should be, harassing the enemy most effectively at no cost whatever."[17]

His most pronounced effect was on the far-flung whaling business. Whale oil was the major contemporary source for both illumination and lubrication, and the disruption of this essential supply from the Pacific cut badly into the British economy. One unnamed member of Parliament mourned that because of what Porter had done in the Galápagos, London "burnt dark for a year."[18] Nor were the psychological results of the captain's derring-do less striking. In the sonorous prose of Washington Irving:

It occasioned great uneasiness in Great Britain. The merchants who had any property afloat in this quarter, trembled with apprehension for its fate; the underwriters groaned at the catalogue of captures brought by every advice, while the pride of the nation was sorely incensed at beholding a single frigate lording it over the Pacific . . . in saucy defiance of their thousand ships; revelling in the spoils of boundless wealth, and almost banishing the British flag from those regions where it had so long waved proudly predominant.[19]

Although Porter showered encomiums upon himself for his accomplishments during the second act of his escapades in the Pacific— namely, his sojourn for seven weeks during the autumn of 1813 in the Marquesas Islands in the central southern part of that ocean— they were largely unwarranted. He told his crew en route why they were going there: "We are bound to the Western Islands, with two objects in view: Firstly, that we may put our ship in condition . . . for our return home. Secondly, I am desirous that you should have some relaxation and amusement after being so long at sea, as from your late good conduct you deserve it."[20] With smug satisfaction he noted the crew's reaction to the above: ". . . they could talk and think of nothing but the beauties of the islands . . . and amply indulged themselves in fancied bliss."[21]

On 25 October the *Essex*, the *Essex Jr.*, and four other prizes, with their English captives, came into Nuku Hiva Island in the Marquesas. That achipelago, the easternmost of Polynesia, lies about 2,500 miles southeast of Hawaii and 850 miles northeast of Tahiti. First discovered and named by the Spaniards in the late 1500s, the Marquesas were forgotten until Captain James Cook's visit in 1774. After that Western ships stopped off there occasionally.

It is easy to follow Porter's stay from his diary-like *Journal of a Cruise Made to the Pacific Ocean* . . . , 2 vols., 1815 and 1822 editions. His initial order of business was to careen and refit the *Essex*, employing the islanders to scrape barnacles from the hull with coconut shells. Some idea of shipboard conditions of that day may be gleaned from Porter's casual comment that when they fumigated the flagship with charcoal fires, they killed "from twelve to fifteen hundred rats." In short, by the time the Marquesas had been reached, rats had outnumbered men almost five to one in a small frigate. Actually they merely exchanged one vermin for another; cockroaches quickly infested the ship.[22] All hands were soon busy constructing a settlement named "Madisonville" and a defensive work called "Fort Madison." In this connection one night Porter found a marine sentry asleep on duty, and asserting that he did not wish to hold a court-martial with the possible imposition of a mandatory death sentence, he instead crept up on him, drew out his pistol and shot him through "the fleshy part of the thigh," which as the captain complacently pointed out, made "every person more vigilant, particularly the marines."[23]

During their Marquesan visit, any vestiges of sexual repression were promptly put in abeyance. Porter, his officers, and men reveled with the "young girls," who were "handsome and well-formed; their skins were remarkably soft and smooth, and their complexions no darker than many brunett[e]s in America." Indeed, it was soon "helter-skelter and promiscuous intercourse, every girl the wife of every man." Such comments in his *Journal* were, of course, grist for the mills of English reviewers (one of whom called Porter, a "hoary proficient in swinish sensualism") and domestic enemies alike. Significantly, some of the steamier passages of his 1815 edition were considerably watered down in that of 1822.[24]

Nuku Hiva, one of the most beautiful islands in the Pacific, was well populated by some 40,000 Polynesians, divided into no fewer than thirty-one separate tribes, among them the "Tickeymahues" and the "Attakakahaneuahs." Porter and his people settled among the Taiis, and, as should have been expected, once he was associated with them, there was no way to avoid participation in their tribal wars. Porter avowed that he had made every effort to befriend the nearby "Happahs," yet he had been given no choice but to fight them. After an American attack had killed no more than four or five, the other three or four thousand sued for peace (Marquesan warfare was supposed to wound, not kill), and were assessed an indemnity of hogs and fruit.[25]

More serious was Porter's war with the potent Taipis, who inhabited a nine-mile-long valley to the northeast of the Taiis. They had launched a series of provocations that the captain found impossible to ignore. Yet his first assault upon the largest and most belligerent tribe in Nuku Hiva was so carelessly planned that it almost cost him his life. He advanced into their territory with only thirty-five Americans and some 5,000 Taiis and Happahs, who fled at the first sign of resistance. Trapped before an impenetrable defense, he and his men finally had to battle their way through the Taipis and escape to the waiting boats at the beach. His second attack was characterized by improved tactics. He led 200 well-armed Americans and their Nuku Hivan allies to scale the 3,000-foot escarpment and then descend into the Taipi Valley, spreading havoc that resulted in "a long line of smoking [*sic*] ruins" that "now marked our traces from one end of the valley to the other; the opposite hills were covered with unhappy fugitives, and the whole presented a sense of desolation

Porter's ships at anchor in the Marquesas Islands where he spent the winter of 1813–14 at Nuku Hiva. He established a camp that he named Madisonville in a bay he named Massachusetts. Porter drew this picture to illustrate his journal of the cruise.

and horror. Unhappy and heroic people!"[26] Positive that he would be castigated both in Britain and America for his assault—and he was—Porter defended himself:

> We were a handful of men among numerous warlike tribes, liable at any moment to be attacked by them and cut off; our only hope of safety was in convincing them of our great superiority over them . . . . I had offered them friendship, and my offers had been rejected with insulting scorn . . . had they [the other tribes] been convinced that the Typees could keep us at bay, they must have felt satisfied that their united forces were capable of destroying us. . . . by reducing the Typees before they could come to an understanding with the other tribes . . . I hoped to bring about a general peace and secure the future tranquility of the island.[27]

During the interim between the Happah and Taipi wars Porter became the U.S. Navy's first active imperialist, extending the boundaries of the United States many thousands of miles to the southwest. On 19 November 1813 he assembled his Americans, English prisoners, and Marquesans to announce that he was annexing Nuku Hiva to his nation. Why? Because the "natives . . . have requested to be admitted into the great American family, whose pure republican policy approaches so near their own . . . . I have taken it upon myself to promise that they shall be so adopted; that our chief shall be their chief . . . ."[28] Unfortunately the news of this elongation of the country arrived in Washington during the summer of 1814, about the same time as the British army that burned the Capitol and the White House, along with some other public buildings, and sent the President into headlong flight to avoid capture. Madison's main biographer neatly describes what ensued: "Having trouble nearer at home, Chief Madison of the Attakakahaneuahs and thirty other tribes did not ask Congress to accept the island . . . ."[29]

Porter received both compliments and castigations then and later for being "the first American naval imperialist"—in the sense of being an annexer of remote, heavily populated areas where the conquerers would go as temporary administrators, soldiers, businessmen, teachers, and missionaries in contrast to permanent settlers of nearby, relatively empty lands. One contemporary newspaper wondered if anyone had ever matched Porter's deeds as "at once an admiral and a governor."[30] The early-twentieth-century naval officer E. L. Beach commented that "Porter's mind was imperial in conception. He had the prescience to see that American control of the Pacific was essential to the national stability, and this is in 1814 [sic], when the United States extended theoretically but little west of the Mississippi."[31] To the contrary, an anti-Porter newspaper thought that the only good that could come from the annexation of Nuku Hiva was that the "feeble and pusillanimous Madison" might be sent there to preside over their many tribes.[32] A modern author judged the episode as amounting to nothing more than "some colorful chapters in his journal and, when he saw fit to interfere in some local feuds, some dead Marquesans."[33]

The last of those quotations gives an accurate summary. Within a matter of months after his departure, everything that Porter had tried to make permanent fell to pieces. Tribal warfare resumed, and mutiny broke out among the few Americans and Britons whom he had left behind to provide a base for his possible return. The prizes he had brought with him were all lost. His lengthy apologia for what he had done in the south central Pacific might have had more merit except that he had no justification for being there for almost two months save to repair ship and provide himself and his men with some sexual gratification. And once he was among the Taiis, he had no choice but to war upon their enemies. His annexation proved farcical, and so totally forgotten was it, that when the French annexed the Marquesans in 1842, Washington uttered not a word of protest.

By early December the American sojourn had to end, much to the dismay of the men who viewed with abhorrence the prospect of harsh sea duty in place of their idyllic sexual delights. A few even tried to run away or mutiny but were quelled by what the captain called "the most exemplary punishment."[34] On the 12th the *Essex* and the *Essex Jr.* weighed anchor while, as then twelve-year-old David Glasgow Farragut could recall with the keenest memory decades later, the flagship's band played a tune most appropriate for their leave taking: "The Girl I Left Behind Me."[35]

If Porter's first act of his Pacific cruise could be greeted with acclamation, and his second with at best mixed reviews, his finale— in theatrical terms—bombed. And it was solely the captain's fault. At Valparaiso, before setting out for the Galápagos Islands, he had been told not only that the *Constitution* had whipped the *Java* but that the *Wasp* had beaten the *Frolic*. This news impelled him to write in his journal that this action "makes us pant for an opportunity of doing something ourselves."[36] In the Marquesas he had been informed that a three-ship British squadron had sailed for the Pacific: the frigate *Phoebe* and the sloop *Cherub*[37] (contemporary British naval nomenclature is incomprehensible) would hunt him down, while the sloop *Raccoon* would go on to Oregon to lay a stronger British claim to that country.[38] Moreover, a rumor was true that additional British warships were being sent around the Horn. Nonetheless, Porter notified the Secretary of the Navy that he was heading for Valparaiso, a port to which the British would be sure to come. He aspired to enhance his fame by doing "something more splendid" than he had as yet been able to accomplish.[39] He would deliberately seek out the stronger English force and fight it.

Can one condone Porter's incredible decision? Was he totally oblivious to the essential American naval strategy of the war? Could he not realize that any number of single-ship U.S. victories could make no difference as to its outcome? Was he so blind that he could not perceive that his one option to aid his nation was to avoid at all costs the *Phoebe* and the *Cherub* if he could—that he should have sailed to the western Pacific and the Indian Ocean to ruin the thriving British merchant marine in those waters? The answer to all these questions must be "yes." Indeed, his avid quest for glory wrote finis to what might have been a turning point in the war.

Five days after he had arrived at Valparaiso the two British men-of-war pulled into that port. The *Phoebe* was commanded by Captain Thomas T. Hillyar, a sober and dedicated professional who had been a close friend of Porter when both were serving in the Mediterranean. As he approached the *Essex*, he could see that Porter had his ship in fighting trim, matches glowing over the cannon and the crew with cutlasses in hand for boarding. Loudly protesting his peaceful intent, the Englishman came close to losing everything when an errant wind almost brought the *Phoebe* into the *Essex*—Porter telling him if the two vessels touched he would attack, but they just missed. The American later wrote that he could have pulverized the *Phoebe* with a single broadside, and he was very likely correct. He claimed that he had withheld fire solely because he recognized Chile's neutral status.[40]

The next day the two commanders agreed that any combat between them would be outside Valparaiso's three-mile limit. Within a week the British ships had been resupplied and stood out to sea to blockade the *Essex* and the *Essex Jr.*, although the latter was so flimsily constructed that she would take no part in any battle. For weeks Porter kept trying to provoke Hillyar into having the two frigates fight *mano a mano* without interference from the *Cherub*, but the Englishman wisely refused. As February dragged into late March 1814, Porter came to the belated conclusion that he must escape. The odds against him would become intolerable should either the *Raccoon* return from Oregon or a second British frigate appear. He was right in his latter expectation; fifteen days after the battle HMS *Tagus* came into Valparaiso.[41]

On 28 March the weather first enticed and then repeatedly betrayed Porter. When a sudden gust pulled out the *Essex*'s anchor cables, he saw an opportunity to slip past his blockaders and run for the open sea. Cramming on full sail he raced out of the harbor, but as he rounded a promontory a vicious gale struck his ship, ripping away her main-topmast, a disaster that made most difficult the operation of a large sailing vessel. Porter probably erred in not pressing on, crippled though he was, taking his chances at close quarters with the enemy; but convinced that he would be safe from attack there, he turned back, coming to "within a pistol shot" of the shore.[42]

Instead the *Phoebe* and the *Cherub* leisurely moved in for the kill, Hillyar knowing that the *Essex* was crammed with short-range carronades but possessed only six long guns, of which only three could be used off the stern during the battle.[43] So the British men-of-war stationed themselves beyond carronade range and proceeded to batter the Americans with their combined total of 32 long guns. Twice Porter attempted to make for the English frigate in hopes of boarding her; twice the weather drove him back toward shore. For two and a half hours the slaughter went on until Porter, finally recognizing the inevitable, surrendered. Of the *Essex*'s complement, fifty-eight had been killed and sixty-five wounded, a startling 60 percent casualty rate, although the captain himself suffered no more than a bruise on the forehead. The British lost only five killed and ten wounded.[44] Porter was sure that his ship had been so thoroughly shot to pieces that she could never sail to England, but he was wrong, and she served for some years in the Royal Navy. The surviving Americans were put in the *Essex Jr.* and returned to the United States just in time to participate in the inept defense of Washington in the summer of 1814.[45]

Porter kept on explaining away his defeat by stressing that in February he had given up his sure victory through his respect for Chilean neutrality and international law, while in March Hillyar had broken both.[46] True enough, but the Englishman's instructions had been explicit—he was to respect the non-belligerency of no port in which he might find the *Essex*.[47] Furthermore, Porter himself had made something of a violation of Chile's neutrality when he had burned two of his English prizes in the harbor, hoping thereby to lure Hillyar into battle with him. The consensus of what had transpired at Valparaiso would seem to be that the English captain all along had realized that "Hard work, not heroics, a policeman's arrest of a burglar, was the task of the *Phoebe* and *Cherub*."[48]

As the Treaty of Ghent concluded the drawn War of 1812, Porter's thoughts, along with those of almost all other U.S. naval officers, were to ensure some kind of a future for himself. Here his premature work as an imperialist again came to the fore. He was the first to advocate seriously using the U.S. Navy to force open Japan. Early in 1815 he wrote to President Madison through the Secretary of the Navy that "the important trade of Japan has been shut against every nation except the Dutch . . . . the time may be favorable for its opening and it would be a glory . . . for us, a nation of only forty years standing to beat down their rooted prejudices—secure to ourselves a valuable trade, and make that people known to the world." Probably his chief reason for his appeal was contained in his conclusion: "the world is at peace . . . . We have ships . . . [and] officers who will require employment."[49] The administration seriously considered his suggestion, but preparations were not completed before a minor squabble with Spain in 1816 led the United States to concentrate its warships in the Caribbean. Even so, one modern authority claims that subsequent American Pacific explorations, including Matthew C. Perry's famous "opening" of Japan in 1853–54, "all developed from the idea which the proposal of 1815 initiated."[50]

The remainder of Porter's life tended to emphasize the administrative and diplomatic, for not only did he have no more American wars to fight, but he would have only one further tour of sea duty, and that amounted to less than two years. His postwar career started auspiciously enough; despite his drubbing by Hillyar, he was treated on his return home as a conquering hero. Along with John Rodgers as its "president" and the Isaac Hull (almost immediately superseded by Stephen Decatur), Porter was granted the signal honor of being an original member of the Board of Navy Commissioners, serving from 1815 to 1822. This body had been established to help the Secretary of the Navy cope with an ever increasing flood of paperwork. After some initial confusion as to the board's responsibilities vis-à-vis the Secretary, it was finally given such duties as investigating "the need for and the location of Navy yards and dry docks"; developing "specified rules of conduct for officers and men"; procuring and stockpiling supplies; deciding upon the proper armaments for ships; recommending such reforms as regulated systems for the appointment, promotion, and dismissal of officers; founding a naval academy; and creating higher ranks in the service.[51] During its early years the board functioned with reasonable efficiency, but by the late 1830s it had hardened into something of a citadel of reaction, tending to oppose such essential innovations for a modern navy as armor plating, steampower, and rifled cannon; thus it had to be replaced by the Navy Bureaus in 1842.

While on the board Porter paid much attention to courts-martial, for he was by nature pugnaciously litigious. With no war on hand, nor even any particular threat of one, the officers were apt to compensate for their lack of official hostilities by an incredible number of private feuds. A few reached "the field of honor," and Porter and Rodgers were close enough during March 1820 to witness the termination of the famous James Barron–Stephen Decatur duel near Washington, which resulted in Decatur's agonizing demise. In less feral situations Porter devoted considerable time to helping his friend Captain Isaac Hull, under siege by a cabal of officers seeking to ruin him in Boston in 1822 and 1823, culminating in the complete vindication of the accused.[52]

Throughout this period Porter acted out a sizable role in U.S.–Latin American relations. From 1810 to 1825 colonial uprisings against their Spanish masters raged in both Americas. But the way of the rebels was hard; the Spaniards and their royalist supporters fought tenaciously to keep Madrid's red and gold standard flying from the Rio Grande to Tierra del Fuego. At first practically every American sided with the revolutionaries as fellow republicans in a world of reactionary monarchy. But Porter inadvertently shattered this relative unanimity, and delayed for several years early American recognition of Argentina and Chile in particular. In Valparaiso during 1813 he had made a friend of José Miguél Carrera, the temporary dictator of Chile. Three years later Carrera came to the United States, seeking aid from Porter and his friends, having been ousted in Santiago by Bernardo O'Higgins, his Chilean nemesis, backed by the brilliant Argentinian General José de San Martín.[53]

The "Porterites" went all out for Carrera, arguing that this deposed ruler of a small and distant country was the only worthy recipient of American recognition as the leader of an independent state. Unfortunately this support brought them into a collision with one who also ardently favored early recognition of Latin-American rebel regimes. This was Henry Clay, who disliked Carrera and threw his full support behind O'Higgins in Chile and San Martín in Argentina. Each faction passed its time denigrating the heroes of the other, which tended both to split the pro-revolutionary forces and reduce national enthusiasm for their cause.[54]

President James Monroe and Secretary of State John Quincy Adams were able to avoid recognizing either group. Although they too favored the rebels, they were convinced that a precipitate recognition of Argentina and Chile could be calamitous. While the royalists, especially in Peru, could fight well, the matter of recognition, they thought, must await more auspicious times. Second, there was always a chance, unlikely though it was, that the ultraconservative powers of Europe might interpret U.S. recognition of lower South America as a challenge to be met, and intervene to restore Spain's American colonies to it. Finally, Adams was immersed in his lengthy and delicate negotiations with Luis de Onís, Spanish Minister to Washington, which finally ended in the pro-American Adams–Onís Transcontinental Treaty of 1819. This treaty gave the United States clear titles to both West and East Florida and drew an excellent western boundary line from the Gulf to the Pacific. A too hasty recognition of Argentina and Chile before ratifications of the pact were exchanged in 1821 might have wrecked everything. But there was no problem recognizing them a year later. So Porter, no matter how much to the contrary had been his original expectations, actually had worked well for his nation's vital interests.[55]

He would have yet another impact upon the Latin American policy of the United States. This, however, would come out of a different matrix and operate with far greater destructive power upon him. Porter had come out of the War of 1812 a relatively wealthy man, thanks to his prize money. Furthermore, as a navy commissioner he was paid $3,500 a year at a time when a "post captain," the highest regular rank in the service, received only $1,200, plus rations. So he splurged in 1816, buying a huge estate atop Meridian Hill, Washington's highest point, and embellishing it with a lavish mansion where he entertained a host of visitors. He became a gentleman farmer, trying to utilize all the latest agricultural fads, all of which failed, as did his investments. By 1823 he had decided that his best chance for financial recovery was to return to sea duty. He resigned as commissioner in exchange for an appointment as commodore of the West India Squadron.[56]

By this time the Gulf of Mexico and the Caribbean had become infested with privateers and pirates (they were practically indistinguishable in their behavior) who caused vast woe to American shippers plying through those waters. One Philadelphian reported that he had kept a careful account of the "piratical acts" committed there from 1815 to 1822, and they numbered precisely "three thousand and two," many of which had been accompanied by deeds of atrocious cruelty.[57] During 1822 and 1823 Commodore James Biddle had been the first officer dispatched to end piracy. But he had been hindered by vessels too deep-drafted for essential close-to-shore maneuverings, as well as by a refusal of Spanish authorities to permit him to chase pirates ashore in Cuba and Puerto Rico. Poor Biddle could accomplish little, and this flagship became afflicted with an unusually lethal form of yellow fever which killed over a hundred of his men, about one-third of his entire complement.[58]

Porter's auspices looked much brighter than Biddle's when he arrived in the West Indies during February 1823. He could take with him several speedy sail- and oar-powered barges able to harry free-booters along the shoreline. In an interesting historical footnote, he also had the *Sea Gull*, a converted Hudson River ferry, the first steamboat ever to participate in naval warfare.[59] By the end of the year he had largely eradicated piracy off Cuba, if not Puerto Rico, an accomplishment for which the President lauded him in the same annual message that contained the Monroe Doctrine.[60] But much of Porter's elan vanished when he fell victim to yellow fever for a second time. He returned to Washington without asking permission to do so, an act that aroused the resentment of President Madison, soon-to-be-President Adams, and Secretary of the Navy Samuel Southard. To their animadversions he replied with choler and impudence. By the time he went back to the West Indies late in 1824 the admin-istration was viewing him as an insolent troublemaker.[61]

Porter had no sooner arrived in the Danish West Indies (the Virgin Islands) during November 1824 than one of his officers told him about his maltreatment in the Puerto Rican town of Fajardo ("Fox-ardo" in contemporary documentation). In search of thieves who had looted an American warehouse and allegedly taken their booty to Fajardo, he had proceeded there out of uniform to make inquiries, was arrested as a trespasser, held in jail for a few hours, and then hooted out of town on his release. Porter listened to this story with mounting fury, and the next day led 200 armed Americans ashore in that Spanish colony. There he dictated at bayonet's point an abject apology to his officer by Fajardo's authorities under a promise to wipe out that settlement if such were not forthcoming. He departed the same afternoon, notified Washington of what he had done, and settled back to await the congratulations that he was sure lay in wait for him.[62]

The reaction of the Monroe Administration was quite the contrary, Adams referring to Porter's descent on Puerto Rico as "a direct, hostile invasion of the island, utterly unjustifiable . . . one of the most high-handed acts I have ever heard of."[63] Instead of being praised, Porter was suspended from his command, brought back to Washington, condemned by a court of inquiry, and court-martialed on two counts:

1. "Disobedience of orders, and conduct unbecoming an officer" in that he had landed "on the island of Porto Rico, in the dominions of his Catholic Majesty the King of Spain, then and still at amity with the United States, in a forceful and hostile manner . . . ."

2. "Insubordinate conduct, and conduct unbecoming an officer"

for, among other misdemeanors, sending one letter to President Adams and four to Secretary Southard of "insubordinate and disrespectful character."[64]

Porter's trial, which took up five hot and tedious weeks in Washington during the summer of 1825, had a pro forma air about it. It seemed certain he would be convicted. Four of his personal enemies sat as his judges, and the administration's animus toward him was incessant. The proceedings were almost interminable; a Porter biographer was on target when he observed that, "Everyone concerned gave evidence at the greatest possible length. The prosecution dragged in everything it could think of, relevant or irrelevant, while Porter on the defense wandered far afield."[65] Indeed he did, to the amount of 50,000 words in his final statement, many of them concentrating on the similarity of what he had done in Puerto Rico and what Andrew Jackson had done when he invaded the Floridas in 1818, arguing that both had the right to ignore international boundaries when "in pursuit of pirates." For identical acts, he pointed out, the first had been pilloried, the second lauded. Adams and Southard vehemently denied that Porter had been in pursuit of anyone at Fajardo, and to this conclusion the judges harkened.[66]

Finally, on 10 August, Porter was found guilty on both counts. For such delinquencies, dismissal from the service was a likely sentence. At the very least a long suspension without pay was expected. Instead the sentence was literally incredible. He was given a six-month suspension at full salary and allowance, that is, given a paid half-year vacation. Furthermore, the court stated that it was sure that he had acted "with an anxious disposition . . . to maintain the honor and advance the interest of the nation and the service."[67] Little wonder that his wife Evalina wrote: "Look at the sentence of the court . . . and it plainly shows that he was to be whipped like a boy for a fault and chuckled into good humor by a sugar plumb [*sic*] . . . ."[68]

What the Porters could not realize was that the international situation for the United States had changed drastically from Jackson in 1818 to Porter in 1824. In the first instance, Adams had been able to use the general's savage irruption into East and West Florida as a massive lever to pry those colonies from Spain, stressing to Luis de Onís that Madrid was so remiss in policing its borders that law and order could be achieved only through an American armed invasion. Spain therefore had to (and did) relinquish control of the Floridas to the United States. But in the second, the picture had changed so decidedly that aggression, so useful before, could have been catastrophic. In 1823, reactionary France, acting as agent for the so-called Holy Alliance, conquered all of Spain from its more liberal rulers, restoring to the throne its deposed, vicious, and worth-less Bourbon king. The Monroe Doctrine had been promulgated during that December to guard against the possibility, remote though it was, that the French might try to restore to Spain its American colonies. In it President Monroe offered Europe a quid pro quo: no further European colonies would be permitted in the Americas be-cause their monarchical system was different from the republicanism of the New World. In return the United States promised not to interfere in Europe's already established American colonies or in that continent's internal affairs.[69]

While such considerations were paramount in the administration, Porter had the ill timing to lead 200 U.S. sailors and marines ashore in a Spanish colony, browbeating its officials into a compulsory apol-ogy on the threat of Fajardo's destruction. This just might be the excuse that the French were looking for to send an armada across the Atlantic. During Porter's trial Monroe summed up well this as-pect of the case against that officer. He concluded that Porter had not been working "on the side of peace," and continued:

> This command was deemed a very important one . . . [and] I knew that it would attract the attention, not of Spain alone . . . but of the new governments, our neighbors, to the south & in certain respects, of several of the powers of Europe. . . . [Porter's orders were] dictated by a desire rather to err . . . on the side of moderation, than to risk a varience, with any of the nations concerned . . . .[70]

Announcing that never again would he associate "with those who were led by men in power to inflict an unrighteous sentence,"[71] Porter resigned from the service during the summer of 1826. This act not only closed twenty-eight years in the U.S. Navy but, of course, terminated any further contributions that he might have made to the American naval tradition. Instead, he spent most of the last seventeen years of his life an exile from his own country.

He had resigned to become from 1826 to 1829 de facto com-manding officer of the new Mexican navy, fighting to keep its in-dependence from Spain. At first he was able to write to his wife with enchanting immodesty, "I have accomplished wonders" with both men and ships, slashing at Spanish lines of supply and communica-tions effectively enough to make any concentrated assault upon Vera Cruz impossible.[72] But the latter portions of his Mexican interlude constituted a trip through hell. His nephew was killed in action against the Spaniards, one son became a prisoner of war, another (his favorite) died of yellow fever at the age of ten, he himself was bitten by a tarantula, evidently Antonio Lopez de Santa Anna twice tried to have him assassinated, in all probability his wife in Pennsylvania was unfaithful to him, and the utter collapse of the Mexican economy plunged him into an abject destitution. As he wrote later in life, "My sufferings in Mexico, the trials of fortitude I underwent, exceed all belief. . . ."[73]

For several months Porter operated his Mexican naval squadron from a base at Key West. This breach of American neutrality, Porter's granting of a letter of marque to a Mexican privateer, and his recruitment of American sailors in New Orleans for service in Mexico strained American–Mexican relations, but not to the point of damaging his reputation among Jacksonian political leaders.

When Porter returned to Washington in 1829, President Jackson offered to reinstate him in the U.S. Navy, but Porter rejected the proposal saying that he would "sooner beg my bread from door to door than to link my reputation with men who could pronounce it a punishable offense to do all in my power to sustain the honor and interest of the flag and country."[74] For six months Porter rejected other offers of various positions as beneath his dignity.

Finally, in the spring of 1830 he accepted a State Department appointment. Thus, his last extended service was diplomatic: first as Consul-General to the Barbary states and then initially as Chargé d'Affaires and then Minister to the Ottoman Empire, at the start of which service he exchanged ratifications of the first Turkish–American treaty, and during which he returned to the United States for only a single brief visit. As a diplomat he enjoyed a relatively placid professional life, keeping busy writing to the Secretary of State at such length and to such an extent that Daniel Webster finally had to tell him point-blank, "do not write so often."[75] His personal relations were another matter. He quarreled with almost all his associates, broke with most of his ten children, and watched his marriage disintegrate into mutual abhorrence, with each accusing the other of madness (probably each was at least partially correct). Porter died at Constantinople during March of 1843 of heart disease, complicated by pleurisy. To a large degree he had written his own epitaph nearly eight years earlier in a letter to his foster son, David Glasgow Farragut:

> My country has thus far taken care of me, and I hope by good conduct to merit what she has done, by endeavoring to serve her to the utmost of my power. There was a time when there was nothing that I thought too daring to be attempted for her; but those times are past, and appear only as a confused and painful dream. A retrospect of the history of my life seems a highly-coloured romance, which I should be very loth to live over.[76]

Porter had demonstrated the courage necessary for battle command in the Quasi-War against France, the Tripolitan War, and the War of 1812, especially in his desperate defense of the *Essex* at Valparaiso. Although his annexation ceremony in 1813 may have been farcical, he became America's first naval imperialist when he took over Nuku Hiva Island, and reinforced this imperialism with his advocacy of using the Navy to open Japan. His impact upon his nation's Latin American policy was marked. When he frustrated General James Wilkinson's amorphous plans at New Orleans during 1809—10, he may have helped to abort a filibustering expedition into Mexico. His advocacy of José Miguél Carrera in Chile from 1815 to 1820 had the positive effect of assisting in delaying what could have been a premature recognition of Argentina and Chile; whereas he had a negative influence when he invaded a Spanish colony at a time when the reactionary European powers might have intervened in the Americas because of it. Clearly his most important contribution to his country was to ensure American whaling supremacy for almost a half-century. This he did by his practical wartime annihilation of the British Pacific whaling fleet, interrupting its momentum to such an extent as to make its postwar restitution impractical.

As a naval personality he exhibited the characteristics of his contemporaries, perhaps to excess. Certainly he was brave and impetuous, and he definitely had his share of pride. His rejection of government positions at a time when he verged on personal bankruptcy almost smacks of hubris.

As a maker of the American naval tradition, and as a representative of the officer corps of the Age of Sail, David Porter stands well to the fore.

FURTHER READING

David Porter was the subject of two earlier biographies: David Dixon Porter's *Memoir of Commodore David Porter* (1875) and Archibald D. Turnbull's *Commodore David Porter* (1929). The first, as might be expected, is hopelessly one-sided, for the son cannot admit the father's failings. Furthermore, for some inexplicable and inexcusable reason he omitted entirely the elder Porter's important contributions to American—Latin American policy. Turnbull's biography appears to be little more than a redoing of David Dixon Porter's, with his mistakes of commission and omission, plus a few new errors.

As to specific works dealing with the varied periods of Porter's life: Basic to his experiences in the Quasi- and Tripolitan Wars are the Navy Department's *Naval Documents* pertaining to both conflicts

(1935–38, 1944). Gardner W. Allen's *Our Naval War with France* (1909) and Fletcher Pratt's *Preble's Boys* are of some value, but a word of warning—Pratt can be totally unreliable, for in my biography of Bainbridge I found that he simply made up names, dates, and events to make a better story. Glenn Tucker's *Dawn Like Thunder* (1963) is excellent on Porter and the Tripolitan War. For his cruise in the *Essex* from 1812 to 1814 I consulted the many histories of the war at sea, among which I judge Theodore Roosevelt's *Naval War of 1812* (1882) and C. S. Forester's *Age of Fighting Sail* the best. For Porter's activities against the British whaling fleet, his sojourn in the Marquesas, and the loss of his ship at Valparaiso I have already called attention to the two editions of his *Journal of a Cruise* (1815 and 1822), with William Gifford's brutal critique in the British *Quarterly Review* sandwiched in between. For Porter as a navy commissioner, Charles O. Paullin's *Commodore John Rodgers* (1910) was most helpful. Three works were basic for my discussion of Porter and U.S. Latin American policy: Laura Bornholdt's *Baltimore and Early Pan-Americanism;* Joseph F. Straub's unpublished doctoral dissertation, "José Miguél Carrera" (1953); and William R. Manning's three-volume *Diplomatic Correspondence of the United States Concerning the Independence of Latin America* (1925).

For background to Porter's campaign in the West Indies during 1823 and 1824, I consulted Gardner W. Allen, *Our Navy and the West Indian Pirates* (1929); Francis B. C. Bradlee, *Piracy in the West Indies and Its Suppression* (1923); and Richard Wheeler, *In Pirate Waters* (1969). In addition to Porter's *Exposition . . . Which Justified the Exposition to Foxardo . . .* (1825) and the entire testimony of both his court of inquiry and court-martial, for the Fajardo invasion see John Quincy Adams, *Memoirs*, Vols. 6 and 7 (1874–77); Paullin's *John Rodgers*; Richard S. West, Jr.'s *The Second Admiral: A Life of David Dixon Porter* (1937); and an excellent modern article, Michael Birkner's "The Foxardo Affair Revisited: Porter, Pirates, and the Problem of Civilian Authority in the Early Republic," *American Neptune* (1982). Porter's calamitous Mexican assignment was much clarified by a truly first-rate unpublished doctoral dissertation, Robert L. Bidwell's "The First Mexican Navy, 1821–1830" (1968), with additional information from Elmer W. Flaccus's "Commodore David Porter and the Mexican Navy," *Hispanic American Historical Review* (1954); and J. Fred Rippy's *Joel R. Poinsett* (1935). Charles O. Paullin's *Diplomatic Negotiations of American Naval Officers* (1912) and Henry M. Wriston's *Executive Agents in American Foreign Relations* (1929) narrate the details of the first Turkish–American Treaty of 1830. The earlier Porter biographies compose most of the secondary information about Porter's last years in Turkey, which he enlivened with a chatty and informational two-volume *Constantinople and Its Environs* (1835).

NOTES

1. David Dixon Porter, *Memoir of Commodore David Porter of the United States Navy*, 19–20.
2. Secretary of the Navy to David Porter, 8 October 1799, *Naval Documents Related to the Quasi-War Between the United States and France*, II, 329.
3. David F. Long, *Nothing Too Daring: A Biography of Commodore David Porter, 1780–1843*, 12–13.
4. Glenn Tucker, *Dawn Like Thunder: The Barbary Wars and the Birth of the U.S. Navy*, 143–44.
5. Secretary of the Navy to David Porter, 30 March 1802, R.G. 45: Secretary of the Navy Letters, National Archives.
6. David F. Long, *Sailor-Diplomat: A Biography of Commodore James Biddle, 1783–1848*, 20–21.
7. Ibid., 26.
8. David Porter to Secretary of the Navy, 5 August 1806, R.G. 45: Letters Received by the Secretary of the Navy from Masters Commandant, National Archives.
9. Fletcher Pratt, *Preble's Boys: Commodore Preble and the Birth of American Sea Power*, 214–15.
10. David Porter to Samuel Hambleton, 12 October 1811, David Porter Papers, Van Ness Collection, Owings Mills, Md.
11. David Dixon Porter to U.S. Minister to Mexico, 5 December 1853, David Porter Papers, Van Ness Collection, Owings Mills, Md.
12. David Porter to Secretary of the Navy, 3 September 1812, R.G. 45: Captains' Letters, National Archives.
13. Leonard F. Guttridge and Jay D. Smith, *The Commodores*, 201.
14. David Porter, *Journal of a Cruise Made to the Pacific Ocean by Captain David Porter, in the United States Frigate Essex, in the Years 1812, 1813 and 1814, Containing Descriptions of the Cape de Verd[e] Islands, Coasts of Brazil, Patagonia, Chile and Peru, and of the Gallapagos [sic] Islands*, I, 59–60.
15. James Fenimore Cooper, *History of the Navy of the United States of America*, II, 121.
16. David Porter, *Journal*, I, 256–57, Long, *Nothing Too Daring*, 98–100.
17. Theodore Roosevelt, *The Naval War of 1812*, 165.
18. Thomas H. Benton, *Thirty Years' View: of, A History of the*

Workings of American Government for Thirty Years, from 1820 to 1850, II, 498.

19. Washington Irving, *The Works of Washington Irving*, VIII, 101–2.

20. David Porter, *Journal*, 1822, II, 3–4.

21. Ibid., II, 3.

22. Ibid., II, 66–67, 129.

23. Ibid., II, 75.

24. Ibid., 1815, II, 62–63. William Gifford, "Review of Porter's Cruize [*sic*] in the Pacific Ocean," *The Quarterly Review*, XIII (July 1815), 383. For instance, Porter in his 1815 *Journal*, I, 114–15, wrote: "A Chilean lady would sooner be caught in bed with a gentleman that be seen walking arm in arm with him. . . ." In his 1822 edition, I, 105–6, he changed it to a much more genteel "would consider it a high indecorum to be seen walking."

25. David Porter, *Journal*, 1815, II, 30–52.

26. Ibid., II, 90–111.

27. Ibid., II, 102–3.

28. Ibid., II, 80–82.

29. Irving Brant, *James Madison, Commander in Chief, 1812–1836*, 275.

30. *Independent Chronicle*, Boston, 13 July 1814.

31. E. L. Beach, "The Pioneer of America's Pacific Empire: David Porter," U.S. Naval Institute *Proceedings*, XXIV (June 1908), 561–62.

32. *Salem Gazette* (Massachusetts), 19 July 1814.

33. J. C. Furnas, *The Anatomy of Paradise: Hawaii and the Islands of the South Seas*, 246.

34. David Porter, *Journal*, 1815, II, 140.

35. Charles L. Lewis, *David Glasgow Farragut: Admiral in the Making*, 324, n. 18.

36. Long, *Nothing Too Daring*, 92.

37. Ibid., 102.

38. Ibid.

39. Ibid., 142.

40. David Porter, *Journal*, 1822, II, 144–46.

41. Ibid., II, 171.

42. Ibid., II, 164.

43. David Porter to Secretary of the Navy, 4 April 1814, Captains' Letters. Long guns and carronades made up the largest naval ordnance of that day. The former had a range of up to three miles but were seldom accurate over a mile. Carronades, named after the river Carron in Scotland on the banks of which they were first manufactured,

were short-ranged, and lighter, having a tremendous shattering effect at close quarters, and more of them could be carried without straining the decks. That is the main reason why almost all men-of-war bore more guns than their design number; the *Constitution*, for example, labeled a 44-gun frigate, usually carried about 55. To his credit, Porter, before he had sailed in the *Essex* for the Pacific, protested most bitterly when many of his long guns were replaced with carronades, forecasting with remarkable accuracy exactly what would happen to him in consequence at Valparaiso.

44. David Porter, *Journal*, 1822, 164–68; Hillyar's Official Report in *The Morning Chronicle* (London), 6 July 1814.

45. Long, *Nothing Too Daring*, 162–70.

46. David Porter to Secretary of the Navy, 4 April 1814.

47. *Independent Chronicle*, 11 July 1814.

48. Charles H. Snider, Jr., *The Glorious "Shannon's" Old Blue Duster and Other Faded Flags of Fadeless Fame*, 174.

49. David Porter to Secretary of the Navy, 21 February 1815, Captains' Letters.

50. A. B. Cole, ed., "Captain David Porter's Proposed Expedition to the Pacific and Japan, 1815," *Pacific Historical Review*, IX (1940), 61–65.

51. David Dixon Porter, *Memoir*, 268.

52. David F. Long, *Ready to Hazard: A Biography of Commodore William Bainbridge*, 262–69.

53. Long, *Nothing Too Daring*, 189–94.

54. Ibid., 194–96.

55. Ibid., 200–202.

56. Ibid., 180–83.

57. *Niles' Weekly Register*, 19 April 1823, XXIV, 98.

58. Long, *Sailor-Diplomat*, 96–100.

59. Richard S. West, Jr., *The Second Admiral: A Life of David Dixon Porter, 1813–1891*, 11.

60. Long, *Nothing Too Daring*, 210–16.

61. Ibid., 217–27.

62. David Porter to Secretary of the Navy, 15 November 1824, Captains' Letters.

63. J. Q. Adams, 24 December 1824, *Memoirs: Comprising Portions of His Diary 1795 to 1848*, VI, 453–54.

64. "Charges and Specifications Against David Porter," 7 July 1825, David Porter Court-Martial, R.G. 125: Records of the Office of the Judge Advocate General (Navy), Records of General Courts-Martial and Courts of Inquiry of the Navy Department, 1799–1867. Porter was succeeded in command of the West India Squadron by

Commodore Lewis Warrington, who, receiving permission from Spanish officialdom to chase pirates inland and enjoying excellent cooperation from the Royal Navy, had eradicated buccaneering in the Gulf of Mexico and the Caribbean by the end of 1826.

65. Archibald D. Turnbull, *Commodore David Porter, 1780–1843*, 278.

66. Long, *Nothing Too Daring*, 254–55.

67. Court-Martial Verdict, 10 August 1825, David Porter Court-Martial.

68. Evalina Porter to press, no date, David Porter Papers, Van Ness Collection, Owings Mills, Md.

69. Long, *Nothing Too Daring*, 254–55.

70. James Monroe, "Rough Notes," 18 July 1825, James Monroe Papers, Series I, XXXIV; James Monroe, "Deposition in answer to the queries of David Porter's court-martial," 25 July 1825, David Porter Court-Martial.

71. David Dixon Porter, *Memoir*, 343.

72. David Porter to Evalina Porter, 11 November 1826, David Porter Papers.

73. David Porter to David Glasgow Farragut, 20 June 1835, in Lewis, *Farragut*, 204–5.

74. David Porter to Mahlon Dickerson, 9 October 1829, Mahlon Dickerson Papers, New Jersey Historical Society, New Brunswick, N.J.

75. Secretary of State to David Porter, 22 September 1841, R.G. 59: Diplomatic Instructions, Turkey, National Archives.

76. David Porter to David Farragut, 20 June 1835; Lewis, *Farragut*, 204–20.

STEPHEN DECATUR: HEROIC IDEAL OF THE YOUNG NAVY

BY JOHN H. SCHROEDER

When Stephen Decatur died in 1820, John Quincy Adams mourned the nation's loss of a hero "who has illustrated its history and given grace and dignity to its character in the eyes of the world." His spirit, noted the Secretary of State, was "as kindly, as generous, and as dauntless as breathed in this nation, or on this earth."[1] Coming as they did from such a critical judge of character as Adams, these remarks reflected the tremendous impact that Decatur had made on his generation. His career had combined stirring military exploits, providential good fortune, and exemplary personal attributes in a manner that captured the imagination of his countrymen. In an era of military heroes, Decatur was the most heroic naval figure of his day. Congress, Presidents, and public officials praised him. Banquets, speeches, toasts, and poetic verses celebrated his achievements. Gifts, awards, and mementoes flowed from grateful countrymen.

From the time of his birth in 1779, Stephen Decatur, Jr., seemed destined for a nautical career. Of maritime stock, he was born near the sea and grew up in a seafaring environment. His paternal grandfather had served in the French navy and migrated via the West Indies to Newport, Rhode Island, where he married an American in 1751. Their son Stephen was born the following year shortly before the family moved to Philadelphia, where he spent his childhood, became a ship master, and married Ann Pine in 1774. During the Revolution, Stephen, Sr., commanded several American privateers, made numerous captures, and collected a considerable amount of prize money. In the meantime, Mrs. Decatur had left Philadelphia during the British occupation and moved to Sinepuxent on the East-

Stephen Decatur. Courtesy of the Smithsonian Institution.

ern Shore of Maryland, where she gave birth to Stephen, Jr., on January 5, 1779. After the Revolution, Stephen, Sr., returned to Philadelphia, commanded merchant ships for the shipping firm of Gurney and Smith, and became part owner with his business associates of the merchant vessels *Pennsylvania* and *Ariel*.[2]

Stephen, Jr., and his younger brother, James, enjoyed a pleasant and typical childhood in Philadelphia. When Stephen was eight, his father took him on a voyage to Europe to help him recover from an attack of whooping cough. That voyage seems to have imparted a strong desire in the boy for a career as a ship captain. But his mother objected to additional cruises, and he spent his next few years as a student at the Protestant Episcopal Academy, where his classmates included Richard Rush and future naval officers Richard Somers and Charles Stewart. Although Decatur later entered the University of Pennsylvania, he was indifferent to academic study and remained only a year before accepting a position as a clerk for Gurney and Smith. In addition to its commercial activities, the firm also built ships and served as the naval agent in Philadelphia. When Congress authorized construction of three frigates for the new Navy, the firm contracted to build the 44-gun *United States*. Decatur, whose pastime was the construction, sparring, and rigging of miniature ships, was sent to New Jersey to supervise the getting out of the keel pieces for the new warship and was on board when the *United States* was launched on July 10, 1797. Fortuitously, Decatur had played a minor role in the construction and the launching of a ship that would carry him to a great triumph fifteen years later.[3]

In the midst of a worsening diplomatic crisis with France in 1798, Decatur received his warrant as a midshipman in the U.S. Navy. The commission was obtained and delivered by Captain John Barry, a close friend of the family and the commander of the *United States*. In the process of supervising construction of the frigate, Barry had been impressed with young Decatur's desire to become a naval officer. Understanding the family's opposition, he did not consult them before obtaining the warrant. Stephen's mother withdrew her objections when Barry arrived in person to deliver it.[4]

Decatur was fortunate to be assigned to the *United States* and to serve under Barry, who, as one of the most distinguished naval officers of the Revolution, provided excellent tutelage for the young officer. During the undeclared naval war with France, Decatur participated in a number of cruises on board the *United States* and one on board the brig *Norfolk*. Although these cruises provided excellent experience and resulted in the capture of several French prizes, the *United States* did not engage in any major naval action. Rather it was his father who distinguished himself by volunteering for action, commanding the *Delaware*, and capturing the French schooner *Crovable* as well as several other prizes. Later, the senior Decatur commanded the frigate *Philadelphia* and captured five more French privateers.

As a young officer, Decatur advanced quickly. He became a lieutenant in 1799, a first lieutenant in 1801, and received his first command in 1803. From the outset, Decatur distinquished himself as a resourceful, able, and courageous officer and impressed others as a likable and exceptionally promising individual. A handsome, athletic man at five foot ten, he was a striking figure. Another officer later remembered Decatur's "peculiarity of manner and appearance . . . I had often pictured myself the form and look of a hero, such as my favorite Homer had delineated; here I saw it embodied."[5]

During these early years, Decatur also demonstrated an acute sense of honor, and this sensitivity to various slights involving him in several affairs of honor as either principal or second. In 1799, the first mate of a merchant ship insulted Decatur and the Navy when the young officer came to collect several seamen who had enlisted in the Navy and later signed on with the merchant ship. Decatur held his temper and left with his enlistees, but later demanded an apology after discussing the matter with his father. When the mate refused to apologize, Decatur challenged the man to a duel and used his excellent marksmanship to wound rather than kill the offender, thus exonerating his own personal honor and courage.

Several years later in the Mediterranean, Decatur served as the second for Midshipman Joseph Bainbridge in a controversial duel with an Englishman who was the secretary to the British governor of Malta. After a scuffle in a theater, the Englishman, who was an experienced duelist, challenged Midshipman Bainbridge. Decatur agreed to serve as a second, but insisted on a distance of only four paces because of Bainbridge's inexperience in duels. When Bainbridge killed the Englishman in the confrontation, the governor objected to the affair and demanded that the two American naval officers be tried in civil court for murder. Commodore Richard V. Morris responded by sending both officers home as passengers on board the *Chesapeake*.

In spite of this potentially damaging incident, Decatur received command of the brig *Argus* and returned to the Mediterranean in late 1803. By the beginning of 1804, Decatur commanded the schooner *Enterprise*, a part of Commodore Edward Preble's naval squadron waging war against Tripoli. The young republic's problems with Tripoli and the other Barbary states dated back to the 1780s when the rulers of these states began to demand tribute from the newly independent United States. The Barbary powers had long preyed on merchant ships plying the Mediterranean trade. If a nation paid tribute, its ships were unhindered. If not, the Barbary corsairs captured merchant vessels and held their crews for ransom. For various reasons, the major naval powers of Europe usually preferred to pay tribute rather than attempt to destroy the Barbary corsairs and impose peace on their rulers.[6]

Initially, the United States signed treaties with each of the four states and continued to pay tribute during the 1790s. Humiliating to the young republic, these agreements reflected American naval weakness in the Mediterranean. When the Pasha of Tripoli demanded increased tribute and declared war against the United States in 1801, the Jefferson administration decided to retaliate and sent a naval squadron to the Mediterranean. For two years, the successive commands of Commodores Richard Dale and Richard V. Morris proved ineffective. Although American naval vessels blockaded Tripoli, captured a number of ships, and scored several victories, their efforts were inconsistent and did not bring Tripoli to terms.

In September 1803, the Navy Department appointed Commodore Edward Preble to command the squadron in the Mediterranean. Although he ranked low in the Navy's list of captains, Preble proved an excellent choice. He was a tough commander known for his foul temper and iron discipline, but he was also an energetic officer determined to prosecute the war vigorously, a quality that his younger officers understood and revered in him. His initial squadron in the Mediterranean consisted of six warships, all commanded by officers under thirty years of age, a group that became known as "Preble's Boys."[7]

Shortly after taking command, Preble suffered a serious setback when the Tripolitans captured the 36-gun frigate *Philadelphia* on 31 October 1803. Under the command of Captain William Bainbridge, the *Philadelphia* had been blockading the port of Tripoli when she ran aground on uncharted rocks in the harbor while pursuing a Tripolitan ship. All attempts to free the American warship failed, and Captain Bainbridge finally surrendered after a four-hour gunboat attack. Two days later, the Tripolitans used a high tide to refloat the *Philadelphia*, recovered her guns, and moved the frigate into the harbor within range of their forts. In one stroke, the Bey had gained a powerful frigate to bolster his defenses as well as 307 captives who could be held for large ransom. When news of the disaster spread, the idea of recapturing or destroying the ship surfaced immediately. From captivity, Captain Bainbridge also suggested the idea in a letter written in lemon juice, which was invisible until subject to heat. Lieutenant Decatur offered to lead such an expedition, as did Lieutenant Charles Stewart. The *Philadelphia* held special significance for Decatur because she had been built and paid for by the citizens of Philadelphia and commanded in the naval war against France by Decatur's father. After the *Enterprise*, commanded by Decatur, captured the Tripolitan ketch *Mastico*, Commodore Preble decided to risk the plan and selected Decatur to lead the mission. The captured vessel offered an ideal means of entering the enemy harbor and approaching the *Philadelphia* without alarm.[8]

On 31 January 1804, Preble ordered Decatur to collect a force of seventy-five men and proceed in the captured ketch, renamed the *Intrepid*, to Tripoli in the company of the *Siren*. Decatur's party was then to "enter that harbor in the night, board the *Philadelphia*, burn her and make good your retreat in the *Intrepid*, if possible, unless you can make her the means of destroying the enemy's vessels in the harbor, by converting her into a fire-ship for that purpose . . . ." Preble's instructions did not provide the option of recapturing and escaping with the *Philadelphia* from Tripoli. Although Decatur's orders were simple, the task he faced was difficult and dangerous. The *Philadelphia* was fully armed, well manned, and anchored within range of more than one hundred shore guns as well as Tripolitan gunboats in the harbor.[9]

Decatur selected volunteers for his force and set sail in early February. After a two-week passage delayed by bad weather, the *Intrepid* entered the harbor on the evening of 16 February. Sicilian Salvatore Catalano piloted the ship to avoid suspicion while the American crew were either dressed as Maltese or concealed. When they approached the *Philadelphia* and were hailed, Catalano replied that the ship was Maltese, and had lost her anchors in a recent storm, and sought permission to moor alongside the frigate for the night. Once the request was granted, a line was attached, and the concealed Americans began to haul the small ship toward the frigate. Not until the *Intrepid* was alongside the *Philadelphia* did the Tripolitans realize the ruse and shout an alarm. However, within five minutes, the Americans, using no firearms, secured the ship from the startled enemy. Twenty Tripolitans died, one was taken prisoner, and the remainder were driven overboard in the attack. The Americans then set the ship on fire and returned to the *Intrepid*, escaping from the harbor under fire from Tripolitan gunboats and shore batteries. In the attack, the *Intrepid* suffered only minor damage; no American was killed, and only one man was injured slightly. The courageous Decatur had been the second man to board and the last to leave the *Philadelphia*.[10]

The news of Decatur's triumph delighted Commodore Preble, who had written to the Secretary of the Navy only a short time before emphasizing that the *Philadelphia* had to be destroyed, but that the mission would "undoubtedly cost many lives . . . ." Now almost miraculously Decatur had returned, the *Philadelphia* had been destroyed, and not a single American life had been lost. Preble immediately wrote to the Secretary praising Decatur's achievement and recommending his "instantaneous promotion to the rank of post captain . . . ."[11] And no less a figure than Lord Nelson termed the feat "the most bold and daring act of the age." In May 1804, Secretary of the Navy Robert Smith conveyed President Jefferson's special thanks and promoted Decatur to the rank of post captain, making him the youngest captain in American naval history. At the same time, the President praised Decatur in a presidential message, and Congress passed a resolution lauding the men of the *Intrepid*, authorizing presentation of a sword to Decatur, and approving two months of extra pay to each man on the mission.[12]

Meanwhile, Preble had imposed a blockade on Tripoli, and in August 1804 he began a series of naval attacks on the city. In the first of these actions, Stephen Decatur commanded one of the two squadrons of attacking gunboats while his younger brother James, a lieutenant, commanded a gunboat in the other squadron. Decatur was towing a captured Tripolitan gunboat out of the harbor when he learned that James had been killed by a Tripolitan commander who had first surrendered and then shot the young lieutenant when he boarded the vessel. Accompanied by ten men, Stephen Decatur sought out and boarded the suspected enemy gunboat. In fierce hand-to-hand fighting, Decatur almost lost his own life before he finally shot and killed the enemy commander. Decatur had been saved only by the selfless action of a devoted sailor, who blocked a blow directed at Decatur with his own head, thereby suffering a serious injury. In the fighting, all twenty-four Tripolitans were either killed or wounded while the Americans suffered only four wounded. Although Decatur was exhilarated by these combat missions, the death of his brother and the subsequent loss of boyhood friend Lieutenant Richard Somers tempered much of his excitement.[13]

Shortly after these events, Decatur received notification of his promotion and assumed command of the *Constitution* and then the *Congress* in November 1804. After a peace treaty was concluded with Tripoli in June, 1805, Decatur returned to Hampton Roads in the *Congress*. There he received a hero's welcome and in the process met his future wife, Miss Susan Wheeler, the daughter of a wealthy merchant who was the mayor of Norfolk. During 1805 and 1806, Decatur was feted and honored on a number of occasions, including a banquet in Philadelphia during which his father commemorated the contribution of his two sons with the moving toast, "Our children are the property of their country."[14]

In the next several years, Decatur's career continued to advance as he performed various duties close to home. In addition to supervising construction of new Jeffersonian gunboats and commanding the Gosport naval yard, Decatur took command of the frigate *United States* in 1810 and helped protect American shipping by cruising along the coast. Although he hoped to be excused from serving,

Battle between American and Tripolitan gunboats (top). Decatur attacking Tripolitan gunboat (bottom). The contemporary woodcut at the top shows the gunboats of the era and Decatur at the point of attack in Tripoli Harbor. The lower painting depicts the vicious hand-to-hand battle. Decatur is pictured in the lower right locked in mortal combat. Courtesy of Naval Historical Foundation.

Decatur was a member of the court-martial that suspended Captain James Barron for five years for his role in the *Chesapeake–Leopard* affair in June 1807. The court found Barron guilty of not clearing his ship for action once the American officer had received the British ultimatum to relinquish the alleged British deserters on board. Thus had been sown the seeds of a quarrel that would surface more than a decade later, with tragic consequences. In contrast to the findings of the Barron court-martial, Decatur presided over an 1811 court of inquiry that completely exonerated Commodore John Rodgers for his role as commander of the *President* in the near destruction of the smaller British *Little Belt* in May of that year.

When Congress declared war on England in June 1812, Commodore John Rodgers had already prepared his five-ship squadron for action and was able to sail from New York within days. The squadron, which included Decatur's *United States*, sailed in pursuit of a large British merchant convoy but experienced a disappointing cruise, capturing only a few British vessels. A few weeks later, the squadron returned to Boston where it was reorganized into three small units under the commands of Rodgers, Bainbridge, and Decatur. Although Decatur's squadron consisted of the *United States* and the *Argus*, the two ships separated after sailing from Boston in October.

Dispersal of the Navy's few warships very much reflected Decatur's own strategic analysis of the manner in which the naval war should be conducted. To counter Britain's huge navy, the United States had only sixteen warships in 1812, eight of them frigates. Like most of his naval colleagues, Decatur feared that the British navy would either destroy or blockade the small U.S. Navy if the United States concentrated its warships in one squadron or based them in one or two ports. Instead, Decatur believed that the American frigates should be fully provisioned and dispatched individually or in pairs without specific instructions as to their cruising grounds. Relying on the situation at hand as well as their good judgment and initiative, American naval commanders could then harass and raid British commerce around the globe. American attacks on British commerce worldwide would force the British, in turn, to disperse their own naval forces along their farflung shipping lanes and thereby diminish British naval power in American waters. Although the potential efficacy of this strategy was exaggerated, the size of the U.S. Navy left the nation's military leaders few other options.[15]

After separating from the *Argus*, the *United States* sailed eastward and by the end of October was cruising between the Azores and the Canary Islands. In the early morning of 25 October 1812, Decatur's crew spotted an approaching ship which proved to be the British frigate *Macedonian* commanded by Captain John Carden. Ironically, Decatur and Carden had met before the war and discussed the comparative merits of their two ships. Although the *United States* was larger and carried more heavy guns, Carden argued that the *Macedonian* would win an encounter because she had a battle-tested crew and her smaller 18-pound guns could be handled more rapidly and effectively than the 24-pounders of the *United States*. In addition, the American frigate was known to be a poor sailer and was supposedly much less maneuverable than the *Macedonian*.[16]

In the battle that settled this argument, Carden enjoyed the wind advantage, but he apparently mistook the *United States* for the smaller American frigate *Essex*, which would have given him a marked advantage in long-range heavy guns. As a result, the British captain kept his distance and unwittingly played into Decatur's own tactics. With superior firepower, Decatur and his well-drilled gun crews capitalized fully and directed a destructive bombardment at the *Macedonian*. At one point, the firing of the American 24-pounders became so rapid that the British mistook the solid sheet of flames for a fire on board the *United States*. Decatur's superior seamanship prevented Carden from using his smaller guns effectively throughout the battle or later from closing to board the *United States*. Finally with his masts destroyed, his guns disabled, and his decks a scene of carnage, Carden was forced to surrender. Of her 301-man crew, the *Macedonian* had lost 104 killed or wounded while the *United States* had lost seven dead and five wounded, and suffered only minor damage.[17]

Not wishing to risk losing his prize should he meet a superior enemy, Decatur decided to return to New London, arriving there on 4 December 1812. In the following weeks, Decatur and his crew were honored by a round of celebrations. The legislatures of Massachusetts, New York, Maryland, Pennsylvania, and Virginia expressed their appreciation, as did official bodies in the cities of New London, New York, Philadelphia, and Savannah.

During 1813, the British responded to the loss of several warships by tightening their blockade of the Atlantic coast and hampering American naval efforts. In New York, the blockade posed a serious problem for Decatur, who, despite his best efforts, was unable to escape with his squadron. In 1814, the Navy Department transferred Decatur to command of the frigate *President*, but he still did not return to sea. During the summer of 1814, the British offensive in Chesapeake Bay and the capture of Washington, D.C., created fears that the British might also attack Philadelphia or New York. In response, the Navy Department ordered Decatur to postpone a cruise in the *President* and to take charge of the naval defenses of New York.

After it became apparent that no British attack on New York was imminent, Decatur proposed an extended cruise against British commerce. With a squadron consisting of the *President* and the sloops *Peacock* and *Hornet*, Decatur would raid British commerce in either the area east of Bermuda or the Bay of Bengal. The Navy selected the latter plan, and Decatur again attempted to slip through the British blockade. On the evening of 14 January 1815, the *President* sailed past Sandy Hook in high winds, but ran aground in the process. Nearly two hours of heavy pounding damaged the *President* and seriously impaired her sailing speed. Unable to return to port because of strong westerly winds, Decatur sailed fifty miles along the Long Island coast in an effort to elude the British. Early the next morning, she encountered a British force of four warships, and a chase ensued with the British frigate *Endymion* closing to firing range by late afternoon. Decatur's plan of boarding and capturing the enemy frigate was foiled as the *Endymion* maintained a safe distance; the two ships exchanged shots and the British ship was forced to retire with damage. Because the presence of the British warships precluded any attempt to capture the *Endymion*, Decatur made a last attempt to escape, but his efforts failed. He was unable to elude the enemy, and finally forced to surrender after two British frigates began to bombard the *President*. In the battle, the Americans lost twenty-four killed and fifty-five wounded, or more than twice the casualties of the British.[18]

Although some naval historians have contended that Decatur might have seriously damaged one or both of the British frigates had he not surrendered prematurely, his countrymen and his naval peers did not question his performance or his courage. Decatur returned to the United States shortly after word of the Treaty of Ghent arrived and was received as a hero in both New London and New York. In April 1815, a naval court of inquiry exonerated Decatur and praised him for his command of the *President*. The court found that misplaced beacon boats had caused the *President* to run aground and sustain damages that eventually led to her capture. Denying that different tactics might have produced success, the court concluded that Decatur had adopted the "proper measures" and made "every possible effort to escape." Moreover, the court considered "the management of the *President*, from the time the chase commenced till her surrender, as the highest evidence of the experience, skill, and resources of her commander, and of the ability and seamanship of her officers and crew." Noting that the *Endymion* had been disabled and would have been captured had other British warships not been present, the court asserted that "In this unequal conflict the enemy gained a ship, but the victory was ours."[19] On 20 April, Secretary of the Navy B. W. Crowninshield conveyed to Decatur the approbation of the President and the Navy Department for "brilliant actions [which] have raised the national honor and fame even in the moment of surrendering your ship to an enemy's squadron of vastly superior force, over whose attack, singly, you were decidedly triumphant . . . ."[20] In the meantime, the Navy Department also signified its high opinion of Decatur by offering him his choice of positions.

Relations with Algiers had deteriorated during the war with England as the Dey demanded additional tribute in 1812 and then captured the brig *Edwin* and enslaved her crew. Only the fact that few American merchant ships plied the Mediterranean during the war prevented more ship seizures. In response, Congress approved President James Madison's request in March 1815 for measures against Algiers. Decatur was selected to command the first of two naval squadrons to be sent to the area, and accepted on the condition that he could return to the United States immediately upon the arrival of the second squadron, which was to be commanded by his senior, Commodore William Bainbridge.

On 20 May, Decatur sailed from New York in the *Guerriere*, and on 15 June reached Gibraltar with a squadron of nine American warships. He immediately sailed in pursuit of an Algerian naval squadron that was rumored to be in the area under the command of Admiral Reis Hammida. On 17 June, the American squadron captured the 46-gun Algerian frigate *Mashuda* and killed the admiral in battle. In addition, thirty other Algerians were killed and more than 400 taken captive. Two days later, the American brig *Epervier* ran the 22-gun *Estedia* aground and captured her. In this encounter, another twenty-three Algerians died, and eighty were taken prisoner.

Decatur then proceeded to Algiers, where he and American Consul-General William Shaler opened negotiations through the Swedish consul on 28 June. Decatur, whose military reputation was well known throughout the region, informed the Algerians of their naval losses and delivered a letter from President Madison that offered the Dey a choice of either peace on terms of equality or war. Decatur and Shaler added a note emphasizing that the terms of any settlement must be based on perfect equality between the two nations, inclusion of the most-favored-nation principle, and an end to the payment of any form of tribute to the Dey. In addition, the Americans refused to accept a temporary truce during the negotiations and insisted that the negotiations be concluded on board the *Guerriere* rather than on shore. The following day, the Algerians agreed to discuss the model treaty presented by the Americans which ended all forms of tribute, provided for the return of all prisoners without the payment of any ransom, and specified that the Dey would pay $10,000 plus a quantity of cotton to idemnify Americans for their losses. In addition, the treaty included a most-favored-nation clause and provided that captives taken in future wars were to be treated as prisoners of war, not slaves. Although he refused to return the captured Algerian ships to the Dey as part of the treaty, Decatur agreed to restore them to Algiers as a gift to the Dey.[21]

When the Algerians pleaded for a temporary truce to make final arrangements, Decatur refused and set off in pursuit of an approaching Algerian cruiser. In the face of such pressure, the Algerians quickly agreed to final terms and returned within a matter of hours to the American squadron with the signed treaty as well as all ten American prisoners. On that same day, 30 June 1815, Consul-General Shaler was received on shore with full honors. Only two weeks after sailing into the Mediterranean, Decatur had, in less than forty-eight hours, concluded a landmark agreement with one of the Barbary states.

Decatur's remarkable success can be attributed in large part to the size of his squadron and the commodore's experience in the Mediterranean. Although negotiations moved with alacrity and the Algerians proved most cooperative, Decatur harbored no illusions about his adversary's motives. In his report to Secretary of the Navy Crowninshield, Decatur noted that the treaty "had been dictated at the mouth of the cannon, has been conceded to the losses which Algiers has sustained, and to the dread of still greater evils apprehended." Decatur added that "the presence of a respectable naval force in his sea will be the only certain guarantee for its observance."[22]

From Algiers, Decatur sailed to Tunis. There he exacted an indemnity of $46,000 for two American merchant ships that Tunis had permitted British men-of-war to capture in the harbor of Tunis during the recent war. Then Decatur proceeded to Tripoli in early August where he imposed a similar indemnity of $25,000 and insisted that ten Christian slaves be released. After sailing through the Mediterranean, Decatur touched at Gibraltar and met the second squadron, returning to New York on 12 November 1815.[23]

As on previous occasions, Decatur's successes in the Mediterranean in 1815 produced a new round of honors and celebrations. Secretary of State James Monroe commended Decatur, and President Madison praised his achievements in a December 1815 message to

Congress. Congress also expressed its appreciation by appropriating $100,000 to indemnify Decatur and his crew for the losses they sustained when the Algerian prizes were returned to the Dey. In 1815 and 1816, Decatur again enjoyed a series of banquets, speeches, and toasts. It was during a banquet in Norfolk, in April 1816, that he added to his legend by uttering his famous toast: "Our Country. In her intercourse with foreign nations, may she always be in the right, but our country, right or wrong." Although long criticized in some circles as a dangerous expression of patriotic duty, Decatur's adage subsequently became a virtual motto of the Navy.[24]

When the retirement of Isaac Hull created a vacancy on the three-man Board of Navy Commissioners, Secretary of the Navy Crowninshield selected Decatur for the prestigious position. With the board located in Washington, Decatur and his wife settled there, bought a home, and then built a mansion facing Lafayette Park across from the White House. In their new residence, Decatur and his wife soon assumed a prominent social role in the official life of the capital. To his new position, Decatur brought the same talent and energy he had shown in his previous commands at sea. In its role of providing professional expertise to the Secretary of the Navy, the board played an active administrative role in the construction of warships, the development of ordnance, the purchase of naval supplies, the creation of numerous regulations, and the supervision of various sensitive personnel matters. The commissioners also provided important advice on strategic questions, as in 1817 when Decatur submitted a report on the best site for a naval depot within Chesapeake Bay and the best means of defending the bay by the use of stationary batteries.[25] The department largely adopted Decatur's recommendations. Although he much preferred the challenge of active sea duty in wartime, Decatur seems to have been relatively content during these postwar years and might have maintained his style of life, had not a tragic duel ended his life prematurely.

The origins of the affair dated back to the *Chesapeake–Leonard* incident and to Decatur's service on the subsequent court-martial that suspended Captain James Barron for five years for neglecting to clear the *Chesapeake* for action once he had received the British captain's ultimatum. Barron subsequently served as a merchant ship master and was out of the country when the War of 1812 began. After his suspension ended in 1813, Barron requested reinstatement to active duty but did not return to the United States. Although the Navy Department placed Barron on half pay as an officer on leave, it did not reinstate him because of additional incriminating charges that another naval officer had levied against Barron in the *Chesapeake* incident. Here the matter stood until Barron returned to the United States near the end of 1818 and applied in person to Secretary of the Navy Smith Thompson for restoration the following February. When these efforts failed, an increasingly embittered Barron blamed Decatur for their failure. As a navy commissioner, Decatur had actively opposed Barron's reinstatement because of his conduct since the *Chesapeake* affair. Moreover, Decatur had stated his position in an outspoken and vigorous manner a number of times.[26]

After he received reports of these statements, Barron, encouraged by other officers who were resentful of Decatur, opened an extended correspondence with his adversary. He began by accusing Decatur of insulting his honor as a naval officer. In the ensuing exchange, which lasted over seven months, Decatur denied that he had any "personal differences" with Barron but admitted that he had openly opposed Barron's reinstatement because his "conduct as an officer since the affair of the *Chesapeake*, has been such as ought to forever bar your readmission in the service . . . . In speaking thus, and endeavoring to prevent your readmission, I conceive I was performing a duty I owe to the service; that I was contributing to the preservation of its respectability." Although he had not actually insulted Barron, Decatur's strong opinions, sense of honor, and standards of conduct led Decatur to assume a position that, while technically correct, did not help avoid a duel. The friction between Barron and Decatur was compounded by the role of Captain Jesse D. Elliott, who resented Decatur's support of Captain Oliver Hazard Perry in a quarrel with Elliott over the latter's role in the Battle of Erie. At any rate, Elliott apparently falsely reported Decatur's remarks to Barron and encouraged him to call Decatur to the field of honor.[27]

Finally, in January 1820, Barron issued the challenge, which Decatur promptly accepted. After arrangements were made by Commodore William Bainbridge and Elliott, acting as seconds for Decatur and Barron, respectively, the two antagonists met at Bladensburg, Maryland, on 22 March 1820. Firing from a distance of eight paces, Barron was wounded in the hip and Decatur mortally wounded in the hip and abdomen. Decatur was carried back to his home, where he lingered briefly but died that same evening.[28]

News of Decatur's death stunned the capital. The nation's loss of a beloved hero created an outpouring of grief as Congress adjourned on the day of his funeral. The services were attended by all of official Washington, including the President and the Chief Justice. With full honors, Stephen Decatur, Jr., dead at age forty-one, was buried at Kalorama, the estate of a close friend in Washington.

During a relatively brief naval career, Stephen Decatur was a central figure in a series of naval actions that elevated him to the stature of an authentic national hero. His role in the destruction of the *Philadelphia* captured the imagination of a nation frustrated by months of indecisive activity in the Mediterranean and the recent loss of an American frigate to Tripoli. Decatur's immediate avenging of his brother's death in hand-to-hand fighting embellished his reputation for personal valor. In 1812, the defeat and capture of the *Macedonian* by the *United States* fueled national pride in the Navy and reaffirmed Decatur's exceptional seamanship. In 1815, the dramatic successes of Decatur's naval squadron in the Mediterranean further enhanced both Decatur's stature and the republic's confidence in the months after the War of 1812. Even the surrender of the *President* to the British in January 1815 did not diminish Decatur's legendary heroism, because of the skillfull manner in which he commanded his damaged frigate against a numerically superior force. In a young republic with only a brief military history, Decatur's were daring exploits indeed.

Of particular significance in these triumphs were Decatur's flawless character and exceptional personal qualities, which seemed to make these achievements possible. As with other military heroes, fortune placed Decatur at the right place at the right time. But in each instance, Decatur's own attributes allowed him to overcome difficult obstacles and achieve victory where lesser men would have failed. With Decatur, a rare combination of courage, resourcefulness, determination, kindness, and judgment produced an exceptional leader revered by his men. Even when he failed and had to surrender the *President*, naval peers and contemporaries agreed that his superior talents had brought him close to success and only very bad luck had prevented his escape. In this *Life of Stephen Decatur* published in 1846, naval officer Alexander Slidell Mackenzie summarized those qualities that made Decatur such an appealing figure to nineteenth-century Americans:

> The fortune of Decatur, like that of Caesar, was dependent mainly upon himself, upon the happy ascendancy within him of the qualities essential to success, of a spirit prone to hardy enterprise, and accurate judgment . . . upon a steady confidence in his own intrepidity and force of character . . . upon his own matchless courage and prowess; upon his celerity of thought and action; and upon that imperturbable calmness of temper which left him, in critical situations, master of himself, of others, and of events.[29]

In addition to these personal characteristics, Decatur manifested an intense sense of honor, a passion for glory, and a love of country.

In an age that romanticized such values, Decatur stood as an exemplary military figure to be emulated and a patriot to be idolized.

Embellishing the Decatur legend were a number of coincidences and fortuitous events that seemed to verify his providential destiny. The fact that the *Philadelphia* had been built by the citizens of his hometown and commanded by his father was auspicious. His role in the birth of the *United States*, which he would first serve in as a midshipman and later command against the *Macedonian*, follows this pattern. Providence also seems to have had a role in the willingness of a loyal seaman to take a blow directed at Decatur in Tripoli in 1804, as well as in Decatur's conversation with Captain John Carden prior to their battle in the War of 1812.

Still, in spite of his dramatic deeds, exemplary character, and heroic stature, historians have not accorded Decatur a place among the top rank of American naval officers. Rather his historical significance is confined largely to his individual achievements and to the high standards of conduct he set for the Navy. Although studies of the period and naval histories tend to note his exploits, they do not dwell on Decatur's importance. Moreover, Decatur has not been the subject of a serious biography in almost half a century.

Stephen Decatur's historical significance as a secondary figure is attributable to several factors. First, the luster of his valorous actions has dimmed considerably as subsequent generations of Americans have adopted new heroes and celebrated more recent military triumphs. Second, his victories tended to be in actions of limited military or strategic significance. Stirring as they were, his successes in Tripoli had little effect on the outcome of that conflict, and his capture of the *Macedonian* did not alter the strategy or the outcome of the War of 1812. His expedition to the Barbary states in 1815 occurred in a secondary diplomatic arena and only hastened the end of hostilities many thought should have been concluded long before. Third, Decatur had little long-range impact on the development of American naval policy or strategy. In fact, to the extent that he championed commerce raiding by single warships, some naval historians would consider Decatur's ideas an impediment to the development of a more realistic strategy of naval warfare.[30] At the same time, it is likely that, had he enjoyed the long career then common in the Navy, Decatur would have left his imprint on American naval development after 1820.

Finally, Decatur later came to symbolize some of the flaws as well as the positive attributes associated with the officer corps in the early Navy. His passion for military glory was widely accepted by contemporaries living in an era of romanticism, but subsequent generations have tended to be more cognizant of the dangers inherent in a quest for personal military glory. Decatur's exaggerated sense of honor and acute sensitivity to slights against himself, his uniform, and his country involved him in a series of affairs of honor and eventually led to his senseless death. Although duels over questions of honor were then common in American naval affairs, Decatur's death stirred a sharp public reaction and encouraged efforts to end the practice of dueling. By 1850, duels among American naval officers had become rare, and the Navy finally made dueling a violation of law in 1862. Clearly this highly individualized code of conduct and means of settling real or imagined personal differences had no place in a modern navy. Likewise, although Decatur's adage "Our country, right or wrong" was initially extolled in the Navy and even suggested as the official motto when the Naval Academy was established in the 1840s, his brand of unquestioning loyalty has long been criticized in nonmilitary circles as a dangerous form of false patriotism. In comparison to the character and achievements of his naval contemporaries, Decatur's shortcomings appear minor, indeed, and his illustrious record of naval combat is unsurpassed. Without peer, Decatur stands as the most exemplary naval hero of his time, and that, in and of itself, remains a considerable historical legacy.

FURTHER READING

In spite of his stature as an early American naval hero, Stephen Decatur has attracted little attention from historians in recent decades. The most authoritative biography remains Charles Lee Lewis, *The Romantic Decatur*. In this well-written and scholarly study, Lewis notes that Decatur lived in "the period of romanticism" and stands as "one of the most romantic characters in American history." Developing Decatur's life and career as a "romantic drama," Lewis concludes that his "heroic deeds, and even his untimely death, have made his the most romantic figure of his generation—the very embodiment of chivalrous patriotic youth." A popular biography is Irwin Anthony, *Decatur*, which extolls Decatur and claims that the "full facts in his case lead on to lyricism." Unfortunately, this narrative lacks critical analysis and is marred by a florid style that is imprecise and often misleading. The standard nineteenth-century biography is Alexander Slidell Mackenzie, *The Life of Stephen Decatur*. Although this biography necessarily lacks historical perspective, it details the various anecdotes, stories, and incidents that comprise the full Decatur legend, and as such is an interesting source of further reading.

Given the paucity of recent material on Decatur, those interested in further reading should consult studies dealing with the most prominent events and personalities associated with Decatur's career. Among the most noteworthy biographies treating aspects of his career are David F. Long, *Nothing Too Daring: A Biography of Commodore David Porter, 1780–1843*; Christopher McKee, *Edward Preble: A Naval Biography, 1761–1807*; and Charles O. Paullin, *Commodore John Rodgers, Captain, Commodore, and Senior Officer of the American Navy, 1773–1838*. For an excellent popular account of Decatur and his contemporaries, see Leonard F. Guttridge and Jay D. Smith, *The Commodores*.

A number of solid accounts exist on the Navy's role in the Barbary Wars. James A. Field, Jr., *America and the Mediterranean World, 1776–1882* is an extensively researched and well written study that traces the Navy's role as one of the four themes that the author develops regarding the American role in the Mediterranean. Fletcher Pratt, *Preble's Boys: Commodore Preble and the Birth of American Sea Power* and Glenn Tucker, *Dawn Like Thunder: The Barbary Wars and the Birth of the U.S. Navy* present solid accounts of the Navy and the Barbary states. For the diplomatic role of the Navy in these wars, see Charles O. Paullin, *Diplomatic Negotiations of American Naval Officers, 1778–1883*. William Shaler, who helped to negotiate the 1815 agreement with Algiers, is treated in "On the Shores of Barbary," in Roy F. Nichols, *Advance Agents of American Destiny*.

For the Navy's role in the War of 1812, the two standard studies are Alfred T. Mahan, *Sea Power in its Relation to the War of 1812* and Theodore Roosevelt, *The Naval War of 1812*. An excellent basic history is Reginald Horsman, *The War of 1812*. In addition to the accounts of the Barron–Decatur affair in the biographies of Rodgers and Porter, the duel is treated in Hamilton Cochran, *Noted American Duels and Hostile Encounters* and Don C. Seitz, *Famous American Duels*.

NOTES

1. Charles Francis Adams, ed., *Memoirs of John Quincy Adams, Comprising Portions of His Diary from 1795 to 1848*, V, 32, 36.
2. For detailed narratives of Decatur's life and career, see Charles Lee Lewis, *The Romantic Decatur* and Alexander Slidell Mackenzie, *Life of Stephen Decatur*.
3. Mackenzie, *Life of Decatur*, 17–18.
4. Lewis, *Romantic Decatur*, 19–20.
5. Remarks of Captain Robert S. Spence as quoted in Mackenzie, *Life of Decatur*, 35–36.
6. For background on American diplomatic relations with the Barbary powers, see James A. Field, Jr., *America and the Mediterra-*

nean World, 1776–1882 and Ray W. Irwin, *The Diplomatic Relations of the United States with the Barbary Powers, 1776–1816.*

7. See Christopher McKee, *Edward Preble: A Naval Biography 1761–1807.*

8. Ibid., 190–91; Mackenzie, *Life of Decatur*, 65.

9. Captain Edward Preble to Lieutenant Stephen Decatur, 31 January 1804, *Naval Documents Related to the United States Wars With the Barbary Powers*, III, 376–77. Hereafter cited as *NDBP*.

10. For descriptions of the action, see Lieutenant Stephen Decatur to Captain Edward Preble, 17 February 1804; Lieutenant Charles Stewart to Captain Edward Preble, 19 February 1804; and Captain Edward Preble to Secretary of Navy, 19 February 1804, *NDBP*, III, 414–15, 415–16, 440–41.

11. Captain Edward Preble to Secretary of Navy, 19 February 1804, *NDBP*, III, 441.

12. *Annals of Congress*, 2nd Session, 8th Congress (1804–5), 16, 17, 682–83.

13. For accounts of these actions, see Captain Edward Preble to Secretary of Navy, 18 September 1804; Narrative of Attacks on Tripoli by Richard O'Brien; and Stephen Decatur to Commodore Edward Preble, 3 August 1804, *NDBP*, IV, 293–310, 341–43, 345.

14. Mackenzie, *Life of Decatur*, 136–38.

15. Stephen Decatur to Secretary of the Navy, 8 June 1812, Captains' Letters, National Archives. On the question of strategy, see Alfred T. Mahan, *Sea Power in its Relation to the War of 1812*, I, 314–19.

16. Mackenzie, *Life of Decatur*, 156–58.

17. For Decatur's account of the battle, Stephen Decatur to Secretary of Navy, 30 October 1812, Captains' Letters; Stephen Decatur to Susan Decatur, 30 October 1812 in Mackenzie, *Life of Decatur*, 371–72. For descriptions of the battle, see Mahan, *Sea Power, 1812*, I, 416–22; Theodore Roosevelt, *The Naval War of 1812*, I, 144–55.

18. Stephen Decatur to Secretary of Navy, 18 January 1815, Captains' Letters. Also, Mahan, *Sea Power, 1812*, II, 397–403; Roosevelt, *Naval War*, II, 144–49.

19. Mahan, *Sea Power, 1812*, II, 401–3; Roosevelt, *Naval War*, II, 144–54; Report of the Court of Inquiry, 17 April 1815, *Niles' Weekly Register*, (29 April 1815) VIII, 147–48.

20. Secretary of Navy to Captain Stephen Decatur, 20 April 1815, *Niles'*, VIII, 148.

21. Stephen Decatur to Secretary of Navy, 19, 20 June and 5 July 1815, *American State Papers*, Class VI, I, 396.

22. Decatur to Secretary of Navy, 5 July 1815, ibid., I, 396. See also Charles Oscar Paullin, *Diplomatic Negotiations of American Naval Officers, 1778–1883,* 110–15; "On the Shores of Barbary," in Roy F. Nichols, *Advance Agents of American Destiny,* 113–24.

23. For correspondence that describes Decatur's activities in Tunis and Tripoli, see *State Papers,* Class VI, I, 397–99. Also, Paullin, *Diplomatic Negotiations,* 115–16.

24. Mackenzie, *Life of Decatur,* 294–96; Lewis, *Romantic Decatur,* 182–83. Also, Peter Karsten, *The Naval Aristocracy: The Golden Age of Annapolis and the Emergence of Modern American Navalism,* 194–95.

25. Stephen Decatur to Secretary of Navy, 2 January 1817 in Mackenzie, *Life of Decatur,* 386–98.

26. Lewis, *Romantic Decatur,* 201–22; Mackenzie, *Life of Decatur,* 303–34. Also, Don C. Seitz, *Famous American Duels,* 176–226.

27. The correspondence between Barron and Decatur is contained in Mackenzie, *Life of Decatur,* 398–440.

28. Lewis, *Romantic Decatur,* 223–37; Seitz, *Famous Duels,* 222–25.

29. Mackenzie, *Life of Decatur,* 350–51.

30. Harold and Margaret Sprout, *The Rise of American Naval Power,* 83–85.

JOHN RODGERS: THE STALWART CONSERVATIVE

BY K. JACK BAUER

Two men stand out as the dominant intellectual and administrative figures of the services during the first third of the nineteenth century. Both had incisive minds that probed the reaches of the professional thinking of their times. Both contributed widely to the improvement of their services, and, in both cases, their thoughts penetrated beyond the conventional. Both men looked toward philosophical concepts that would not become commonplace until late in the century. Yet both were men of their times, famed for their tempers and caustic pens. One was Brevet Lieutenant General Winfield Scott; the other, Commodore John Rodgers.

More than any of their contemporaries, Scott and Rodgers must be credited with introducing professionalism into their services. Scott did so through his training of troops, his writings, and his leadership in the post–War of 1812 army. Rodgers introduced effective systems of discipline and training for the notoriously unruly crews who drifted onto the decks of American men-of-war, and, through his leadership of the Board of Naval Commissioners, channeled the organizational energies of the Navy into the creation of a highly regarded professional force.

John Rodgers, Sr., was born in Scotland about 1726 and emigrated to America prior to 1760, the time of his marriage to Elizabeth Reynolds. The young couple settled in what is today Havre de Grace, Maryland. By the time of the Revolution Rodgers was a man of substance and a militia officer.[1] Among the couple's eight children was a son born on 11 July 1772 and named after his father.

Early in his childhood young John Rodgers was attracted to the sea, and, in 1786, he convinced his father to apprentice him to a highly respected Baltimore mariner. Between 1786 and 1791 Rodgers learned his profession in voyages to Europe and the West Indies. As often happened, he became a mate before his eighteenth birthday and a master before his twenty-first. His apprenticeship taught Rodgers the necessity of taut discipline. A mate quickly learned that only discipline, often enforced with fist, brass knuckle, belaying pin, or cat, kept a crew in line. After the formation of the Navy, many claimed that one could differentiate between those captains who came from the merchant service and those whose entire service had been in the Navy by the discipline enforced on board their ships.[2] John Rodgers carried that education with him to the grave.

In 1793 Rodgers received command of the ship *Jane* owned by Samuel and John Smith, and during the next five years he sailed her to British and French ports. He then shifted to the ship *Hope* in 1797, only to lose her to a French privateer and the L'Orient prize court. When Rodgers returned home, he received an appointment in the expanding U.S. Navy, probably through his Baltimore connections and his politician brother-in-law William Pinkney.[3]

In March 1794, because of seizures of American vessels by Algerian corsairs, Congress had authorized the construction of six frigates. Although a diplomatic settlement with the Barbary state delayed the establishment of a permanent naval force, new difficulties with France brought authorization in July 1797 to complete three vessels.[4] One was the *Constellation* (36). Her captain was Thomas Truxtun; and Rodgers, whose commission bore a 9 March 1798 date, served as first lieutenant, or executive officer.[5] The young officer could not have found a better teacher than Truxtun, who issued detailed orders that prescribed responsibilities and acceptable conduct and established a precise training routine.

At the end of 1797 Truxtun received command of a small squadron cruising in the northern Leeward Islands where, on 9 February 1798, the *Constellation* overpowered the French frigate *L'Insurgente* (36). During the action Rodgers commanded a section of main deck guns and led the eleven-man boarding party that took charge of the prize. Before Rodgers and his men could complete the transfer of the French crew to the *Constellation*, the wind rose, and it was two days before the vessels could resume the transfer. With the boarding party outnumbered thirteen to one by the remaining Frenchman, Rodgers had the prisoners collected in the lower deck and placed sentries at the companion hatches to shoot anyone attempting to climb up.[6]

Truxtun gave Rodgers temporary command of the prize and sought to have him promoted to permanent command, but Rodgers held the post for only about three months because Secretary of the Navy

John Rodgers. Courtesy of the Naval Historical Center.

Benjamin Stoddert ruled that he was too junior to command a frigate.[7] Rodgers was promoted to captain on 5 March and, shortly thereafter, assumed command of the sloop-of-war *Maryland* (20) under construction in Baltimore. When he placed her in commission in September, Rodgers showed Truxtun's influence by imposing very precise regulations to govern activities on board his vessel.[8] Such careful discipline came to be the hallmark of his command.

The *Maryland* drew a quiet assignment off Surinam, where she remained until August 1800.[9] Her return home coincided with the signing of a peace convention with France. In March Rodgers headed the *Maryland* for France with the courier bearing certification of American ratification. He reached Havre in early May and returned to Baltimore in late August.[10] By then the Peace Establishment naval force was set. Initially it appeared Rodgers would be retained, but on 22 October, Secretary Robert Smith, the brother of Rodgers's former employers, penned an unhappy letter informing him of his release.[11]

Rodgers soon reentered the merchant service, sailing his schooner *Nelly* to Cap Francois, Haiti. There he made the acquaintance of the American commercial agent, Colonel Tobias Lear, and his son, Benjamin Lincoln Lear, who would later figure extensively in Rodgers's life. When French troops attacked the former slaves holding the town, Rodgers led a band of blacks who evacuated Americans and other whites along with much of their property. The French commander rewarded Rodgers's heroics by granting him an import permit, but when Rodgers returned with two vessels, the friendship proved fickle. Both ships and their cargoes were seized. When Rodgers protested, he was first cast into prison and then summarily expelled from the island. He returned to Baltimore in May.[12]

The hero of Cap Francois journeyed to Havre de Grace to recover and await the outcome of developments in Washington. During his absence war had broken out with Tripoli and a squadron was organized for service in the Mediterranean. It appeared that recently discharged officers such as Rodgers would be recalled. The wait was softened by Rodgers's introduction to Minerva Denison, the blond seventeen-year-old daughter of a local landowner. He was soon smitten although the two were not married until 1806.[13] As he anticipated, Rodgers was restored to the Navy List. Recommissioned on 25 August 1802, he received command of the small frigate *John Adams* (28). She joined the squadron under Commodore Richard V. Morris at Malta in early January 1803.[14]

The commodore proved both to lack drive and to attract ill luck. After a winter storm prevented Rodgers and the boats of the squadron from raiding Tripoli harbor, Morris led his vessels to Tunis, where he hoped to settle a lingering dispute over a partially Tunisian-owned prize. The Bey first threatened war unless the case were tried in a Tunisian court, and then seized Morris to enforce demands for $22,000 that he claimed the United States owed him. The Americans capitulated in both cases.[15] Finally in April, a month after the winter storms abated, Morris headed back to Tripoli. En route, a fire on board the flagship exploded some powder.[16]

After escorting the damaged vessel to Malta, Rodgers, in the *John Adams*, established a blockade at Tripoli, and on 12 May seized the Moroccan ship *Meshouda* attempting to enter the port. Soon afterward Rodgers concluded that peace was possible if the whole squadron concentrated off Tripoli. He hastened to Malta, but found Morris preferred to continue the blockade strategy although his squadron was too small to accomplish it. The two men returned to Tripoli where they intercepted and burned several coastal traders trying to run into the port. Late in May, a dying wind frustrated another attack on the harbor. Despite the setback, Morris opened discussions with the Tripolitans, but soon discovered that their demands were too high for serious negotiations. When the blockaders destroyed a 22-gun polacre trying to put to sea on 22 June, Morris decided the threat to American shipping was over and withdrew the blockaders in order to deal with Algiers and Morocco.[17]

Before he could carry out his new mission, Morris received recall orders. He transferred command to Rodgers on 12 September. Breaking his pennant in the *New York* (36), the new commodore prepared to visit Morocco only to find Commodore Edward Preble, the commander of the replacement Mediterranean squadron, already at Gibraltar. After an explosion of temper over Preble, his junior, flying a commodore's broad pennant in his presence, Rodgers volunteered to accompany the new commander to Morocco before returning home. The incident demonstrated Rodgers's ability, like that of Winfield Scott, to fly into a towering rage when provoked but then act magnanimously once his passion cooled.[18]

The expedition arose from the seizure of American craft by Moroccan cruisers. The appearance of Rodgers and Preble with four vessels at Tangier had a calming effect. The emperor of Morocco hastened to repudiate the captures. The Americans, for their part, returned two Moroccan prizes (including the *Meshouda*). With the Moroccan crisis settled, Rodgers sailed for home in late October, arriving in Washington on 2 December.[19] The tour in the Mediterranean solidified Rodgers's reputation as one of the more competent of the junior captains and, as his relations with Morris and Preble proved, a man willing to put the good of the service ahead of personal gain.

Following his return Rodgers superintended construction of *Gunboat No. 1* at Washington Navy Yard. Rodgers used his stay in Washington to secure a midshipman's warrant for his younger brother, George Washington Rodgers. The younger Rodgers served until 1832, but never achieved distinction. Rodgers also found time to press his suit of Minerva Denison. They became engaged and made plans for a wedding in the fall of 1804.[20]

Rodgers did not remain on shore to see his gunboat complete, or to take his marriage vows. In April, he hoisted the commission pennant on the frigate *Congress* (36) which was assigned to a new Mediterranean force under Commodore Samuel Barron. The squadron sailed on 4 July making the crossing in thirty-eight days.[21] On his arrival Barron discovered that the emperor of Morocco had again "begun to be unreasonable" and the Bey of Tunis was "refractory and has made many threats." Barron split his squadron. Rodgers remained at Gibraltar with the *Congress* and *Essex* (32) while the rest of the squadron sailed to Tripoli. Rodgers visited Tangier in mid-August and quickly concluded that the threat was exaggerated. He promptly headed the *Congress* toward Tripoli.[22]

Barron, who was sick from a liver ailment, left Rodgers to manage the Tripoli blockade while he sought relief in Syracuse. Even when his illness worsened, Barron refused to surrender command. This refusal exasperated latent antagonism between Rodgers and the Barrons, both the commodore and his brother James. The roots of their hostility are obscure, but it reached such intensity that Rodgers considered challenging his superior. Nor was Rodgers's temper improved by Barron's shifting him to the *Constitution* (44) with orders to Lisbon for repairs. The work occupied most of the winter of 1804–5, the *Constitution* rejoining the squadron in March 1805. She took her turn before Tripoli the following month and seized a Tunisian xebec trying to run the blockade with two prizes.[23]

Barron's continuing poor health finally convinced him that he must give up command. On 22 May he formally transferred responsibility to Rodgers. Including vessels en route, Rodgers's command consisted of twelve cruising vessels, a pair of bomb ketches, and ten gunboats, the largest squadron yet assembled under the American flag. While the two commodores completed the transfer, Tobias Lear, Rodgers's Cap Francois friend, plunged into negotiations with Tripoli. With Rodgers's full support he strove for a quick settlement, apparently out of fear for the safety of the *Philadelphia* prisoners. On 4 June he signed a treaty that abolished tribute, but included $60,000 ransom for Bainbridge and his crew.[24]

Rodgers next turned his attention to Tunis where the Bey demanded the return of the xebec captured by the *Constitution* in April. Rodgers arrived off Tunis on 1 August with thirteen vessels. He demanded that the Bey negotiate or declare war. The Tunisian backed down. Rodgers, who doubted the Bey's sincerity, insisted that the ruler prove it by sending an ambassador to Washington.[25] The remainder of Rodgers's tour was quiet. The squadron sailed the western Mediterranean until it went into winter quarters at Syracuse. Rodgers took formal leave of his command on 29 May 1806 and reached Washington in late July.[26] He had proved himself as a squadron commander.

But he had not conquered his temper. Rodgers's animosity toward the Barrons, especially James, boiled over upon receipt of reports of slanderous newspaper accounts that he believed they had planted. On his return to the United States, Rodgers challenged James Barron to a duel, but it never occurred.[27]

Rodgers's return permitted him to reschedule his marriage. It took place on 21 October at the Denison family's Sion Hill mansion. The naval officer, now thirty-four, and his bride, twenty-two, had a successful marriage that produced eleven children, ten of whom lived to adulthood. Three sons followed their father into the Navy, and a fourth joined the Coast Survey. Secretary Smith contributed to the happiness of the newlyweds by assigning Rodgers to superintend the construction of *Gunboat No. 7* at Havre de Grace and to prove cannon being cast nearby.[28]

The Jefferson administration faced the nearly impossible task of protecting the rights of American commerce during the Napoleonic Wars. Because the United States possessed the largest neutral merchant marine and traded with all the belligerents, her vessels were subject to the ebb and flow of their unilateral trade restrictions. Moreover, the British navy, finding volunteers infrequent and crew shortages common, resorted to impressing British subjects on board foreign merchantmen. Many British boarding officers were not too careful in screening the crews of American craft, so numerous Americans reluctantly entered the king's service.

The worst incident occurred in June 1807 when the British *Leopard* (50) fired into and removed four men from the *Chesapeake* (36), flying the broad pennant of James Barron as commander-designate of the Mediterranean squadron. During the excitement that followed, Rodgers received command of the New York Station, a force that soon numbered three bomb ketches and thirty-one gunboats.[29]

Rodgers's activities in New York were interrupted by assignment as president of Barron's court-martial for inadequate defense of the *Chesapeake*. The choice of Rodgers was unusual considering his known animosity toward Barron, but he seems to have presided with reasonable evenhandedness. The trial took place in Norfolk between 3 January and 22 February 1808. The court found Barron guilty of neglecting to clear his ship for action and sentenced him to five years' suspension.[30]

In March, Rodgers returned to New York. Meanwhile, Congress recognized the failure of the total embargo of foreign trade and directed the fitting out of additional vessels to patrol American waters. Rodgers received command of the force with the *Constitution* as his flagship along with Secretary of the Navy Paul Hamilton's admonition that "we must place ourselves in an attitude for war." The assignment allowed Rodgers to exercise fully his technical interests. He devised a set of night signals for his vessels; urged the adoption of a standardized system for determining the sizes of masts; and took charge of the Navy's part in the September 1810 torpedo experiments conducted by Robert Fulton. Believing Fulton's ideas were "the most . . . visionary . . . to have originated in the brain of a man not actually out of his sense," Rodgers provided the *Argus* (16) as the target for a simulated attack. Her commander, Master Commandant James Lawrence, so draped the brig with nets, grappling hooks, and even a swinging scythe that Fulton's attack was frustrated. Although the inventor insisted that the naval officers had used unfair defenses, subsequent demonstrations of underwater weapons proved no more promising.[31]

During the summer of 1810 Hamilton divided the patrol force into two divisions, one under Rodgers and the other under Commodore Stephen Decatur. Fearful of another *Chesapeake* incident, the Secretary exhorted his commanders to "support at any risk & cost the dignity of your flag." Rodgers, in turn, directed his subordinates to return two shots for one if fired upon and to employ "the utmost extent of all your force" if a cannonball actually struck.[32]

Rodgers's force cruised the cost without incident until April 1811. Then a British vessel, believed to be the frigate *Guerriere* (38), removed a sailor from a brig off New York. Ordered by Secretary Hamilton to see that such insolence ceased, Rodgers hastened to sea in the *President* (44). At noon on 16 May, lookouts spotted the topsails of a warship, and the *President* gave chase. She did not get close enough to hail until 10:12 P.M. After an exchange of hails the quarry—later identified as HMS *Little Belt* (20), with Captain Arthur B. Bingham, RN in command—fired, and a general action ensued. When it ended about 15 minutes later, the *Little Belt* was a shambles, with thirteen men dead, plus nineteen wounded. The *President*, by comparison, suffered only one man injured and little physical damage. After determining that the Britisher needed no assistance, Rodgers ordered his vessel to New York. She entered port on the twenty-fifth.[33] Because British reports of the engagement differed markedly from his own, especially as to who fired the first shot, Rodgers requested a court of inquiry. It met with Decatur as president and absolved the Americans of firing the first shot, as have American historians in the succeeding years.[34] The action served as a tonic to American self-confidence, but it also intensified anti-British feeling.

Early 1812 brought belated efforts to prepare for possible hostilities with Britain. In January Rodgers received orders to plan a telegraph line between New York and Washington. He soon concluded that the system was impractical, although a shorter line operated between Sandy Hook and New York City. In mid-March Secretary Hamilton warned Rodgers to prepare for active service, but to keep his squadron at New York.[35]

The Secretary also queried his senior officers on the best strategy to harass British trade with the least danger to the small U.S. Navy. Rodgers recommended an immediate offensive in order to strike before the British forces could concentrate. He proposed deploying light craft in the West Indies to harry trade; using two or three frigates and a sloop to raid shipping near the British Isles; and deploying the remaining frigates, operating as a squadron, along the U.S. or Canadian coast. He suggested that the latter attack targets of opportunity and shift areas of operation frequently to force wide deployment of British cruisers. Such a strategy, Rodgers believed, would negate the British superiority in numbers and permit American vessels caught abroad by the outbreak of hostilities to reach their home ports in relative safety. Most of the other officers recommended single-ship cruisers. In response, Hamilton ordered Rodgers to concentrate or disperse his vessels as circumstances dictated.[36]

In June Hamilton directed Rodgers to prepare for immediate service and ordered Decatur to reinforce him. War with Britain was declared on the eighteenth. Two days later, prior to receiving the news, Rodgers, with the *President* and the *Hornet* (18), dropped down to Sandy Hook where the *Argus* and Decatur, with his two frigates, joined. The two commodores signed an interesting agreement, intended to protect their widows should either husband be killed. They agreed that for the duration of the war they would share equally in prize money and that, if one were killed, his widow would continue to receive her husband's share. Official news of war arrived at mid-afternoon on 21 June. The combined squadrons immediately put to sea in search of a 110-ship convoy bound from Jamaica to Britain.[37]

On 23 June, while seeking the convoy, the American squadron sighted and chased the British frigate *Belvidera* (32) off Nantucket but could not catch her, although the *President* got within range. Rodgers, himself, fired the first shot of the chase, but later suffered a broken leg when one of his vessel's guns shattered. The Americans fruitlessly pursued the convoy nearly to the English Channel. From there, Rodgers ran south to Madiera and then across the Atlantic to the Grand Banks before returning to Boston on 31 August. The cruise netted seven prizes and proved Rodgers's strategy; most of the American merchantmen at sea got home safely.[38]

Secretary Hamilton concluded that the squadron would accomplish more if broken into three divisions. That permitted attacks on British trade in three different areas while forcing the Royal Navy to continue its use of small squadrons in order to ensure a successful encounter with the Americans. The three divisions put to sea in October. Rodgers in the *President*, with the *Congress* in company, sortied on 8 October. Off Newfoundland, Rodgers took the packet *Swallow* carrying $175,000 in specie. Rodgers's division then sailed east to the vicinity of Madiera and south to the Cape Verdes before returning to Boston on the last day of the year. The cruise yielded only two prizes.[39]

In late February, the new Secretary of the Navy, William Jones, fearful of a strengthening of the British blockade, ordered all possible vessels to sea to raid shipping from Cape Clear to the Cape of Good Hope. Rodgers led his division to sea on the last day of April 1813. It separated when free of the British cordon. Rodgers in the *President* followed a roundabout route from Newfoundland to the Azores, the Shetland Islands, and the North Sea before entering Bergen, Norway. From there she returned home, passing north of Ireland and through the Grand Banks. Off Nantucket she had the good fortune to meet and decoy under her guns the tender *Highflyer*. Rodgers's vessel made port at Providence, Rhode Island, on 27 September. The cruise resulted in twelve prizes, but only the *Highflyer* reached port safely.[40] The *President* went to sea again on 4 December 1813, avoided a British squadron looking for her, and steered for the West Indies. Once again Rodgers had poor luck and failed to locate any convoys. The big frigate ran past the blockaders into New York on 18 February 1814.[41]

Shortly afterward Secretary Jones offered Rodgers his choice of commands. He selected the frigate *Guerriere* (44) under construction in Philadelphia. He also assumed temporary command of the Delaware River gunboat flotilla.[42] In July as the result of British raids, Rodgers sent some men to protect installations at the head of Chesapeake Bay. The attacks were the precursor to a campaign against Washington and Baltimore. In mid-August Secretary Jones ordered Rodgers to bring 300 of his men to Baltimore. They departed New Castle, Delaware, on 23 August and marched day and night to reach Baltimore on the evening of the twenty-fifth. On arrival Rodgers learned of the British rout of American forces at Bladensburg the preceding day. The naval contingent immediately began constructing defenses in coordination with the local militia and volunteers under Rodgers's former employer, militia Major General Samuel Smith.

During 1–5 September Rodgers led a mixed force of sailors and militia in an abortive attempt to trap and destroy a small British squadron retiring down the Potomac River.[43]

Secretary Jones then ordered Rogers back to Baltimore to help expedite the construction of its defenses and revive the spirits of its inhabitants. He played his roles well. Baltimore, Rodgers told its doubt-ridden mayor, "can be defended, and shall be." He suggested scuttling merchant vessels to block the entrance into the harbor and consulted with Robert Fulton on the possible installation of mines. Rodgers's 2,400-man naval brigade formed the city's southern defenses which protected the flanks of Fort McHenry. The sailors came under heavy fire during the bombardment of Fort McHenry and on the night of 13–14 September turned back a British landing along Ferry Branch that, if successful, would have opened the way into the city. While Secretary Jones's claim that the naval brigade had saved the city was an overstatement, it is clear that Rodgers, by his stalwart courage, and his men, by their steadfastness and efficiency, had played a major role in defeating the British attack.[44] The sailors remained in Baltimore until 20 September when rumors of an impending British attack on the Delaware River hastened them back to Philadelphia.[45]

The need for reorganization of the Navy Department had become evident to Jones as he struggled to direct the Navy's war effort without a staff of professional advisors. As he prepared to leave office in late 1814, he organized his thoughts in reports to the President and Congress. He suggested the creation of a Board of Inspection composed of three officers and two civilians, each with an area of specific oversight to share reponsibility with the Secretary. President James Madison took a more direct course and offered the secretaryship to Rodgers. The commodore rejected the appointment because it would remove him from service. Congress, after soliciting comments from senior officers, rewrote the plan to provide for a board of three senior captains to be attached to the Secretary's office. In keeping with the tradition of civilian control, the board was forbidden to exercise "control and direction of the naval forces of the United States" and limited to "ministerial duties . . . relative to the procurement of naval stores and materials, and the construction, armament, equipment, and employment, of vessels of war, as well as all other matters connected with the naval establishment of the United States." The legislation became law on 7 February 1815.[46]

The creation of the new body came at a critical time. Not only had the Navy Department acquired a new head, Benjamin Crowninshield, but the war with Britain had come to an end. In selecting the new commissioners, Crowninshield asked Rodgers for advice. He received critical thumbnail sketches of each of the captains and the recommendation that he appoint William Bainbridge, Isaac Hull, and Charles Morris or Hull, David Porter, and Morris. When Rodgers, who had been offered either the presidency of the board or command of the expedition fitting out for operations against Algiers, chose the former, President Madison designated Porter and Hull as his companions.[47] Rodgers was both the natural and the best choice for president of the board. The second ranking officer, he was intellectually the broadest and most generally competent of the senior captains. His interest in the technical side of his profession was well-established, and he, better than any of his contemporaries, recognized the value of local control of the sea.

The Board of Naval Commissioners met on 25 April. Rodgers took the chair as the senior officer. It is difficult to identify from the record precisely what role he played in any particular decision. The board's journal records actions but not discussions, and its correspondence was always signed by the senior officer. Moreover, apparently none of its members kept memoirs.[48]

Rodgers celebrated his new post by purchasing "Bellevue," a house on Georgetown Heights beyond Rock Creek. By 1820 the growing family, now numbering six children and their grandmother Denison, had outgrown the house. Rodgers then purchased a pair of row houses on "P" Street, Southwest, near the Washington Arsenal on Greenleaf Point, which he converted into a single structure. It proved ample, despite the arrival of four more children between 1821 and 1829, until he moved to Madison Place on Lafayette Park in 1835.

The presidency of the Board of Naval Commissioners automatically thrust Rodgers into the malestrom of official Washington society. Both the stout but well-proportioned commodore and his slim blond lady enjoyed their social life. They entertained frequently, and Rodgers, like many other abstainers of the era, had a reputation for keeping a fine cellar. Until he freed them in 1822, Rodgers owned eight house slaves and their three children. The adults continued in his employ after manumission.

Coincident with moving to Washington, Rodgers acquired part interest in a lumber, brick, and lime business. The commodore also invested in canals and speculated moderately in Washington real estate. He subsequently served as a director of the Bank of Columbia and the Bank of the United States, and as president of the Potomac Fire Insurance Company. When combined with his substantial salary as a navy commissioner, his outside income permitted Rodgers to live a life of comparative luxury and ease. It also allowed him the leisure to undertake substantial civic duties as a member of the Board of Public Health and as an alderman.[49]

No sooner had the Board of Naval Commissioners organized than it wrangled with Secretary Crowninshield over its sphere of responsibilities. Board members believed that Crowninshield should accept their recommendations about squadron organization and officer assignments, but the Secretary argued that these matters were his to decide and that the board's powers were limited to administrative matters. When President Madison ruled in favor of his civilian secretary, Rodgers evidently accepted the defeat in good grace, as did Porter, but Hull did not. In July he left he board and returned to command of the Boston Navy Yard.[50] Stephen Decatur replaced Hull on 2 January 1816, but his presence was about as welcome as a sea anemone in a seaman's boot. While Rodgers and Porter were close personal and professional friends, the latter and Decatur were often at odds. Apparently Rodgers, who was on good terms with both men, had to serve as peacemaker.[51]

Prior to Decatur's arrival the board had considered building navy yards and had concluded that three, if properly equipped, would meet the nation's needs. One should be Boston; the others, new establishments in Rhode Island and Virginia. Each yard should contain a dry dock adequate to deck a ship-of-the-line and be large enough to berth five ships-of-the-line and ten frigates. The commissioners followed this report with another recommending the annual construction of a ship-of-the-line, a frigate, and two sloops-of-war. They pointed to the importance of early procurement of timber and championed the use, wherever possible, of American copper, hemp, and canvas. They also advocated establishment of a national gun foundry and a naval academy, and supported merit promotion, as well as the weeding out of incompetent officers, all advanced concepts for that date.[52]

In large part because of the recommendations of the board and those of Secretary Crowninshield, Congress in 1816 enacted a program of gradual increase of the Navy. The law authorized the construction of nine ships-of-the-line and twelve frigates over the next eight years.[53] The supervision of their design and construction became one of the major responsibilities of the commissioners. The concern with ship design was mirrored by the board's interest in ordnance developments—notably exploding shells, experimental batches of which it bought in 1817 and 1819.[54]

One task assigned to the board in its chartering legislation was a long overdue revision of the Naval Regulations. The commissioners completed their revision in April 1817, but Congress ignored both that revision and one proposed in 1832. As a result, most secretaries and the board resorted to circulars and general orders to standardize activities within the service.[55]

When Crowninshield resigned in September 1818, former President Madison recommended that the office of Secretary of the Navy be abolished and the duties assigned to the president of the Board of Naval Commissioners. President Monroe viewed that as a great threat to civilian control and refused either to consider it or to appoint Rodgers as Acting Secretary. Monroe, on the other hand, offered to appoint Rodgers Secretary if the naval officer would shed his uniform, but as the President expected, he did not want to surrender the security of his service career.[56]

The issue of the continued appropriations called for under the Gradual Increase Act engaged the board in extensive correspondence in 1820. In January Rodgers responded to a request from Representative Stephenson Archer for the board's view of the efficacy of reducing the appropriation. Rodgers, in a strong letter, pointed out that timber exposed to the weather deteriorated, and therefore suspended vessels would have to be enclosed in expensive shiphouses. That killed thought of suspending the program but not of stretching out the funding. In December 1820 Secretary Smith Thompson, on the grounds of political expediency, secured Rodgers's agreement to lengthen the time to complete funding. Rodgers's price was the construction of shiphouses, but the House of Representatives refused to fund them.[57] During the early 1820s Rodgers became interested in marine railways as a possible alternative to the expensive dry docks which Congress was loath to provide. He initially mentioned them in an 1821 report and the following year submitted plans for one to Secretary Thompson. That year a marine railway was installed at the Washington Shipyard following his design. Not until 1827 would Congress authorize dry docks.[58]

Rodgers played only a minor role in the duel between Stephen Decatur and James Barron. He refused to be Decatur's second and advised his friend against the meeting. Nevertheless, Rodgers was nearby when the two men met and was one of those who rushed to Decatur's assistance. He subsequently served as a witness to the dying man's will and as a pallbearer at his funeral.[59]

In 1820 the inventor John Stevens proposed the construction of a fleet of steamers for defense of the nation's harbors. Rodgers responded by pointing out that the board had found all plans so far submitted inadequate. That was scarcely surprising because steam crafts were still in their infancy and had yet to prove themselves in other than protected waters. The board had purchased engines in

1817 and 1819, but had been prevented from installing them in hulls because of the lack of reasonable designs.[60]

During 1822 the board considered the composition of an anti-piracy squadron for the Caribbean. In December Porter left the board to command the force. As a result, Rodgers now had to work with two new commissioners, Isaac Chauncey, who followed Porter, and Charles Morris, who arrived on 3 March 1823. Alone among the senior officers, Morris possessed a breadth and depth of mind approaching that of Rodgers. The two men worked well together and between them dominated the board for the remainder of its life.

Porter's anti-piracy mission ran afoul of a yellow fever epidemic during the summer and fall of 1823. In September Rodgers volunteered to visit the squadron's base at Thompson's Island (Key West) with a party of surgeons to determine "the origin of the disease" and the fitness of the site as a rendezvous for the squadron. He spent most of October and early November in Florida, but by then the fever season was nearly past. The surgeons improved the hospital, but otherwise the commissioner found no need to shift the base. Other problems soon arose from Porter's poor judgment, which opened a gulf between the two former friends.[61]

In May 1824 Secretary Samuel L. Southard decided to offer Rodgers command of the Mediterranean Squadron. It was being strengthened because of the complications caused by the Greek Revolution to a force appropriate for the Navy's senior officer. Moreover, Rodgers appeared to be the logical person to initiate discussions of a possible commercial treaty with the Ottoman Empire because the intermediary in the talks would be the Capudan Pasha, or commander of the Turkish navy. A third inducement to Rodgers's appointment was the squadron's slack discipline. Rodgers accepted and left the board on 15 December with President Monroe's thanks for his "zeal, intelligence, and skill."[62]

Rodgers's flagship, the newly completed ship-of-the-line *North Carolina*, departed Hampton Roads 27 March 1825 and reached Gibraltar 30 April. The Mediterranean force promptly came under the Rodgers System, "the ruling feature of which," one midshipman wrote, "is, to render every one as uncomfortable as possible." It embraced constant ship's work, tight discipline, and limited shore leave. In early July the squadron cruised to the eastern Mediterranean. At Poros, the first stop in the Aegean, Rodgers's fabled temper appeared when a shore party chose to go swimming rather than visit the local ruins. There are other tales during the cruise of his knocking down a seaman who did not rise when he entered the forecastle and his hitting a pilot over the head with a spyglass hard enough to kill

The Mediterranean Squadron, 1825. Rodgers was a member of the Board of Naval Commissioners from 1815 to 1837, except for the three years, 1824–27, that he commanded the Mediterranean Squadron from on board the ship-of-the-line *North Carolina*, shown leading the frigates *Constitution* and *Brandywine* and the sloops *Erie* and *Ontario* out of Port Mahon in January 1825. Courtesy of the Naval Historical Foundation.

him. The squadron continued its cruise to Greece, unsuccessfully seeking the Capudan Pasha. With bad weather approaching, Rodgers led his vessels into winter quarters at Port Mahon.

In the spring of 1826 the squadron sailed eastward again. In July Rodgers finally made contact with the Capudan Pasha, who agreed to support the American diplomatic efforts. During the exchange of visits, the Turk honored Rodgers by hoisting the Sultan's personal flag. The American reciprocated by having his vessels pass through the Turkish fleet and man their rigging as they passed the Capudan Pasha's flagship. Although he could press the American cause no further because of the complexities of Ottoman politics, Rodgers set in motion the steps that led to the Commercial Treaty of 1830.

The remainder of Rodgers's tour was uneventful although in January 1827 the *North Carolina* ran into a vicious mistral that put over 135 of her crew on the sick list. The following May, Rodgers sailed for home via Gibraltar and the West Indies, arriving in Hampton Roads on 29 July. Rodgers's command of the Mediterranean Squadron had been a success. He had pried ajar the Ottoman door and restored discipline where it was lacking.[63]

Since the Board of Naval Commissioners again had two vacancies, Rodgers quickly reclaimed his old office. He took his seat on 8 October 1827, joining Lewis Warrington (in office since January) and his long-time friend Thomas Tingey, who took his seat on 24 September but died on 27 October. That slot remained vacant for a year until Commodore Daniel T. Patterson reported.[64]

Tragedy struck in April 1828 when Rodgers's son, Frederick, was drowned in Norfolk harbor, along with two other midshipmen, when their boat capsized. The impact was so great that Rodgers's biographer believes that neither parent fully recovered. They clearly had some second thoughts about allowing John, Jr. to enter the Navy, but these shortly disappeared, and young Rodgers embarked on a career nearly as distinguished as his father's.[65]

The relations between Rodgers and Andrew Jackson's first Secretary of the Navy were notably poor. Rodgers considered Secretary John Branch to be especially dull and ignorant of naval matters. By the spring of 1831 Rodgers was so annoyed by Branch's incompetence that he told John Quincy Adams that he was "repeatedly upon the point" of resigning. Nor were his relationships with other Jacksonian politicians much better. When two arrived in his office to confront the old sailor with charges of peculation, Rodgers suggested that they make use of the door because it would save him the mortification of having to kick them out. They abandoned their investigation.[66]

During the spring and summer of 1832 a cholera epidemic swept the country. When Benjamin Lincoln Lear, the son of Tobias and a close friend of the Rodgers family, was stricken in September, John Rodgers personally nursed the ailing man until he died on 1 October. Two days later Rodgers came down with the malady and was confined to his home until 19 November. He never fully recovered, but he continued to attend to office business and generally made the annual inspection tours. Yet, his strength was limited and he spent long periods away from Washington "for his health," as the board's journal laconically noted. In July–September 1834 he visited Sweet Sulphur Springs, Virginia, and spent July and August 1835 in New York City.[67]

During the mid-1830s the board belatedly turned its attention once again to steam warships. The failure of the board, or that of the secretaries, to integrate steam power into the fleet had left the U.S. Navy in the wake of the more progressive European services. In 1834 the board secured the plan for a large steam engine, and the next year Secretary Mahlon Dickerson authorized the construction of one of the 1816 batteries. Rodgers's personal role in this is unclear, but he was a close confidant of Dickerson, who seldom took significant steps without his advice.[68] The board followed this in 1836 with a major study of the naval requirements of the country. While it noted the expanse of American trade and the coastline to be protected, it declined to estimate the force required to protect them, a clear indication that the board could not agree. Instead, board members assumed that in wartime the Navy could recruit 30,000 seamen, who, they calculated, would permit manning fifteen ships-of-the-line, twenty-five frigates, twenty-five sloops-of-war, twenty-five steamers, and twenty-five smaller craft. The commissioners refused to set a peacetime standard. The imprecision of the report is a good gauge of the deterioration of Rodgers's control over the board. Prior to his illness such a report would have been both stronger and more precise.[69]

Although Rodgers continued to attend meetings and sign correspondence, his health deteriorated. Finally, on 1 May 1837 he resigned his seat, "intending," as the board's secretary noted, "to take a voyage to Europe for the benefit of his health." That day he received a warm note from Secretary Dickerson conveying his best wishes and relaying President Jackson's regret that circumstances had forced the resignation.[70]

Accompanied by Butler, his faithful valet, Rodgers sailed from New York on 10 May. He visited English friends and returned to the United States in late August, apparently not much improved.

After a few weeks in Washington, he moved to the Naval Asylum in Philadelphia where his health continued to deteriorate until he died in the arms of the devoted valet on 1 August 1838. His funeral took place during the afternoon of 3 August at Christ Church Burying Ground in Philadelphia, and was an impressive affair organized by Commodore Charles Stewart with militia units, marines, naval officers in full dress, dignitaries, and several thousand onlookers. The pallbearers were Commodores Stewart, Biddle, and W. Branford Shubrick, Major Hartman Bache of the Topographical Engineers, and Army Ordnance Captain William A. Thornton. The Episcopal burial service was read by the Rev. Dr. Stephen Higginson Tyng. In 1839 the body was transferred to the Congressional Cemetery in Washington where Rodgers lies next to his wife and surrounded by family and numerous comrades in arms.[71]

John Rodgers was the dominant figure in the Navy for a quarter of a century—twenty-five years that encompassed the glories of the single-ship encounters of the War of 1812, the gradual increase and the worldwide expansion of naval responsibilities, and the shift of technologies that introduced the exploding shell and steam power into the Navy. No other American naval officer has had so long a period of influence, and few have presided over such radical changes in the naval force and its responsibilities.

Rodgers personally bridged the first generation of naval officers who had been reared in the merchant service and learned naval practice in the makeshift Continental Navy, and the later, more sophisticated professionals whose education was in a navy shaped by Truxtun, Preble, and Rodgers. It would be argued, especially by the *enfant terribles* of the next generation of naval officers such as Matthew Perry and Matthew Maury, that the old hero was an archconservative who resisted change. Conservative he was, in the sense that he would not abandon the tried and true simply because it stood in the way of the latest fad. He bore the brunt of the assault of those who worried about the slow adoption of steam power by the United States. Yet, there is only slim evidence to connect Rodgers to that delay. Certainly a naval board that recommended the use of steamers for anti-piracy operation in 1822 was not backward; nor is it surprising that the board moved slowly after the *Sea Gull* failed to produce significant results. Neither should it be overlooked that under Rodgers's leadership, the board revised naval regulations, improved the service's financial and accounting systems, introduced purchasing by contract, and developed checks against fraud and misapplication of public funds, thereby establishing precedents and standards that would be followed, in some cases, for half a century.

Thomas Hart Benton, a man not readily impressed by his contemporaries, considered Rodgers "the complete personation of my
idea of the perfect naval commander."[72] And so he was, for in him
we can identify the intellect, presence, courage, and drive of a dominant leader. He possessed them in better balance than any of his
contemporaries in the Navy and to a degree matched by few since.

FURTHER READING

There are three major collections of John Rodgers's papers. The
largest is in the Rodgers Family Papers of the Naval Historical Foundation on deposit at the Library of Congress. The second is in the
New-York Historical Society, and the third at the Historical Society
of Pennsylvania. A small group exists at Georgetown University.
Numerous letters can be found in the correspondence of his contemporaries in service. Most of Rodgers's official correspondence is
preserved in the National Archives. Most valuable for this study
were the Secretary of the Navy's Letters to Officers of Ships of War,
Personal Letterbook, and the Circulars and General Orders files; the
Letters to the Secretary from Captains; and the papers of the Board
of Naval Commissioners, notably its Journal. All are contained in
Record Group 45, the Naval Records Collection of the Office of
Naval Records and Library.

Nearly all the surviving Rodgers correspondence concerning his
service in the Quasi-War with France and in the Barbary Wars is
reprinted in the two Office of Naval Records and Library compila-
tions *Naval Documents Related to the Quasi-War Between the United
States and France* and *Naval Documents Related to the United States
Wars with the Barbary Powers*. The same will be true of the War of
1812 material when the series currently under way at the Naval
Historical Center under the editorship of Dr. William S. Dudley is
completed. Some of the more important reports are included in
*American State Papers, Documents Legislative and Executive of the Con-
gress of the United States, Naval Affairs*, as are many significant Board
of Naval Commissioners documents. Additional material is repro-
duced in the author's *The New American State Papers: Naval Affairs*.
Some not otherwise found appear in Charles W. Goldsborough,
United States Naval Chronicle.

The only full-length biography of Rodgers is that written by Charles
O. Paullin (1910), who also prepared the sketch of Rodgers for the
Dictionary of American Biography. Leonard F. Guttridge and Jay D.
Smith, *The Commodores* is an anti-Rodgers collective biography that
introduces some recent research. Few of the recent biographies of
his contemporaries add much to our knowledge of Rodgers, but the

three by David F. Long, *Nothing Too Daring, Ready To Hazard*, and *Sailor-Diplomat*, as well as Samuel Eliot Morison's majestic *Old Bruin*, deal with him at some length, but not so favorably as Christopher McKee in *Edward Preble* or Robert Erwin Johnson in *Rear Admiral John Rodgers*. Few memoirs by Rodgers's contemporaries allot him much space.

For a detailed study of the Quasi-War the student must still return to Gardner W. Allen, *Our Naval War with France*, or the early general histories of Thomas Clark and James Fenimore Cooper. Allen's *Our Navy and the Barbary Corsairs* is still the best study of the Barbary Wars, although a number of modern works exist, notably Glenn Tucker, *Dawn Like Thunder*. The classic studies of naval operations during the War of 1812 by Alfred Thayer Mahan and Theodore Roosevelt and the generally reliable *Pictorial Field-Book of the War of 1812* by Benson J. Lossing have not been displaced by modern works. John K. Mahon, *The War of 1812*, is a good recent overview of the conflict.

No study of the naval commissioners exists. The best account we have is in Charles O. Paullin, *Paullin's History of Naval Administration*, a reprinting of his 1905–14 series in the U.S. Naval Institute *Proceedings*. Harold and Margaret Sprout, *The Rise of American Naval Power*, and Robert Greenhalgh Albion, *Makers of Naval Policy*, consider naval policy, while Howard I. Chapelle, *History of the American Sailing Navy*, discusses the role of the Board of Naval Commissioners in the design of warships. The author's *Ships of the Navy, Combat Vessels* provides data for the craft, while James L. Mooney et al., *Dictionary of American Naval Fighting Ships* sketches their operational history. Unfortunately, we have no study of ordnance or of the naval supply system during the naval commissioners' period.

Rodgers's diplomatic activities in the Mediterranean are studied in Charles O. Paullin's *Diplomatic Negotiations of American Naval Officers*. They are less fully discussed in James A. Field, Jr., *America and the Mediterranean World*. The significance of Rodgers as a disciplinarian is developed in James E. Valle, *Rocks and Shoals*.

NOTES

1. Although the surviving records show him only as a captain, Rodgers was always called "Colonel" in his later years.
2. See comments of David Porter in David F. Long, *Nothing Too Daring: A Biography of David Porter 1780–1843*, 7, and Gardner W. Allen, *Our Naval War with France*, 135.
3. Details of Rodgers's early life are supplied by Charles Oscar

Paullin, *Commodore John Rodgers, Captain, Commodore, and Senior Officer of the American Navy, 1773–1838*; Paullin, "John Rodgers," in Allen Johnson and Dumas Malone, eds., *Dictionary of American Biography*, XVI, 75–76. The capture of the *Hope* is noted in "Abstract of the Cases of Capture . . . ," Office of Naval Records and Library, *Naval Documents Related to the Quasi-War Between the United States and France*, I, 28. (Hereafter cited as *NDQW*.) Rodgers's account is in his *Appel a la Loyaute de la Nacion francaise contra les Pirateriers Exercees par les Armateurs*.

4. *The Public Statutes at Large of the United States of America* (hereafter U.S. Stat.), I, 350–51, 453–54; Charles Oscar Paullin, *Paullin's History of Administration*, 91, 97.

5. Paullin, *Administration*, 97; Paullin, *Rodgers*, 33.

6. McHenry to Truxtun, 30 May 1798; Truxtun to Stoddert, 27 October 1798, 14 February 1799; Rodgers to Stoddert, 15 February 1799, *NDQW*, I, 92–93, 508–9, *NDQW*, II, 329–30, 336–37; Stoddert to Truxtun, 8 December 1798, K. Jack Bauer, ed., *The New American State Papers: Naval Affairs*, IV, 19–21; Charles W. Goldsborough, ed., *United States Naval Chronicle*, 90–91, 132; James Fenimore Cooper, *The History of the Navy of the United States of America*, I, 297–98, 300; Allen, *Naval War*, 94–98; Paullin, *Rodgers*, 40–47, 51; Long, *Nothing Too Daring*, 9.

7. Stoddert to Truxtun, 16 January, 13 March, 19 June; Truxtun to Rodgers, 15 February, 7 March, 11 May; Truxtun to Stoddert, 14 February; Stoddert to Adams, 25 May 1799, *NDQW*, II, 229–30, 243, 252, 358–59, 427, 450–51, III, 166, 322. Rodger's commission is in Rodgers Family Papers, Library of Congress (hereafter RFP), series 3A, vol. 1.

8. K. Jack Bauer, *Ships of the Navy 1776–1969: Combat Vessels*, 23; Stoddert to Rodgers, 13 June, 17 July, 30 July 1799, *NDQW*, III, 355, 507, 568; Paullin, *Rodgers*, 56–60.

9. Stoddert to Rodgers, 5 September 1799, Rodgers to Stoddert, 20 September 1800, *NDQW*, IV, 158, VI, 312, 364–66; Paullin, *Rodgers*, 63–68.

10. Stoddert to Rodgers, 26 January, 7 March, 18 March 1801, *NDQW*, VII, 105, 141, 148; Allen, *Naval War*, 221; Paullin, *Rodgers*, 68–70.

11. Actg. Sec. Navy to Truxtun, 11 June 1801, Smith to Rodgers, 22 October 1801, Office of Naval Records and Library, *Naval Documents Related to the United States Wars with the Barbary Powers* (hereafter *NDBP*), I, 488–89, *NDQW*, VII, 292.

12. Rodgers to James Madison, June 1802, Notice of Expulsion, 29 April 1802, RFP, ser. 3A, vol. 1; Paullin, *Rodgers*, 77–82.

13. Paullin, *Rodgers*, 82–91.

14. Office of Naval Records and Library, *Register of Officer Personnel United States Navy and Marine Corps and Ships' Data 1801–1807*, 47; Cooper, *History of the Navy*, I, 353–54; Smith to Rodgers, 25 August, 18 September 1802, *NDBP*, II, 250, 276; Christopher McKee, *Edward Preble: A Naval Biography*, 110; Gardner W. Allen, *Our Navy and the Barbary Corsairs*, 106.

15. Morris to Smith, 30 March 1803, *NDBP*, II, 381–85; Charles Oscar Paullin, *Diplomatic Negotiations of American Naval Officers 1778–1883*, 65–67; Paullin, *Rodgers*, 102–3; Allen, *Barbary Corsairs*, 121–22.

16. Allen, *Barbary Corsairs*, 122–23; McKee, *Preble*, 111–12, 115–16; Cooper, *History of the Navy*, I, 363; Paullin, *Rodgers*, 103–5.

17. Paullin, *Rodgers*, 105–10; Allen, *Barbary Corsairs*, 125–31; McKee, *Preble*, 116–20; Cooper, *History of the Navy*, I, 363–71; Rodgers to Morris, 30 June, Rodgers to Smith, 4 December 1803, *NDBP*, II, 459–60, 465–66.

18. Smith to Morris, 21 June 1803, Smith to Rodgers, 21 June 1803, Preble to Rodgers, 15 September 1803, Rodgers to Preble, 15 September 1803, *NDBP*, II, 457, III, 46–47; Allen, *Barbary Corsairs*, 133–34; Paullin, *Rodgers*, 110–11.

19. Paullin, *Rodgers*, 112–13; Allen, *Barbary Corsairs*, 143–45; Cooper, *History of the Navy*, II, 8–9; McKee, *Preble*, 148–72.

20. Smith to Rodgers, 21 December 1803, *NDBP*, III, 282–83; *Register*, 81; Robert Erwin Johnson, *Rear Admiral John Rodgers 1812–1882*, 4; Edward W. Callahan, ed., *List of Officers of the Navy of the United States and of the Marine Corps from 1775 to 1900*, 469; Paullin, *Rodgers*, 115, 119.

21. Rodgers to Smith, 30 June, 12 August 1804, *NDBP*, IV, 239, 402–3; *Register*, 70.

22. Barron to Rodgers, 14 August, Rodgers to Smith, 17 August, 30 August 1804, *NDBP*, IV, 414, 423, 487–88. The quotation is from Rodgers to Smith, 12 August 1804, *NDBP*, IV, 403.

23. Rodgers to Smith, 6 November, 30 December 1804, 27 January, 30 January, 4 February, 5 February 1805, *NDBP*, V, 124n, 225, 314–15, 321–22, 328, 332; Allen, *Barbary Corsairs*, 220–21; McKee, *Preble*, 310, 329; Paullin, *Rodgers*, 121–27.

24. Barron to Rodgers, 22 May 1805, *NDBP*, VI, 31–32; Allen, *Barbary Corsairs*, 221–23, 252; Cooper, *History of the Navy*, II, 82–85; Paullin, *Negotiations*, 86–87.

25. Rodgers to Smith, 1 September 1805, *NDBP*, VI, 259–63; Allen, *Barbary Corsairs*, 267–69; Cooper, *History of the Navy*, II, 97–99; Paullin, *Rodgers*, 146–59.

26. Rodgers to Hugh Campbell, 31 August 1805, Rodgers to Smith, 1 September, 30 October 1805, 3 January, 14 February, 5 March, 19 March, 23 May, 26 May, 26 July 1806, Rodgers to Navy Agents, 29 May 1806, Smith to Rodgers, 22 March 1806, *NDBP*, VI, 258–63, 298, 331–32, 369, 380–81, 396–97, 399, 431–35, 438, 461; Allen, *Barbary Corsairs*, 270–71; James A. Field, Jr., *America and the Mediterranean World 1776–1882*, 54; Paullin, *Rodgers*, 159–66.

27. Paullin, *Rodgers*, 174–83; David F. Long, *Ready to Hazard: A Biography of Commodore William Bainbridge, 1774–1833*, 110.

28. R.G. 45: Record of Officers, C. 245, National Archives; Smith to Rodgers, 3 October 1806, R.G. 45: Secretary of the Navy Letters, VII, 243; Paullin, *Rodgers*, 172–73.

29. Smith to Rodgers, 9 July, 22 October, 23 October 1807, R.G. 45: Secretary of the Navy Letters, VII, 434, 522–23, 573; Paullin, *Rodgers*, 187–91.

30. Smith to Rodgers, 13 November, 9 December, 19 December 1807, R.G. 45: Secretary of the Navy Letters, VII, 529, 561–62, 571; Long, *Ready to Hazard*, 110–12; Long, *Nothing Too Daring*, 37–38; Paullin, *Rodgers*, 193–97. Extensive material on the trial is in *NDBP*, VI, 561–70.

31. Hamilton to Madison, 25 July 1809, Hamilton to Rodgers, Bainbridge, Decatur, Smith, and Evans, 6 August 1809, Bauer, *State Papers*, I, 60–63; Cooper, *History of the Navy*, II, 116; R.G. 24: Record of Officers, D; Paullin, *Rodgers*, 200–202, 204–7; Hamilton to Rodgers, 19 December 1809, R.G. 45: Secretary of the Navy Letters, VIII, 581; Wallace Hutcheon, Jr., *Robert Fulton: Pioneer of Underwater Warfare*, 108–12.

32. Hamilton to Rodgers, 2 June, 5 June, 9 June, 10 June 1810, Bauer, *State Papers*, II, 5–7; Rodgers to Hamilton, 4 August 1810, R.G. 45: Captains' Letters, XIX.

33. Rodgers to Minerva Rodgers, 23 May, 25 May 1811, RFP, ser. 2, Box 20; Log of *Little Belt*, copy in R.G. 45: Area File, A-7; Samuel Eliot Morison, *Old Bruin: Commodore Matthew C. Perry, 1794–1858*, 29–32; Benson J. Lossing, *The Pictorial Field-Book of the War of 1812*, 181–84; Alfred Thayer Mahan, *Sea Power in Its Relations to the War of 1812*, I, 258–59; Paullin, *Rodgers*, 220–29.

34. Paullin, *Rodgers*, 237–41; Cooper, *History of the Navy*, II, 122–32; Lossing, *Field-Book*, 184–85.

35. Hamilton to Rodgers, 14 January, 17 March, 3 April, 4 April, 14 May 1812, R.G. 45: Secretary of the Navy Letters, IX, 540, 580, X, 6, 9, 38; Lossing, *Field-Book* 183n; Paullin, *Rodgers*, 244–45.

36. Hamilton to Rodgers, 21 May, 22 June 1812, R.G. 45: Sec-

retary of the Navy Letters, X, 41, 69–70; Rodgers to Hamilton, 3 June 1812, Decatur to Hamilton, 8 June 1812, R.G. 45: Captain's Letters, XXIII; Frank L. Owsley, Jr., "Paul Hamilton," in Paolo E. Coletta, Robert G. Albion, and K. Jack Bauer, eds., *American Secretaries of the Navy*, I, 96–97; Edward K. Eckert, *The Navy Department in the War of 1812*, 19; Paullin, *Rodgers*, 245–46.

37. Hamilton to Rodgers, 5 June, 18 June 1812, Hamilton to Decatur, 2 June 1812, R.G. 45: Secretary of the Navy Letters, X, 49, 59, 61; Hamilton, Circular, 19 June 1812, Bauer, *State Papers*, IV, 135; Rodgers to Hamilton, 19 June, 21 June 1812, R.G. 45: Captains' Letters, XXIV; Rodgers and Decatur Agreement, 21 June 1812, R.G. 45: Area File, A-7. Decatur asked to be excused from the agreement following his capture of the *Macedonian*. Decatur to Rodgers, 17 January (1813), RFP, ser. 2, Box 21.

38. Rodgers to Hamilton, 1 September 1812, Bauer, *State Papers*, IV, 144–45; Cooper, *History of the Navy*, II, 149–53; Lossing, *Field-Book*, 435–36; Mahan, *Sea Power, 1812*, I, 319–25; Theodore Roosevelt, *The Naval War of 1812*, 73–78; Paullin, *Rodgers*, 250–58.

39. Hamilton to Rodgers and Decatur, 9 September 1812, Hamilton to Rodgers, Bainbridge, and Decatur, 2 October 1812, R.G. 45: Secretary of the Navy Letters, X, 146–47, 167; Rodgers to Hamilton, 31 December 1812, R.G. 45: Captains' Letters, XXV; Mahan, *Sea Power, 1812*, I, 403–5; Paullin, *Rodgers*, 260–62; Roosevelt, *Naval War*, 106–7.

40. Jones, Circular, 22 February 1813, Jones to Rodgers, 29 April 1813, Bauer, *State Papers*, IV, 152–53, 156–57; Rodgers to Jones, 27 September 1813, R.G. 45: Captains' Letters, XXXI; Robert Wilden Neeser, *Statistical and Chronological History of the United States Navy 1775–1907*, II, 128–29; Paullin, *Rodgers*, 264–71.

41. Rodgers to Jones, 19 February 1814, R.G. 45: Captains' Letters, XXXIV; Cooper, *History of the Navy*, II, 297–98; Paullin, *Rodgers*, 272–73; Roosevelt, *Naval War*, 286.

42. Jones to Rodgers, 12 March, 16 April 1814, R.G. 45: Secretary of the Navy Letters, XI, 239, 279; Minerva Rodgers, Recollections of Trip to Baltimore by John Rodgers, RFP, ser. 1, Box 19d.

43. Jones to Rodgers, 19 August, 23 August, 29 August 1814, R.G. 45: Secretary of the Navy Letters, XI, 409, 431, 434–35; Rodgers to Jones, 14 July, 23 August, 27 August, 29 August 1814, Porter to Jones, 23 August, 27 August 1814; R.G. 45: Captains' Letters, XXVIII; Rodgers to Minerva Rodgers, 23 August, 24 August 1814, RFP, ser. 1, Box 14, ser. 2, Box 20; Mahan, *Sea Power*

1812, II, 350; Cooper, *History of the Navy*, II, 307; Paullin, *Rodgers*, 282–89; Long, *Nothing Too Daring*, 169–71.

44. Rodgers to Jones, 24 September 1814, R.G. 45: Captains' Letters, XXXIX; Rodgers to Minerva Rodgers, 28 August 1814, RFP, ser. 1, Box 14; Jones to Rodgers, 5 September 1814, R.G. 45: Secretary of the Navy Letters, XI, 412; Jones to E. Jones, 20/21 September 1814, quoted in Eckert, *Navy Department*, 29; Lossing, *Field-Book*, 948–49, 954, 956; Paullin, *Rodgers*, 289–97.

45. Jones to Rodgers, 19 September 1814, R.G. 45: Secretary of the Navy Letters, XI, 418–419; Rodgers to Jones, 21 September, 23 September 1814, R.G. 45: Captains' Letters, XXXIX; Rodgers to Minerva Rodgers, 23 September 1814, RFP, ser. 2, Box 20.

46. Madison to Rodgers, 24 November 1814, RFP, ser. 2, Box 22; Jones to President of the Senate, 15 November 1814, Rep. William Reed, Report, 9 January 1815, *American State Papers. Documents Legislative and Executive of the Congress of the United States. Naval Affairs*, I, 320–24, 354–59; *Public Statutes at Large*, III, 202–3; Paullin, *Naval Administration*, 166–67; Irving Brant, *James Madison*, VI, 346.

47. Paullin, *Naval Administration*, 168–69; Paullin, *Rodgers*, 301–3; Robert Greenhalgh Albion, *Makers of Naval Policy 1798–1947*, 49; Rodgers to Minerva Rodgers, 14 February, 27 February 1815, RFP, ser. 2, Box 20.

48. Record of Officers, E (M330, R3); Rodgers, Commission, 28 February 1815, RFP, ser. 3A, vol. 2; R.G. 45: Journal of the Board of Naval Commissioners (BNC), I, 1–4; Paullin, *Naval Administration*, 170–71.

49. Johnson, *Rodgers*, 7, 36; Paullin, *Rodgers*, 362–82.

50. BNC Journal, I, 6–7, 10, 13, 15–17; Crowninshield to BNC, 29 April, 18 May, 23 May, 13 June 1815, R.G. 45: BNC Letters Received, I, 3–4; Paullin, *Naval Administration*, 171–73; Brant, *Madison*, VI, 388; Long, *Ready to Hazard*, 195; Gardner W. Allen, *Commodore Hull: The Papers of Isaac Hull*, 39.

51. BNC Journal, I, 60; Charles Lee Lewis, *The Romantic Decatur*, 181; Archibald Douglas Turnbull, *Commodore David Porter 1780–1843*, 249.

52. BNC Journal, I, 9–10, 48; Rodgers to Crowninshield, 2 May 1815, Bauer, *State Papers*, VI, 190–91; Edwin M. Hall, "Benjamin Crowninshield," in Coletta, *Secretaries*, I, 117–18; Paullin, *Rodgers*, 309–10. When asked to recommend a Virginia site, the commissioners could not agree.

53. *Public Statutes at Large*, III, 321.

54. Crowninshield to Rodgers, 20 December 1816, 10 February,

20 February 1818, BNC Letters Received, I, 57, 107, 109; BNC Journal, I, 63.

55. BNC Journal, I, 86; Monroe to Senate, 20 April 1818, *American Papers*, I, 510–24; James E. Valle, *Rocks and Shoals*, 62.

56. Charles Francis Adams, ed., *Memoirs of John Quincy Adams, Comprising Portions of His Diary from 1795 to 1848*, IV, 132–44 *passim*. In December 1818 Rodgers had Porter plant an item in the *National Intelligencer* claiming that he was not offered the post. His motivation is uncertain. Adams, *Adams*, IV, 185. Monroe's opposition to Rodgers's serving as Acting Secretary vanished by 1823 when he occupied the post between 1 and 16 September. BNC Journal, IV, n.p.

57. Rodgers to Calhoun, 24 December 1818, Rodgers to Thompson, 17 January, 31 January, 9 December 1820, *American Papers*, I, 583–84, 647–52, 677–80; Craig Symonds, *Navalists and Anti-Navalists*, 225–27; Paullin, *Naval Administration*, 177–78; For Rodgers's interest in ship preservation, see Charles Haines, "Ship Preservation in the Old Navy," *The American Neptune*, XLII (1982), 279–81.

58. Rodgers to Thompson, 18 January 1821, 23 December 1822, *American Papers*, I, 735, 873–76; Paullin, *Rodgers*, 389.

59. Paullin, *Rodgers*, 384–86; Long, *Ready to Hazard*, 234, 239; Alexander Slidell Mackenzie, *Life of Stephen Decatur*, 384–86.

60. Rodgers to Crowninshield, 20 January 1818, Rodgers to Thompson, 31 January 1820, 4 January 1821, *American Papers*, I, 481, 652, 685.

61. Rodgers to Thompson, 2 February 1822, Rodgers to Sen. James Pleasants, 8 February 1822, Monroe to Senate, 9 December 1822, Thompson to Pleasants, 11 December 1822, Southard to Rodgers, 29 September 1823, Rodgers to Southard, 16 November, 14 November 1823, *American Papers*, I, 786, 815, 822, II, 175–76, 1121; *Public Statutes at Large*, IV, 72; Long, *Nothing Too Daring*, 219–24; BNC Journal, IV.

62. Adams, *Adams*, VI, 358; Morison, *Old Bruin*, 86; Southard to Rodgers, 15 September 1824, RFP, ser. 1, Box 14; James M. Merrill, "Midshipman DuPont and the Cruise of the *North Carolina*, 1825–1827," *The American Neptune*, XL (1980), 211–25; Field, *America and Mediterranean*, 118.

63. BNC Journal, IV; Merrill, "Cruise," 212–23; Field, *America and Mediterranean*, 190–19, 134–35; Paullin, *Negotiations*, 137–40; Paullin, *Rodgers*, 327–58; Morison, *Old Bruin*, 75, 90, 95–101; Rodgers to Secretary of the Navy, 7 July, October 1825, 18 July, 11 September 1826, *American Papers*, II, 112, 733, Bauer, *State Papers*, II,

313–28. The correspondence relating to the Turkish mission is reprinted in *House Executive Document 250, 22nd Congress, 1st Session*, 14–51. Rodgers, "Memorandum of the Conversation with the Capudan Pacha at Tenedos," is in RFP, ser. 1, Box 14, and his correspondence with the Turk is in ser. 2, Box 22.

64. BNC Journal, VIII, 30, 90, 961. Rodgers's commission, 1 October 1827, is in RFP, ser. 1, Box 17.

65. Adams, *Adams*, VII, 501; Johnson, *Rodgers*, 9–10; Paullin, *Rodgers*, 383–84.

66. Adams, *Adams*, VIII, 354, 540.

67. BNC Journal, XI, 341–71, 538–42, 588–93, XII, 321–40, XIII, 285–316, 344–51; Paullin, *Rodgers*, 393–94.

68. W. Kemble to Rodgers, 29 January 1834, Dickerson to Rodgers, 26 June 1835, *House Documents 423, 25th Congress, 2nd Session*, 3–4; W. Patrick Strauss, "Mahlon Dickerson," Coletta, *Secretaries*, I, 155; Paullin, *Rodgers*, 390–91.

69. Rodgers to Dickerson, 2 March 1836, *American Papers*, IV, 400–403.

70. BNC Journal, CIV, 406; Dickerson to Rodgers, 1 May 1837, RFP, ser. 2, Box 21.

71. Rodgers to Minerva Rodgers, 7 May, 9 May 1837, RFP, ser. 1, Box 14; Long, *Nothing Too Daring*, 164n; Paullin, *Rodgers*, 369, 395–99.

72. Thomas Hart Benton, *Thirty Years' View*, II, 144–45.

Isaac Hull.

R. F. Stockton. Courtesy of Naval Photographic Center.

THE TWILIGHT OF THE
SAILING NAVY

ISAAC HULL: BULWARK OF THE SAILING NAVY

BY LINDA M. MALONEY

The one fact that is universally known about Isaac Hull is that he was a bona fide war hero. As "the conqueror of the *Guerriere*," he made his imperishable mark in the Navy in 1812, and the reputation has followed him. But from our perspective it may be more useful to see Hull as a man in transition. He entered the Navy as a lieutenant at its very beginning in 1798, and he died a commodore in 1843, just as steam was making serious inroads on sail, and the introduction of rifled guns was about to put a permanent end to the era of the wooden warship. Hull's career is interesting as an example of adaptation to changing circumstances. He spent almost all of his first fifteen years in the Navy afloat; of his remaining thirty years of service, two-thirds were served on shore in navy yards. From an era of almost uninterrupted war and international tension, the United States passed in 1815 into a period of thirty years of peace; from operations, the emphasis shifted to building. Isaac Hull's career mirrored this change. When, within a few years of his death, the country went to war again, the Navy would reflect the changes wrought during peacetime.

Hull was probably the nearest to a self-made man that the officer corps of his generation could boast. Like everyone else, of course, he received his initial appointment by political preferment: his uncle, William Hull, was a prominent Boston Republican and friend of the *Constitution*'s first commander, Samuel Nicholson. That was how Isaac Hull came to be named fourth lieutenant of the new frigate, the appointment dating from his twenty-fifth birthday, 9 March 1798. These political connections were no substitute for ability, however. By the end of *Constitution*'s second cruise, all four of the officers

Isaac Hull. The engraving below the portrait represents the climactic moment in the battle between the *Constitution* and the *Guerriere*. This was
the first American naval victory in the War of 1812. It destroyed the
myth of British invincibility and earned for the ship the nickname "Old
Ironsides."

above Hull, including the captain, had been removed from the ship—
some from the Navy—and he found himself first lieutenant. He
continued to impress his commanding officers with his competence
and good sense. Thus, in 1805, when the Secretary of the Navy
recommended Hull to President Jefferson for promotion to captain,
he mentioned that "he is a favorite nephew of our good friend General Hull, who interests himself much in his advancement," but was
also aware that "his character in the Navy is remarkably high."[1]

Hull's beginnings were anything but auspicious. Second son of a Connecticut family of declining fortunes, he went to sea before the mast as a young boy and never had anything that could be called an education. He got his navigational mathematics at night school, between voyages. He commanded merchant ships for four years, from 1794 to 1798, but his three ventures were disastrous: two captures by the French and one financial failure. When Stephen Higginson remarked in 1798 that the officers of the *Constitution* were almost all "incapable of getting their living in the common pursuits of life" and, therefore, turned to the Navy as a last resort, he could well have been thinking of Isaac Hull.[2]

But Isaac Hull was a navy man born. In the service he had at last found his appointed niche in life. So devoted to the Navy was he, that he never took leave of absence to make a merchant voyage, even when he desperately needed money. He never took leave for any reason until 1835, when, after thirty-seven years of service, he spent two years in Europe for his wife's health. Then, at what for most men would be retirement age even in civilian life, he returned to make one last cruise in command.

No one had to teach Hull to love the Navy. It was his element. But he did learn from some of the older men how (and how not) to be a good officer. His first commander, Samuel Nicholson, was an object lesson in what *not* to do; but the second, Silas Talbot, was probably the major influence in Hull's career.

Talbot's revolutionary service had been in the Army and in privateering. This service had several important implications for young Hull, who was Talbot's first lieutenant. First, Talbot was a competent seaman but had no pretense to a particular skill. He gave his executive officer a free hand in running the ship, and Hull made the most of the opportunity to master his profession. Not only that; he learned how to command, and how to delegate. When Charles Morris became Hull's first lieutenant in 1810, he noted that "Captain Hull . . . gives his first lieutenant every opportunity of displaying taste or talent that they can desire."[3] That was the legacy of Silas Talbot.

Hull learned something else from Talbot, perhaps owing to the latter's background: to spare the cat. To rule with the lash was certainly not politic in privateers, and in the less-confined situation of the Army, its use was not so frequent as in the Navy. Officers brought up on shipboard, amid men closely packed and far from the law, found security in the terror of the lash. Silas Talbot punished lightly and infrequently, at no cost to order or discipline. There were officers—such as Alexander Murray—whose slovenly ships showed that, for them, sparing the cat was merely another expression of indolence. But the *Constitution*, under Talbot, and later under Hull, was shipshape, orderly, and fully controlled by a captain who commanded the respect of his men. When Hull left the frigate in 1812, his men begged him to remain with them. And, instructing his own nephew as a young officer, Isaac Hull adjured him "not to suffer yourself or any under you to punish the men unnecessarily."[4]

Hull was so fond of Talbot that, after the latter's resignation from the Navy in 1801, he toyed with the idea of joining him in a settlement in the West. But chronic lack of funds and love for the Navy combined to keep him where he was. Hull was by this time so proficient an officer that he easily dominated his last commander, Hugh G. Campbell, in the intervening year before he received his first independent command in the schooner *Enterprise*. During the cruise under Campbell, Hull became legendary in the Navy for his coolness in rescuing the frigate *Adams* from the rocks near Algeciras. In the *Enterprise*, and later in the brig *Argus*, he gained further reputation in the eyes of both senior and junior officers; one of the latter dubbed him "the active Captain Hull."

By the time Edward Preble arrived to command the Mediterranean squadron in 1803, Isaac Hull was thirty years old. Though he became known as one of "Preble's boys," he was so with a difference. Preble seems never to have regarded Hull as under his tutelage, but judged him from the first as a reliable subordinate. One of his first actions was to detach the *Argus* for independent service, remarking to the Secretary of the Navy that "I have made choice of this vessel more particularly on account of the judgment, prudence and firmness of her commander, Lieutenant Commandant Hull, on whose discretion I rely with confidence."[5]

After participating in Preble's attacks on Tripoli, an object lesson in daring and resourcefulness in the use of a small force, Hull was chosen for another independent assignment. He was sent, with the *Argus* and another brig, to furnish naval support for William Eaton's land expedition against Tripoli. It was Hull's naval guns that ensured the capture of Derna and held it until the peace treaty and evacuation of the American forces. In a sense, the naval operation at Derna was Preble in miniature. But it would be a long time before Hull again had occasion to practice fleet maneuvers, and never in war.

One of the most striking features of young Isaac Hull's character was his amiability. There is no evidence that in the first forty years of his life he ever had a serious personal quarrel. After the Tripolitan War, he remained a close friend of Edward Preble and of William Eaton, but also of their mortal enemy, John Rodgers. Some people found this trait peculiar, even contemptible. William Bainbridge wrote to Rodgers in 1814, with more than a touch of condescension, that "Hull is as fat and good-natured as ever,"[6] and it was Bainbridge who finally succeeded in provoking Hull to resistance in 1815. But, serious though that falling-out was, it did not lead to a duel, as so often happened in those days. Hull loathed dueling and was frustrated as a commander because it was not forbidden by naval regulations. More than once a midshipman in his frigate was killed in a duel, and he found himself powerless to punish the deed. In his own case, his sense of humor would have made him admit that he presented all too broad a target!

Following the Tripolitan War, Hull, now a captain, spent most of the next two years supervising the building of gunboats in Connecticut and Rhode Island. He also got his father named Navy Agent for Connecticut, and the two of them executed contracts for boarding pikes, cutlasses, and pistols for the Navy. There were then no cost-plus contracts; Hull made the government's dollars go as far they could. At the same time, he respected the workmen and realized that quality work could only be had for quality wages. He cautioned the Navy Department about one would-be contractor: "He is very close and will be very apt to screw the carpenters so close after having made his own contract as to oblige them to slight their work unless they have good looking to."[7] Subsequently Hull learned that this same man had tried to get the pike and cutlass contract by advising the successful bidder, Nathan Starr, to "put on a good price, that the government were able to pay," and then underbidding him. This provoked a rare angry outburst from Hull: he informed Robert Smith that "[Van Deusen's] only object is gain and . . . almost any advantage would be taken by him to obtain that object . . . . This is the first letter I ever had occasion to write to the injury of any person nor should I be induced to do it now were I not compelled to do so by what I consider my duty."[8] The whole episode was an object lesson in government contracts and shipbuilding that Hull would make use of as a navy yard commander in later years.

Shortly before the end of the embargo, Hull was ordered to his first frigate command in the *Chesapeake*, which he retained for seven months until the ship was laid up. The dull-sailing and unhappy *Chesapeake* was stationed at Boston for most of that period, and although Hull enjoyed the social life, he chafed at the enforced inactivity. In the summer of 1809 he made a cruise in Long Island Sound to acquaint his midshipmen with sea duty. There was a particular glut of midshipmen at this time because the recently built gunboats had already been laid up and their officers reassigned. Hull had more than a dozen of these young officers. He spent a month in the sound, instructing them in the navigation and working of the ship, and also in harbor mapping. This kind of concern for his subordinates, especially the youngest, was typical of Hull throughout his career.

After laying up the *Chesapeake*, Hull spent nearly a year at Boston on recruiting duty, a service universally detested by the officers. With the merchant fleet once more at sea, sailors were hard to come by, and even harder to keep once they were signed on. Hull's recruits were berthed in the *Chesapeake*, which was at the wharf, and it was all too easy for the men to escape. Hull appealed to the new Secretary of the Navy, Paul Hamilton, to let him fit out a gunboat as a receiving ship and anchor her in the harbor where desertion was at least a little more complicated. He incautiously wrote that "we . . . have been obliged either to lock them up in the storerooms, or put them in irons every night to prevent their getting away . . . ."[9]

Hamilton, who was unfamiliar with the Navy and had never met the genial Hull, was shocked at this apparent brutality. He wrote Hull to stop it at once, adding a homily on punishment: "Degrading punishments are calculated to produce debasement of mind, which in time dries up all the springs of honorable action, and renders men callous to every generous impulse and a fit instrument for the basest purposes . . . ."[10]

Hull, who thought all this came with rather ill grace from a slave-holder, apologized for giving the Secretary the wrong impression. He explained that the men in irons were those who had shipped with the naval recruiters after having signed on and deserted from a merchantman. "With the two months' advance from the merchant ship, and the advance and bounty from the recruiting officers and other expenses brought them in debt from fifty to eighty dollars." Strenuous measures had to be taken to prevent a second desertion, this time at government expense.

As for the men in the storerooms, Hull thought he was doing them a favor by berthing them there, for they were short of warm clothing and could get some protection from the cold by rolling up in the old sails. Hull intended to leave no impression that he was less than sensitive to his duty toward the men under his command. "I am aware," he wrote, "that every attention ought to be paid to the happiness and comfort of men that enter the public service and that punishment ought not to be inflicted before a crime has been committed, and that only in proportion to the offense. Ever since I have had the honor of commanding men I have punished with great caution and have ever made it a rule not to punish a man before I had informed myself perfectly as to his guilt."[11]

In May 1810 Hull was ordered to command the frigate *President*. Within a few weeks he exchanged her for the *Constitution* because John Rodgers, the senior captain, was dissatisfied with the latter's sailing. Hull was delighted to get command of his old favorite, but her poor condition presented a special challenge. He quickly discovered that the principal cause of the difficulty was the ship's foul bottom. After nearly ten years of continuous salt-water service, she had accumulated an enormous load of oysters, barnacles, and mussels. Hull's first move was to take the ship up the Delaware as far as Brandywine Creek, where he lay for some weeks. As the shellfish died, he had the bottom worked over with an iron scraper he had devised, following this up by a scrubbing with river reeds. By the end of the summer, the ship's sailing was again at least respectable, and she performed creditably on a cruise to Europe in 1811–12. But she really needed a thorough overhaul of her copper. This she finally got in the spring of 1812. She was hove out at the Washington Navy Yard under Hull's supervision, where the copper was cleaned, repaired, and replaced as necessary. Only a few days after she was righted, and while she was still in the Potomac, war was declared.

The deeds of the *Constitution* in July and August of 1812 are well known but bear retelling because too little notice has been paid to the work Isaac Hull did *before* that critical time to make the successes possible. He had, first of all, restored the ship from a lumbering hulk to a first-class sailer. Without the work that brought this about, the *Constitution* would almost certainly have fallen to the enemy at dawn on 18 July 1812, when she found herself amid five British ships. Instead, Hull was able to turn to the south, set every sail, and make a run for it. For three desperate days and nights, Hull, his officers, and his 400-man crew worked to outdistance their pursuers. During the years 1810 to 1812 Hull had rebuilt the crew. The enlistments of most of his petty officers, the linch-pins of a ship's operation, had expired; they had left the Navy, and he had been forced to train a virtually green crew. A few courts-martial and even some floggings, both of which Hull loathed, had been necessary, but these combined with the use of "positive reinforcement" had good effect. Just before putting to sea Hull wrote that "I am in hopes . . . the moment the ship goes to sea to give them rest, and get them in heart, after which I shall have a tolerable good crew."[12] The role of Charles Morris, Hull's first lieutenant, was crucial in the escape. It was he who suggested a kedging maneuver during the chase in which a boat would carry the *Constitution*'s anchor ahead of the ship and drop it to the bottom, after which the men at the capstan would warp the ship ahead. While they strained on the capstan bars, another boat took a

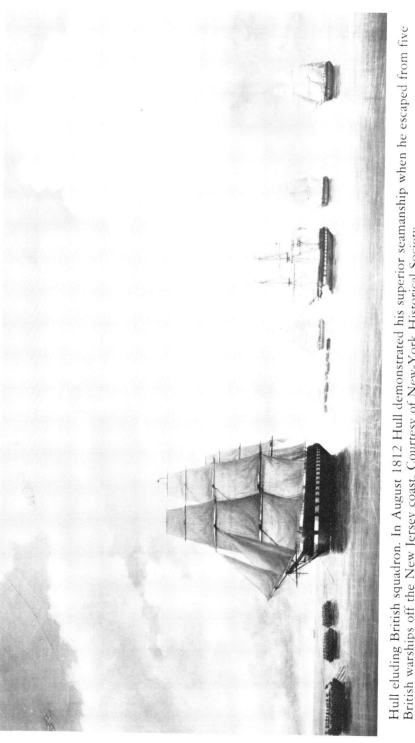

Hull eluding British squadron. In August 1812 Hull demonstrated his superior seamanship when he escaped from five British warships off the New Jersey coast. Courtesy of New-York Historical Society.

second anchor farther ahead. Many lieutenants would have feared to make suggestions to their commanding officer, and indeed Morris had been trying desperately to get out of the *Constitution* for six months before she sailed. He saw more opportunity for advancement in an independent command and had been in none too gracious a mood when he rejoined the ship only days before she sailed. Instead of resenting his attitude, Hull sympathized with Morris and did everything he could to make Morris's position in the *Constitution* advantageous to him. This treatment gave the lieutenant the confidence to suggest the kedging maneuver. Each time there was a breath of wind, Hull sent men to the yards to pour buckets of water on the sails to make them hold more wind. Twice during the chase when the ship surged forward before a breeze, Hull managed to retrieve all the boats that he had sent ahead to tow the ship or drop her anchor during the calms. The boats were hooked on and run up on the spare outboard spars without causing the frigate to lose way, and also without cutting any boat adrift and leaving its occupants to be captured. The second instance occurred during the night, and only a man of Hull's skill could have managed it. Few would have tried, and the admiration of the men saved was unlimited. After almost three full days a squall bore up on the *Constitution* near nightfall, and Hull took advantage of it and the subsequent darkness to widen the gap between his ship and the enemy.

The chase brought the crew together, and afterward the "Constitutions" were ready for anything. Their commander gave them public praise: "notwithstanding the length of the chase, and the officers and crew being deprived of sleep, and allowed but little refreshments during the time, not a murmur was heard to escape them."[13] The whole episode convinced the men that they had an unbeatable combination of ship, captain, officers, and crew.

Just before leaving Boston on their second sortie Hull wrote that "I have great confidence in the men, and they appear in good spirits."[14] Within a month the whole world would know Hull was right. On 2 August 1812, Hull and the *Constitution* spotted the *Guerriere* sailing alone and closed for battle. For three-quarters of an hour the ships maneuvered for position. Then Hull closed to within 200 yards of the enemy and opened fire. Broadsides were exchanged until Hull gained enough of a lead to cross the enemy's bow and pour a raking broadside into her. When the ships became entangled, riflemen in the tops and massed on the quarterdecks of both ships prevented boarding parties from lodging footholds on each other. By now the *Guerriere* had lost her mizzenmast. As the ships drifted apart, the foremast on the *Guerriere* fell against her mainmast, and both masts fell over the side. His ship was now a riddled hulk, and the *Guerriere's* captain had no choice but to surrender.

Hull's victory helped destroy the myth that Britain was invincible at sea and helped redress the shock many felt when they learned that Isaac's uncle, William Hull, had surrendered Detroit four days earlier without firing a shot. Returning with the *Guerriere's* battle flag, he once more gave the honor to Morris, the officers, and men: ". . . it gives me great pleasure to say that from the smallest boy in the ship to the oldest seaman not a look of fear was seen."[15]

The crew's feeling about Hull, in contrast with another commander, became public when Hull resigned the command of the *Constitution* soon afterward. As Hull's pennant was lowered and William Bainbridge's hoisted, the ranks broke, and the men rushed to surround Hull, begging him to stay with them, promising even to fight a line-of-battle ship under his command.[16] Bainbridge was forced to send the armorer and several other men out of the ship because they adamantly refused to sail with him.[17]

Hull always took a special interest in men who had been injured in the public service and in the surviving families of those killed. Richard Dunn, who lost his leg in the *Guerriere* engagement, became Hull's "shadow" for more than ten years, as Hull found work for him in the navy yard at Portsmouth and later at Boston. Hull believed, as a matter of policy, that a naval pension was granted for injuries suffered, and should not bar the recipient from earning wages in the public service. In other words, he thought it shocking that a pension granted because of an injury should become a means of keeping the recipient poor by depriving him of the opportunity to work as he was capable. He discussed the matter at length with the Accountant of the Navy in 1814. The two of them were in agreement, but report had it that the Secretary of the Navy was opposed to the practice; so Hull and the Accountant kept the matter between them, and Hull's pensioners went on drawing their pay.[18]

Isaac Hull's marriage in January 1813 made shore duty more attractive than it had been in his bachelor days. From that time on, most of his service was in navy yards. He replaced Bainbridge at Boston while the latter was cruising in the *Constitution*. When Bainbridge returned in February 1813, he expected to resume the station, so Hull moved on to Portsmouth, New Hampshire, where he commanded from March 1813 to March 1815. The public reaction to Hull's victory, followed by those of Decatur and Bainbridge, had spurred Congress to vote an expansion of the Navy, including its first three line-of-battle ships. One of these was to be built at Portsmouth. As in the past, the captain who supervised construction would be entitled to the command.

Hull had a great many obstacles to overcome in this assignment. For one thing, Portsmouth had never been a fully operational navy yard before this, so he had to organize the whole operation from scratch and build everything he needed to carry it forward. His most important contribution was the "ship house" or enclosed building ways, which was Hull's original suggestion though it has been claimed for Bainbridge. After Hull's ship, the *Washington*, was launched, the house covered the unfinished *New Hampshire* from 1817 until she was launched in 1864. The site is still the location of the largest enclosed building ways in the United States.

The second big problem at Portsmouth was a shortage of live oak timber for the frame of the ship. This timber had been cut and stored in the 1790s, but in the intervening years pieces had been "borrowed" as needed to repair existing ships. Several hundred pieces were miss-

Launching the USS *Washington*. During his long career, Hull, an able administrator, commanded the Boston, Portsmouth, New Hampshire, and Washington Navy Yards. The USS *Washington* was launched at Portsmouth on 1 October 1814. Courtesy of the Naval Historical Center.

ing at Portsmouth, and although two frames had been deposited at Boston, William Bainbridge insisted on taking everything he needed to build his ship, the *Independence*, before he would spare any pieces for Portsmouth. Hull had to make do with white oak, a less durable material, in several critical places.

These wartime battleships were based on plans drawn up by Joshua Humphreys, but the plans suffered heavy alterations at the hands of Secretary of the Navy William Jones, with advice liberally supplied by Bainbridge. Hull disapproved of many of the changes, but his objections were overridden. Both he and Bainbridge had difficulty finding adequate builders. Bainbridge had the talented Hartt father and son, but he quarreled with them early on. Hull had to manage with local workmen who had never before built anything larger than a 200-ton merchantman. That meant that a large proportion of the day-to-day supervision fell on his shoulders. The best naval architects of the day, Noah Brown and Henry Eckford, were on the lakes, building ships at furious speed for emergency defense. Hull and Bainbridge had to be content to work more deliberately, though both were chafing to get their ships launched in order to break the British blockade.

That blockade was a major source of anxiety to Hull. Particularly in 1814, the British intensified their raids on the coast of New England. Hull was theoretically responsible for defending the entire coast of New Hampshire and Maine, with a naval force of one or two brigs and a flotilla of gunboats at Portsmouth and Portland. An adequate defense was patently impossible. Army support was minimal, and the few guns mounted to defend Portsmouth harbor were served by a highly unreliable militia. The *Washington*, on the stocks, was completely vulnerable, making Hull all the more anxious to launch. But the whole tense summer of 1814, and a series of night alarms, had to be passed before she went afloat on 1 October.

By that time the United States was nearly bankrupt. Hull had nothing with which to pay his workmen and suppliers but virtually worthless Treasury notes; so little further progress was made on the *Washington* before the war ground to its exhausted halt in February 1815. Hull gave no thought to possible further glory. While John Rodgers regretted "that anything occurred to prevent my trying [a new frigate's] *stings* on John Bull's hide,"[19] Hull had had all the war he wanted, and then some. "I have to congratulate you on the news of peace," he wrote an army friend, "and I hope it will be many years before we are again involved in war."[20]

The experience of the War of 1812 had focused public attention on the Navy. It seemed to the friends of that service an opportune

time to effect some changes, such as establishing the ranks of commodore and admiral, improvement of building facilities, and reorganization of naval administration. Hull took a keen interest in these
matters. The rank question was a particular sore point. He had no
personal stake—or so he thought at the time—because he was ninth
on the captains' list and very unlikely ever to be an admiral. But he
thought that rank ought to be regularized "to prevent every midshipman that has command of a gunboat on a separate station taking
on himself the name of *Commodore*."[21] At that time there were six
"commodores" junior to Hull, two of them masters-commandant.
While there were ten grades of officers in the Army, plus the possibility of brevet appointments, the naval officer could aspire to only
three promotions. Often he was a captain at age thirty, with no higher
rank to hope for. But nothing was done about the rank question. It
would prove to be an even greater problem for Hull in later years.

The eventual result of the deliberations of 1814–15 was the reorganization of the Navy Department by creation of a Board of Navy
Commissioners, to consist of three captains. They were to oversee
the "practical" aspects of administration, including supervision of
navy yards, procurement, and other technical matters outside the
Secretary's ken. The new Secretary, B. W. Crowninshield, solicited
the advice of John Rodgers on the composition of the first board
and received in reply a famous letter filled with scathing pen portraits
of most of the captains. The only individuals who escaped undamaged
were Hull, David Porter, and Charles Morris. Rodgers described
Hull as "a man of most amiable disposition, and although he does
not pretend to much science is however an excellent seaman and at
the same time unites all the most essential qualifications necessary
for such a situation."[22]

Rodgers eventually accepted appointment as chairman of the navy
board, and persuaded Hull to join him, along with David Porter.
Hull was very hesitant, because of the expense and political friction
he foresaw at Washington. But his wife was nursing a dying mother,
and he did not want to take the *Washington* to sea, leaving her in
that situation. So he accepted the appointment. But it turned out as
he foresaw. Even before Hull reached the capital on 25 April 1815,
a jurisdictional quarrel had erupted between the commissioners and
the Secretary. Hall was appalled to find himself in the middle of such
an acrimonious dispute, which was being carried on partly in the
newspapers. He beat a hasty retreat. When William Bainbridge left
Boston for the Mediterranean on 2 July, Hull already had his bags
packed. He left Washington the next day and took over the navy
yard command two weeks later.

The Hull family, now augmented by Mrs. Hull's two sisters and Isaac Hull's two nieces, settled in for a happy peacetime life at Boston. But they reckoned without William Bainbridge. The latter had reached the Mediterranean just in time to find that Stephen Decatur had defeated the Algerian fleet and concluded a peace treaty with the Dey. That, and an attack of measles, put the commodore in a very bad mood. He blew into Boston on 19 November 1815, convinced that he had been unjustly ordered away from his station and that he had every right to resume it, just as he had done in 1813. But this time, to his astonishment, Isaac Hull refused to move at his convenience. Hull now had heavy family responsibilities and his finances were, as usual, precarious. One of his reasons for leaving Washington had been that he could not afford to live there. He appealed to the Secretary, and his claim to remain in command was upheld.

Unfortunately for Hull, the department tried to ease the situation by making Bainbridge commander afloat at Boston. This led to a running jurisdictional quarrel during the whole of the next four years. When the Monroe administration came into office in 1817, Bainbridge renewed his claim with full vigor, but again without success. He had one big advantage: the commandant's clerk at the yard, Benjamin Fosdick, was his appointee and confidante. Evidently Fosdick reported to Bainbridge the contents of Hull's correspondence with the Navy Department almost before Hull had read or written it. Not long after Bainbridge left Boston, Fosdick did too, and some months later it was learned that he had taken with him a large sum of money that he had obtained by falsifying the payrolls. Hull's swift action resulted in Fosdick's capture and the recovery of the money, but his enemies made it appear that Hull was somehow responsible for the defalcation.

During his early years at Boston, Hull was frustrated in his desire to expand and improve the yard because the navy commissioners wanted to draw up a master plan before deciding which yards to expand and which to close. (They never did close any, but some emerged as more important than others.) An order in April 1817 to dismiss all blacks and foreigners from government service reduced the Boston yard's work force to thirteen. But soon afterward the decision was taken to retain the station as a major building and outfitting yard. Employment took a permanent upturn, and Hull did not inquire too closely about citizenship. During his tenure Hull laid down two ships-of-the-line, with ship houses to cover them. He also built a range of brick storehouses with sail and mold lofts over them, and a brick wall around the yard in which were incorporated quarters for officers.

Hull had his own ideas about the direction which naval policy ought to take in these years. He wrote to Senator Samuel W. Dana of Massachusetts:

> I should be for repairing and keep[ing] in commission the ships we now have afloat, and build and launch about twenty heavy sloops of war . . . . Continue to build now and then a line of battle ship and collect as much timber for that class of ships as you please and put it in dock. But such ships as you build and do not want afloat, build houses over them and let them stand under cover until they are wanted. They then can be caulked, coppered and launched before you could get crews for them.

He pointed out that if heavy ships were launched in time of peace, "the moment they are in the water they become a great expense to the nation and soon go to decay, and become an eyesore to those that gave the money to build them."[23] But Hull knew that these ideas, though good taxpayer politics, would not set well with his brother officers, so he asked Dana not to let it be known the suggestion came from him.

The proposed sloops-of-war, Hull thought, would make good training vessels for young officers, of whom he had far too many in the yard. Their idleness, for want of regular duty, was bad for them and set a bad example; besides, each of them monopolized a seaman as his servant. The question of adequate employment for officers in peacetime was not solved by Hull or any of his successors. These young men, many of them married, could not live on half pay, which was twenty dollars a month for a lieutenant and ten for a midshipman. They needed their full salary and allowances (chamber money, rations, fuel and candles, servant's pay), but they found little to do in the navy yards apart from standing watch, and they were making no professional advancement. They were a constant source of trouble: quarreling, drinking, dueling, sometimes even stealing. Hull got along well enough with most of them, but there were one or two who were more than he could handle.

The first source of trouble was Captain John Shaw, who was just two places below Hull on the captains' list and one of those junior "commodores" about whom Hull had complained in 1814. When he took over from Bainbridge as commander afloat in November 1819, he impudently hoisted a commodore's pennant in the *Independence*. Hull kept quiet about it for the time being, but when Secretary of the Navy Smith Thompson issued a circular on 1 May 1820, on the subject of commodores—perhaps in response to a private suggestion by Hull—he immediately asked for a definition of the rank, and whether the department considered it as applying either to him or to Shaw. Thompson replied that "no captain in the Navy of the United States is considered by the Department as holding the station of commodore or entitled to wear a broad pennant of any kind unless he shall have been by the President of the United States or the Secretary of the Navy directly appointed to the command of a Squadron of vessels on separate service."[24] Thus, neither Hull nor Shaw was entitled to be "commodore," which meant that Shaw was going to have to remove the stars from his epaulets and the pennant from his masthead.

The summer went by, and no change was made. Finally, in September, Hull made an official complaint. A few months later the commissioners paid a visit to the navy yard, and John Rodgers told Shaw to haul down the pennant, or else. The result was that Shaw opened a correspondence with all the "commodores" junior to Hull to incite them to rescue their threatened dignity, and incidentally to supply him with any damaging information about Hull they might have. While that was going on, the crisis of Fosdick's theft occurred, providing Shaw with further ammunition. Moreover, he entered into alliance with Lieutenant Joel Abbot, one of the idle young officers at Boston who was angry at Hull because the Navy Department— over Hull's protests—had cut off extra allowances to the supernumerary lieutenants. The two of them set to work to blacken Hull's reputation in every conceivable manner. They were abetted by Bainbridge, who returned to Boston, and renewed his application for command, in 1820. Again unsuccessful, he turned his hand to orchestrating the attack on Hull, remaining discreetly in the background throughout. The assault was made more effective, and eventually became a national scandal, because the cause was taken up by the old Federalist faction, which was now adopting the Jacksonian movement. Hull, despite his horror of politics, was identified with the old-line Republicanism of John Quincy Adams and the incumbent Monroe administration.

The result of all this was a series of bitter trials in 1822, carried out against a background of lurid abuse in the Federalist–Jacksonian press. Shaw's court-martial in March sentenced him to six months' suspension, a light sentence that he professed to regard as a personal triumph. Abbot got two years' suspension. But the public attack continued at such volume that Hull was forced to ask for a court of inquiry on his own conduct. Some of Hull's actions had been well-intentioned but indiscreet. For example, in 1816 he had bought a piece of land adjacent to the yard. He had first begged the Navy Department to buy the property, which was needed to expand the yard, but they had refused. Later, when it was decided that the yard should, indeed, be enlarged, Hull sold the land to the Navy, at a very small profit. That transaction was paraded in 1822 as an example of "peculation." The court of inquiry, headed by John Rodgers, found Hull's conduct, except for such minor indiscretions, "correct and meritorious."

After all these trials, Hull was glad to leave Boston the following year to take command of the Pacific squadron, hoisting his first commodore's pennant in the frigate *United States*. The years of his cruise, 1824–27, saw the final actions of the wars for independence in Peru and Chile. Hull was "neutral in favor of the revolution," but he behaved with scrupulous correctness and was a credit to the diplomacy of American naval officers. A British colleague described him, on board the *United States* at Callao in 1826: "He is a stout, thick set, rather shortish man, has a pleasing, rather handsome, countenance, and very much beloved by his officers and men. Indeed, he brought to my recollection several of the captains of the *old school*."[25] When out of earshot—which was not very far in those days—his officers and men called him "Uncle Isaac."

On his return to the United States, Hull assumed command of the Washington Navy Yard. That place had been in the doldrums during the declining years of its former commander, Thomas Tingey. It had ceased to be a building yard for large vessels because of the shallow water in the Potomac, but it was politically expedient to keep it as an active establishment. During Hull's tenure, 1829–35, the new direction of the yard became clear: it was to be the Navy's principal ironworking establishment. Hull, working closely with John Rodgers and the other commissioners, developed the facilities there for production of anchors, chain cables, and cambooses (ships' galleys), as well as lesser ironwork for ships. Only one naval ship was launched at Washington during this time: the schooner *Experiment*, built on the principle of lamination, without an interior frame. She was an unhandy craft, but much safer than anyone supposed. Her active career was brief, simply because no officer wanted to risk his life in her.

Hull left Washington in 1835 and, for the first time since he entered the Navy, took leave of absence for travel abroad. He and his wife spent two years in Europe, but the financial panic of 1837 broke just as they were preparing to return home. The expenses of the trip and the precarious situation of his private affairs made it imperative for Hull to seek active duty again. In 1838 he served a few months as chairman of the board to revise the tables of allowances for naval ships and then, in the fall, accepted the plum of naval commands, the Mediterranean squadron, with his flag in the new ship-of-the-line *Ohio*.

It was an ambitious undertaking for a man of sixty-five. His health was poor: he had just undergone a throat operation and suffered from chronic lung ailments. During the cruise he had two strokes. Also, Hull was by this time almost totally deaf. These conditions made him very dependent on his wife, so that she and her sister accompanied him on the cruise as a matter of course. It was then quite the usual thing for squadron commanders and even junior officers to take their families on board; the petty officers also brought along wives, who frequently acted as maids for the officers' ladies. But in the *Ohio* this caused trouble. The navy commissioners had decided, as an experiment, to berth the ship's lieutenants on the orlop deck, far down in the ship. These gentlemen supposed that the experiment would be brief, and that once the ship was at sea they would be able to move up to the captain's quarters on the gundeck, the captain and commodore sharing the poop. The presence of the Hull family, however, meant that the status quo would have to be maintained. The lieutenants and surgeon started an uproar in the newspapers, alleging irreparable damage to their health. Hull, who had endured many a gale in a schooner, and once roasted through a Norfolk summer in a gunboat, thought this conduct rather unbecoming to naval officers, not to say ungentlemanly. As the cruise went on, things only got worse. The presence of a captain in the ship insulated Hull from direct contact with his aggrieved subordinates. His deafness further isolated him, as most of the ship's tidings came to him through his wife and, of course, from her own point of view. She told him that the officers treated her in an insulting manner— which, judging by their own letters, was true. Hull found this behavior intolerable and finally, in April 1840, sent the malcontents home.

Secretary of the Navy James K. Paulding had, up to this time, sided with Hull and, as Hull interpreted his letters, given him authority to punish the offending officers.[26] But once in the United States, the officers had the Secretary's ear as well as the backing of influential friends. (One of the most vocal complainants was Lieutenant Samuel F. DuPont.) Paulding accepted their whole story, even the notion that Mrs. Hull had taken command of the *Ohio*, and ordered them all restored to their places in the squadron. Hull was first astonished, then crushed. He wrote Paulding:

> It is somewhat remarkable that this station, the Mediterranean, was the scene of my early services in our then infant Navy; I witnessed

its rise, its progress and its advancement, bound myself to it, and hoped its course would be ever onward. And that now, it is the scene of my last services and I am here, I fear, to be a witness, of its fall, retrogradation and ruin, but my hopes and wishes are, to live long enough to see harmony and union, discipline and subordination, restored among its officers.[27]

It was not just Hull, or his family, who caused all this unhappiness. There was a serious breakdown of naval discipline in those years. Hull's Pacific cruise had been pacific indeed; but by the 1840s the situation of peacetime officers was becoming unendurable. Hull had been a lieutenant at twenty-five and a captain at thirty-three. Many of his lieutenants were now past forty, with command rank a distant dream. With all these smoldering wicks in the ships, there were plenty of explosions. Not only the *Ohio*, but the squadron's other ships, the *Brandywine* and the *Cyane*, were wracked with quarrels from start to finish. When the *Cyane* returned to the United States in 1841, nearly every officer in her was court-martialed, including the captain.

The miserable climax of this dismal cruise was the war scare of 1841, growing out of the Maine boundary dispute. On receiving several alarming reports via France and Spain, Hull called a council of his officers and decided to sortie from the Mediterranean to avoid being bottled up. By 6 April the ships were off Malaga, where they received reassurances that war was not imminent, but the *Brandywine*, which had been separated during a storm, went directly to the United States. Her captain, William C. Bolton, was subsequently tried and reprimanded for disobedience of orders. That ended the cruise on a sour note.

Further evidence of the topsy-turvy state of the Navy came from the *Cyane* trials. The court at Norfolk had given Master Commandant William K. Latimer a mild reprimand and a suspension, cashiered some of the junior officers, and sentenced Lieutenant Sylvanus Godon, one of the chief *Ohio* complainers before his transfer to the *Cyane*, to two years' suspension. But Godon and the others appealed to the Secretary, Abel P. Upshur, who proved even more pliant than Paulding. Every one of the sentences on the junior officers was overturned. Latimer was retried, and was passed over for promotion in 1842. Hull was so disgusted that he gave serious thought to resigning from the Navy and leaving the United States to settle in Europe. But it was too late. His health was badly undermined, and after a long winter of chest pain and cough, he died in February 1843.

In his last years Isaac Hull thought the Navy, and the country, were in a deplorable state, and so they were. And yet he and the other old pioneers had built better than they knew. The young officers who had been so troublesome to Hull proved themselves competent commanders in the Mexican War and later—on both sides—in the Civil War. They also presided over an era of social reform that made the Navy a better place for Hull's beloved Jack Tars. Hull and his generation were like fathers—often resented when in authority, remembered with affection when they are gone. Thus, the "old school" gave birth to the new.

FURTHER READING

Apart from popular material on Hull's exploits in the War of 1812, there is little to be found in printed sources. He has had only one full-length biography: Bruce Grant, *Isaac Hull, Captain of Old Ironsides*, which was compiled somewhat hastily to coincide with the sesquicentennial of the *Constitution*'s launch. A brief and partly accurate sketch appeared in Fletcher Pratt, *Preble's Boys*. Leo T. Malloy has compiled *Commodore Isaac Hull, U.S.N., His Life and Times*, not so much a life of Hull as a collection of interesting lore relating to the Derby locality and its notable personalities. A selection of Hull's papers, with some biographical continuity supplied, may be found in Gardner W. Allen, *Commodore Hull: The Papers of Isaac Hull*.

For Hull in the War of 1812, see Linda McKee [Maloney], "By Heaven, That Ship is Ours!," *American Heritage*, XVI, no. 1 (December 1964), pp. 4–11, 94–98. Less well-known episodes are treated in the author's articles, "A Forgotten Watchword," U.S. Naval Institute *Proceedings*, LXXIX, no. 10 (October 1963), p. 176, and "A Naval Experiment," *The American Neptune*, XXXIV, no. 3 (July 1974), pp. 188–96. See also "The U.S. Navy's Pacific Squadron: 1824–1827," in Robert William Love, Jr., ed., *Changing Interpretations and New Sources in Naval History.*

Important collections of Hull's papers may be found at the USS *Constitution* Museum in Boston and at the New-York Historical Society, as well as in the National Archives.

NOTES

1. Robert Smith to Thomas Jefferson, 27 March 1805, Thomas Jefferson Papers, Library of Congress.

2. Stephen Higginson to Timothy Pickering, 9 June 1798, American Historical Association, *Annual Report*, 1896, I, 806.

3. Charles Morris to Lemuel Morris, 20 July 1810, New-York Historical Society.

4. Isaac Hull to Joseph B. Hull, 7 June 1835, Hull Papers, USS *Constitution* Museum.

5. Preble to Robert Smith, 23 October 1803, *Naval Documents Related to the United States Wars with the Barbary Powers*, III, 161.

6. William Bainbridge to John Rodgers, 9 March 1814, Rodgers Family Papers, Series II, Library of Congress.

7. Hull to Charles W. Goldsborough, 27 December 1807, Boston Public Library.

8. Hull to Smith, 10 April 1808, R.G. 45: Captains' Letters, National Archives.

9. Hull to Paul Hamilton, 1 April 1810, Hull LB, New-York Historical Society.

10. Paul Hamilton to Hull, 8 April 1810, R.G. 45: Letters to Officers, Ships of War (OSW), National Archives.

11. Hull to Paul Hamilton, 16 April 1810, Hull LB, New-York Historical Society.

12. Hull to Paul Hamilton, 10 July 1812, R.G. 45: Captains' Letters, National Archives.

13. *Niles' Weekly Register*, II, 381.

14. Hull to Paul Hamilton, 2 August 1812, R.G. 45: Captains' Letters, National Archives.

15. Hull to Paul Hamilton, 30 August 1812, R.G. 45: Captains' Letters, National Archives.

16. Amos A. Evan, "Journal Kept on Board the United States Frigate *Constitution*, 1812 . . . ," *Pennsylvania Magazine of History*, XIX, entry for 15 September 1812.

17. *Constitution* log, 16 September 1812, R.G. 24: National Archives; Bainbridge to Paul Hamilton, 17 September 1812, R.G. 45: Captains' Letters, National Archives.

18. Hull to Thomas Turner, 2 January [1814], R.G. 217: Letters Received by the Accountant of the Navy, National Archives; Turner to Hull, 18 January 1814, Accountant's LB.

19. Rodgers to B. W. Crowninshield, 13 February 1815, B. W. Crowninshield Papers, Peabody Museum of Salem.

20. Hull to Samuel Storer, 21 February 1815, Hull LB, New-York Historical Society.

21. Hull to David Daggett, 18 November 1814, Hull LB, New-York Historical Society.

22. Rodgers to Crowninshield, 11 February 1815, B. W. Crowninshield Papers, Peabody Museum of Salem.

23. Hull to Samuel W. Dana, 8 March 1820, FDR Library.

24. Thompson to Hull, 17 May 1820, R.G. 45: Secretary of the Navy Letters to Commandants, National Archives.

25. "John Cunningham's Journal," *The Mariner's Mirror*, IX, 334.

26. James K. Paulding to Hull, 27 December 1838, 16 December 1839, Hull Papers, USS *Constitution* Museum.

27. Hull to Paulding, 5 December 1840, R.G. 45: Captains' Letters, National Archives.

ROBERT F. STOCKTON: NAVAL OFFICER AND REFORMER

BY HAROLD D. LANGLEY

Robert Field Stockton (1796–1866) was one of the most intelligent and versatile officers of the U.S. Navy in the Age of Sail. His background, education, philosophy, and personal qualities all contributed to making him an effective and highly esteemed officer and man. He was the first career naval officer to be elected to the U.S. Senate, and he was also mentioned as a candidate for President. But Stockton did not find political life particularly appealing, nor would he consent to any compromise of the principles that he believed to be right. He returned to private life and devoted himself to his family. He is well remembered for his contributions to the development of steam power in the Navy and to ending the practice of punishment by flogging.

The Stockton family had a long and honored association with New Jersey. Robert Stockton's immigrant ancestors were Quakers who acquired a large tract of land in the Princeton area. His paternal grandfather, Richard Stockton, was a member of the first graduating class of Princeton College, a lawyer, a member of the Executive Council of the Colony, and an associate justice of its Supreme Court. When the Revolution began, he sided with the rebels and was a signer of the Declaration of Independence. While a chairman of a committee of the Continental Congress, he was captured by the British in New York and imprisoned for a month. The hardships that he endured in prison undermined his health and he never fully recovered. He died in 1781.[1]

The future commodore's father, Richard Stockton, was the eldest son of the signer of the Declaration of Independence. A prominent lawyer, and a Federalist, he had a political career that included a

273

Robert F. Stockton. Courtesy of the Chicago Historical Society.

term in the U.S. Senate (1796–99), four unsuccessful bids for the governorship of New Jersey (1801–4), and a term in the U.S. House of Representatives (1813–15).[2] From the experiences of his grandfather and his father, young Robert Stockton learned of the demands and obligations of public service and a sense of duty to his country. From his lawyer father he learned to think critically and to get to the heart of every question. His father's example in politics and in law taught him the virtue of patience and discretion and the importance of principles. He was raised in a Federalist environment and had much admiration for the men of that persuasion whom he met through his father. In later life he said that if he had been of age in those days, he would probably have been a Federalist himself.[3]

As a young man Robert F. Stockton led a rather sheltered life. Much of the time he was privately tutored. For the most part, his contacts with other boys his age was limited to those who lived near his home.

During the brief period that Robert attended a local school, he proved himself among his peers and gained a reputation for personal courage and for coolness and self-possession in times of crisis. He made an effort to be respectful and courteous to all whom he met, but was quick to repay any insult or act of aggression. He cultivated a high-minded and generous attitude. For school bullies he had nothing but contempt. Whenever he found one of them preying on a weaker boy, he assisted the victim.[4]

In 1808, at the age of thirteen, he entered Princeton College where he distinguished himself in mathematics, languages, and elocution. He does not seem to have had a clear idea of what he wanted to do in life. No doubt he gave some thought to following in his father's footsteps, but the study of the law held no great appeal. In his more reflective moments Stockton may well have decided that it would be hard to surpass his grandfather and his father in the field of law. Possibly he was looking for a more active career. Whatever the case may have been, this was the time when the English-speaking world was reading about the life and exploits of Horatio Lord Nelson, the British naval officer who died in the act of defeating the combined French and Spanish fleets in 1805. Young Stockton was inspired by Nelson's exploits and dreamed of emulating him.[5] For a long time there seemed to be little hope of a naval career in the United States. Under President Jefferson the naval force had been cut back, and a heavy reliance was placed on gunboats. With no Navy to protect them on the high seas, American merchant ships were caught in the middle of a war between France and Great Britain and were seized by both sides for blockade violations. The impressment of American seaman by British naval officers was a further gross abuse of national pride and honor. These events undoubtedly fanned the patriotic ardor of young Stockton.

It was not until 1811 that he was able to apply for a midshipman's warrant. When he was accepted, he still had a year and a half to go to finish college. Why his father let him drop out of school is not known. Very possibly the father felt that a little time at sea would be a maturing experience. Ordered to join the frigate *President*, then at Newport, Rhode Island, Stockton left Princeton in February 1812 and reported to Commodore John Rodgers, the most widely known senior officer of the Navy.[6] So began a long and important association for young Stockton.

The *President* and the *Essex* sailed for New York on 28 March, and Stockton got his first taste of sea duty when the ships encountered a heavy gale that carried them south of the Delaware Bay. When war was declared in June, Rodgers promptly took his squadron to sea. Six days later, off Nantucket, they sighted the British 32-gun frigate *Belvidera* and gave chase. A running fight ensued. On board the *President* a bow gun exploded, killing one midshipman and wounding fourteen men, including Rodgers. The *President* lost ground, sustaining some damage from British shot, and Rodgers was unable to overtake the enemy vessel. The pursuit was called off and the rest of the squadron came up to join the flagship.[7]

Ever since he reported for duty, Stockton had observed Rodgers and the other officers on board the ship, noting their strengths and weaknesses. He could not help but be impressed with Rodgers, especially after he was wounded. With a fractured leg, Rodgers was supported by two of his men while he continued to command.[8] Here was an officer whom Stockton could emulate.

Rodgers had also taken the measure of Stockton. The military deportment and coolness in battle of this young and inexperienced officer were impressive. Rodgers and other officers noted that Stockton was prompt in his discharge of every duty; that he was quick to anticipate what was needed in every given situation; and that he was courteous, respectful, and had a sprightly disposition. Stockton's brief experience in battle had whetted his appetite for more excitement. The young midshipman's outlook and manner also made him a favorite with the crew, to whom he became known as "Fighting Bob."[9]

At the time of the British campaign against Baltimore, Rodgers was ordered to report to Washington, and he brought Stockton with him. Impressed with Stockton, Secretary of the Navy William Jones had the young man assigned to him as an aide. While on this duty Stockton volunteered to ride over to British-occupied Alexandria to investigate some cannonading. His coolness and willingness to take chances added to the regard with which he was held by his civilian superior.[10]

But the life of an aide to the Secretary did not commend itself to Stockton. He requested and received permission to return to Rodgers, who was then involved in preparing the defense of Baltimore. A part of those preparations involved the training of seamen to execute the rudiments of military drill and maneuvers. Although they were eager to fight, Rodgers had great difficulty in fashioning the men into an effective land force.[11] Stockton undoubtedly reached Baltimore in time to participate in some of the training. Many years later, in California, Stockton would be called upon to transform another body of sailors into infantry and would draw upon the experience of Rodgers.

Stockton took part in the defense of Fort McHenry, and exposed himself to enemy fire on several occasions to carry messages to and from Rodgers's headquarters. For his gallantry in action here and in other battles, Stockton received honorable notices from his superiors. On 9 December 1814 he was promoted to lieutenant.[12]

It had long been obvious that Stockton would never return to college to complete his studies. His early years in the Navy were spent in mastering the details of his profession. He then turned to educating himself through books on a variety of topics. He read history, international law, ethics, moral philosophy, and religion. His favorites were the Bible and the works of Cicero, Shakespeare, and Lord Bacon. A Princeton professor who knew him well later said that Stockton was one of the best-informed men he had ever met. No matter what the subject under discussion, Stockton could make some worthwhile observations on the topic. Princeton gave him an honorary M.A. degree in 1821.[13]

In the war with Algiers Stockton showed an unusual interest in the effects of naval gunnery. While the frigate *Guerriere* was closing to attack the Algerian frigate *Mishouri*, Stockton, in the accompanying schooner *Spitfire*, requested permission to station himself on his ship's bowsprit to observe the effect of the broadside. His request was approved. The *Spitfire* moved close to the stern of the enemy ship. From his precarious perch he observed two of the *Guerriere's* broadsides. To his commanding officer he reported that the *Guerriere* was firing widely, and suggested that the *Spitfire* aim its long 32-pound cannon on the cabin windows of the pirate vessel. This was done, and in a half hour the Algerian ship was taken.[14] The incident was an early indication that Stockton was studying the most effective way to use guns, in a manner well beyond the other lieutenants. It was also a way of bringing himself to the attention of his superiors.

After the war with Algiers Stockton returned to the Mediterranean in the new ship-of-the-line *Washington*, the flagship of Commodore Issac Chauncey. Peacetime routine was dull, and there were few opportunities for officers to advance themselves. Frustration often prompted younger officers to utter hostile and unguarded remarks that led to duels. Discipline among the officers deteriorated. Two events that took place in the squadron greatly influenced Stockton. Captain John Orde Creighton of the *Washington* was brought to trial for striking a midshipman, accusing him of lying, and threatening to throw him overboard. The court-martial board, with Oliver Hazard Perry presiding, did not allow the midshipman to present the testimony of two lieutenants, and arbitrarily ended the trial. The court found Creighton not guilty. This verdict so outraged the midshipmen of the squadron that fifty-one of them sent a petition to Congress asking for protection from tyrannical officers. It was the view of members of Congress that the petition was insubordinate, and they took no action on it.[15]

Another outrage took place when Commodore Oliver Hazard Perry, acting in an arbitrary manner, removed from command John Heath, the captain of the marines on *Java*. When the relief from command was not followed by charges, Heath sent a note to Perry asking what the next step was to be. Perry summoned Heath to his cabin, and, during a high-pitched discussion, struck the marine. Heath proferred charges, with Perry making counter charges. The same court that had tried Creighton now tried Perry, and Creighton was one of the judges. The court found both men guilty, but sentenced them only to a reprimand. Once again the verdict outraged the junior officers. Fifty of them, midshipmen, liuetenants, and marines, sent a memorial to the Congress protesting the partiality of the court-martial.[16] Stockton signed this memorial, which marked the real beginning of his interest in naval reform.

Stockton could do little to reform the Navy as a whole, but he could do something about those under his immediate command. He set about teaching his subordinates his philosophy of command. Stockton believed that a commander must inspire his officers to respect him and to be deferential to his position and sense of honor. It was the commander's obligation to demonstrate to all his dedication to justice and fairness. An officer was expected to be a gentleman, and a gentleman should not do wrong himself or allow anyone else to do it without punishment. As for the subordinates, they must respect and obey their superiors. One of the basic lessons that all officers must learn, according to Stockton, was that they remain cool under all circumstances. "Remember Gentlemen," he would say, "that there is always time enough to fight; keep cool; never get in a passion, under the grossest provocation."[17]

The young lieutenant applied this principle in an effort to curtail dueling. Stockton himself was a good shot, and he fought duels with British officers in the Mediterranean in the interest of demanding respect for the officers of the U.S. Navy, not to avenge his personal honor. When an American midshipman challenged him to a duel, Stockton met the man ashore at the appointed place. The midshipman fired and missed. Stockton fired into the air. The seconds determined that honor had been satisfied. All involved in this encounter became firm friends of Stockton, and the midshipman became a zealous upholder of shipboard discipline. Increasingly Stockton devoted himself to compromising disputes between officers and discouraging duels. His success in this effort led others to enlist his effort to arbitrate questions. In Stockton's view, it was rarely necessary for a gentleman to fight a duel. A gentleman was always willing to make whatever explanations were proper. If the offended person was also a gentleman, he would be satisfied with honest explanations.[18] This code of conduct was palatable to junior officers because it came from someone who had proved his personal courage on a number of occasions.

Because he had some knowledge of the law and was a good speaker, Stockton found himself in demand as a counsel in courts-martial. In this as in other things, he was a conscientious officer, and he had some successes in this area as well. It may well have pleased him to reflect that by a strange quirk of fate he was now acting as a lawyer, as his father and grandfather had done before him.[19]

As a result of several disciplinary problems in the squadron, Commodore Charles Stewart relieved four officers and sent them to the sloop-of-war *Erie*, under Stockton's command, for passage home. Stockton made the journey during the winter, and arrived in late January 1820 wihout any mishaps. Smith Thompson, the Secretary of the Navy, expressed his satisfaction with Stockton's report of his voyage, and added that it was "evidence of your active exertion, and prudence as commander of the ship."[20]

For his next assignment, Stockton asked the Secretary "for the most dangerous, the most difficult and the most unpromising employment at the disposal of the government." This turned out to be an assignment in the schooner *Alligator* to the west coast of Africa where he was to seize any American ships that were involved in slave trade. While he was in Washington on official business, Stockton was approached by two leaders of the American Colonization Society and asked if he would acquire some land on the west coast of Africa that could become a colony for the resettlement of ex-slaves. He was willing to undertake the mission, provided that he was not bound by detailed instructions and was free to exercise his own discretion. The society agreed to these terms. Stockton was to work with Dr. Eli Ayres, the society's agent in Africa, who also held a commission as a naval surgeon. In the fall of 1821 Stockton went to sea again in the *Alligator*.[21]

Given the humanitarian nature of the enterprise, it seemed appropriate to Stockton to put into action some of his ideas on leadership. He decided to see whether discipline could be maintained without the use of the cat-o'-nine tails. Remembering Captain John

Orde Creighton's penchant for flogging men, Stockton was determined to have none of that on board his ship. So, while the ship was
still within sight of the shore, he ordered that the cat-o'-nine tails
be thrown overboard. He would command obedience and discipline
by other means. The experiment proved to be a success, and thereafter Stockton became an advocate of the abolition of flogging.[22]

As for the mission of the Colonization Society, Stockton explored
the coast of Africa and determined that the region around Cape
Mesurado would be suitable for the proposed colony. With some
difficulty and with the threat of force he persuaded the local tribal
rulers to cede the area. The colony subsequently established became
the Republic of Liberia. Stockton developed a strong interest in the
work of the society, and a few years later, when he returned to New
Jersey, he organized a branch of that society in his native state and
served as its first president.[23]

Turning his attention now to the slave trade, Stockton zealously
seized ships that he suspected were American vessels operating under
foreign flags. Unfortunately, four of them turned out to be French,
and a minor diplomatic crisis resulted. A Portuguese slaver made
the mistake of firing on him, and he seized that as a prize as well.
The Secretary of the Navy was obliged to tell Stockton to restrict
his activities to ships flying the American flag.[24]

The *Alligator* under Stockton's command was next assigned to the
West Indies as a part of the government's effort to eliminate piracy
in that area. The ship became a part of the newly created West India
squadron under Commodore James Biddle. In the course of this
duty Stockton went to Charleston, South Carolina, where he met
and fell in love with Harriett Maria Potter, the only daughter of John
Potter, a wealthy merchant. His overtures were encouraged, and the
couple were married in Charleston on 4 March 1823. The marriage
brought Stockton control of property in the South and close ties
with his wife's father and friends. As a result, Stockton developed a
great sympathy for the people and problems of the South.[25]

When Stockton took his bride to Princeton, and while on leave
from active service, he found himself caught up in the politics of the
day. The question was who would succeed James Monroe in the
presidential election of 1824. The Federalists had ceased to be a
force on the national scene, but were still active in some states. In
the dominant Democratic–Republican party of Monroe there were
five major figures competing for the office. Secretary of State John
Quincy Adams was the candidate from the Northeast. Senator Andrew Jackson of Tennessee and Representative Henry Clay of Ken-
tucky were the candidates of the West. There were two candidates

from the South: Secretary of War John C. Calhoun of South Carolina and Secretary of the Treasury William H. Crawford of Georgia. In the election no clear victor emerged, and the question was referred to the House of Representatives. As a result, Adams became the President and Calhoun the Vice-President. Clay was subsequently appointed Secretary of State in the new administration. The Jacksonians charged that the will of the people had not been done, and that Adams had won the office through bargain and corruption. Thus the campaign of 1828 started four years early.[26]

Stockton's father was a Federalist, and Robert had grown up with a strong sense of respect for men of that persuasion. In 1824 he favored John Quincy Adams, but he was disappointed in his actions as President. At Princeton Stockton established a newspaper and began to write occasional editorials for it. Not surprisingly he was drawn into politics. He became an ardent supporter of Andrew Jackson and shared the widespread enthusiasm that followed the triumph of the general in the presidential elections of 1828 and 1832.[27]

Meanwhile he was recalled to active duty in November 1826 and given the job of superintending the survey of the harbors of Savannah and Beaufort. Southerners were very anxious to see a naval base established in Georgia or the Carolinas, and the survey was a part of that effort. While engaged in this work, Stockton received word of the death of his father in March 1828. He requested and received a leave of absence to settle his affairs. So began a decade of activity in New Jersey.[28]

With the death of his father, Stockton came into possession of the family homestead, "Morven," as well as land and other capital. This inheritance, together with other property that he inherited and that which he acquired by purchase and by marriage, made him quite comfortable.[29] He was now prepared to risk it all to support internal improvement in his native state.

The people of New Jersey noted New York's success with the Erie Canal and believed that they could reap similar benefits by linking the Delaware and Hudson rivers. Several groups sought governmental assistance for at least three competing routes. When Congress refused to provide aid, the state legislature turned to private investors and chartered several canal companies. The first one, chartered for the New Brunswick to Bordentown route, was unable to sell its stock, and the second one, the Delaware and Raritan Canal Company, was doing little better when Stockton bought a controlling interest in 1830. One of the major problems facing the company was the legislature's chartering of the Camden and Amboy Railroad Company at the same time. Stockton knew that the canal could not succeed if it had to compete with a virtually parallel railroad from the very beginning. To meet the challenge he applied to the state for the right to build another railroad from Trenton to New Brunswick. He argued that unless he could build the proposed route, the Camden and Amboy Railroad would be a monopoly. The state responded by consolidating the two companies and by giving the combined company the authority to build the Trenton–New Brunswick connection. As a result both the canal and railroad lines were built, and New Jersey enjoyed a system that not only did not incur any public debt, but actually paid large sums to the state for charter rights and transit duties.[30] Before all this became a reality, however, the very difficult problem of raising capital had to be overcome. Rebuffed by New York and Philadelphia investors, Stockton turned to his father-in-law, John Potter, who raised between a third and a half of the required funds in Charleston, South Carolina. On the New Jersey front, the struggle to build and maintain the company developed Stockton's political and managerial skills to a high degree. Yet for the rest of his life he was very defensive about his association with a monopoly.[31]

In 1838 Stockton traveled to England to obtain a loan to help the company to weather the financial crisis caused by the panic of 1837. His success in negotiating a large loan at a low interest rate added to his reputation in the business community. The trip was also to have enormous implications for the Navy, for it was at that time that he met John Ericsson, a Swedish engineer.[32]

Ericsson was trying to convince the officials of the Royal Navy of the value of his iron-hulled steam vessel powered by a screw propeller. A ride in the craft convinced Stockton that it was just what his company needed. He ordered one of the boats and had Ericsson design a 50-horsepower engine for it.[33]

A few months after Stockton returned from Europe, the Navy Department ordered him to sea as the executive officer in the ship-of-the-line *Ohio* under command of Commodore Isaac Hull. Stockton was now a master commandant, having been promoted to that rank on 27 May 1830.[34] After his many years ashore, the return to active duty must have had its difficult moments. Stockton was now forty-two and had been used to a very comfortable existence. Now he must adjust to the rigor and discomfort of shipboard life.

During the crossing of the Atlantic Ocean, Stockton had additional opportunities to observe the state of naval discipline. Commodore Hull was a humane officer who enjoyed the respect and affection of the crew; it was his habit to reduce the sentences of men convicted of offenses. The ship itself was in the charge of Captain Joseph Smith, a tall officer with a penetrating eye, who had a strong interest in temperance and who called himself the seamen's friend. But in his zeal to stop drunkenness and other evils, he punished the men severely by flogging. As a result he lost the respect of the men and failed in his efforts to improve them. It seems likely that this experience simply reinforced Stockton's view that flogging could be eliminated and that there were better and more effective ways to lead men.[35]

In Europe Stockton was detached from the ship to carry dispatches to the American Minister to Great Britain. While in that country he studied the latest improvements in naval architecture and visited navy yards, depots, and manufacturing plants. The trip to England provided an opportunity to witness the trials of the iron screw steamer he had ordered from Ericsson. They were most impressive. Named the *Robert F. Stockton*, the completed vessel crossed the Atlantic under sail in 1839 and was used for many years as a tugboat on the Delaware and Raritan Canal.[36]

Stockton was most impressed with Ericsson's work, and saw opportunities for the application of his genius in America. His encouraging comments came at a time when the British admiralty rejected Ericsson's design for a screw steamer. Stockton had Ericsson build a model of a screw steamer for naval use that was sent to the Navy Department. The warm encouragement of Stockton led Ericsson to emigrate to the United States. Meanwhile Stockton learned that he had been promoted to captain on 8 December 1838. He returned to the United States full of enthusiasm for modernizing the Navy.[37]

Back home Stockton found resistance to his ideas in official circles. Among the older naval officers and even the Secretary of the Navy there was a hostility to moving toward steam-powered warships. The only thing that Stockton could hope for was a change in administration, and the election of 1840 was approaching.

Thoroughly disenchanted with the Van Buren administration, Stockton took a leave of absence and worked actively in New Jersey to support the Whig Party candidate, General William Henry Harrison. Harrison died in April 1841, and the new President, John Tyler, and his Secretary of the Navy, George E. Badger, were more receptive than their predecessors to building steam vessels and improving the naval forces of the nation.[38]

Much encouraged by the change, Stockton sent the model of the steam warship to the new Secretary of the Navy in April 1841. As a result, the Navy Department authorized the construction of "a steamer of six hundred tons on the plan proposed by Captain Stockton; steam to be the main propelling power upon Ericsson's plan." Thus Ericsson's genius and Stockton's connections and sponsorship combined to produce the first steam-powered screw vessel in the U.S.Navy. When completed, the vessel was a full-rigged ship of 954 tons that used steam as auxiliary power. For armament it carried twelve 42-pound carronades and two 12-inch wrought iron guns reinforced by tiers of hoops. One of these, known as the "Oregon," had been designed by Ericsson in England and brought to the United States. The other gun, known as "the Peacemaker," was forged for Stockton by the Hamersley forge and bored and finished under Ericsson's direction. The names of the guns had a special significance at a time when there was a diplomatic crisis with Great Britain over the Oregon Territory.[39]

In the process of building the ship, additional funds were required, and Stockton put his own money into the project. By the time the vessel was finished he had developed a proprietary attitude toward it and considered it "his" ship. It was named the USS *Princeton* in honor of the captain's home town. An unfortunate change took place in Stockton at this time, as he encouraged the notion that the ship was the product of his ideas alone. Evidence of this is contained in Stockton's 5 February 1844 letter to the Secretary of the Navy, in which he described the virtues of the *Princeton* and her guns without mentioning John Ericsson. When the *Princeton* went to Washington to demonstrate her capabilities to government officials, Ericsson was left in New York angry at his exclusion from the official party.

On 28 February 1844 the *Princeton* made a cruise down the Potomac to show the power of her large guns. On board were the President, members of his cabinet, members of Congress, and a number of ladies. Earlier Ericsson had suggested that the demonstration be done with a gun of his own design, but Stockton preferred the one with which he was associated. The assembled guests were impressed by the power of the cannon, and on the way back to Washington the captain was requested to fire it one more time. He consented, but on this occasion the gun exploded, killing the Secretaries of State and Navy, as well as four other persons. Stockton himself was badly scorched, but he continued to give his attention to all around him. Subsequently he asked for a court of inquiry to investigate the accident.

Shortly after the news of the explosion reached Ericsson in New York, he received a letter from one of the *Princeton*'s officers requesting that he come to Washington for the investigation. This Ericsson refused to do, nor would he accept any responsibility for the accident. The court exonerated Stockton of any blame for the explosion of the gun, but he never forgave Ericsson, and in retaliation for what he considered Ericsson's failure to support him, he used his influence to prevent the government from paying Ericsson for his services in building the *Princeton*. This was the most petty and dishonorable aspect of his naval career, and it tarnished his reputation as an exponent of the new technology in warfare.[40]

Before the diplomatic crisis with Great Britain over Oregon was settled, a new threat of war with Mexico emerged as a result of efforts to bring the republic of Texas into the Federal Union. The problem for Mexico was that Texas, in arguing that its border was the Rio Grande, was asserting control over a region well beyond the actual settlements of the republic. For anti-slavery-minded northerners, the admission of Texas ran a risk of increasing the power of the southerners in the Senate, as well as bringing on a war. The decision on Texas was so controversial that it was not until the closing days of the Tyler administration that it was admitted to the Union by a joint resolution of Congress. A troublesome issue was thus removed from the public agenda before the newly elected James K. Polk took office.[41]

From Stockton's point of view, the admission of Texas was a highly desirable thing. A thorough-going expansionist, he believed that God had ordained the Americans to occupy the areas of the West.[42] Given this point of view and his close association with the outgoing administration, it is not surprising that Stockton was chosen by President Tyler to carry to Texas the news that Congress had approved the annexation. It was now up to the Texas legislature to accept this and to enter the Union as a state. The business was not without risk. At the news of the passage of the joint resolution in Texas, the Mexican government broke off diplomatic relations with the United States. The Mexican minister at Washington went home to his country to help organize resistance to the United States.[43]

As Stockton saw it, the new Democratic administration headed by President Polk had come into office on a platform that promised the reoccupation of the Oregon Territory and the annexation of Texas. These actions might provoke a war with Great Britain, with Mexico, or with both. If war came with both, and Stockton had a chance to make a choice, he wanted to test his skill against the British on the high seas. He had not forgotten the thrill of combat under John Rodgers. Of the two contestants, Britain was the bigger threat. Therefore, it seemed wise to resolve the Mexican question as quickly as possible in order to be free to cope with Great Britain, if necessary. In Texas it was reported that the Mexicans were preparing for war and might possibly have the assistance of a European power. There seemed to be no time to lose. Why wait until the Mexicans were ready to fight? Why not resolve the question according to the United States' own time table?[44]

For Stockton this meant that someone in Texas had to take the initiative. When he arrived in Texas he found that Texas politicians were quibbling over the terms of the annexation and that European diplomats were trying to convince them not to accept the incorporation. Fearing that Texas might yet be lost to the Union, Stockton suggested to Texas President Anson Jones that Texas should become more hostile toward Mexico, arguing that if Mexico went to war the United States could neutralize the threat before any Europeans got involved. Jones hoped to establish more friendly relations with Mexico and rejected Stockton's suggestion that Texas manufacture a war for the convenience of the United States. While there was strong pro-annexation sentiment among the Texas people, their leaders were not enthusiastic about risking war. Most likely Stockton talked about his ideas with the American Chargé d'Affaires in Texas. If so, he learned quickly that Polk's administration was committed to resolving the problems with Mexico through diplomacy. Disgusted at the turn of events, Stockton returned to the East, reaching Philadelphia in June 1845.[45]

The commodore's action in Texas was an example of his boldness. The record shows that he had no authorization from the President or the Navy Department to do as he did. Stockton was prepared to take risks because he was convinced that if he were successful, the administration would overlook some irregularities. Also, he believed that Mexico would fight, and he communicated these thoughts to his superiors.

In the fall of 1845 Stockton was given the command of the frigate *Congress* and instructions to carry a U.S. commissioner to the Hawaiian Islands. The captain also carried sealed orders that were not to be opened until he was beyond the Virginia Capes. Stockton was very much afraid that he was being sent to the Pacific just as war with Mexico was about to break out. His old ship, the *Princeton*, had been assigned to Commodore David Conner in the Gulf of Mexico. If war should come instead with Great Britain, he would be far from that as well. But orders were orders, and Stockton was determined to do his best in any situation into which fate cast him.[46]

While the *Congress* was preparing for sea, her chaplain received a consignment of 300 to 400 books for the ship's library. These were on religious as well as miscellaneous subjects, and they came from the American Tract Society, the Sunday School Union, and the Presbyterian Board of Publications. Knowing that there was no appropriation for such books, Stockton purchased them himself for his crew. In addition, the American Tract Society supplied Bibles for the crew. Delighted with this windfall, Chaplain Walter Colton wrote in his journal: "No national ship ever left a port of the United States more amply provided with books suited to the habits and capacities of those on board."[17]

Religious ideas were important in shaping Stockton, so it followed in his mind that they could influence others. Born a Presbyterian, he became an Episcopalian at the time of his marriage and subsequently served as a vestryman at Trinity Church in Princeton. As a naval officer he insisted that religious services be performed on board his ship every Sunday. He cultivated the friendship of chaplains and supported their work. Among the people he was close to was Chaplain Charles S. Stewart, who had a strong opinion about the degrading effects of punishment by flogging. His ideas reinforced Stockton's own views. In human affairs Stockton believed that people responded to reason, and that kindness begat kindness. He was not above flogging if all other possibilities were exhausted, but unlike many other officers in his day, he did not consider it his first recourse. He took pains to make his men believe that as their commander he was like a parent, stern and demanding at times but always concerned, sympathetic, and forgiving. This approach was very effective on board his ships.[48]

Stockton's efforts to promote harmony in the *Congress* included keeping the men informed of their mission. When Stockton opened his sealed orders, he learned that after he discharged his passengers in Hawaii he was to sail for Oregon and California. He promptly shared this information with his crew. No one knew what to expect when the *Congress* anchored in Monterey Bay on 15 July 1846 and found a squadron under the command of Commodore John D. Sloat in control of the area. Stockton promptly went to confer with the senior officer.[49] So began one of the most controversial aspects of Stockton's career.

The meeting between Sloat and Stockton produced some surprises. The senior commander told Stockton that his health was bad and that he intended to transfer the command as soon as possible. It developed that the previous May, while Sloat's squadron was at Mazatlan, Mexico, he had received a message from the squadron's surgeon, then in Guadalajara, that there had been fighting between Mexican and American troops along the Rio Grande. Sloat promptly relayed this information to the American consul at Monterey, California, by way of Captain William Mervine in the sloop-of-war *Cyane*. Sloat remained in Mazatlan until he learned of General Zachary

Taylor's victories at Palo Alto and Resaca de la Palma. Further confirmation of the war came from Mexico City by way of another message from the squadron's surgeon. It was not until 8 June, or twenty-two days after the first report of fighting, that Sloat sailed for Monterey in the *Savannah*, to arrive there on 1 July. Five days later he learned that a small group of soldiers under Brevet Captain John C. Fremont of the Topographical Engineers had abandoned their scientific survey work and were actively supporting a revolt by American settlers. Sonoma and San Francisco were under control of this group. What was Sloat to do?

It probably seemed reasonable to him that Fremont had acted under orders from Washington. If so, it was important to have a meeting with him as soon as possible to determine what was to be done. Meanwhile Sloat was concerned that the British had their eyes on California, and he wanted to forestall any movement by them in that direction. Accordingly, he ordered the seizure of Monterey and San Francisco. These things were accomplished on 7 and 9 July, respectively. Sonoma was also occupied. Fremont hastened to Monterey and met with Sloat, in a meeting unsatisfactory to both. Fremont wanted an official endorsement of what he had done thus far and support for further operations in California. Sloat was surprised and shocked to learn that Fremont had acted on his own authority and without knowing about the war with Mexico. This news induced Sloat to break off the meeting. He was delighted when Stockton arrived, and was only too happy to turn the naval and land command over to the younger officer. The change of command arrangements were completed on 29 July, and Sloat departed for home.[50]

While seizing Monterey, Commodore Sloat had issued a proclamation announcing the outbreak of war and the annexation of California. It spoke of the advantages the area would have as a part of the United States, and promised that all who did not wish to remain there could return to Mexico after the war. The real estate titles of the Californians and the church would be recognized. Items furnished to the Americans would be bought at a fair price. This moderate and statesman-like document was in accord with American consul Thomas Larkin's hopes that the conquest of California would be peaceful. He knew that long before the arrival of Fremont or Sloat Californians were discontented under Mexican rule.[51]

Stockton's assessment of the situation was different. He knew that the U.S. government was anxious to acquire California. He was suspicious of the British naval vessel in California waters and thought the British might support Mexican efforts to resist the American occupation. But even if no British support were forthcoming, Mexico was bound to react to the loss of California. It seemed wise to complete the conquest as soon as possible before the Mexicans discovered how very small and scattered the American forces were.[52]

Stockton's force consisted of the *Portsmouth* at San Francisco, whose men were holding the garrisons ashore; the frigate *Savannah* at Monterey; and the *Warren* at Mazatlan. This left only the frigate *Congress* and the sloop-of-war *Cyane* and 160 men under Fremont to seize and control the rest of California. To Stockton it seemed clear that he must move quickly with all the men he could muster.

On his own authority, he designated Fremont's organization "the California battalion of United States troops," and promoted their leader to the rank of major. Arrangements were made to establish volunteer garrisons at Sutter's Fort, Sonoma, San Juan Batista, and Santa Clara. Stockton informed Walter Colton, the chaplain of the *Congress*, that he would function as the mayor of Monterey until further notice.[53]

The commodore's supreme confidence in his own judgment and his "take charge" personality led him to issue a rather arrogant and bombastic proclamation that blamed the Mexicans for the war and for outrages against Fremont and his scientific group. To avenge these wrongs, points had been seized in California. Mexican officials had departed, and anarchy reigned until Stockton brought order. General Jose Maria Castro, the Mexican commander in California, was to be driven out of the country. Local officials must recognize American authority. Consul Larkin told the authorities in Washing-

Stockton's squadron off La Paz, Mexico. Stockton took command of American naval forces in the Pacific early in the Mexican War and blockaded the Mexican coast. Combining his forces with those of John C. Fremont and Stephen W. Kearney, he helped seize California for the United States. Courtesy of the Franklin D. Roosevelt Library.

ton that the assertions in the proclamation did not come from him. One of Stockton's subordinate officers considered the proclamation rather unintelligible.[54] It was not a happy note on which to begin. One can only assume that Stockton was trying to intimidate the Mexicans with rhetoric.

Stockton's strategy was to increase Fremont's strength as quickly as possible, moving Fremont's battalion via the *Cyane* to San Diego. After acquiring horses there it would move inland to prevent Castro's retreat from Los Angeles. Then Stockton would land his sailors and marines at San Pedro and move against Castro. While Stockton was transforming his men into infantry, Larkin tried to arrange a truce and a conference between the commanders. Stockton refused to talk to Castro unless California declared its independence under the protection of the United States. Castro could agree to no such terms, but his force was too small to oppose the Americans. He left California. Stockton's force marched to Los Angeles where it was joined by Fremont's followers.[55] Here Stockton issued a new proclamation stating that California belonged to the United States and would soon have a government and laws similar to those of other American territories. An election date for civil officers was announced. Meanwhile, a civil and military government would be in power with Stockton as governor.

In forming a civil government the commodore exceeded his instructions and the provisions of the Constitution. Stockton justified his actions on the grounds that it was important for the tranquility of the area to have a functioning civil government that could protect civil property rights, maintain the American presence, and free his forces for an attack on Mexico. He was also concerned about the influx of Mormons into the area. As events later proved, neither the President nor the Secretary of the Navy accepted these arguments.[56]

No sooner had Stockton reported to the Secretary of the Navy that peace reigned in California than a revolt broke out in Los Angeles and spread to other points. All the territory south of San Luis Obispo reverted to Mexican control. An army expedition under General Stephen Watts Kearney marched overland from New Mexico, suffered a defeat in a battle with the Mexicans in California, and joined Stockton at San Diego. The balance of power in California now shifted; the combined army and naval units along with Fremont's forces defeated the Mexican troops that opposed them, and the reconquest of California was completed in January 1847.[57]

When the fighting stopped, a smoldering feud between Stockton and Kearney intensified over the issue of who was in control of the area. Kearney pointed to his instructions from the President stating that he was to establish a new territorial government in California as he had already done in New Mexico. Stockton based his claims on the Navy Department's orders to Sloat. The commodore argued that the general's orders had been superseded by events. Stockton then proceeded to appoint Fremont the governor. In February new orders came from Washington placing the authority in Kearney's hands.[58]

The commodore left California on 20 June and traveled overland to Washington where he visited President Polk on 25 November. Later Stockton returned to Washington to give testimony in court-martial proceedings against Fremont. The court found Fremont guilty of mutiny, disobedience, and prejudicial conduct and sentenced him to be dismissed from the service. Polk approved all but the mutiny finding and restored Fremont to duty. Instead, that officer resigned.[59]

It had become clear to Stockton that while the authorities in Washington disapproved of his actions in California, the general public did not. On his return from the West he was cheered by crowds and offered testimonial dinners, which he declined until after he returned home when he attended a reception in his honor in New Jersey and a banquet in Philadelphia.[60]

While all this was personally gratifying, Stockton was worried about the debate on Negro slavery and Southern threats to secede from the Union. Stockton believed that God had plans for the United States, and the breakup of the Union would retard them. He was, therefore, willing to support any compromise that would hold the states together. The commodore did not believe that the Federal government had a right to interfere with slavery in the states. His own connection with the South through his wife naturally gave him a good insight into the views of southerners. But his own views of the blacks and their future was unique.

As Stockton saw it, God intended to use the blacks in America as the means of civilizing Africa. He believed that no white man could survive there. The slaves and their ancestors had been taken from their tribal environment and exposed to the superior civilization of the Anglo-Saxons. Slavery was a time of suffering, but it was an ordeal through which the blacks must go to prepare them for the work ahead. Their situation was similar to that of the Jews in Egyptian bondage before Moses led them to the promised land. The establishment of Liberia was a step toward the development of Africa, and as such, freed blacks should be encouraged to settle there. Slavery would end when God was ready to use the blacks for his work in Africa. Until that time slaves had to be trained to be self-supporting. This comfortable philosophy allowed Stockton to believe that there was cruelty and injustice in the institution of slavery, but that slavery itself was not a sin. It was the duty of the states to correct injustices. Abolitionists would drive the southern states out of the Union, and would not free any slaves.[61]

These views and his national stature made Stockton an appealing compromise candidate in some circles, but he was not interested in political office. He resigned his commission in the Navy on 28 May 1850 to devote himself to private affairs. In a letter to a Trenton newspaper in November 1850, Stockton turned down the suggestion that his name should be placed in nomination for the U.S. Senate. He hoped that the honor would go to someone who was pledged to uphold the Union. Members of the New Jersey state legislature believed that no one had a stronger dedication to the Union than Stockton. He was elected as a Democrat to the Thirty-second Congress, which met in special session on 4 March 1851.[62]

During his time in the Senate he made speeches advocating improved harbor defenses and against intervention in European affairs, but his most famous effort came about as a result of an attempt to reintroduce punishment by flogging in the Navy.[63]

Flogging in the Navy and merchant marine had been abolished by a provision in an appropriation bill passed on 28 September 1850. The President signed the bill into law and Congress adjourned on the same day. Because no substitute punishments were indicated,

Flogging. Stockton was a strong opponent of shipboard punishments such as this flogging being administered on board the USS *Cyane* c. 1842. Courtesy of the Naval Historical Center.

there was a feeling in some parts of the Navy that the measure was hasty and ill-conceived. The Secretary of the Navy received letters from officers who asked for instructions on how to deal with unruly seamen. The Secretary asked Congress to revise the whole system of punishments at once. On 17 December 1851 Senator Richard Broadhead of Pennsylvania introduced a memorial signed by a large number of citizens urging that punishment by flogging be reintroduced. This stirred Stockton to action. After expressing his amazement that any group of people would advocate such a thing, Stockton gave notice that he would oppose the suggestion.

When the proposition was considered on 7 January 1852, Stockton was ready. He spoke with feeling about the superiority of the American sailor and how he had proved his worth in war and peace. Said Stockton: "The theory that the Navy cannot be governed, and that our national ships cannot be navigated without the use of the lash, seems to me to be founded in that false idea, that sailors *are not men* — not American citizens — have not the common feelings, sympathies, and honorable impulses of our Anglo-American race." The commodore related how men would undergo all sorts of hardship for a commander they loved and who they believed cared for them. Punishment by flogging destroyed a sailor's self-respect, pride, and patriotism. A new and more civilized age had dawned. In the state prisons the worst offenses were no longer punished by flogging. Why then, he asked, did people want to restore "this relic of barbarism" to the Navy?

Stockton went on to describe his own quarter century of association with seamen in various parts of the world. He told what they had done as infantry in the California campaigns. "American sailors, as a class," said Stockton, "have loved their country as well, and have done more for her in peace and war, then any other equal number of citizens." Yet the sailor enjoyed little in the way of comfort; was treated as an outcast on shore; and often died poor. Some now argued that he should again be flogged like a felon. As far as he was concerned, said Stockton, he would rather see the Navy abolished than to see flogging restored. Officers of the Navy who thought that the sailor was more influenced by fear than by affection were wrong. "You can do infinitely more with him by rewarding him for his faithfulness than by flogging him for his delinquencies," said Stockton. It was much more effective to punish minor infractions by stopping the sailor's allowance of tobacco, tea, sugar, or coffee. To improve the Navy and its discipline, Stockton recommended a system of rewards and punishments, the abolition of the grog ration, and a restructuring of the recruiting service.

Efforts to refute Stockton's arguments were made by George E. Badger of North Carolina, a former Secretary of the Navy, and by Stephen Mallory of Florida, but they were futile. No one could bring to the subject the range of firsthand experience and conviction that the commodore possessed. The petition to reestablish flogging was referred to the Committee on Naval Affairs where it died. The Congress now had to consider a new code of discipline. This code was not completed and enacted into law until 1862.[64]

In beating back the effort to restore flogging, Stockton reached the apex of his career as a naval reformer. He was the right man in the right place to win the battle. No one could match his credentials. He had had a wide-ranging and full career, and had proved himself successful in business, in politics, and as a naval officer. On board his own ship he had demonstrated that a system of humane discipline was not only possible, but also efficient. It was now up to other officers to learn how to apply those lessons. He had repaid his own men for their devotion. In the Senate of the United States he had proclaimed the virtues of the American sailor. By his action in stopping the restoration of a cruel punishment he helped to start a systematic reexamination of the whole body of regulations. The result was both a new code and a fresh perspective on how the Navy should function.

By the time the new regulations came about, Stockton was long gone from the Senate. He had been a reluctant candidate for the honor, and when his wife's father died, he found himself obliged to deal with many additional questions in regard to the estate. Accordingly he resigned his seat in the Senate on 10 January 1853, and served from then until his death as president of the Delaware and Raritan Canal Company. He was mentioned as a possible presidential candidate by the new American Party in 1856, but he seems to have given little encouragement to such talk. The widening sectional rift of the following years worried him. By 1859 the extreme positions of the Democrats and the Republicans on the slavery issue led him to return to politics. Now he embraced the American Party, arguing that if it immediately reorganized itself and softened its stand against immigrants it could attract the conservative, patriotic, and moderate men who loved the Constitution and wished to preserve the Union.[65] When remnants of the American and Whig parties later combined to form the Constitutional Union party, they accepted Stockton's ideas but turned to others for candidates. When Lincoln and the Republicans won the election of 1860 and the secession of the southern states threatened the future of the Union, Stockton tried to help. As a delegate to the Peace Conference in Washington in that year, he tried unsuccessfully to work out a compromise solution to the crisis. During the Civil War Stockton was deeply distressed by the suffering on both sides and withdrew from active participation in public affairs. The nation was in the midst of determining a reconstruction policy for the South when Stockton died on 7 October 1866.[66]

His naval career had been a checkered one, broken by various leaves of absence. He had the typical experiences of the day: combat against the British during the War of 1812, tours in the Mediterranean and chasing pirates in the Caribbean, and surveying expeditions along the coast. In addition, Stockton shared the aggressive spirit of his contemporaries as demonstrated by his belligerent actions against Mexico. It is for these things that he is best remembered, but in a way this is wrong, for Stockton was not a typical or average officer. He was unlike most of his fellow officers in that the sea was not his entire life. Ashore he had a highly successful business career; was a popular, if reluctant, politician; and was active in reform movements such as the American Colonization Society. An early advocate of "White Man's Burden," Stockton believed that Americans were divinely ordained to inspire the "lesser peoples" of the world. Within the Navy he was an early exponent of steam propulsion. Through his influence, John Ericsson, the future designer of the *Monitor*, came to America, and with Ericsson, he supervised the construction of the USS *Princeton*, the first American screw-propeller-driven sloop-of-war.

Stockton was also a reformer. He ran the ships under his command without the lash, serving as an example of a new style of leadership, and in the Senate prevented the reintroduction of flogging. In these and other ways Stockton was a link between the Old Navy of sailing ships and men driven to their work and the New Navy of steam propulsion and professionalism.

FURTHER READING

Manuscript materials relating to Robert F. Stockton's career in the Navy can be found in the records of the Navy Department now in the custody of the National Archives and Records Service, Washington, D.C. Many of these records have been microfilmed. Stockton letters may be found in Letters Received by the Secretary of the Navy From Officers Below the Rank of Commander, Microcopy M-148; Captains' Letters, M-125; Letters Received by the Secretary of the Navy From Commanding Officers of Squadrons, M-89; and a letter of 1826 from Stockton in Correspondence of the Secretary of the Navy Relating to African Colonization, M-205. Official letters to Stockton may be found in Letters Sent by the Secretary of the Navy to Officers, M-149.

Private papers relating to Stockton's career include the Stockton Papers at Princeton University Library. While these contain some letters on naval matters, they are mainly of interest for Stockton's business interests. At the same institution are the Papers of Samuel Southard, who was a New Jersey senator and who served as the Secretary of the Navy. His papers contain a few letters by or about Stockton. There are letters of Stockton on official matters in the John Rodgers Papers in the Library of Congress. Letters on a personal level are in the Daniel Webster Papers in the Library of Congress. Stockton's letter to the Board of Managers of the American Colonization Society, dated 16 December 1821, relating to the acquisition of the land that became Liberia is in the Peter Force Papers, Series 9, roll 111, at the Library of Congress. The text of the contract between King Peter and the other African chiefs and Stockton and Eli Ayres has been separated from the above letter and was filmed as an enclosure in the folder "U.S. Army Inspection of Small Arms, Regulations 1823, August" on the above reel.

Stockton's ideas on reform are most easily studied in his speeches in Congress, published in the *Congressional Globe*, 32nd Congress, many of which were also reprinted as separate items, and in the open letters published in his biography. Shortly before he resigned from the Navy he sent a reply to a circular letter of the Secretary of the Navy requesting the views of various officers on flogging and the spirit ration. The replies of the officers were bound together under the title "Corporal Punishment and the Spirit Ration, Reports of Officers, 1850," Record Group 45, National Archives. Stockton's letter, dated 6 February 1850, is number 17 in the volume.

There are only two biographies of Stockton, one published and one unpublished. The first, prepared by his friend and neighbor Samuel J. Bayard, *A Sketch of the Life of Com. Robert F. Stockton*, was a campaign biography for the Presidential election of 1856. It is uncritical, but it contains information found in no other source. It also reflects Stockton's ideas about aspects of his career and on public issues. The book amounts to a summing up of his life when Stockton was at the height of his career.

The second biography is an unpublished typescript manuscript by Alfred Hoyt Bill, entitled "Fighting Bob; The Life and Exploits of Commodore Robert Field Stockton, United States Navy," in the Princeton University Library. The work is not documented but was prepared with the help of information from Stockton's descendants, and shows some signs of reliance on published and unpublished sources. It is only mildly critical of Stockton on a few matters, such as the fight with Ericsson. Bill completed the manuscript sometime in the late 1950s or early 1960s and doubtless intended to publish it in book form with sources before he died. Earlier he had produced a book on the home of the Stocktons, now the residence of the governors of New Jersey. That book, *A House Called Morven: Its Role in American History, 1701–1954*, contains brief sketches of the commodore and his father, among others, in relation to the history of the house.

Brief accounts of aspects of Stockton's career can be found in Charles O. Paullin's *Commodore John Rodgers, Captain, Commodore, and Senior Officer of the American Navy, 1773–1838*; David F. Long's *Ready to Hazard: A Biography of Commodore William Bainbridge, 1774–1833*; Philip J. Staudenraus, *The African Colonization Movement, 1816–1865*; John Elfreth Watkins, *Biographical Sketches of John Stevens, Robert I. Stevens, Edwin A. Stevens, John S. Darcy, John P. Jackson, Robert F. Stockon*; William Conant Church, *The Life of John Ericsson*; Frank M. Bennett, *The Steam Navy of the United States*; James Phinney Baxter, *The Introduction of the Ironclad Warship*; and Richard P. McCormick, *The Second American Party System: Party Formation in the Jacksonian Era*. For details on the development of the *Princeton*'s guns, see Lee M. Pearson, "The 'Princeton' and the 'Peacemaker': A Study in Nineteenth-Century Naval Research and Development Procedures," *Technology and Culture*, VII, 163–83. An excellent contemporary account of the tragedy in the *Princeton* by Representative George Sykes of New Jersey may be found in St. George L. Sioussat, ed., "the Accident on Board the U.S.S. 'Princeton', February 28, 1844: A Contemporary New-Letter," *Pennsylvania History*, VII, 1–29. A general overview of the policies and personalities of the various Secretaries of the Navy under whom Stockton served may be found in Paolo Coletta, ed., *American Secretaries of the Navy, 1775–1972*, I, 93–361.

Stockton's role in the Mexican War is treated in a very critical manner in Glenn W. Price, *Origins of the War With Mexico: The Polk–Stockton Intrigue*. Price's conclusions are disputed by Charles Sellers in his *James K. Polk: Continentalist, 1843–1846*; in David M. Pletcher, *The Diplomacy of Annexation: Texas, Oregon, and the Mexican War*; and in K. Jack Bauer, *The Mexican War, 1846–1848*. The fullest account of the California campaign is in Hubert Howe Bancroft, *History of California*. Briefer accounts are in Justin W. Smith, *The War With Mexico*; K. Jack Bauer, *Surfboats and Horse Marines: U.S.*

Naval Operations in the Mexican War, 1846–48; Allan Nevins, *Fremont, Pathmarker of the West*; Dwight L. Clarke, *Stephen Watts Kearney: Soldier of the West*. A modern popular account of the war in California is in David Nevin, *The Mexican War*, a volume in the Time–Life series on the Old West. An excellent, balanced account of the California campaign and the war is K. Jack Bauer, *The Mexican War, 1846–48*. The most recent study of the California campaign is Neal Harlow, *California Conquered: War and Peace on the Pacific, 1846–50*. Most modern writers tend to be very critical of Stockton's personal traits, especially his arrogance and quest for glory in California. My own feeling is that in most things except his attitudes toward his men, his outlook and stance was very similar to that of many wealthy civilians of his times. For a naval chaplain's favorable view of Stockton, see Walter Colton, *Three Years in California*, and his *Deck and Port; or, Incidents of a Cruise in the United States Frigate Congress to California*. For an enlisted man's view of Stockton, see Joseph T. Downey, *The Cruise of the Portsmouth, 1845–47: A Sailor's View of the Naval Conquest of California*, edited by Howard Lamar.

For a full account of the efforts of Stockton and other reformers to abolish flogging in the Navy, see Harold D. Langley, *Social Reform in the U.S. Navy, 1798–1862*. On Stockton's efforts to save the Union, see Robert Gray Gunderson, *Old Gentleman's Convention: The Washington Peace Conference of 1861*.

NOTES

1. Richard B. Morris, "Richard Stockton," *Dictionary of American Biography*, edited by Dumas Malone, XVII, 46–47. Hereafter cited as *DAB*.

2. Walter R. Fee, "Richard Stockton, *DAB*, XVII, 47–48. The Stockton family background is discussed in Alfred Hoyt Bill, *A House Called Morven: Its Role in American History, 1701–1954*.

3. Bill, *Morven*; Samuel J. Bayard, *A Sketch of the Life of Com. Robert F. Stockton*, 131.

4. Bayard, *Stockton*, 11; Alfred Hoyt Bill, "Fighting Bob; The Life and Exploits of Commodore Robert Field Stockton, United States Navy," unpublished typescript manuscript, Princeton University Library.

5. Bayard, *Stockton*, 11–12.

6. Edward W. Callahan, ed., *List of Officers of the Navy of the United States and of the Marine Corps from 1775 to 1900*, 524. Stockton's service record is in the Records of the Bureau of Naval Personnel, Record Group 24, Abstracts of Service of Naval Officers 1798–1892, Microcopy M-330, roll 19, 73; Bayard, *Stockton*, 13.

7. Charles O. Paullin, *Commodore John Rodgers, Captain, Commodore, and Senior Officer of the American Navy, 1773–1838: A Biography*, 246–56.

8. Ibid., 255.

9. Bayard, *Stockton*, 15.

10. Paullin, *Rodgers*, 260–61, 284–89; Bayard, *Stockton*, 18–19.

11. Paullin, *Rodgers*, 290–91.

12. Ibid., 294–95; Callahan, *List*, 524; Bayard, *Stockton*, 20–22.

13. Bayard, *Stockton*, 12; Bill, "Fighting Bob," 43.

14. Bayard, *Stockton*, 2; Leonard F. Guttridge and Jay D. Smith, *The Commodores*, 278.

15. Guttridge, *Commodores*, 283; U.S. Congress, *American State Papers: Naval Affairs*, I, 453–55.

16. Congress, *State Papers*, I, 502.

17. Bayard, *Stockton*, 28–29.

18. Ibid., 29–36.

19. Ibid., 36.

20. Ibid., 36–38; R.G. 45: Secretary of the Navy Letters, National Archives.

21. R.G. 45: Officers' Letters; R.G. 24: Abstracts of Service of Naval Officers, 1798–1892, National Archives. Stockton was given the command of the *Alligator* on 21 August 1821. Bill, "Fighting Bob," 43; Bayard, *Stockton*, 39.

22. Bayard, *Stockton*, 40; Bill, "Fighting Bob," 44.

23. Bill, "Fighting Bob," 40–47, 54; Philip J. Staudenraus, *The African Colonization Movement, 1816–1865*, 50–51. Stockton's letter to the American Colonization Society on the selection of the site is dated 16 December 1821 and is in the Peter Force Collection, Library of Congress, Series 9, roll 110.

24. Bayard, *Stockton*, 48–53. Stockton's seizure of the Portuguese ship *Marrianna Flora* was subsequently upheld by the U.S. Supreme Court, which reversed a decision of a district court. For Justice Joseph Story's statement of the majority opinion see Henry Wheaton, *Reports of Cases Argued and Adjudged in the Supreme Court, 1816–1827*, XI, 50–52. Judge Story also upheld Stockton's seizure of the French ship *Jeune Eugenie* in the Circuit Court; see William Powell Mason, *Reports of Cases in the Circuit Court of the United States for the First Circuit from 1816 to 1830*, II, 409–63. On the diplomatic aspects, see Charles Francis Adams, ed., *Memoirs of John Quincy Adams*, VI, 21–23, 27–29, 31. Additional information on Stockton's seizures is in Correspondence of the Secretary of the Navy Relating to African Colonization, 1819–1844, Microcopy M-205, National Archives, which includes letters sent and received, 91 (letters sent) and 65, 67

(letters received). Other correspondence is in Letters to Officers, M-149, roll 14. The letter of the Secretary of the Navy cited is on page 202. For an overview of the slave trade problem, see Peter Duignan and Clarence Clendenen, *The United States and the African Slave Trade, 1819–1862.*

25. Bayard, *Stockton*, 53–54; Bill, "Fighting Bob," 49–55; Letters to Officers, M-149, roll 14, 261.

26. Robert V. Remini, *The Election of Andrew Jackson*, 11–120.

27. For a succinct account of political developments in New Jersey, see Richard P. McCormick, *The Second American Party System: Party Formation in the Jackson Era*, 124–34. The newspaper that Stockton owned was *The Princeton Courier*. Stockton was a delegate from Somerset County to the Democratic–Republican (the dominant party of President Adams) state convention in September 1826. See Bayard, *Stockton*, 56–64; Bill, "Fighting Bob," 52.

28. Letters to Officers, M-149, roll 17, 52, 56, 177, 328, 469, 504.

29. When his great uncle Elias Boudinot died in 1821, Stockton received a bequest of $10,000. In 1826 Stockton built a house 100 yards east of "Morven." On the death of his father, the bulk of the estate was left to Robert. A trust fund of between $60,000 and $80,000 was established with Stockton and Samuel Bayard as trustees to provide for Richard Stockton's widow and four daughters. According to Bill, some provisions in the father's will were so complicated that the courts were still trying to resolve them fifty years after Richard's death. When Robert was in Georgia in 1827 he bought a large sugar plantation near Cumberland Island and eighty or ninety slaves to work it. See Bill, "Fighting Bob," 51–53, 55–57.

30. Bayard, *Stockton*, 65–68; Bill, "Fighting Bob," 59–64.

31. George R. Taylor, *The Transportation Revolution, 1815–1860*, 51. Potter had made his own fortune in Anglo-American trade between the American Revolution and the War of 1812. See Bill, "Fighting Bob," 49–50. For Stockton's reply to a published letter from the citizens of Toms River, New Jersey on the monopoly, see Bayard, *Stockton*, 68–75. McCormick points out that in New Jersey the Jacksonians became identified with the Camden and Amboy Railroad and the Whig Party with the New Jersey Railroad. See McCormick, *Party System*, 131.

32. Bayard, *Stockton*, 66; Bill, "Fighting Bob," 64.

33. Bayard, *Stockton*, 66; Bill, "Fighting Bob," 74; William Conant Church, *The Life of John Ericsson*, I, 92–93; John Elfreth Watkins, *Biographical Sketches of John Stevens, Robert I. Stevens, Edwin A. Stevens, John S. Darcy, John R. Jackson, Robert F. Stockton*, 16.

34. Callahan, *List*, 524.

35. For an enlisted man's view of life in the *Ohio* under Captain Smith, see F. P. Torrey, *Journal of the Cruise of the United States Ship Ohio, Commodore Isaac Hull, Commander, In the Mediterranean, In the Years 1839, '40, '41*, 48–50; and R. F. Gould, *The Life of Gould, An Ex-Man-of-War's Man With Incidents on Sea and Shore*, 137–38.

36. Bayard, *Stockton*, 76–77; Church, *Ericsson*, I, 94–96; James Phinney Baxter, *The Introduction of the Ironclad Warship*, 12–13.

37. Church, *Ericsson*, I, 121, 123; Callahan, *List*, 524. The *Ohio* sailed for the Mediterranean on 6 December 1838, two days before Stockton was promoted to captain. He learned of this later when he was in England.

38. Bayard, *Stockton*, 77–79; Bill, "Fighting Bob," 78–79. Bill points out that Stockton cultivated the friendship of President Tyler and entertained him at "Morven." Tyler offered Stockton the post of Secretary of the Navy, which the captain declined.

39. Church, *Ericsson*, I, 117–24; Frank M. Bennett, *The Steam Navy of the United States*, 61–63.

40. Church, *Ericsson*, I, 125–54; Bennett, *Steam*, 70–71; Baxter, *Ironclad*, 13–14. In 1853 the U.S. Court of Claims decided the issue in favor of Ericsson, but Congress never appropriated the money to pay him.

41. For a recent study of the domestic and foreign implications of the annexation, see David M. Pletcher, *The Diplomacy of Annexation: Texas, Oregon, and the Mexican War*, 139–207.

42. Bayard, *Stockton*, Appendix, 70–71.

43. Ibid., 93; Pletcher, *Annexation*, 184–85.

44. Bayard, *Stockton*, 93–95. In a letter to Secretary of the Navy George Bancroft of 24 October 1845, Stockton spoke of his hopes. Among other things, he wrote: "My great object in the first place was to be prepared, in the event of a war with Mexico, to try to do something creditable to the Navy." Letters Received by the Secretary of the Navy: Captains' Letters, M-125, roll 324, 205.

45. For a highly critical assessment of this episode, see Glenn W. Price, *Origins of the War With Mexico: The Polk–Stockton Intrigue*, Chapter 4. This interpretation is corrected in Charles Sellers, *James K. Polk: Continentalist, 1843–1846*, 220–26; Pletcher, *Annexation*, 197–200; and K. Jack Bauer, *The Mexican War, 1846–1848*, 6, 9.

46. Bayard, *Stockton*, 95–96; Bill, "Fighting Bob," 91–95; K. Jack Bauer, *Surfboats and Horse Marines: U.S. Naval Operations in the Mexican War, 1846–48*, 8–10.

47. Reverend Walter Colton, *Deck and Port; or, Incidents of a Cruise in the United States Frigate Congress to California*, 19; Harry

R. Skallerup, *Books Afloat and Ashore: A History of Books, Libraries, and Reading Among Seamen During the Age of Sail*, 94–96.

48. Harold D.Langley, *Social Reform in the U.S. Navy, 1798–1862*, 184–85; Colton, *Deck and Port*, 44–45.

49. Bayard, *Stockton*, 97–98; Bauer, *Surfboats*, 158; Justin W. Smith, *The War With Mexico*, I, 336. Smith says of Stockton: "The new Commodore seems to have been a smart, but vain, selfish, lordly and rampant individual, thirsting for glory; and little glory could be seen in following after his predecessor under so mild a policy."

50. Bauer, *Surfboats*, 158–63; Bauer, *Mexican War*, 164–73; Allen Nevins, *Fremont, Pathmarker of the West*, I, 253–89; Hubert Howe Bancroft, *History of California*, V, 199–214, 224–54.

51. Bancroft, *California*, V, 234–38.

52. Bayard, *Stockton*, 118; Bancroft, *California*, V, 251–54; Bauer, *Surfboats*, 161–62.

53. Bauer, *Mexican War*, 168–74; Bancroft, *California*, V, 253–54; Reverend Walter Colton, *Three Years in California*, 17.

54. Bancroft, *California*, V, 255–60. Bancroft says that the proclamation "was made up of falsehood, of irrelevant issues, and of bombastic ranting in about equal parts . . . ." He says it was "unworthy" of Stockton, and was dictated by Fremont and Lieutenant Archibald Gillespie, USMC to advance their own interests. Stockton adopted their views because they exaggerated the problems he faced and the glory that success would bring. It would make a good impression in the United States, and in the event that war had not been declared, it would help to lay a foundation for his own defense and that of the U.S. government. For the reactions of Larkin and others to the proclamation, see the recent study of the war by Neal Harlow, *California Conquered: War and Peace on the Pacific, 1846–1850*, 142.

55. Bancroft, *California*, V, 261–81; Smith, *Mexico*, I, 336–37; Bauer, *Surfboats*, 165–68; Bauer, *Mexican War*, 174–76; Harlow, *California*, 142–51.

56. Bancroft, *California*, V, 281–85; Smith, *Mexico*, I, 336–37; Bauer, *Surfboats*, 165–68; Bauer, *Mexican War*, 174–76; Harlow, *California*, 151–54. Stockton's proclamation is published in Congress. House. *Message from the President . . . at the Commencement of the Second Session of the Twenty-Ninth Congress*. House ex. doc. 4, 29th Cong., 2nd Sess., 669–70.

57. Bancroft, *California*, V, 288–407; Smith, *Mexico*, I, 238–346; Bauer, *Surfboats*, 171–200; Bauer, *Mexican War*, 183–93; Harlow, *California*, 159–232.

58. Bancroft, *California*, V, 411–31; Bauer, *Surfboats*, 202–4; Bauer, *Mexican War*, 194–95; Harlow, *California*, 235–41; Dwight

L. Clarke, *Stephen Watts Kearney: Soldier of the West*, 256–78; Bill, "Fighting Bob," 139–41; Congress. Senate. *Report of the Secretary of the Navy, Communicating Copies of Commodore Stockton's Despatches Relating to the Military and Naval Operations in California.* Senate ex. doc. 31, 30th Cong., 2nd Sess., February 16, 1849, 1–37.

59. Bayard, *Stockton*, 154–67; Bill, "Fighting Bob," 143–51; Nevins, *Fremont*, I, 327–42.

60. Bayard, *Stockton*, 169.

61. Stockton's ideas are set forth in his letter to Daniel Webster of 25 March 1850, which is printed in the appendix to Bayard, *Stockton*, 70–79.

62. Bayard, *Stockton*, 185–86; Bill, "Fighting Bob," 162–64. Bill says that Stockton was elected "by means of a secret bargain with the Whigs in the legislature . . . ," 162.

63. Stockton's speeches are in the *Congressional Globe*, 32nd Congress, 1st session, XXIV, parts 1 and 2.

64. *Congressional Globe*, 32nd Congress, 1st session, XXIV, Part 1, 218–23. Mallory's speech is in the appendix to vol. XXV, 108–19. On 2 March 1855 Congress passed "An Act to Provide a More Efficient Discipline for the Navy, that established a system of summary courts martial for minor offenses." This, in turn, led to a major revision of the regulations of 1800 and to the enactment of a new code on 27 July 1862. See *U.S. Statutes at Large*, XII, Chapter 204, 603.

Stockton's views on flogging while he was an officer are set forth in his letter of 6 February 1850 to Secretary of the Navy William B. Preston, in Corporal Punishment and the Spirit Ration, R.G. 45: Reports of Officers, 1850, National Archives, letter #17.

65. Bill, "Fighting Bob," 164–69. Bill says that it was believed that Stockton resigned in anticipation of being named Secretary of the Navy in the incoming administration of Democrat Franklin Pierce. If so, it did not seem to affect Stockton's friendship with the President. Subsequently Pierce was entertained at Stockton's home, "Morven." Bill also states that Stockton was hurt by association with the canal company monopoly in New Jersey, and by his reactions to a collision of two trains on his line in New Jersey. Stockton refused to pay any compensation for the casualties or the loss of property. The commodore embraced the principles of the American Party in anticipation of getting the nomination of that group for the presidency. But, says Bill, public response to his name was so lukewarm that he withdrew it. Millard Fillmore became the party's nominee. Stockton never sought public office again, although he returned to the Democratic Party after the election of 1856.

66. Robert Gray Gunderson, *Old Gentlemen's Convention: The Washington Peace Conference of 1861*, 12, 64, 67–70. Bill points out that during the Civil War Stockton kept away from all public demonstrations as much as he could. In 1863 his wife died, and he spent increasing amounts of time at his beach house in Sea Girt. Although loyal to the Union, he was largely a "silent and melancholy spectator" of the war. Bill, "Fighting Bob," 176–80.

BIBLIOGRAPHY

DOCUMENTARY SOURCES

Manuscripts

Library of Congress, Washington, D.C.
  William Bainbridge Papers
  Peter Force Collection
  Benjamin Franklin Papers
  Thomas Jefferson Papers
  John Paul Jones Papers
  James Monroe Papers
  David Porter Papers
  David Dixon Porter Papers
  Rodgers Family Papers
  Daniel Webster Papers
National Archives, Washington, D.C.
  Records of the Bureau of Naval Personnel (Record Group 24)
  Naval Records Collection of the Office of Naval Records and
      Library (Record Group 45)
  General Records of the Department of State (Record Group 59)
  Records of the Office of the Secretary of War (Record Group 107)
  Records of the Office of the Judge Advocate General (Record
      Group 125)
  Records of the U.S. Marine Corps (Record Group 127)
  Records of the General Accounting Office (Record Group 217)
  Records of the Continental and Confederation Congresses and the
      Constitutional Convention (Record Group 360)
Naval Historical Center, Washington, D.C.
  Biographical Files, Historical Research Branch

William L. Clements Library, Ann Arbor, Mich.
  Oliver Hazard Perry Papers
Henry E. Huntington Library, San Marino, Calif.
  Charles T. Harbeck Papers
Boston Public Library, Boston, Mass.
  Manuscript Collections
Princeton University Library, Princeton, N.J.
  Stockton Papers
  Papers of Samuel Southard
Pierpont Morgan Library, New York, N.Y.
  Manuscript Collections
Historical Society of Pennsylvania, Philadelphia, Pa.
  Dreer Collection
Guy W. Bailey Memorial Library, Burlington, Vt.
  Horace B. Sawyer Papers
Franklin D. Roosevelt Library, Hyde Park, N.Y.
  Letters of Isaac Hull
Peabody Museum, Salem, Mass.
  Benjamin W. Crowninshield Papers
New-York Historical Society, New York, N.Y.
  Isaac Hull Letterbook and Papers
  Rodgers Family Papers
United States Naval Academy Museum, Annapolis, Md.
  John Paul Jones Papers
The Historical Society of Delaware, Wilmington, Del.
  Letters of Thomas Macdonough
American Philosophical Society, Philadelphia, Pa.
  Papers of Benjamin Franklin
USS Constitution Museum, Boston, Mass.
  Isaac Hull Papers
Public Archives of Canada, Ottawa, Ont.
  Manuscript Collections
Scottish Record Office, Edinburgh, Scotland
  Kirkcudbright Sheriff Clerk's Records
Papers in Private Hands
  David Porter Papers, Van Ness Collection, Owings Mill, Md.
  Selkirk Family Papers, Sir David Hope-Dunbar, Kirkcudbright,
    Scotland

Printed Source Materials

Adams, J. Q. *Memoirs: Comprising Portions of His Diary from 1795
  to 1848*. Edited by Charles Frances Adams, 12 vols. Philadelphia:
  Lippincott, 1874–77.

"John Cunningham's Journal." *The Mariner's Mirror*, IX (1923), 334.

Knopf, R. C., transcriber. *Anecdotes of the Lake Erie Area: War of 1812*. Columbus: Ohio Historical Society, 1957.

Manning, William R., ed. *Diplomatic Correspondence of the United States Concerning the Independence of Latin America*, 3 vols. New York: Oxford University Press, 1925.

Mason, William Powell. *Reports of Cases Argued and Determined in the Circuit Court of the United States for the First Circuit*, 5 vols. Boston: Wells and Lilly, 1819–31.

Middlebrook, Louis F. *The Log of the Bon Homme Richard*. Mystic: The Marine Historical Association, 1936.

Morris, Charles. *Autobiography*. Boston: A. Williams for the Naval Institute, 1880.

Morris, Gouverneur. *A Diary of the French Revolution, 1789–1793*, 2 vols. Boston: Houghton Mifflin, 1939.

Naval Documents Related to the Quasi-War Between the United States and France, 7 vols. Washington, D.C.: Government Printing Office, 1935–38.

Naval Documents Related to the United States Wars with the Barbary Powers, 7 vols. Washington, D.C.: Government Printing Office, 1939–44.

Paullin, Charles Oscar, ed. *Out-Letters of the Continental Marine Committee and Board of Admiralty, August, 1776–September, 1780*, 2 vols. New York: Naval History Society, 1914.

———. *The Battle of Lake Erie: A Collection of Documents*. Cleveland: The Twofant Club, 1918.

Porter, David. *Constantinople and Its Environs: In a Series of Letters, Exhibiting the Actual State of the Manners, Customs, and Habits of the Turks, Armenians, Jews, and Greeks*. By an American, Long Resident at Constantinople. 2 vols. New York: Harper, 1835.

———. *An Exposition of the Facts and Circumstances Which Justified the Expedition to Foxardo, and the Consequences Thereof, Together with the Proceedings of the Court-of-Inquiry Thereon, Held by Order of the Hon. Secretary of the Navy*. Washington: Davis & Force, 1825.

———. *Journal of a Cruise Made to the Pacific Ocean by Captain David Porter, in the United States Frigate Essex, in the Years 1812, 1813 and 1814, Containing Descriptions of the Cape de Verd[e] Islands, Coasts of Brazil, Patagonia, Chile and Peru, and of the Gallapagos [sic] Islands*, 2 vols. Philadelphia: Bradford and Inskeep, 1815.

———. *Journal of a Cruise Made to the Pacific Ocean by Captain David Porter, in the United States Frigate Essex, in the Years 1812, 1813 and 1814, Containing Descriptions of the Cape de Verd[e] Islands, Coasts of Brazil, Patagonia, Chile and Peru, and of the Gallapagos* [*sic*] *Islands, 2nd edition, To Which is now added an introduction, in which the charges contained in the Quarterly Review, of the first edition of this Journal, are examined.* New York: Wiley & Halsted, 1822.

Preble, George H., ed. *Diary of Ezra Green, M.D., Surgeon on board the Continental Ship-of-War Ranger Under John Paul Jones, from November 1, 1777 to Sept. 27, 1778 . . . . Boston: D. Clapp, 1875.*

The Public Statutes at Large of United States of America, 12 vols. Boston: Little, Brown, 1845–65.

Register of Officer Personnel, United States Navy and Marine Corps and Ships' Data, 1801–1807. Washington, D.C.: Office of Naval Records and Library, 1945.

Rodgers, John. *Appel a la Loyaute de la Nacion francaise contra les Pirateriers Exercees par les Armateurs.* N.p., n.p., 1797.

Smith, Philip Chadwick Foster. *The Frigate Essex Papers: Building the Salem Frigate, 1798–1799.* Salem: Peabody Museum, 1974.

Smith, Paul H., ed. *Letters of the Delegates to Congress*, 10 vols. to date. Washington, D.C.: Library of Congress, 1976–   .

Torrey, F. P. *Journal of the Cruise of the United States Ship Ohio, Commodore Isaac Hull, Commander, In the Mediterranean, In the Years 1839, '40, '41.* Boston: n.p., 1841.

Wheaton, Henry. *Reports of Cases Argued and Adjudged in the Supreme Court, 1816–1827*, 12 vols. Philadelphia: n.p., 1816–27.

SECONDARY SOURCES

Books

Adair, Douglass. *Fame and the Founding Fathers: Essays by Douglass Adair.* Edited by Trevor Calhoun. New York: Norton, 1974.

Adams, Henry. *The War of 1812.* Edited by H. A. DeWeerd. Washington, D.C.: Infantry Journal Press, 1944.

Albion, Robert G. *Makers of Naval Policy 1798–1947.* Annapolis: Naval Institute Press, 1980.

Allen, Gardner W. *A Naval History of the American Revolution*, 2 vols. Boston: Houghton Mifflin, 1913.

———. *Our Naval War with France.* Boston: Houghton Mifflin, 1909.

———. *Our Navy and the Barbary Corsairs.* Boston: Houghton Mifflin, 1905.

———. *Our Navy and the West Indian Pirates.* Salem: Essex Institute, 1929.

Anthony, Irwin. *Decatur.* New York: Charles Scribner's Sons, 1931.

Appleton's Cyclopaedia of American Biography, 6 vols. New York: Appleton, 1887–89.

Bancroft, Hubert Howe. *History of California*, 7 vols. San Francisco: A. L. Bancroft & Co., 1884–90.

Barnes, James. *Commodore Bainbridge, From the Gunroom to the Quarter-Deck*. New York: Appleton, 1897.

Bass, William P. and Ethel L. *Constitution, Second Phase, 1802–07— Mediterranean, Tripoli, Malta & More*. Melbourne: Shipsresearch, 1981.

Bauer, K. Jack. *The Mexican War, 1846–1848*. New York: Macmillan, 1974.

———. *Ships of the Navy, 1776–1969: Volume I, Combat Vessels*. Troy: Rensselaer Polytechnic Institute, 1970.

———. *Surfboats and Horse Marines: U.S. Naval Operations in the Mexican War, 1846–48*. Annapolis: Naval Institute Press, 1969.

Baxter, James Phinney. *The Introduction of the Ironclad Warship*. Cambridge: Cambridge University Press, 1933.

Benjamin, Park. *United States Naval Academy*. New York: Putnam, 1900.

Bennett, Frank M. *The Steam Navy of the United States: A History of the Growth of the Steam Vessel of War in the U.S. Navy, and of the Naval Engineer Corps*. Pittsburgh: W. T. Nicholson, 1896.

Benton, Thomas H. *Thirty Years' View; or, A History of the Workings of the American Government for Thirty Years, from 1820 to 1850*, 2 vols. New York: Appleton, 1854.

Berton, Pierre. *Flames Across the Border: The Canadian–American Tragedy, 1813–1814*. Boston: Little, Brown, 1982.

———. *The Invasion of Canada, 1812–1813*. Boston: Little, Brown, 1980.

Bidwell, Robert L. "The First Mexican Navy, 1821–1830." Unpublished doctoral dissertation, 1968.

Bill, Alfred Hoyt. *A House Called Morven: Its Role in American History, 1701–1954*. Princeton: Princeton University Press, 1954.

Bornholdt, Laura A. *Baltimore and Early Pan-Americanism: A Study in the Background of the Monroe Doctrine*. Smith College Studies in History, No. 34. Northampton: Smith College, 1949.

Bradlee, Francis B. C. *Piracy in the West Indies and Its Suppression*. Salem: Essex Institute, 1923.

Brant, Irving. *James Madison, Commander in Chief, 1812–1836*. Indianapolis: The Bobbs-Merrill Co., Inc., 1961.

Buell, Augustus C. *Paul Jones, Founder of the American Navy: A History*, 2 vols. New York: Charles Scribner's Sons, 1900.

Calvert, James. *The Naval Profession*. New York: McGraw-Hill, 1965.

Channing, Edward. *History of the United States*. New York: Macmillan, 1917.

Chapelle, Howard I. *History of the American Sailing Navy*. New York: Bonanza Books, 1949.

Church, William Conant. *The Life of John Ericsson*, 2 vols. New York: Scribner, 1890.

Clark, William Bell. *Ben Franklin's Privateers*. New York: Greenwood Press, 1969.

———. *Gallant John Barry, 1745–1803: The Story of a Naval Hero of Two Wars*. New York: Macmillan, 1938.

Clarke, Dwight L. *Stephen Watts Kearney: Soldier of the West*. Norman: University of Oklahoma, 1961.

Clowes, William Laird. *The Royal Navy, A History from the Earliest Times to the Present*. London: Sampson, Low, Marston & Co., 1901.

Cochran, Hamilton. *Noted American Duels and Hostile Encounters*. Philadelphia: Chilton Books, 1963.

Coles, Harry L. *The War of 1812*. Chicago: University of Chicago Press, 1956.

Coletta, Paolo E., Albion, Robert G., and Bauer, K. Jack, eds. *American Secretaries of the Navy*, 2 vols. Annapolis: Naval Institute Press, 1980.

Colton, Walter. *Deck and Port; or, Incidents of a Cruise in the United States Frigate Congress to California*. New York: B. W. Evans, 1860.

———. *Three Years in California, 1846–1849*. New York: A. S. Barnes, 1850.

Cooper, James F. *The Battle of Lake Erie; or Answers to Messers. Burges, Duer, and Mackenzie*. Cooperstown: H. & E. Phinney, 1843.

———. *The History of the Navy of the United States of America*, 2 vols., 2nd ed. Philadelphia: Lea & Blanchard, 1840.

———. *Lives of Distinguished American Naval Officers*, 2 vols. Philadelphia: Carey and Hart, 1846.

Crawford, M. MacDermot. *The Sailor Whom England Feared*. London: E. Nash, 1913.

Cunningham, Noble E. *The Process of Government under Jefferson*. Princeton: Princeton University Press, 1978.

Davenport, Charles Benedict. *Naval Officers: Their Heredity and Development*. Washington, D.C.: Carnegie Institution of Washington, 1919.

Dearborn, Henry A. S. *The Life of William Bainbridge, Esq., of the United States Navy*. Edited by James Barnes. Princeton: Princeton University Press, 1931.

Dearden, Seton. *A Nest of Corsairs: The Fighting Karamanlis of Tripoli*. London: John Murray, 1976.

DeKoven, Mrs. Reginald (Anna). *The Life and Letters of John Paul Jones*, 2 vols. New York: Charles Scribner's Sons, 1913.

Dillon, Richard. *We Have Met the Enemy: Oliver Hazard Perry, Wilderness Commodore*. New York: McGraw-Hill, 1978.

Dobbins, W. D. *History of the Battle of Lake Erie (September 10, 1813), and Reminiscences of the Flagships "Lawrence" and "Niagara."* Erie: Ashby and Vincent, 1876.

Downey, Joseph T. *The Cruise of the Portsmouth, 1845–1847: A Sailor's View of the Naval Conquest of California*. Edited by Howard R. Lamar. New Haven: Yale University Press, 1958.

Duignan, Peter and Clendenen, C. J. *The United States and the African Slave Trade, 1619–1862*. Palo Alto: Stanford University Press, 1963.

Dutton, Charles J. *Oliver Hazard Perry*. New York: Longmans, 1935.

Eckert, Edward K. *The Navy Department in the War of 1812*. Gainesville: University of Florida Press, 1973.

Emerson, George D., compiler. *The Perry Victory Centenary: Report of the Perry's Victory Centennial Commission, State of New York*. Albany: J. B. Lyon, 1916.

Everest, Allan S. *The War of 1812 in the Champlain Valley*. Syracuse: Syracuse University Press, 1981.

Ferguson, Eugene S. *Truxtun of the Constitution*. Baltimore: Johns Hopkins University Press, 1956.

Field, Edward. *Esek Hopkins, Commander-in-Chief of the Continental Navy During the American Revolution, 1775–1778*. Providence: Preston and Rounds, 1898.

Field, James A., Jr. *America and the Mediterranean World, 1776–1882*. Princeton: Princeton University Press, 1969.

Fink, Leo Gregory. *Barry or Jones, "Father of the United States Navy."* Philadelphia: Jefferies and Manz, 1962.

Forester, C. S. *The Age of Fighting Sail: The Story of the Naval War of 1812*. New York: Doubleday, 1956.

Fowler, William M., Jr. *William Ellery: A Rhode Island Politico & Lord of Admiralty*. Metuchen: Scarecrow Press, 1973.

Furnas, J. C. *The Anatomy of Paradise: Hawaii and the Islands of the South Seas*. New York: William Sloane Associates, 1948.

Golder, Frank A. *John Paul Jones in Russia*. Garden City: Doubleday, Page & Company, 1927.

Goldsborough, Charles W. *United States Naval Chronicle*. Washington, D.C.: printed by J. Wilson, 1824.

Grant, Bruce. *Isaac Hull, Captain of Old Ironsides: The Life and Fighting Times of Isaac Hull and the U.S. Frigate Constitution*. Chicago: Pellegrini & Cudahy, 1947.

Griffin, Martin I. J. *Commodore John Barry: The Record of His Services for Our Country*. Philadelphia: published by the Author, 1903.

Gunderson, Robert Gray. *Old Gentlemen's Convention: The Washington Peace Conference of 1861.* Madison: University of Wisconsin Press, 1961.

Gurn, Joseph. *Commodore John Barry: Father of the American Navy.* New York: P. J. Kennedy, 1933.

Guttridge, Leonard F. and Smith, Jay D. *The Commodores.* New York: Harper & Row, 1969.

Hagan, Kenneth J., ed. *In Peace and War.* Westport: Greenwood, 1978.

Hammersly, Sydney E. *The Lake Champlain Naval Battles of 1776–1814: Hudson–Champlain, 1959, 350th Anniversary Edition.* Waterford: Col. Sydney E. Hammersly, 1959.

Hannon, Bryan. *Three American Commodores.* New York: n.p., 1935.

Hapgood, Hutchins. *Paul Jones.* New York: Houghton Mifflin, 1901.

Harlow, Neal. *California Conquered: War and Peace on the Pacific 1846–1850.* Berkeley: University of California Press, 1982.

Harris, Thomas. *The Life and Services of Commodore William Bainbridge, United States Navy.* Philadelphia: Carey, Lea & Blanchard, 1837.

Hitsman, J. Mackay. *The Incredible War of 1812, A Military History.* Toronto: University of Toronto Press, 1965.

Horsfield, John. *The Art of Leadership in War: The Royal Navy from the Age of Nelson to the End of World War II.* Westport: Greenwood Press, 1980.

Horsman, Reginald. *The War of 1812.* New York: Alfred A. Knopf, 1969.

Hutcheon, Wallace, Jr. *Robert Fulton: Pioneer of Underwater Warfare.* Annapolis: Naval Institute Press, 1981.

Irving, Washington. *The Works of Washington Irving,* 12 vols. New York: G. P. Putnam's Sons, 1883.

Irwin, Ray W. *The Diplomatic Relations of the United States with the Barbary Powers, 1776–1816.* Chapel Hill: University of North Carolina Press, 1931.

James, William. *Full and Correct Account of the Chief Naval Occurrences of the Late War Between Great Britain and the United States,* 2 vols. London: T. Egerton, 1818.

Johnson, Allen and Malone, Dumas, eds. *Dictionary of American Biography,* 20 vols. New York: Charles Scribner's Sons, 1928–36.

Johnson, Gerald W. *The First Captain: The Story of John Paul Jones.* New York: Coward-McCann, 1947.

Johnson, Robert Erwin. *Rear Admiral John Rodgers.* Annapolis: Naval Institute Press, 1967.

Karsten, Peter. *The Naval Aristocracy: The Golden Age of Annapolis and the Emergence of Modern American Navalism.* New York: The Free Press, 1972.

Knox, Dudley W. *A History of the United States Navy.* New York: Putnam, 1936.

Langley, Harold D. *Social Reform in the U.S. Navy, 1798–1862.* Urbana: University of Illinois Press, 1967.

Lewis, Charles L. *Admiral DeGrasse and American Independence.* Annapolis: Naval Institute Press, 1945.

———. *David Glasgow Farragut: Admiral in the Making,* 2 vols. Annapolis: Naval Institute Press, 1941–43.

———. *The Romantic Decatur.* Philadelphia: The University of Pennsylvania Press, 1937.

Long, David F. *Nothing Too Daring: A Biography of Commodore David Porter, 1780–1843.* Annapolis: Naval Institute Press, 1970.

———. *Ready to Hazard: A Biography of Commodore William Bainbridge, 1774–1833.* Boston: University Press of New England, 1981.

———. *Sailor-Diplomat: A Biography of Commodore James Biddle, 1783–1848.* Boston: Northeastern University Press, 1983.

Lorenz, Lincoln. *John Paul Jones, Fighter for Freedom and Glory.* Annapolis: Naval Institute Press, 1941.

Lossing, Benson J. *Pictorial Field-Book of the War of 1812.* New York: Harper and Brothers, 1868.

Macdonough, Rodney. *Life of Commodore Thomas Macdonough, U.S. Navy.* Boston: The Fort Hill Press, 1909.

———. *The Macdonough–Hackstaff Ancestry.* Boston: Press of Samuel Usher, 1901.

MacKenzie, Alexander S. *The Life of Commodore Oliver Hazard Perry,* 2 vols. New York: Harper's, 1840.

———. *The Life of Stephen Decatur.* Boston: Charles C. Little and James Brown, 1846.

Maclay, Edgar Stanton. *A History of the United States Navy from 1775 to 1893.* New York: D. Appleton and Co., 1894.

Mahan, Alfred Thayer. *Sea Power in its Relations to the War of 1812.* Boston: Little, Brown and Co., 1919.

———. *Types of Naval Officers.* London: Sampson Low, Marston & Co., 1904.

Mahon, John K. *The War of 1812: A Military History.* Gainesville: University of Florida Press, 1972.

[Malcolm, John.] *Memoirs of Rear-Admiral Paul Jones.* Edinburgh: Oliver & Boyd, 1830.

Malloy, Leo T. *Commodore Isaac Hull, U.S.N., His Life and Times.* Darby: n.p., 1964.

Marcus, G. J. *A Naval History of England: The Formative Centuries.* Boston: Little, Brown, 1961.

McCormick, Richard P. *The Second American Party System: Party Formation in the Jacksonian Era.* Chapel Hill: University of North Carolina Press, 1966.

McCusker, John J. *Alfred: The First Continental Flagship.* Washington, D.C.: Smithsonian Institution Press, 1973.

McKee, Christopher. *Edward Preble: A Naval Biography, 1761–1807.* Annapolis: Naval Institute Press, 1972; reprinted, New York: Arno Press, 1980.

Meyers, Frank C. "Congress and the Navy: The Establishment and Administration of the American Revolutionary Navy by the Continental Congress." Unpublished doctoral dissertation, University of North Carolina, 1972.

Millett, Allan R. *Semper Fidelis: The History of the United States Marine Corps.* New York: Macmillan, 1980.

Mills, James C. *Oliver Hazard Perry and the Battle of Lake Erie.* Detroit: J. Phelps, 1913.

Mooney, James L., ed. *Dictionary of American Naval Fighting Ships,* 8 vols. Washington, D.C.: Government Printing Office, 1959–81.

Morgan, William James. *Captains to the Northward: The New England Captains in the Continental Navy.* Barre: Barre Press, 1959.

Morison, Samuel Eliot. *John Paul Jones: A Sailor's Biography.* Boston: Little, Brown, 1959.

———. *Old Bruin: Commodore Matthew C. Perry, 1794–1858.* Boston: Little, Brown, 1967.

Moskin, J. Robert. *The U.S. Marine Corps Story.* New York: McGraw-Hill, 1977.

Muller, Charles G. *The Proudest Day: Macdonough on Lake Champlain.* New York: John Day, 1960.

Neeser, Robert Wilden. *Statistical and Chronological History of the United States Navy, 1775–1907,* 2 vols. New York: Macmillan, 1909.

Nevin, David. *The Mexican War.* Alexandria: Time–Life Books, 1978.

Nevins, Allan. *Fremont, Pathmarker of the West,* 2 vols. New York: Longmans, Green, 1955.

Nichols, Roy F. *Advance Agents of American Destiny.* Philadelphia: University of Pennsylvania Press, 1956.

Nicolay, Helen. *Deactur of the Old Navy.* New York: D. Appleton-Century Co., 1942.

Niles, John M. *Life of Oliver Hazard Perry: with an Appendix Comprising a Biographical Memoir of the Late Captain James Lawrence; with Brief Sketches of the Events in the Lives of Commodores Bainbridge,*

Decatur, Porter and Macdonough [*with a*] *View of the Rise, Present Condition, and Future Prospects of the Navy of the United States* [*and*] *a List of the Officers of the Navy and Vessels-of-War of the United States,* 3rd ed. Hartford: O. D. Cooke, 1821.

Paullin, Charles Oscar. *Commodore John Rodgers, Captain, Commodore, and Senior Officer of the American Navy, 1773–1838.* Cleveland: The Arther H. Clark Company, 1910.

―――. *Diplomatic Negotiations of American Naval Officers, 1778–1883* Baltimore: The Johns Hopkins Press, 1912.

―――. *The Navy of the American Revolution: Its Administration, Its Policy, and Its Achievements.* Cleveland: Burrows Brothers, 1906.

―――. *Paullin's History of Naval Administration, 1775–1911.* Annapolis: Naval Institute Press, 1968.

Pletcher, David M. *The Diplomacy of Annexation: Texas, Oregon, and the Mexican War.* Columbia: University of Missouri Press, 1973.

Porter, David Dixon. *Memoir of Commodore David Porter of the United States Navy.* Albany: J. Munsell, 1875.

Potter, E. B., ed. *Sea Power,* 2nd ed. Annapolis: Naval Institute Press, 1981.

Pratt, Fletcher. *Preble's Boys: Commodore Preble and the Birth of American Sea Power.* New York: Sloane, 1950.

―――. *The Navy.* Garden City: Doubleday, 1938.

Price, Glenn W. *Origins of the War With Mexico: The Polk–Stockton Intrigue.* Austin: University of Texas Press, 1967.

Remini, Robert V. *The Election of Andrew Jackson.* Philadelphia: Lippincott, 1963.

Rider, Hope S. *Valour Fore & Aft: Being the Adventures of the Continental Sloop Providence, 1775–1779, Formerly Flagship Katy of Rhode Island's Navy.* Annapolis: Naval Institute Press, 1977.

Rippy, James F. *Joel R. Poinsett, Versatile American.* Westport: Greenwood, 1968.

Roosevelt, Theodore. *The Naval War of 1812.* New York: G. P. Putnam's Sons, 1882.

Sabine, Lorenzo. *Life of Edward Preble.* Boston: Little and Brown, 1847.

Sands, Robert. *Life and Correspondence of John Paul Jones, Including His Narrative of the Campaign of the Liman.* New York: A. Chandler, 1830.

Schulte Nordholt, Jan Willem. *The Dutch Republic and American Independence.* Translated by Herbert H. Rowen. Chapel Hill: University of North Carolina Press, 1982.

Seitz, Don C. *Famous American Duels.* New York: Thomas Y. Crowell Company Publishers, 1929.

————. *Paul Jones, His Exploits in English Seas During 1776–1780*. New York: Dutton, 1917.

Sellers, Charles. *James K. Polk: Continentalist, 1843–1846*. Princeton: Princeton University Press, 1966.

Sherburne, John Henry. *Life and Character of the Chevalier John Paul Jones*. New York: Wilder & Campbell, 1825.

Skallerup, Harry R. *Books Afloat and Ashore: A History of Books, Libraries, and Reading Among Seamen During the Age of Sail*. Hamden: Archon Books, 1974.

Skelton, William B. "The United States Army Officer Corps, 1784–1861: A Social History." In progress.

Smith, Justin W. *The War With Mexico*, 2 vols. New York: Macmillan, 1919.

Smith, Myron J., Jr. *Navies in the American Revolution: A Bibliography*. Metuchen: Scarecrow Press, 1973.

Snider, Charles H., Jr. *The Glorious "Shannon's" Old Blue Duster and Other Faded Flags of Fadeless Fame*. Toronto: McClellan and Stewart, 1923.

Sprout, Harold and Margaret. *The Rise of American Naval Power*, revised edition. Princeton: Princeton University Press, 1967.

Stackpole, Edouard A. *A Nantucketer Who Followed an Ideal in a Far Country*. N.p., n.d.

Staudenraus, Philip J. *The African Colonization Movement, 1816–1865*. New York: Columbia University Press, 1961.

Stewart, Charles W., compiler. *John Paul Jones Commemoration at Annapolis, April 24, 1906*. Washington, D.C.: Government Printing Office, 1907.

Straub, Joseph F. "Jose Miguel Carrera." Unpublished doctoral dissertation, 1953.

Symonds, Craig. *Navalists and Anti-Navalists*. Newark: University of Delaware Press, 1980.

Taylor, George R. *The Transportation Revolution, 1815–1860*. New York: Harper & Row, 1951.

Thomson, Valentine. *Knight of the Seas*. New York: Liveright, 1939.

Toussaint, Auguste. *Les Frères Surcouf*. Paris: Flamarion, 1979.

Tucker, Glenn. *Dawn Like Thunder: The Barbary Wars and the Birth of the U.S. Navy*. Indianapolis: Bobbs-Merrill, 1963.

————. *Poltroons and Patriots: A Popular Account of the War of 1812*, 2 vols. Indianapolis: Bobbs-Merrill, 1954.

Turnbull, Archibald D. *Commodore David Porter, 1780–1843*. New York: Century, 1929.

Valle, James E. *Rocks and Shoals: Order and Discipline in the Old Navy, 1798–1861*. Annapolis: Naval Institute Press, 1980.

Walsh, John Evangelist. *Night on Fire: The First Complete Account of John Paul Jones' Greatest Battle*. New York: McGraw-Hill, 1978.

Ward, James H. *Manual of Naval Tactics*. New York: D. Appleton, 1859.

Warner, Oliver. *Command at Sea: Great Fighting Admirals from Hawke to Nimitz*. New York: St. Martin's Press, 1976.

Watkins, John Elfreth. *Biographical Sketches of John Stevens, Robert L. Stevens, Edwin A. Stevens, John S. Darcy, John P. Jackson, Robert F. Stockton*. Washington, D.C.: Press of W. F. Roberts, 1892.

West, Richard S., Jr. *The Second Admiral: A Life of David Dixon Porter, 1813–1891*. New York: Coward-McCann, 1937.

Wheeler, Richard. *In Pirate Waters: Captain David Porter, U.S. Navy and America's War on Piracy in the West Indies*. New York: Thomas Y. Crowell, 1969.

White, Leonard D. *The Jeffersonians: A Study in Administrative History, 1801–1829*. New York: Macmillan, 1951.

Wriston, Henry M. *Executive Agents in American Foreign Relations*. Baltimore: The Johns Hopkins Press, 1929.

Articles

Beach, E. L. "The Pioneer of America's Pacific Empire: David Porter." U.S. Naval Institute *Proceedings*, XXIV (1908), 561–62.

Birkner, Michael. "The Foxardo Affair Revisted: Porter, Pirates, and the Problem of Civilian Authority in the Early Republic." *The American Neptune*, XLII (1982), 165–78.

Chamberlain, Waldo. "The Tradition of the Offensive in the United States Navy." U.S. Naval Institute *Proceedings*, LXVII (1941), 1375–84.

Clark, Ellery H., Jr. "Famous Swords at the United States Naval Academy," U.S. Naval Institute *Proceedings*, LXVI (1940), 1769–75.

———. "United States Place Names Honoring the Navy." U.S. Naval Institute *Proceedings*, LXXIV (1948), 452–55.

Cole, A. B., ed. "Captain David Porter's Proposed Expedition to the Pacific and Japan, 1815." *Pacific Historical Review*, IX (1940), 61–65.

Cooke, Mary Lewis and Lewis, Charles Lee. "An American Naval Officer in the Mediterranean, 1802–7." U.S. Naval Institute *Proceedings*, LXVII (1941), 1533–39.

Cox, Richard J. "An Eye Witness Account of the Battle of Lake Erie." U.S. Naval Institute *Proceedings*, CIV (1978), 72–73.

Darling, Charles H. "Thomas Macdonough: An Address Before the Vermont Historical Society, October 27, 1904." Vermont Historical Society *Proceedings* (1905), 57–89.

Duval, Ruby R. "The Perpetuation of History and Tradition at the United States Naval Academy Today." U.S. Naval Institute *Proceedings*, LXIV (1938), 669–77.

Dye, Ira. "Early American Merchant Seafarers." American Philosophical Society *Proceedings*, CXX (1976), 331–60.

Estes, J. Worth. "Naval Medicine in the Age of Sail: The Voyage of the New York, 1802–1803." *Bulletin of the History of Medicine*, LVI (1982), 238–53.

Flaccus, Elmer W. "Commodore David Porter and the Mexican Navy." *Hispanic American Historical Review*, XXXIV (August 1954), 365–73.

Folsom, William R. "The Battle of Plattsburgh," *Vermont Quarterly*, XX (1952), 234–59.

Forester, C. S. "Victory on Lake Champlain." *American Heritage*, XV (1963), 4–11, 88–90.

Gifford, William. "Review of Porter's Cruize [*sic*] in the Pacific Ocean." *The Quarterly Review*, XIII (July 1815), 383.

Gilman, Emma C. "Hero of the Battleship 'Saratoga'—Macdonough of Connecticut." *Connecticut Magazine*, XI (1907), 553–59.

Haines, Charles. "Ship Preservation in the Old Navy." *The American Neptune*, XLII (1982), 279–81.

Hill, Henry W. "Otter Creek in History." Vermont Historical Society *Proceedings*, VIII (1913–14), 125–48.

Macdonough, Rodney. "The Hero of Lake Champlain's Great Naval Battle." *Vermonter*, II (1897), 149–54.

———. "A Paper on Commodore Thomas Macdonough, United States Navy." *Papers of the Historical Society of Delaware*, XVIII (1907), 3–22.

Maloney, Linda. "A Naval Experiment." *The American Neptune*, XXXIV (1974), 188–96.

———. "The U.S. Navy's Pacific Squadron: 1824–1827." In Robert William Love, Jr., ed., *Changing Interpretations and New Sources in Naval History*. New York: Garland, 1980, 180–91.

Mahan, Alfred Thayer. "Commodore Macdonough at Plattsburgh." *North American Review*, CC (August 1914), 203–21.

McCusker, John J., Jr. "The American Invasion of Nassau in the Bahamas." *The American Neptune*, XXV (1965), 189–217.

McKee [Maloney], Linda. "A Forgotten Watchword." U.S. Naval Institute *Proceedings*, LXXIX (1963), 176.

———. "By Heaven, That Ship Is Ours!" *American Heritage*, XVI, no. 1, (December 1964), 4–11, 94–98.

Merrill, James M. "Midshipman DuPont and the Cruise of the *North Carolina*, 1825–27." *The American Neptune*, XL (1980), 211–25.

Muller, Charles G. "Commodore & Mrs. Thomas Macdonough." *Delaware History*, IX (1960–61), 341–54.

Murphy, W. S. "Four American Officers of the War of 1812." *Irish Sword*, VI (1963), 4.

Oliver, Frederick L. "Commodore Oliver Hazard Perry of Newport, Rhode Island." U.S. Naval Institute *Proceedings*, LXXX (1954), 777–83.

Pearson, Lee M. "The 'Princeton' and the 'Peacemaker': A Study in Nineteenth-Century Naval Research and Development Procedures." *Technology and Culture*, VII (1966), 163–83.

Pratt, Fletcher. "The Basis of Our Naval Traditions." U.S. Naval Institute *Proceedings*, LXIII (1937), 1107–14.

Sykes, George. "The Accident on Board the U.S.S. 'Princeton', February 28, 1844: A Contemporary Newsletter." *Pennsylvania History*, VII (1937), 1–29.

Tucker, Spencer C. "The Carronade." U.S. Naval Institute *Proceedings*, IC (1973), 65–70.

Vandergrift, L. C. "Memoir of Commodore Macdonough," *Papers of the Historical Society of Delaware* (1895), 3–14.

NOTES ON AUTHORS

William M. Fowler, Jr., is Professor of History at Northeastern University and Managing Editor of the New England Quarterly. He has written extensively about the early history of the Navy. Among his books are *Rebels Under Sail: The American Navy During the Revolution; William Ellery: A Rhode Island Politico and Lord of Admiralty; The Baron of Beacon Hill: A Biography of John Hancock*; and *Jack Tars and Commodores: The American Navy, 1783–1815*.

James C. Bradford is Assistant Professor at Texas A&M University where he teaches American and naval history. He did undergraduate work at Michigan State University and earned his Ph.D. at the University of Virginia. He taught Early American and naval history at the U.S. Naval Academy from 1973 to 1981. He is currently editing a comprehensive microfilm and select letterpress edition of the Papers of John Paul Jones.

William James Morgan is the U.S. Navy's Senior Historian Emeritus. Upon retirement in 1982 he received the Navy's highest civilian award, the Distinguished Civilian Service Medal. He served as a naval officer in World War II and the Korean War. He did his undergraduate work at Fordham University, and took his M.A. at Columbia University and Ph.D. at the University of Southern California. He is editor of the multivolume series *Naval Documents of the American Revolution*. Other publications include *Captains to the Northward: The New England Captains in the Continental Navy, The Autobiography of Rear Admiral Charles Wilkes*, "American Privateering in America's War for Independence" in *Course et Piraterie, La Commission Inter-*

nationale d'Historie Maritime and *The American Neptune*, and "Documenting the American Navies of the Revolution" in *Versatile Guardian: Research in Navy History.*

Christopher McKee is the Samuel R. and Marie-Louise Rosenthal Professor and Librarian of the College at Grinnell College. He is the author of *Edward Preble: A Naval Biography, 1761–1807* and various articles, including "Fantasies of Mutiny and Murder: A Suggested Psycho-history of the Seaman in the United States Navy, 1798–1815" in *Armed Forces and Society*, and contributes the chapters on the nineteenth-century Navy to the *Supplements to A Guide to the Sources of United States Military History*, edited by Robin Higham and Donald J. Mrozek. Professor McKee is currently completing a book on the social history of the origins of the officer corps of the U.S. Navy during the years 1794–1815.

Craig L. Symonds is Associate Professor of History at the U.S. Naval Academy. He received his Ph.D. from the University of Florida. While in the Navy he was stationed at the Naval War College where he taught courses in strategy. He is the author of *Charleston Blockade, Navalists and Antinavalists*, and *A Battlefield Atlas of the Civil War* and the editor of *New Aspects of Naval History.*

John K. Mahon was educated at Swarthmore College (B.A., 1934) and the University of California, Los Angeles (Ph.D., 1950), served in the army during World War II, and was Civilian Historian for the Office of the Chief of Military History, 1951–53. He has been on the faculty of the University of Florida since 1954 and served as Chairman of the History Department, 1965–73. In 1977 and 1978 he was the Harold K. Johnson Visiting Professor of Military History at the U.S. Army Military History Institute, Carlisle Barracks. Professor Mahon is the author of twenty-five journal articles and four books including *The War of 1812* and *History of the Second Seminole War, 1835–1842*. His offices in professional associations include Trustee of the American Military Institute, 1951, 1968–73, 1980–83 and President of the Florida Historical Society, 1980–82.

Edward K. Eckert, Professor of History at St. Bonaventure University, is the author of *The Navy Department in the War of 1812* and *Ten Years in the Saddle* with Nicholas J. Amato, plus over twenty articles in leading historical journals. He specializes in nineteenth-century American naval and military history. Professor Eckert has just completed a book on Jefferson Davis's symbolism to the post–Civil War

South, and is currently at work on a biography of Davis. Married and the father of three sons, Eckert enjoys traveling with his family to out-of-the-way historic spots.

David F. Long, Dartmouth University, A.B, 1939, and Columbia University A.M. and Ph.D. (1948, 1950), has taught history at the University of New Hampshire since 1948, specializing in the history of American foreign relations. This led him to his present interest in early U.S. naval biographies of David Porter, William Bainbridge, and James Biddle because naval officers conducted most of the diplomatic relations with what we now call the "Third World" until late in the nineteenth century. He has published six books, most of them concerning his twin interests. He has also had four Fulbright grants, three teaching (two separate lectureships at the University of Sri Lanka in the late 1950s, and one at Makerere University at Kampala, Uganda, 1964) and one research (Korea, 1974). Under the title "Diplomatic Activities of U.S. Naval Officers, 1798–1883," he is currently entirely reworking Charles O. Paullin's *Diplomatic Negotiations of American Naval Officers, 1778–1883*.

John H. Schroeder received his Ph.D. in History from the University of Virginia in 1971. Since then, he has been a member of the Department of History at the University of Wisconsin–Milwaukee where he is an Associate Professor. He is the author of *Mr. Polk's War: American Opposition and Dissent, 1846–1848*, and has written numerous articles and reviews on early American history including "Jacksonian Naval Policy, 1829–1837," which is forthcoming in the selected proceedings of the Fifth Naval History Symposium. Professor Schroeder is currently completing work on a study of the U.S. Navy and American commercial diplomacy from 1829 to 1861.

K. Jack Bauer is Professor of History at Rensselaer Polytechnic Institute. He holds an A.B. from Harvard College and an M.A. and a Ph.D. from Indiana University. Dr. Bauer is the author or editor of numerous books and articles on military and naval history, including *Surfboats and Horse Marines, Ships of the Navy, Combat Vessels, The Mexican War 1846–1848, American Secretaries of the Navy* (co-editor), *The New American State Papers: Naval Affairs*, and *Ports of the West* (co-editor). He has recently completed a biography of Present Zachary Taylor. Dr. Bauer has served on the staffs of the National Archives, Historical Branch of the Marine Corps, and Historical Division of the Navy and has been the John F. Morrison Visiting Professor of Military History at the Army's Command and General Staff College. He is a Trustee of the American Military Institute and a former Vice President of the North American Society for Oceanic History.

Linda M. Maloney is a native of Houston, Texas. She holds the A.B. and Ph.D. degrees, in history and American studies, from Saint Louis University, as well as an M.A. in religious studies from the same institution. In addition, she holds the degree of Master of International Business Studies from the University of South Carolina. She has published articles related to the career of Isaac Hull in several journals, including the U.S. Naval Institute *Proceedings*, *American Heritage*, and *The American Neptune*, and is the author of a biography of Hull that has not yet been published. Her ongoing interest in the role of women in society has led her most recently to studies in theology at the University of Tübingen, West Germany.

Harold D. Langley is a Curator in the Division of Naval History, National Museum of American History, Smithsonian Institution, and an Adjunct Professor of History at The Catholic University of America in Washington, D.C. His undergraduate education was completed at The Catholic University, and he received his M.A. and Ph.D. degrees from the University of Pennsylvania. He is the author of *Social Reform in the U.S. Navy; 1798–1862*, the editor of *To Utah With the Dragoons*; the co-editor of *Roosevelt and Churchill: Their Secret Wartime Correspondence*; and the editor of *So Proudly We Hail: The History of the United States Flag*. In addition, he contributed five chapters to *American Secretaries of the Navy, 1775–1972*, edited by Paolo E. Coletta, and a chapter on "The Sailor's Life" in the volume *Fighting For Time* in the series *The Image of War, 1861–1865* edited by William C. Davis. The author of twenty-eight articles, mainly on aspects of naval and diplomatic history, Dr. Langley is currently doing research on the history of medicine in the U.S. Navy.

INDEX